Lecture Notes in Artificial Intelligence 10023

Subseries of Lecture Notes in Computer Science

LNAI Series Editors

Randy Goebel
University of Alberta, Edmonton, Canada
Yuzuru Tanaka
Hokkaido University, Sapporo, Japan
Wolfgang Wahlster
DFKI and Saarland University, Saarbrücken, Germany

LNAI Founding Series Editor

Joerg Siekmann
DFKI and Saarland University, Saarbrücken, Germany

More information about this series at http://www.springer.com/series/1244

Cheng-Lin Liu · Amir Hussain
Bin Luo · Kay Chen Tan
Yi Zeng · Zhaoxiang Zhang (Eds.)

Advances in Brain Inspired Cognitive Systems

8th International Conference, BICS 2016
Beijing, China, November 28–30, 2016
Proceedings

 Springer

Editors
Cheng-Lin Liu
Institute of Automation
Chinese Academy of Sciences
Beijing
China

Amir Hussain
Computing Science and Mathematics
University of Stirling
Stirling
UK

Bin Luo
Anhui University
Anhui
China

Kay Chen Tan
National University of Singapore
Singapore
Singapore

Yi Zeng
Institute of Automation
Chinese Academy of Sciences
Beijing
China

Zhaoxiang Zhang
Institute of Automation
Chinese Academy of Sciences
Beijing
China

ISSN 0302-9743   ISSN 1611-3349   (electronic)
Lecture Notes in Artificial Intelligence
ISBN 978-3-319-49684-9   ISBN 978-3-319-49685-6   (eBook)
DOI 10.1007/978-3-319-49685-6

Library of Congress Control Number: 2016957381

LNCS Sublibrary: SL7 – Artificial Intelligence

Printed on acid-free paper

This Springer imprint is published by Springer Nature
The registered company is Springer International Publishing AG
The registered company address is: Gewerbestrasse 11, 6330 Cham, Switzerland

Preface

Welcome to the proceedings of BICS 2016 – the 8th International Conference on Brain Inspired Cognitive Systems. BICS has now become a well-established conference series on brain-inspired cognitive systems around the world, with growing popularity and increasing quality. BICS 2016 followed on from BICS 2004 (Stirling, Scotland, UK), BICS 2006 (Island of Lesvos, Greece), BICS 2008 (Sao Luis, Brazil), BICS 2010 (Madrid, Spain), BICS 2012 (Shenyang, China), BICS 2013 (Beijing, China), and BICS 2015 (Hefei, China). Beijing, as the capital of the People's Republic of China, is the nation's political, economic, and cultural center as well as China's most important center for international trade and communications.

This volume of *Lecture Notes in Artificial Intelligence* constitutes the proceedings of BICS 2016. In this context, BICS 2016 aimed to provide an open academic forum for researchers, engineers, and students to discuss the emerging areas and challenges, to present the state of the art of brain-inspired cognitive systems research and applications in diverse fields, and to exchange their fantastic ideas. The conference featured plenary lectures given by world-renowned scholars, regular sessions with broad coverage, and some special sessions focusing on popular and timely topics.

The conference received 43 submissions from more than 129 authors in 19 countries and regions across four continents. Based on a rigorous review process carried out by the Program Committee members and reviewers, 32 high-quality papers were selected for publication in the conference proceedings. These papers cover many topics of brain-inspired cognitive systems – related research including biologically inspired systems, cognitive neuroscience, models of consciousness, and neural computation.

Many organizations and volunteers made great contributions toward the success of this event. We are grateful to the Institute of Automation of the Chinese Academy of Sciences for their financial support and the Institute of Electrical and Electronic Engineers (IEEE) for their technical support. We would also like to sincerely thank all the committee members for their great efforts and time in organizing the event. Special thanks go to the Program Committee members and reviewers whose insightful reviews and timely feedback ensured the high quality of the accepted papers and the smooth flow of the symposium. We would also like to thank the publisher, Springer, for their cooperation in publishing the proceedings in the prestigious series of *Lecture Notes in Artificial Intelligence*. Finally, we would like to thank all the speakers, authors, and participants for their support.

November 2016

Cheng-Lin Liu
Amir Hussain
Bin Luo
Kay Chen Tan
Yi Zeng
Zhaoxiang Zhang

Organization

General Chairs

Cheng-Lin Liu   Institute of Automation, Chinese Academy of Sciences,
                         China
Amir Hussain   Stirling University, Scotland, UK

Program Chairs

Bin Luo   Anhui University, China
Kay Chen Tan   National University of Singapore, Singapore

Publicity Chairs

Cesare Alippi   Politecnico di Milano, Italy
Haibo He   University of Rhode Island, USA
Hussein Abbass   University of New South Wales, Australia
Erik Cambria   NTU, Singapore

Local Organization Chair

Yi Zeng   Institute of Automation, Chinese Academy of Sciences,
                        China

Publication Chair

Zhaoxiang Zhang   Institute of Automation, Chinese Academy of Sciences,
                        China

Program Committee

Andrew Abel   Stirling University, Scotland, UK
Peter Andras   Keele University, UK
Xiang Bai   Huazhong University of Science and Technology, China
Vladimir Bajic   KAUST, Thuwal, Saudi Arabia
Yanchao Bi   Beijing Normal University, China
Erik Cambria   Nanyang Technological University, Singapore
Lihong Cao   Communication University of China, China
Mingming Cheng   Nankai University, China
Yongsheng Dong   Xi'an Institute of Optics and Precision Mechanics, Chinese
                        Academy of Sciences, China

Marcos Faundez Zanuy	Tecnocampus, Barcelona, Spain
Yachuang Feng	Xi'an Institute of Optics and Precision Mechanics, Chinese Academy of Sciences, China
Alexander Gelbukh	CIC IPN, Mexico
Hugo Gravato Marques	ETH Zurich, Zurich, Switzerland
Claudius Gros	Goethe University Frankfurt, Germany
Xiaolin Hu	Tsinghua University, China
Tiejun Huang	Peking University, China
Amir Hussain	Stirling University, Scotland, UK
Rongrong Ji	Xiamen University, China
Yi Jiang	Institute of Psychology, Chinese Academy of Sciences, China
Jingpeng Li	Stirling University, Scotland, UK
Yongjie Li	University of Electronic Science and Technology of China, China
Cheng-Lin Liu	Institute of Automation, Chinese Academy of Sciences, China
Huaping Liu	Tsinghua University, China
Weifeng Liu	China University of Petroleum, China
Xiaoqiang Lu	Xi'an Institute of Optics and Precision Mechanics, Chinese Academy of Sciences, China
Bin Luo	Anhui University, China
Mufti Mahmud	University of Padova, Italy
Zeeshan Malik	Stirling University, Scotland, UK
Deyu Meng	Xi'an Jiaotong University, China
Junaid Qadir	National University of Sciences and Technology, Islamabad
Simone Scardapane	Sapienza University of Rome, Italy
Bailu Si	Shenyang Institute of Automation, Chinese Academy of Sciences, China
Mingli Song	Zhejiang University, China
Dacheng Tao	University of Technology, Sydney, Australia
Yonghong Tian	Peking University, China
Isabel Trancoso	INESC-ID, Portugal
Stefano Vassanelli	University of Padova, Italy
Liang Wang	Institute of Psychology, Chinese Academy of Sciences, China
Zhijiang Wang	Institute of Mental Health, Peking University, China
Qi Wang	Northwestern Polytechnical University, China
Hui Wei	Fudan University, China
Jonathan Wu	University of Windsor, Canada
Qiang Wu	University of Technology Sydney, Australia
Erfu Yang	University of Strathclyde, Glasgow, UK
Tianming Yang	Institute of Neuroscience, China
Shan Yu	Institute of Automation, Chinese Academy of Sciences, China

Contents

An Improved Recurrent Network for Online Equality-Constrained Quadratic Programming

Ke Chen[1] and Zhaoxiang Zhang[2(✉)]

[1] Department of Signal Processing,
Tampere University of Technology, Tampere, Finland
`ke.chen@tut.fi`
[2] CAS Center for Excellence in Brain Science and Intelligence Technology,
CASIA, Beijing, China
`zhaoxiang.zhang@ia.ac.cn`

Abstract. Encouraged by the success of conventional GradientNet and recently-proposed ZhangNet for online equality-constrained quadratic programming problem, an improved recurrent network and its electronic implementation are firstly proposed and developed in this paper. Exploited in the primal form of quadratic programming with linear equality constraints, the proposed neural model can solve the problem effectively. Moreover, compared to the existing recurrent networks, i.e., GradientNet (GN) and ZhangNet (ZN), our model can theoretically guarantee superior global exponential convergence performance. Robustness performance of our such neural model is also analysed under a large model implementation error, with the upper bound of stead-state solution error estimated. Simulation results demonstrate theoretical analysis on the proposed model for online equality-constrained quadratic programming.

Keywords: Recurrent networks · Online equality-constrained quadratic programming · Global exponential convergence · Robustness analysis

1 Introduction

Quadratic programming with equality constraints is one of the basic and classic problems widely encountered in the fields of science and engineering, e.g., computer vision and pattern recognition [1,2], digital signal processing [3], and robotics [4–7]. A number of machine learning techniques are designed based on quadratic programming with equality constraints, such as ridge regression [1,2], least square support vector machines [8–10] and primal support vector machines [11]. In mathematics, the following formulation about equality-constrained quadratic programming (QP) is depicted as:

$$\min \quad \frac{1}{2}\boldsymbol{x}^T \boldsymbol{Q} \boldsymbol{x} + \boldsymbol{x}^T \boldsymbol{q} \tag{1}$$

$$\text{s.t.} \quad \boldsymbol{A}\boldsymbol{x} = \boldsymbol{b} \tag{2}$$

where Hessian matrix $\boldsymbol{Q} \in \mathbb{R}^{n \times n}$ is symmetric and positive definite. In addition, $\boldsymbol{q} \in \mathbb{R}^n$, $\boldsymbol{A} \in \mathbb{R}^{m \times n}$, $\boldsymbol{b} \in \mathbb{R}^m$ are coefficients and $\boldsymbol{x} \in \mathbb{R}^n$ is the unknown vector

© Springer International Publishing AG 2016
C.-L. Liu et al. (Eds.): BICS 2016, LNAI 10023, pp. 1–10, 2016.
DOI: 10.1007/978-3-319-49685-6_1

to be optimised. It is worth mentioning here that other optimisation problems can be derived from the above formulation:

- when Hessian matrix Q is a null matrix [i.e., each element of Q is zero], QP (1) and (2) can be reduced to linear programming with equality constraints;
- when each entry of vector q is zero, QP (1) and (2) can be a special case of equality-constrained quadratic programming without linear term $x^T q$;
- when every elements in coefficients A and b are zero, QP (1) and (2) can be reduced to quadratic function minimization.

For addressing such a problem, the straight-forward solution is matrix-inverse based [1,2,8,9]. It is known that the computational complexity of matrix inversion is proportional to the cube of the matrix's dimensionality. Owing to the development of in-depth research, numerical algorithms performed on serial-processing digital computers are adopted and widely used to approximate matrix-inverse [3,11]. However, the numerical algorithms are still very computationally expensive for large scale or real-time applications in view of at least $O(n^2)$ complexity [12]. Alternatively, neural dynamic approaches in a parallel-processing manner are thus proposed [13–17]. Numerous dynamic and analog solvers based on recurrent neural networks have been developed and investigated for a number of linear algebra problems as well as their applications [13–26]. Because of its parallel distributed nature and convenience of hardware implementation [26], the neural dynamic approach is thus regarded as a powerful candidate for online computation.

A kind of primal recurrent neural network (i.e., GradientNet) was proposed by Wang [14,17] for real-time equality-constrained quadratic programming with global asymptotical convergence achieved. Recently, a novel descent method was proposed by Zhang et al. to develop an implicit neural system (i.e., ZhangNet) for solving online time-varying problems [16,27], which can also be applied to coping with QP (1) and (2). Both recurrent networks based on gradient descent and Zhang descent respectively can effectively solve QP (1) and (2). This paper proposes an improved network to achieve superior global convergence performance and stable robustness even with a large realisation error.

The main contributions and novelties of this paper are three folds:

- A novel recurrent neural network in the form of an implicit neural dynamical system together with its electronic implementation is firstly proposed for online equality-constrained QP (1) and (2).
- Our neural dynamic model can achieve superior global convergence performance with its exponential convergence rate estimated in comparison with the GradientNet [14] and more recent ZhangNet [16].
- With considering a large implementation error, the investigation of robustness properties of the proposed network is presented with its steady-state solution error bound estimated, which substantiates that our dynamic system is still global stable under noises.

Simulative results demonstrate global convergence and robustness analysis on the proposed model for online quadratic programming (1) and linear equality constraint (2).

2   Problem Formulation and Solvers

To solve equality-constrained quadratic programming (1)–(2), the following Lagrangian formulation of the primal problem of QP can be firstly defined as:

$$L(\boldsymbol{x}, \boldsymbol{c}) = \frac{1}{2}\boldsymbol{x}^T \boldsymbol{Q}\boldsymbol{x} + \boldsymbol{x}^T \boldsymbol{q} + \boldsymbol{c}^T(\boldsymbol{A}\boldsymbol{x} - \boldsymbol{b}),$$

where vector $\boldsymbol{c} \in \mathbb{R}^m$ is Lagrangian multipliers. With respect to $\boldsymbol{x}$ and $\boldsymbol{c}$, the following formulation can thus be obtained:

$$\begin{cases} \frac{\partial L(\boldsymbol{x},\boldsymbol{c})}{\partial \boldsymbol{x}} = \boldsymbol{Q}\boldsymbol{x} + \boldsymbol{A}^T\boldsymbol{c} + \boldsymbol{q} = 0, \\ \frac{\partial L(\boldsymbol{x},\boldsymbol{c})}{\partial \boldsymbol{c}} = \boldsymbol{A}\boldsymbol{x} - \boldsymbol{b} = 0. \end{cases} \tag{3}$$

Equation (3) can thus be reformulated into the following linear equations [14]:

$$\boldsymbol{M}\boldsymbol{y} = \boldsymbol{v}, \tag{4}$$

where coefficients

$$\boldsymbol{M} = \begin{bmatrix} \boldsymbol{Q} & \boldsymbol{A}^T \\ \boldsymbol{A} & \boldsymbol{0}_{m \times m} \end{bmatrix} \in \mathbb{R}^{(m+n) \times (m+n)}, \quad \boldsymbol{v} = \begin{bmatrix} -\boldsymbol{q} \\ \boldsymbol{b} \end{bmatrix} \in \mathbb{R}^{m+n},$$

and $\boldsymbol{y} = [\boldsymbol{x}, \boldsymbol{c}]^T \in \mathbb{R}^{m+n}$ denotes the unknown vector to be solved.

In addition, the following condition for unique solution to linear equations (4) is also presented here to lay a basis for further theoretical analysis.

Unique Solution Condition – Linear equations (4) have an unique solution [i.e., QP (1) and (2) exist an unique global optimal solution] if and only if matrix $\boldsymbol{Q}$ is positive definite and matrix $\boldsymbol{A}$ has full rank.

GradientNet [14, 23] based on norm-based energy function and ZhangNet [16, 27] based on vector-formed error function attempt to solve QP (1)–(2) online. On one hand, the formulation of GradientNet is presented as

$$\dot{\boldsymbol{y}}(t) = -\gamma \boldsymbol{M}^T \boldsymbol{M}\boldsymbol{y}(t) + \gamma \boldsymbol{M}^T \boldsymbol{v}, \tag{5}$$

where design parameter $\gamma > 0 \in \mathbb{R}$ is used to adjust the convergence rate and $\boldsymbol{A}^T$ denotes the transpose of coefficient matrix $\boldsymbol{A}$. On the other hand, ZhangNet for QP (1)–(2) can be depicted as

$$\boldsymbol{M}\dot{\boldsymbol{y}}(t) = -\gamma \boldsymbol{M}\boldsymbol{y}(t) + \gamma \boldsymbol{v}. \tag{6}$$

This paper proposes a novel recurrent neural network based on a novel descent different gradient descent in (5) and Zhang descent in (6), which can be formulated as the following:

$$\boldsymbol{M}\dot{\boldsymbol{y}}(t) = -\gamma(\boldsymbol{M}\boldsymbol{M}^T + \boldsymbol{I})(\boldsymbol{M}\boldsymbol{y}(t) - \boldsymbol{v}). \tag{7}$$

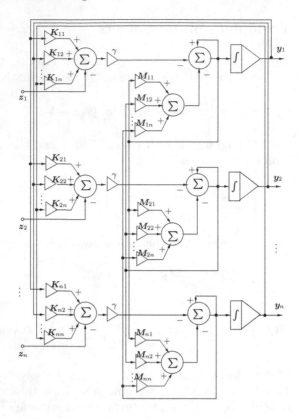

Fig. 1. Circuit schematics of our network (7) in the form of neural model (8)

where $I \in \mathbb{R}^{(m+n)\times(m+n)}$ denotes the unit matrix (or termed, the identity matrix). Following our neural model (7), ith element's dynamic equation ($i = 1, 2, \cdots, m+n$) can be presented as:

$$\dot{\boldsymbol{y}}_i = -\left(\sum_{j=1, j\neq i}^{m+n} \boldsymbol{M}_{ij}\dot{\boldsymbol{y}}_j\right) + (1 - \boldsymbol{M}_{ii})\dot{\boldsymbol{y}}_i - \gamma\left(\sum_{j=1}^{m+n} \boldsymbol{K}_{ij}\boldsymbol{y}_j - \boldsymbol{z}_i\right), \quad (8)$$

where $\boldsymbol{M}_{ij}$, $\boldsymbol{K}_{ij}$, and $\boldsymbol{z}_i$ denote the corresponding elements of time-invariant coefficients $\boldsymbol{M}$, $\boldsymbol{K} = (\boldsymbol{M}\boldsymbol{M}^T + \boldsymbol{I})\boldsymbol{M}$, and $\boldsymbol{z} = (\boldsymbol{M}\boldsymbol{M}^T + \boldsymbol{I})\boldsymbol{v}$, respectively. The architecture of the realization of (7) in the form of (8) is shown in Fig. 1.

3   Theoretical Analysis

3.1   Convergence Analysis

Global exponential convergence properties of our neural network (7) is investigated. In addition, two propositions about global convergence by GradientNet (5) and ZhangNet (6) for (1)–(2) are also presented for the comparative purpose.

Proposition 1. Given a symmetric and positive matrix $Q \in \mathbb{R}^{n \times n}$, a full rank matrix $A \in \mathbb{R}^{m \times n}$, coefficient vectors $q \in \mathbb{R}^n$ and $b \in \mathbb{R}^m$, the state vector $x(t) \in \mathbb{R}^n$ of GradientNet (5), starting from any initial state $x(0) \in \mathbb{R}^n$, will exponentially converge to global optimal solution x^* with its corresponding Lagrangian multiplier vector c^* [i.e., the theoretical solution y^* of linear equations (4)]. In addition, the exponential convergence rate is the product of γ and the minimum eigenvalue $\alpha > 0$ of $M^T M$, where $M = [Q, A^T; A, 0_{m \times m}] \in \mathbb{R}^{(m+n) \times (m+n)}$. □

Proposition 2. Given a symmetric and positive matrix $Q \in \mathbb{R}^{n \times n}$, a full rank matrix $A \in \mathbb{R}^{m \times n}$, coefficients $q \in \mathbb{R}^n$ and $b \in \mathbb{R}^m$, the state vector $x(t) \in \mathbb{R}^n$ of ZN model (6), starting from any initial state $x(0) \in \mathbb{R}^n$, will exponentially converge to global optimal solution x^* with its corresponding Lagrangian multiplier vector c^* [i.e., the exact solution y^* of linear equations (4)] having the convergence rate γ. □

It is evident that, in addition to having the same design parameter γ, the minimum eigenvalue α of $M^T M$ will determine the convergence rate of GN model (5) and ZN model (6). In details, when $\alpha > 1$, GN model (5) can outperform ZN model (6); when $\alpha = 1$ GN model (5) and ZN model (6) have the same convergence rate; when $\alpha < 1$, superior convergence can be achieved by ZN model (6) compared to GN model (5).

Theorem 1. Given a symmetric and positive matrix $Q \in \mathbb{R}^{n \times n}$, a full rank matrix $A \in \mathbb{R}^{m \times n}$, coefficients $q \in \mathbb{R}^n$ and $b \in \mathbb{R}^m$, the state vector $x(t) \in \mathbb{R}^n$ of our model (7), starting from any initial state $x(0) \in \mathbb{R}^n$, will exponentially converge to the global optimal solution x^* with its corresponding Lagrangian multiplier vector c^* [i.e., the theoretical solution y^* of linear equations (4)]. In addition, the exponential convergence rate is the product of γ and the minimum eigenvalue $\beta = \alpha + 1 > 1$ of $M^T M + I$, where $M = [Q, A^T; A, 0_{m \times m}] \in \mathbb{R}^{(m+n) \times (m+n)}$ and I is the $m + n$ dimensional unit matrix. Evidently, global exponential convergence rate $\gamma\beta$ of (7) is higher than $\gamma\alpha$ of (5) and γ of (6). □

3.2 Robustness Analysis

When our neural model (7) is applied to solving online QP (1) and (2), the following theorem about its steady-state solution-error bound is analysed to show its robustness properties. Before that, perturbed neural model with the consideration of a large implementation error is depicted as the following:

$$M\dot{y}(t) = -\gamma(MM^T + I)(My(t) - v) + \Delta r(t), \qquad (9)$$

where $\Delta r(t)$ denotes the large model implementation error.

Theorem 2. Consider a symmetric and positive matrix $Q \in \mathbb{R}^{n \times n}$, a full rank matrix $A \in \mathbb{R}^{m \times n}$, coefficients $q \in \mathbb{R}^n$ and $b \in \mathbb{R}^m$. Given $\|\Delta r(t)\|_2 \leqslant \zeta$ at any time instant $t \in [0, \infty)$, starting from any initial states $x(0) \in \mathbb{R}^n$ and

Lagrangian multipliers $c(0) \in \mathbb{R}^m$, the steady-state solution-error bound of the perturbed model (9) for solving online QP (1) and (2) can be written tightly as

$$\lim_{t \to \infty} \|y(t) - y^*\|_2 \leqslant \frac{\zeta}{\gamma\beta\sqrt{\alpha}}, \tag{10}$$

where design parameter γ of model (9) should be large enough, $\alpha > 0$ is the minimal eigenvalue of matrix $M^T M$, and $\beta > 1$ is the minimal eigenvalue of matrix $M^T M + I$. As the design-parameter γ increases, the steady-state solution-error in (10) decreases. On the other hand, it follows from (10) that as ζ decreases, the steady-state solution-error in (10) decreases.   □

4   Simulative Examples

In order to demonstrate superior global exponential convergence and robustness, we will consider the following example of quadratic programming with equality constraints as:

$$Q = \begin{bmatrix} 3 & -1 & 1 \\ -1 & 4 & 2 \\ 1 & 2 & 1 \end{bmatrix}, \quad q = \begin{bmatrix} -6 \\ 15 \\ 9 \end{bmatrix}, \quad A = \begin{bmatrix} 1 & 2 & 2 \\ 3 & 2 & 1 \end{bmatrix}, \quad b = \begin{bmatrix} 12 \\ -9 \end{bmatrix}.$$

As a result, the coefficients of linear equations (4) can be presented as

$$M = \begin{bmatrix} 3 & -1 & 1 & 1 & 3 \\ -1 & 4 & 2 & 2 & 2 \\ 1 & 2 & 1 & 2 & 1 \\ 1 & 2 & 2 & 0 & 0 \\ 3 & 2 & 1 & 0 & 0 \end{bmatrix}, \quad v = \begin{bmatrix} 6 \\ -15 \\ -9 \\ 12 \\ -9 \end{bmatrix},$$

where the optimal solution $x^* = [-1.7857, -10.5357, 17.4286]^T$ and the corresponding optimal Lagrangian multipliers $c^* = [1.1786, -5.9286]^T$. Evidently, related to the coefficient matrix M of linear equations (4), the minimal eigenvalue α of $M^T M$ and the minimal eigenvalue β of $M^T M + I$ are 0.4016 and 1.4016 respectively.

Computer simulation results about global convergence are shown in Figs. 2 and 3. With the design parameter $\gamma = 100$, the convergence rate for our model (7) is $\gamma\beta = 140.16$ and thus the convergence time to a tiny solution error $\exp(-7)$ from a initial solution error is 49.9 ms, which is illustrated as the left plot of Fig. 2. When the design parameter γ increasing to 1000 [the convergence rate $\gamma\beta = 1401.6$], as illustrated in the right plot of Fig. 2, the convergence time to a tiny solution error $\exp(-7)$ from a initial solution error is 4.99 ms. Evidently, global convergence can be expedited by increasing the design parameter γ.

For the comparative and illustrative purposes, Fig. 3 shows solution error by our model (7), GradientNet (5), and ZhangNet (6) from zero initial state for online quadratic programming with equality constraints. With the design parameter $\gamma = 100$ and $\gamma = 1000$, the convergence time to a tiny solution

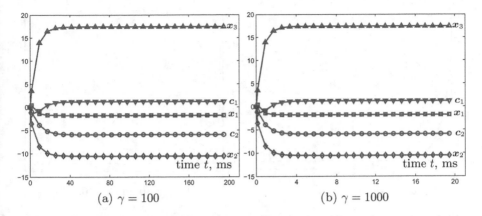

Fig. 2. Exponential convergence of state vectors $x(t)$ and $c(t)$ by our model (7) for QP (1) and (2) from the initial states $x(0) = 0_n$ and $c(0) = 0_m$ with $\gamma = 100$ and $\gamma = 1000$.

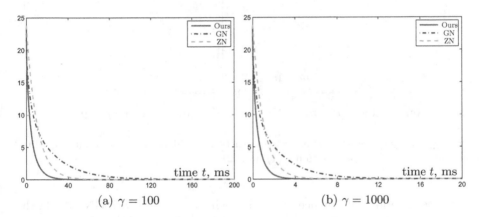

Fig. 3. Solution error by the proposed model (7), GradientNet (GN) (5), and ZhangNet (ZN) (6) for QP (1) and (2) from zero initial state with design parameter $\gamma = 100$ and $\gamma = 1000$ (Color figure online)

error $\exp(-7)$ by GN model (5) is 174.3 ms and 17.43 ms respectively, which are shown via dash-dotted blue curves in Fig. 3. In addition, global exponential convergence of solution error by Zhang model (6) is also illustrated in Fig. 3 as dash green curves, of which convergence time to a tiny solution error $\exp(-7)$ is 70 ms and 7 ms for $\gamma = 100$ and $\gamma = 1000$. Evidently, solution error by our model (7), which is shown as solid red curves, can be more convergent to zero than the other curves generated by GN (5) and ZN (6). It is worth pointing out here that, from comparison between GN (5) and ZN (6) for QP (1) and (2) in Fig. 3, ZN (6) outperform GN (5) because of the minimal eigenvalue $\alpha = 0.4016$ of matrix $M^T M$ is less than 1. From the analysis in Sect. 3, ZN (6) cannot theoretically

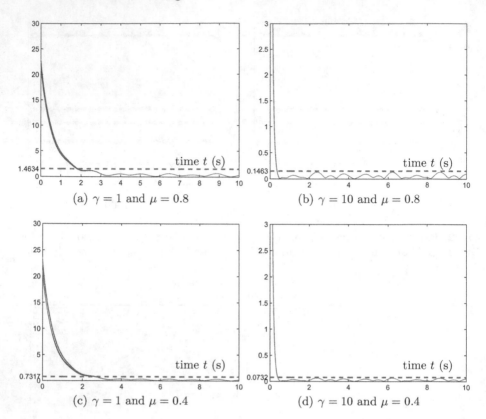

Fig. 4. Convergence of solution error by perturbed neural model (9) for online equality-constrained quadratic programming (1) and (2)

guarantee superior convergence performance in comparison with GN (5). On the other hand, from simulative results in Figs. 2 and 3, our model (7) can always achieve superior global exponential convergence compared to GN (5) and ZN (6), which substantiates the aforementioned theoretical analysis in Theorem 1.

To verify our robustness analysis in Theorem 2, another simulation for showing the convergence of solution error $\|\boldsymbol{y}(t) - \boldsymbol{y}^*\|_2$ synthesized by perturbed model (9) is conducted with considering the following large model implementation error:

$$\Delta\boldsymbol{r}(t) = \mu \left[\sin(3t), \cos(3t), \sin(5t), -\cos(5t), 0.8\right]^T,$$

where $\|\Delta\boldsymbol{r}(t)\|_2 \leqslant \zeta = \sqrt{2.64}\mu$ and μ is used to adjust the scale of the implementation error. With simulation results shown in Fig. 4, we can see that starting from randomly-generated initial states $\boldsymbol{x}(0) \in [-2,2]^3$ and Lagrangian multipliers $\boldsymbol{c}(0) \in [-2,2]^2$, the solution error of the analysed model (9) can always converge to and/or stay within the presented upper error bounds $\zeta/(\gamma\beta\sqrt{\alpha}) = 1.4634$ with $\gamma = 1$ and $\zeta = \sqrt{2.64}\mu = 1.2998$ for $\mu = 0.8$. Such a steady-state solution-error is decreased [e.g., $\zeta/(\gamma\beta\sqrt{\alpha}) = 0.1463$ with $\gamma = 10$ and $\zeta = 1.2998$] and the convergence is also expedited when design parameter γ is increased. Compared to the bottom two plots of Fig. 4, when ζ decreases from 1.2998 to 0.6499 [i.e., μ decreases from 0.8 to 0.4], the steady-state solution error bound also decreases [i.e., from 1.4634 to 0.7317 for $\gamma = 1$ and from 0.1463 to 0.0732 for $\gamma = 10$]. Simulative observations demonstrate robustness analysis on (9) with a large implementation error presented in Theorem 2.

5   Conclusion

A novel neural network (7) for real-time equality-constrained quadratic programming is proposed in this paper. Global exponential convergence analysis is investigated with global exponential convergence rate estimated. Compared to other existing neural networks, i.e., GradientNet (5) and recently-proposed ZhangNet (6), superior global exponential convergence to the optimal solution by our model (7) can be reached. Moreover, with the consideration of a large model-implementation error, the solution error for steady-state states by our perturbed model (9) is always upper bounded with the estimated error bound. Computer simulation results can substantiate the efficacy and robustness on our model for online quadratic programming with equality constraints.

Acknowledgements. This work was funded by the Academy of Finland under No. 267581 and 298700.

References

1. Chen, K., Loy, C.C., Gong, S., Xiang, T.: Feature mining for localised crowd counting. In: British Machine Vision Conference, pp. 21:1–21:11 (2012)
2. Chen, K., Gong, S., Xiang, T., Loy, C.C.: Cumulative attribute space for age and crowd density estimation. In: IEEE Conference on Computer Vision and Pattern Recognition, pp. 2467–2474 (2013)
3. Leithead, W., Zhang, Y.: $O(N^2)$-operation approximation of covariance matrix inverse in Gaussian process regression based on quasi-Newton BFGS method. Commun. Stat. Simul. Comput. **36**(2), 367–380 (2007)
4. Wang, J., Zhang, Y.: Recurrent neural networks for real-time computation of inverse kinematics of redundant manipulators. In: Machine Intelligence: Quo Vadis, pp. 299–319 (2004)
5. Zhang, Y.: A set of nonlinear equations and inequalities arising in robotics and its online solution via a primal neural network. Neurocomputing **70**(1), 513–524 (2006)
6. Zhang, Y., Li, K.: Bi-criteria velocity minimization of robot manipulators using LVI-based primal-dual neural network and illustrated via PUMA560 robot arm. Robotica **28**(04), 525–537 (2010)
7. Zhang, Y., Ma, W., Li, X.D., Tan, H.Z., Chen, K.: Matlab simulink modeling and simulation of LVI-based primal-dual neural network for solving linear and quadratic programs. Neurocomputing **72**(7), 1679–1687 (2009)

8. Suykens, J.A., Vandewalle, J.: Least squares support vector machine classifiers. Neural Process. Lett. **9**(3), 293–300 (1999)
9. Suykens, J.A., Van Gestel, T., De Brabanter, J., De Moor, B., Vandewalle, J., Suykens, J., Van Gestel, T.: Least Squares Support Vector Machines, vol. 4. World Scientific, Singapore (2002)
10. Wang, Z., Chen, S.: New least squares support vector machines based on matrix patterns. Neural Process. Lett. **26**(1), 41–56 (2007)
11. Chapelle, O.: Training a support vector machine in the primal. Neural Comput. **19**(5), 1155–1178 (2007)
12. Zhang, Y., Leithead, W.E., Leith, D.J.: Time-series Gaussian process regression based on Toeplitz computation of $O(N^2)$ operations and $O(N)$-level storage. In: IEEE Conference on Decision and Control, pp. 3711–3716 (2005)
13. Hopfield, J.J., Tank, D.W.: Neural computation of decisions in optimization problems. Biol. Cybern. **52**(3), 141–152 (1985)
14. Wang, J.: Recurrent neural network for solving quadratic programming problems with equality constraints. Electron. Lett. **28**(14), 1345–1347 (1992)
15. Zhang, Y.: Towards piecewise-linear primal neural networks for optimization and redundant robotics. In: IEEE International Conference on Networking, Sensing and Control, pp. 374–379 (2006)
16. Zhang, Y., Li, Z.: Zhang neural network for online solution of time-varying convex quadratic program subject to time-varying linear-equality constraints. Phys. Lett. A **373**(18), 1639–1643 (2009)
17. Zhang, Y., Yang, Y., Ruan, G.: Performance analysis of gradient neural network exploited for online time-varying quadratic minimization and equality-constrained quadratic programming. Neurocomputing **74**(10), 1710–1719 (2011)
18. Chen, K.: Recurrent implicit dynamics for online matrix inversion. Appl. Math. Comput. **219**(20), 10218–10224 (2013)
19. Chen, K., Yi, C.: Robustness analysis of a hybrid of recursive neural dynamics for online matrix inversion. Appl. Math. Comput. **273**, 969–975 (2016)
20. Chen, K.: Improved neural dynamics for online Sylvester equations solving. Inf. Process. Lett. **116**(7), 455–459 (2016)
21. Chen, K.: Robustness analysis of Wang neural network for online linear equation solving. Electron. Lett. **48**(22), 1391–1392 (2012)
22. Chen, K.: Implicit dynamic system for online simultaneous linear equations solving. Electron. Lett. **49**(2), 101–102 (2013)
23. Zhang, Y., Chen, K., Tan, H.Z.: Performance analysis of gradient neural network exploited for online time-varying matrix inversion. IEEE Trans. Autom. Control **54**(8), 1940–1945 (2009)
24. Chen, K., Guo, D., Tan, Z., Yang, Z., Zhang, Y.: Cyclic motion planning of redundant robot arms: simple extension of performance index may not work. In: International Symposium on Intelligent Information Technology Application, pp. 635–639 (2008)
25. Chen, K., Zhang, L., Zhang, Y.: Cyclic motion generation of multi-link planar robot performing square end-effector trajectory analyzed via gradient-descent and Zhang et al's neural-dynamic methods. In: International Symposium on Systems and Control in Aerospace and Astronautics, pp. 1–6 (2008)
26. Mead, C., Ismail, M.: Analog VLSI Implementation of Neural Systems. Springer Science & Business Media, New York (1989)
27. Zhang, Y., Ge, S.S.: Design and analysis of a general recurrent neural network model for time-varying matrix inversion. IEEE Trans. Neural Netw. **16**(6), 1477–1490 (2005)

Towards Robot Self-consciousness (I): Brain-Inspired Robot Mirror Neuron System Model and Its Application in Mirror Self-recognition

Yi Zeng[1,2(✉)], Yuxuan Zhao[1], and Jun Bai[1]

[1] Institute of Automation, Chinese Academy of Sciences, Beijing, China
yi.zeng@ia.ac.cn
[2] Center for Excellence in Brain Science and Intelligence Technology,
Chinese Academy of Sciences, Shanghai, China

Abstract. Mirror Self-Recognition is a well accepted test to identify whether an animal is with self-consciousness. Mirror neuron system is believed to be one of the most important biological foundation for Mirror Self-Recognition. Inspired by the biological mirror neuron system of the mammalian brain, we propose a Brain-inspired Robot Mirror Neuron System Model (Robot-MNS-Model) and we apply it to humanoid robots for mirror self-recognition. This model evaluates the similarity between the actual movements of robots and their visual perceptions. The association for self-recognition is supported by STDP learning which connects the correlated visual perception and motor control. The model is evaluated on self-recognition mirror test for 3 humanoid robots. Each robot has to decide which one is itself after a series of random movements facing a mirror. The results show that with the proposed model, multiple robots can pass the self-recognition mirror test at the same time, which is a step forward towards robot self-consciousness.

Keywords: Robot self-consciousness · Mirror self-recognition · Mirror neuron system · Associative learning

1 Introduction

Self consciousness is of vital importance for an agent with real intelligence. Machine consciousness is a grand challenge for Artificial Intelligence research. In order to identify whether an animal species is with self consciousness, the Mirror Self-Recognition test is proposed [1]. Only a few animal species are considered to be with self consciousness. Besides human, animals that are considered to be with self-consciousness include: chimpanzees [1], orangutans [2], bonobos [3], gorillas [4,5], Asiatic elephant [6], dolphins [7], orcas [8], Eurasian [9], etc.

Recent findings proofed the possibility of training rhesus monkeys to be with self consciousness [10]. With this possibility as a support, we hypothesize that

© Springer International Publishing AG 2016
C.-L. Liu et al. (Eds.): BICS 2016, LNAI 10023, pp. 11–21, 2016.
DOI: 10.1007/978-3-319-49685-6_2

machine with a brain-inspired computational model can be trained to have self consciousness.

For mammalian brain, especially human brain, multiple brain regions are involved in self consciousness. They closely interact with each other and collectively form a comprehensive neural pathway. Two sub systems need to be paid more attention to. Namely, the Mirror Neuron System (MNS) [11], and the Cortical Midline Structures (CMS) [12]. The medial prefrontal cortex (MPFC) is a very important region in CMS for self consciousness [13]. The ventromedial prefrontal cortex (VMPFC) mostly responds to self, while the dorsomedial prefrontal cortex (DMPFC) primarily responds to others [14]. For the mirror self-recognition test, especially for a robot self-consciousness model, we hypothesize that mirror neuron system (MNS) learns the correlation of the original agent and the agent in the mirror, then MPFC is activated by the mirror neuron system to realize the robot self. Hence, creating a computational model for mirror neuron system (MNS) is a first preparation for realizing robot self-consciousness.

In order to create a robot with self-consciousness, in this paper, we propose a brain-inspired Robot Mirror Neuron System Model (Robot-MNS-Model) and we apply it to humanoid robots for mirror self-recognition. Although this investigation will be a long term exploration[1], the efforts in this paper try to have a step forward towards robot self-consciousness.

2   Brain-Inspired Robotic Mirror Neuron System Model

As a core architecture for the computational model of robot self-consciousness, we propose a Robotic Mirror Neuron System model (Robot MNS Model).

2.1   The Architecture of the Robotic Mirror Neuron System

The architecture of the Robot MNS Model is shown in Fig. 1. The model is mainly based on the understanding of human mirror neuron system introduced in [11,15], and is with reconsideration to adapt to robotics.

The motion detection module receives visual inputs and detects motions in the visual sequence. It is composed of Extrastriate Body Area (EBA) and MT/V5. EBA is sensitive to human body and its parts, no matter they are static or moving [16]. MT/V5 is with the ability of motion detection, and responds to stimuli which are moving towards a certain direction with a certain speed [17]. In this model, EBA is with the function of body part detection, while MT/V5 is for orientation and speed detection of moving objects. Both EBA and MT/V5 transmit information to posterior superior temporal sulcus (pSTS). pSTS is sensitive to biological motion, and its function is to visually encodes biological motion [18]. The inferior parietal lobule (IPL) integrates visual inputs from pSTS and motion inputs from vPMC. Namely, IPL, which is one of the most important core area in mirror neuron system and for this model, does consistency checking on observed

---

[1] Robot Self-Consciousness Project: http://bii.ia.ac.cn/robot-self.

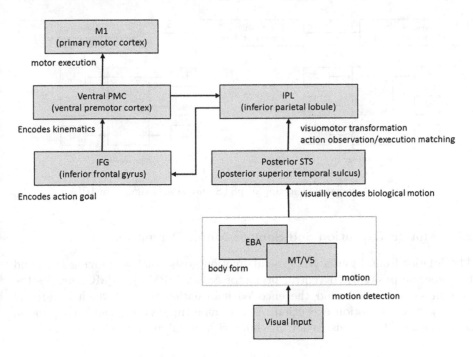

Fig. 1. The architecture of the robotic mirror neuron system model

action and motion execution [18,19]. The inferior frontal gyrus (IFG) encodes action goals, and it responds to goal driven motions [19]. In this model, IFG generates motion goals, and transmit information on motion goals to vPMC. It also make inference on motion intention based on inputs from IPL. The Ventral premotor cortex (Ventral PMC) encodes kinematics based on motion goal from IPL, the encoded information are sent to M1 for concrete motor execution, and to IPL for information integration. M1 encodes the strength and orientation of motion and controls the concrete motion execution [20].

In the robotic mirror neuron system model, motion goal generation and motion understanding are associated with IFG. The neural pathway of the proposed model is mainly based on understandings from [11,15,21,22]. In this model, there are mainly two pathways. Namely, The somato motion perception pathway (IFG → vPMC → IPL), and the visual motion perception pathway (visual inputs → EBA & MT/V5 → pSTS → IPL). Both pSTS and vPMC send signals to IPL. If the signals from these two regions co-occur with each other in the same time slot (in this investigation, the time slot is consistent with the slot for STDP) and the sequences of movements are consistent with each other, new connections will be formed or existing connections will be strengthened to represent their consistency, then IPL activates mPFC and the robot recognizes the moving agent is itself. Figure 2 presents the associative learning process between pSTS and vPMC signals in IPL.

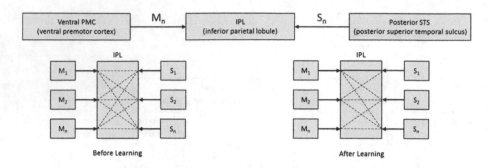

Fig. 2. Associative learning of pSTS and vPMC signals in IPL

2.2 Motion Execution and Somato Motor Perception

The inferior frontal gyrus (IFG) sends motion goals (such as moving left hand to a specific position) to ventral premotor cortex (vPMC). vPMC encodes the motion sequence and send the encoded information to M1, which is directly related to robot motion execution. At the same time, vPMC sends the motion sequence to IPL for consistency checking with visual motion perception.

2.3 Motion Detection

Here we propose a multiple brain region coordinated computational model for the visual dorsal pathway to simulate the cognitive function of motion detection. The model is a spiking neural network model, which is enlightened by the work introduced in [23].

As a preprocessing step, the image is firstly transformed to three spatial-temporal scales through convolutions with different Gaussian kernels. This is to simulate the effect of retina and can help to detect targets in different scales in the scene.

After preprocessing, the image is fed as input to V1. As is pointed out by neural scientists, most neurons in V1 related to motion can exhibit a crucial characteristic: direction selectivity. To clarify this, it is necessary to introduce the concept of spatial-temporal space. As a 2-D image, a resolution cell(or a pixel) can be located by its (x, y) spatial coordinates in the scene. However, for an image sequence, a third dimension t should be appended to describe the temporal change of this resolution cell. Thus, the image sequence can be described as a 3-D subspace with x, y, and t axis. A basic unit in motion can be represented as its spatial change of (x, y) with the temporal sequence t. In other words, this unit in motion is actually a trajectory in this 3-D subspace.

For a neuron related to motion in V1, direction selectivity means this neuron can reach its maximal response in a particular direction in the spatial-temporal space within its receptive field. This implies that this neuron responds to motion not simply in a spatial direction, but also in a specific speed. To simulate this physiological effect in a mathematical form, we sample the 3-D spatial-temporal space in 28 dimensions, corresponding to 28 different motion directions and speeds. In fact, these directions correspond to different functional columns in V1.

As a further step, neurons from V1 are connected to MT. Different from the neurons in V1, the neurons in MT respond to motion in a specific direction, regardless of the speeds. Hence, this is a projection process from 3-D spatial-temporal space to 2-D spatial space. the input of MT neurons is in fact the linear transformation to the output of V1 neurons. In our simulation, we sample 8 spatial directions in MT, corresponding to motions in these 8 directions.

LIP takes the role of decision making in motion detection. Its function is similar to the output layer of artificial neural network. In [23], the output is the firing rates in 8 directions. In our investigation, however, what we concern is the degree of motion, regardless of the directions. To this end, we consider only the maximal firing rates of all the 8 directions. Since this maximal firing rate implies the intention of motion, we can use it to detect the targets in motion.

One key issue in the network is direction selectivity in V1. In [23], an algebra model is proposed, and the process can be briefly described as follows.

After preprocessing, the motion descriptors are calculated based on the input image sequence.

$$L_{kr}(x, y, t) = \alpha_{v1lin} \sum_{T=0}^{3} \left[\sum_{Y=0}^{3-T} \left[\frac{3!}{X!Y!T!} (\widehat{u}_{k,x})^X (\widehat{u}_{k,y})^Y (\widehat{u}_{k,t})^T \frac{\partial^3 f_r(x, y, t)}{\partial x^X \partial y^Y \partial t^T} \right] \right] \quad (1)$$

In this equation, X, Y and T are two spatial directions and the temporal dimension respectively. r is the scalar, which is 0, 1 or 2. k is one of the 28 spatial-temporal directions. α_{v1lin} is a tuning parameter. $L_{kr}(x, y, t)$ is the motion descriptor.

Then, the descriptors are translated to the responses of simple V1 cells.

$$S_{kr}(x, y, t) = \frac{\alpha_{filt \to rate, r} \alpha_{v1rect} L_{kr}(x, y, t)^2}{\alpha_{v1norm} \exp\left(\frac{-(x^2 + y^2)}{2\sigma_{v1norm}^2}\right) * \left(\frac{1}{28} \sum_{k=1}^{28} L_{kr}(x, y, t)^2\right) + \alpha_{v1semi}^2} \quad (2)$$

Here, σ_{v1norm} is the Gaussian kernel. $\alpha_{filt \to rate, r}$, α_{v1rect}, α_{v1norm} are parameters to be tuned. The responses of V1 simple cells are then further filtered as the responses of V1 complex cells.

$$C_{kr}(x, y, t) = \alpha_{v1comp} \exp\left(\frac{-(x^2 + y^2)}{2\sigma_{v1comp}^2}\right) * S_{kr}(x, y, t) \quad (3)$$

σ_{v1comp} is the Gaussian kernel. α_{v1comp} is the tuning parameter. This responses can be taken as the firing rate.

Enlightened by [24], we propose to use the classical Integrate and Fire (IF) model to generate spikes.

$$\begin{cases} \frac{dV}{dt} = G_\theta^{exc}(x_0, y_0, t)(E^{exc} - V(t)) \\ \quad + G_\theta^{inh}(x_0, y_0, t)(E^{inh} - V(t)) - g^L V(t) \\ \text{Spikes when } V = 1 \text{ and resets } V \text{ to } 0 \end{cases} \quad (4)$$

For the purpose of direction selectivity, the key is that the excitatory and inhibitory conductances are functions of the direction θ and spatial-temporal location (x, y, t). For excitatory conductance:

$$G_\theta^{exc}(x, y, t) = (F_\theta^e + F_\theta^o) * L(x, y, t) \quad (5)$$

$L(x, y, t)$ is the input sequence. $*$ is the convolution operator. F_θ^e and F_θ^o can be describes as:

$$\begin{cases} F_\theta^e(x, y, t) = G_\theta^e(x, y)P_i(t) \\ F_\theta^o(x, y, t) = G_\theta^o(x, y)P_j(t) \end{cases} \quad (6)$$

G_θ^e and G_θ^o are two Gaussian kernels respectively. $P_i(t)$, $P_j(t)$ are subtractions of two Γ functions.

$$P_\alpha(t) = T_{\alpha,\tau}(t) - T_{\alpha+2,\tau}(t) \quad (7)$$

Here $T_{\alpha,\tau}(t)$ is the Γ function. The inhibitory conductance is described as follows.

$$G_j^{inh} + = G_{max}^{inh} e^{-\frac{d_j^4}{2R^2}} \quad (8)$$

where j is the index of the neuron's spatial temporal neighbor. G_{max}^{inh} is a parameter, describing a maximal contribution of its neighbors. d_j is the spatial-temporal distance, and R is the radius of the scope that can contribute to the inhibitions.

3   Sensory-Motor Associative Learning

In the mirror neuron system, IPL integrates visual and motor information through associative learning. If motor information from vPMC match the visual information from pSTS, and the information are sent to IPL at the same time slot, then they are associated together in IPL. Associations are formed through Spike-Timing-Dependent-Plasticity (STDP) [25,26]. The weight of association among visual inputs and motor outputs ($W_{\text{motor-visual}}$) is based on a set of calculations in Eq. 9.

$$\Delta W = \begin{cases} A_+ \times e^{(\Delta t/\tau_+)} \; if \; \Delta t < 0 \\ A_- \times e^{(\Delta t/\tau_-)} \; if \; \Delta t \geq 0 \end{cases}$$

$$\Delta t = t_{\text{motor}} - t_{\text{visual}}$$

$$W(t)_{\text{motor-visual}} = W(t-1)_{\text{motor-visual}} + \Delta w_{\text{motor-visual}}$$

$$(9)$$

ΔW is the adjustment function for STDP. A_+ and A_- are the maximum and minimum value of synaptic changes respectively. τ_+ and τ_- are time constants for synaptic updates. Δt is the time slot between the time for motor output (t_{motor}) and the time for visual recognition of movement (t_{visual}). In order to keep the biological plausibility, according to [25], $A_+ = 0.777$, $A_- = -0.237$, $\tau_+ = 16.8$ ms, $\tau_- = -33.7$ ms. If mortal signals are transmitted to IPL before visual signals, then the synaptic connectivity will be strengthened, if visual signals come first, it will be weakened.

When there are not only one robot moving in front of a mirror, the robots need to decide which one is itself. The self recognition weight, denoted as $self_{weight}$, is proposed to evaluate which one is the specific robot itself.

$$\theta_{predict} = \max W_{motor}$$

$$Confidence_i = \begin{cases} 1 & |\theta_{predict} - \theta_{visual}| \le \theta_{threshold} \; and \; t_{motor} - t_{visual} < t_{threshold} \\ 0 & \text{otherwise} \end{cases} \qquad (10)$$

$$Self_{weight} = \left(\sum_{i=1}^{n} Confidence_i \right) / n$$

$\theta_{predict}$ is the predicted angle based on motor information. If $\theta_{predict}$ and θ_{visual} are close to each other within a certain threshold ($\theta_{threshold}$), at the same time, t_{motor} is before t_{visual} and they are close to each other within the time slot $t_{threshold}$, the confidence value for the robot under state i is (confidence$_i$) is 1. $Self_{weight}$ is the average value for all the n states during robot movements.

4   Robots Mirror Self-recognition Test

In order to validate the proposed Brain-inspired Robot Mirror Neuron System model, we deploy the computational model to humanoid robotics and challenge the model with the robots mirror self-recognition test. Three robots are required to recognize itself and distinguish itself from others in front of a mirror. The prior knowledge for robots are as the following: If two robots are on its right, then it is in Position 1. If two robots are on its left and right respectively, then it is Position 2. If two robots are on its left, then it is in Position 3. Hence, the judgement process can be described as Eq. 11. During the mirror test, they are required to identify which position it belongs to, and in this way, it obviously needs to know which one is itself first.

$$Position\ ID = \begin{cases} 1 & \text{LeftCount=0 \& RightCount=2} \\ 2 & \text{LeftCount=1 \& RightCount=1} \\ 3 & \text{LeftCount=2 \& RightCount=0} \end{cases} \qquad (11)$$

The robots are assigned random movements if they do not have any obvious solution to a specific task. All of their sensory functions (vision, audition) and

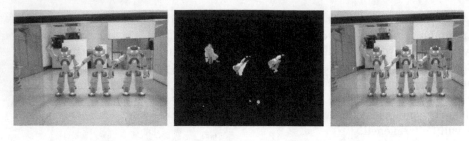

Fig. 3. Visual inputs and motion detection for robots mirror self-recognition

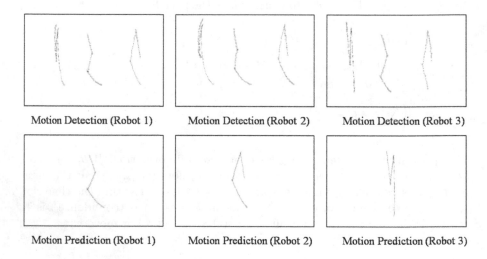

Fig. 4. Motion detection and motion prediction by different robots

motor function are activated with attempts to achieve the goal. Since the robots are in front of a mirror, and their vision systems are active, functions of their visual systems are active. Hence, motion detection from dorsal ventral pathway is functioning. Figure 3 presents the visual inputs of robots and their motion detection.

Robots will keep random movement until they can confirm their positions (i.e. identify which one it is). Figure 4 presents a sample for motion detection of their moving hands through visual inputs of the three robots and motion pathway prediction based on each robot's actual motor outputs.

Figure 5 presents the beliefs of each robots after each random movement. The darkness of each square is negative relevant to the belief values. After movement 2, Robot 2 is not aware which one is itself, while after movement 3, each robot can identify themselves in the mirror.

In order to test the proposed robot mirror neuron system model, 9 sets of robot mirror self-recognition tests are made. For each test, the position of the three robots are changed. Hence they need to re-recognize themselves after each

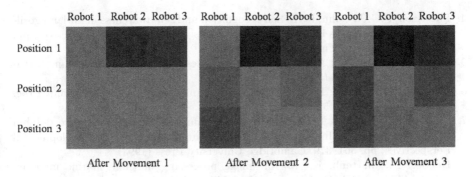

Fig. 5. Beliefs of their positions after different random movements

test. The three robots successfully passed all the 9 tests. Videos on the robots mirror self-recognition test is available at the Robot Self-consciousness Project page[2].

5 Conclusion

With the long term goal of building a robot with consciousness, especially with self-consciousness, as a first step, this paper provides an attempt to build a brain-inspired robot mirror neuron system model. Then we apply the model to robots with the purpose of passing the mirror self-recognition test. The evaluation indicates that the proposed model is biologically plausible and computationally feasible as a core component for robot self consciousness. Mirror Neuron System is only part of the neural pathway for self consciousness.

In order to provide a more comprehensive model and increase the level of self consciousness for robots, our current and future work is to extend the model to involve more regions and pathways that are relevant to self consciousness.

Acknowledgment. This study was funded by the Strategic Priority Research Program of the Chinese Academy of Sciences (XDB02060007), and Beijing Municipal Commission of Science and Technology (Z151100000915070, Z161100000216124).

References

1. Gallup, G.G.J.: Chimpanzees: self recognition. Science **167**(3914), 86–87 (1970)
2. Suarez, S.D., Gallup, G.G.J.: Self-recognition in chimpanzees and orangutans, but not gorillas. J. Hum. Evol. **10**(2), 175–188 (1981)
3. Walraven, V., van Elsacker, L., Verheyen, R.: Reactions of a group of pygmy chimpanzees (Pan paniscus) to their mirror-images: evidence of self-recognition. Primates **36**(1), 145–150 (1995)

---

[2] Robot Self-Consciousness Project: http://bii.ia.ac.cn/robot-self.

4. Patterson, F.G.P., Cohn, R.H.: Self-recognition and self-awareness in lowland gorillas. In: Self-Awareness in Animals and Humans: Developmental Perspectives, pp. 273–290. Cambridge University Press (1994)
5. Posada, S., Colell, M.: Another gorilla recognizes himself in a mirror. Am. J. Primatol. **69**(5), 576–583 (2007)
6. Plotnik, J.M., Waal, F.D., Reiss, D.: Self-recognition in an Asian elephant. Proc. Natl. Acad. Sci. **103**(45), 17053–17057 (2006)
7. Marten, K., Psarakos, S.: Evidence of self-awareness in the bottlenose dolphin (Tursiops truncatus). In: Self-Awareness in Animals and Humans: Developmental Perspectives, pp. 361–379. Cambridge University Press (1994)
8. Delfour, F., Martenb, K.: Mirror image processing in three marine mammal species: killer whales (Orcinus orca), false killer whales (Pseudorca crassidens) and California sea lions (Zalophus californianus). Behav. Process. **53**(3), 181–190 (2001)
9. Prior, H., Schwarz, A., Gntrkn, O.: Mirror-induced behavior in the magpie (Pica pica): evidence of self-recognition. PLOS Biol. **6**(8), e202 (2008)
10. Chang, L., Fang, Q., Zhang, S., Poo, M., Gong, N.: Mirror-induced self-directed behaviors in rhesus monkeys after visual-somatosensory training. Curr. Biol. **25**(2), 212–217 (2015)
11. Iacoboni, M., Dapretto, M.: The mirror neuron system and the consequences of its dysfunction. Nat. Rev. Neurosci. **7**(12), 942–951 (2006)
12. Northoff, G., Heinzel, A., de Greck, M., Bermpoh, F., Dobrowolny, H., Panksepp, J.: Self-referential processing in our brainła meta-analysis of imaging studies on the self. NeuroImage **31**, 440–457 (2006)
13. Heatherton, T.F.: Neuroscience of self and selfregulation. Ann. Rev. Psychol. **62**, 363–390 (2011)
14. Denny, B.T., Kober, H., Wager, T.D., Ochsner, K.N.: A meta-analysis of functional neuroimaging studies of self-and other judgments reveals a spatial gradient for mentalizing in medial prefrontal cortex. J. Cogn. Neurosci. **24**(8), 1742–1752 (2012)
15. Thakkar, K.N., Peterman, J.S., Park, S.: Altered brain activation during action imitation and observation in schizophrenia: a translational approach to investigating social dysfunction in schizophrenia. Am. J. Psychiatry **171**(5), 539–548 (2014)
16. Peelen, M.V., Wiggett, A.J., Downing, P.E.: Patterns of fmri activity dissociate overlapping functional brain areas that respond to biological motion. Neuron **49**(6), 815–822 (2006)
17. Perrone, J.A., Thiele, A.: Speed skills: measuring the visual speed analyzing properties of primate MT neurons. Nat. Neurosci. **4**(5), 526–532 (2001)
18. Grossman, E.D., Blake, R.: Brain areas active during visual perception of biological motion. Neuron **35**(6), 1167–1175 (2002)
19. Hamzei, F., Vry, M.S., Saur, D., Glauche, V., Hoeren, M., Mader, I., Weiller, C., Rijntjes, M.: The dual-loop model and the human mirror neuron system: an exploratory combined fMRI and DTI study of the inferior frontal gyrus. Cereb. Cortex **26**(5), 2215–2224 (2016)
20. Georgopoulos, A.P., Schwartz, A.B., Kettner, R.E.: Neuronal population coding of movement direction. Science **233**(4771), 1416–1419 (1986)
21. Sasaki, A.T., Kochiyama, T., Sugiura, M., Tanabe, H.C., Sadato, N.: Neural networks for action representation: a functional magnetic-resonance imaging and dynamic causal modeling study. Front. Hum. Neurosci. **6**, 236 (2012)
22. Mehta, U.M., Thirthalli, J., Aneelraj, D., Jadhav, P., Gangadhar, B.N., Keshavan, M.S.: Mirror neuron dysfunction in schizophrenia and its functional implications: a systematic review. Schizophrenia Res. **160**(1–3), 9–19 (2014)

23. Beyeler, M., Richert, M., Dutt, N.D., Krichmar, J.L.: Efficient spiking neural network model of pattern motion selectivity in visual cortex. Neuroinformatics **12**(3), 435–454 (2014)
24. Escobar, M.J., Wohrer, A., Kornprobst, P., Vieville, T.: Biological motion recognition using a MT-like model. In: Proceedings of the 3rd IEEE Latin American Robotic Symposium, pp. 47–52 (2006)
25. Bi, G., Poo, M.: Synaptic modification by correlated activity: Hebb's postulate revisited. Annu. Rev. Neurosci. **24**, 139–166 (2001)
26. Song, S., Miller, K.D., Abbott, L.F.: Competitive hebbian learning through spike-timing-dependent synaptic plasticity. Nat. Neurosci. **3**(9), 919–926 (2000)

Implementation of EEG Emotion Recognition System Based on Hierarchical Convolutional Neural Networks

Jinpeng Li[1,2], Zhaoxiang Zhang[1,2,3], and Huiguang He[1,2,3(✉)]

[1] Research Center for Brain-Inspired Intelligence, Institute of Automation,
Chinese Academy of Sciences, Beijing, China
{lijinpeng2015, zhaoxiang.zhang, huiguang.he}@ia.ac.cn
[2] University of Chinese Academy of Sciences (UCAS), Beijing, China
[3] Center for Excellence in Brain Science and Intelligence Technology,
Chinese Academy of Sciences, Beijing, China

Abstract. Deep Learning (DL) is capable of excavating features hidden deep in complex data. In this paper, we introduce hierarchical convolutional neural networks (HCNN) to implement the EEG-based emotion classifier (positive, negative and neutral) in a movie-watching task. Differential Entropy (DE) is calculated as features at certain time interval for each channel. We organize features from different channels into two dimensional maps to train HCNN classifier. This approach extracts features contained in the spatial topology of electrodes directly, which is often neglected by the widely-used one-dimensional models. The performance of HCNN was compared with one-dimensional deep model SAE (Stacked Autoencoder), as well as traditional shallow models SVM and KNN. We find that HCNN (88.2% ± 3.5%) is better than SAE (85.4% ± 8.1%), and deep models are more favorable in emotion recognition BCI (Brain-computer Interface) system than shallow models. Moreover, we show that models learned on one person is hard to transfer to others and the individual difference in EEG emotion-related signal is significant among peoples. Finally, we find Beta and Gamma (rather than Delta, Theta and Alpha) waves play the key role in emotion recognition.

Keywords: Emotion recognition · EEG · Deep Learning · HCNN · Brain wave

1 Introduction

The computational models of emotion is one of the major interests for psychologists, because they might help them understand the mechanism of emotion processing. The emotion recognition system is also an exciting researching topic for computer scientists and engineers, for such system is vital in multiple applications, e.g. workload estimation [1], driving fatigue detection [2], and BCI equipment [3].

There are many physiological signals to help us recognize the emotion state of one subject, which could be divided into two categories. One is called the 'external clues', e.g. facial expression and gesture [4]. Signals of this kind are highly related to the

C.-L. Liu et al. (Eds.): BICS 2016, LNAI 10023, pp. 22–33, 2016.
DOI: 10.1007/978-3-319-49685-6_3

personal habit of subjects, and thus could not be universally used. The favorable physiological signals should be able to describe across different cultures and language backgrounds [5]. The second kind of signals are called the 'internal clues', and among which, electroencephalograph (EEG) is widely used. EEG is reliable for emotion recognition, because it has high accuracy and relatively objective evaluation in comparison with the 'external' ones. The great assumption is that the brain contributes, or even determines the emotion state of one person. EEG devices often have multiple channels (electrodes) to collect electric potentials from different positions. The electrodes are either implantable (i.e. capable of being implanted in living brain tissue through operation) or non-implantable. The former has higher signal-to-noise ratio (SNR), but not fit to the daily use. The latter collects signals on the scalp, and it is noninvasive and wearable. That is favorable to commercial BCI systems (the application demands require the signal-collecting method to be as convenient as possible, e.g. the recent dry EEG equipment even omits the conductive paste). However, the SNR is low. The useful information for emotion recognition is submerged in the noise. Therefore, traditional feature-extraction methods (e.g. PCA and Fisher Projection) are insufficient to excavate patterns hidden deep in EEG signals, because the cost of traditional feature selection methods increases quadratically with respect to the number of features considered [6]. We need more powerful models to learn the most efficient features in the EEG signal.

Since the work of Hinton and Krizhevsky in 2012 [7], Deep Learning (DL) has dominated the machine learning research, and becomes the absolute winner in complex tasks such as image classification [8] and machine translation [9]. DL is capable of learning features automatically, because the DL structures trained under explicit goals (minimize the classification error) in turn possess powerful representational ability. The most important structures include HCNN [7], SAE [10], and DBN [11].

We could analyze EEG signal either in the time domain or in the frequency domain, or the combination of them. The time-domain analyze usually brings heavy computational burden, and not resistant to noise. Consequently, researchers tend to seek for the emotion-related patterns in frequency or time-frequency domain. There are five bands of brain wave that interest the researchers the most: Delta, Theta, Alpha, Beta and Gamma. Delta wave (1–3 Hz) is the slowest 'sleep wave'. Theta wave (4–7 Hz) is believed to be active in light meditation and sleeping. Alpha wave (8–13 Hz) is the 'deep relaxation wave', which is linked with our sense of happiness. Beta wave (14–30 Hz) is the 'waking consciousness and reasoning wave'. Gamma wave (31–50 Hz) has the highest frequency, and little is known about it. Initial research shows Gamma waves are associated with bursts of insight and high-level information processing. Li and Lu [12] proposed that Gamma wave was suitable for EEG-based emotion classification with emotional still images as stimuli. Therefore, Delta, Theta and Alpha might be favorable in resting-state emotion reading. Beta and Gamma waves are tightly-related to rational activities, and thus good for task-evoked emotion reading.

Fourier power might be a choice to characterize the signals, but EEG signal is not a stationary process. Hadjidimitriou et al. [13] employed three kinds of time-frequency distributions (spectrogram, Hilbert-Huang spectrum and Zhao-Atlas-Marks transform) as features to classify ratings of liking and familiarity. Yang Li et al. [14] applied wavelet energy to compensate for the influence of non-stationary character. Lu et al. [5]

used DE as features to classify three emotion states: positive, negative and neutral. They organized features in one-dimensionality and used DBN (Deep Belief Networks) to realize the classifier, and then they investigated the critical frequency bands and channels. The accuracy they obtained was as high as 86.08%.

In this paper, we extract DE features in a movie-watching task, and in order to maintain the information contained in the positional relationship between the electrodes, we organize them as two-dimensional maps to train HCNN classifiers on each frequency bands. The performance is compared with other models. We will also illustrate the relationship between the five frequency bands and the emotion states.

2 Methods

2.1 Short-Time Fourier Transform and Differential Entropy

Fourier Transform (FT) is often used to analyze the frequency configuration of a time-domain signal, and it is widely used in EEG decomposition. However, the FT operation assumes that brain wave activities are stationary, which is a false hypothesis apparently. Therefore, the time series should be cut into small time segments, and within each segment, the brain electric activities are approximately considered as stationary. The idea is called the Short-time Fourier Transform (STFT). STFT decomposes a function of time (EEG signal) into the frequencies that make it up at fixed time intervals. The calculation formulation of STFT is:

$$X(\tau, \omega) = \int_{-\infty}^{\infty} x(t)\omega(t - \tau)e^{-j\omega t}dt \tag{1}$$

Where $x(t)$ is the original signal, $\omega(t)$ is the window function. Hanning Window usually emerges in applications that require low aliasing and less spectrum leakage.

DE [15] is the extension of the Shannon entropy (1), which is an efficient definition of the complexity of a discrete random variable (i.e. if we want to know a random variable thoroughly, how much information do we need). The more information contained in a time series, the more complex it is. DE could be simply understood as the continuous edition of Shannon entropy, and thus a good kind of feature to characterize EEG time series.

$$h(x) = -\sum_{i=1}^{N} p(x_i)\log(p(x_i)) \tag{2}$$

$$h(x) = -\int f(x)\log(f(x))dx \tag{3}$$

If the random variable obeys the Gaussian distribution $N(\mu, \sigma^2)$, the differential entropy in (3) can simply be calculated by the following formulation:

$$h(x) = -\int_{-\infty}^{\infty} \frac{1}{\sqrt{2\pi\sigma^2}}\exp\frac{(x-\mu)^2}{2\sigma^2}\log\frac{1}{\sqrt{2\pi\sigma^2}}\exp\frac{(x-\mu)^2}{2\sigma^2}dx = \frac{1}{2}\log 2\pi e\sigma^2 \tag{4}$$

2.2   Two-Dimensional Feature Organization

In order to maintain the information of EEG placement as much as possible, we organize features (DE in this paper) extracted from 62 channels as two-dimensional maps at a time interval of one second. The configuration of the DE map is illustrated in Fig. 1. In this paper, we organize the DE features in such configuration to feed HCNN for training. However, the map size is two small and the 'pixel values' are too 'concentrated', so we introduce sparsity to generate sparse DE maps that are more suitable for HCNN dispose: all-zero rows and columns are added on alternate rows and columns. All-zero frames are also added on the four edges of maps to maintain patterns hidden in peripheral electrodes. The detailed operation of sparsity will be discussed further. After the sparse operation, the DE map is 20 * 20, and the size is sufficient to train a small-scale HCNN.

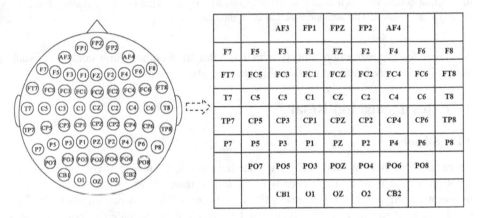

Fig. 1. The organization of DE map. Left: the 62-channel EEG placement in this experiment. Right: the placement is approximately expressed as a map, and each 'pixel' corresponds to a certain electrode. Through this method, the spatial relationship of electrodes are taken into consideration. (F: Frontal, T: Temporal, C: Central, P: Parietal, O: Occipital, Z: Midline).

2.3   HCNN

Here we consider a four-layer HCNN, which consists of two convolution layers and two pooling layers. The layer number is quite limited because the input map size is rather small, and if extra layers are introduced, after more convolution and pooling operations, the two-dimensional character of maps will vanish.

Consequently, the network parameters (e.g. the network depth, the number of feature maps in each layer and the kernel number for each layer) should be carefully appointed to fit different input size and various training goals. From layer to layer, the features becomes increasingly global and abstract, which is similar with the way the human visual cortex works (especially the primary visual cortex in the ventral pathway). The sigmoid function and the pooling operation also endow the network with

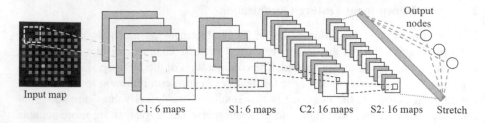

Fig. 2. The HCNN structure. The input map is 20 * 20. C1 is a convolution layer: the kernel size is 5, and the step is 1, then 6 16 * 16 maps are formed. S1 is a maxpooling layer, and the scale size is 2, so 6 8 * 8 maps are obtained. C2 is the second convolution layer: the kernel size is 3, and step is 1, then 16 6 * 6 maps are formed. S2 is another maxpooling layer, and scale size is also 2, so 16 3 * 3 maps are obtained here. All maps in S2 are stretched and concatenated to generate a 144-D vector according to their spatial positions. Finally, the vector is fully-connected to 3 output nodes, in which each node corresponds to a certain kind of emotion state: positive, negative and neutral. The activate function is sigmoid.

nonlinear feature-extraction ability, which is vital in accomplishing complex visual goals. The HCNN structure used in this paper is shown in Fig. 2.

3   Experiments and Results

3.1   Stimulus

There are four healthy male subjects, and they watch 15 movie slices cut from six emotion-related movies. Each slice is about four minutes long (~ 240 s). During the movie-watching process, 62-channel EEG signals are collected simultaneously [5]. The movie list is shown in Table 1. The selected 15 movie slices include five positive ones, five negative ones, and five neutral ones. For each subject, the 15 slices are displayed according to the order shown in Fig. 3, which also shows the duration of each slice. The experiment lasts 3394 s in total. Then the experiment is repeated three times to compensate for the influence of time, as well as to increase the data amount. The duration between adjacent experiments is about one week. Therefore, for one subject

Table 1. The movie list.

Movie slices sources	Label
Tangshan Earthquake	Negative
1942	Negative
Lost in Thailand	Positive
Flirting Scholar	Positive
Just Another Pandora's Box	Positive
World Heritage in China	Neutral

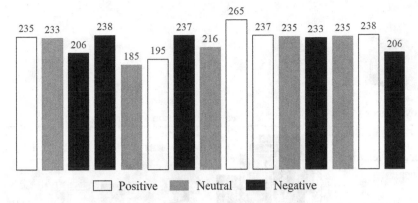

Fig. 3. The slice order (from left to right) and duration (in second).

on one frequency band, we acquire 10182 labeled samples. Self-assessment is done during the experiment to eliminate the influence irrelevant factors [16].

The dataset was originally contributed by Baoliang Lu et al. For more detailed information about the data [5] or download it for scientific research use, please log on to the website (http://bcmi.sjtu.edu.cn/ ~ seed/index.html).

3.2 Train HCNN

The training process is shown in Fig. 4. The subject is invited to watch movie slices to evoke the electric potential signals that are related to emotion activity. At the same time, EEG signals are recorded on 62 channels. The recorded signals then go to the preprocessing module. The raw EEG data (1000 Hz) is downsampled to 200 Hz sampling rate, and in order to filter the noise and remove the artifacts, the EEG data is processed with a bandpass filter between 0.3 Hz to 50 Hz. Therefore, the high frequency noise is excluded, but the five frequency bands we are interested are maintained. After preprocessing, the EEG signals are ready to provide features.

The feature-extraction and organization operation plays the key role in the present experiment, and it is described as follows: primarily, the signals are divided into multiple 1-s segments according to their durations (we assume that the signal is approximately a stationary process in such short time interval), and in every segment, 256-point STFT with nonoverlapped Hanning window is performed, DE is then calculated on each of the five frequency bands. Secondly, for each frequency band, we organize the DE features as two-dimensional maps according to the method described in Fig. 1. We also introduce sparsity by adding all-zero rows and columns to the DE maps, which is good for HCNN training. Finally, the sparse maps of one frequency band, together with the movie-slice labels, are used as the teacher signals to train a HCNN in full-supervised learning algorithm. At the end of this stage, five HCNNs are trained, each one is special for one frequency band. The emotion-related patterns might hide in each of the five frequency bands, but the discriminative capacity is different.

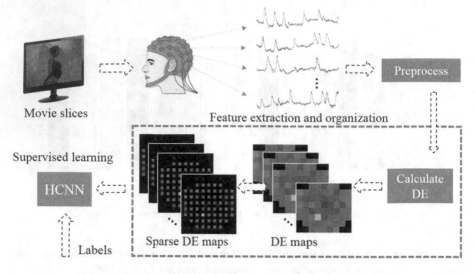

Fig. 4. The training process.

We will examine the performance of the five classifiers and find the most efficient bands for emotion recognition.

For each subject on each of the frequency band, 10182 labeled samples are collected. We use 75% ($\sim$74000) of the samples to train the HCNN, and the remaining 25% ($\sim$2800) are for test (the test samples are not included in the training samples). The initial values of the networks are randomly-appointed. The learning rates are all set to 1, the batch size is 50, and the learning epoch is 600. All the experiments are done in MATLAB (R2014a) software.

3.3 Train SAE and Shallow Classifiers

In order to see the different performance of other classifiers, we also implement the emotion classifiers with other models, i.e. the shallow models kernel-SVM, KNN and one-dimensional deep model SAE.

For kernel-SVM, the penalty factor c and the parameter g are determined by grid search (the searching regions are all from 2^{-8} to 2^{8}) and three-fold cross validation. The kernel is RBF (Radial Basis Function). SVM algorithm is efficient in applications where the sample amount is small and the computing capacity is limited.

For KNN, we choose five nearest neighbors to determine the predicted label of each test sample. The distance is simply defined as Euclidean distance. The memory-based KNN algorithm is simple, but the computation burden is relatively heavy.

SAE is the cascade-connected architecture of several Autoencoders (AE). AE is capable of learning the compressed representation of data, and thus widely used for dimensionality-reduction and deep network pre-training (kind of greedy algorithm). The input layer is composed by 400 neurons. The second layer is a hidden layer, where 200 neurons are assigned. The third layer is also a hidden layer, where 100 neurons are assigned. The last layer is the output layer with three neurons, and each neuron corresponds to one kind of emotion state.

We also investigate the consistency of emotion-related electric responses among different peoples. Here we define three HCNN training strategies.

A. Train and test HCNN on data acquired from one same subject (shown in Fig. 4).
B. Train the HCNN on the data acquired from three other subjects, and then test HCNN on a new subject.
C. Pre-train the HCNN on the data of three other subjects, and fine-tune it by the data of a new subject, and then test the HCNN on the new subject.

3.4 Results

Before showing the classification performance, we plan to illustrate the complexity of the previous task. We introduce Adjusted Cosine Similarity (ACS) as criterion to measure the similarity of features for three emotion states. ACS computes the cosine value of two sets of spatial vector, and the bigger the value is, the smaller the angel is, so the more confidence we acquire to assert that the two vectors are the same. Different from traditional cosine similarity (who simply compare similarity on the basis of spatial angel), ACS also take numerical magnitude into consideration. It not only measures similarity in direction sense, but also reflects the magnitude of feature vectors. We computed the mean ACS for each pair of the three kinds of emotion-states on wave band Beta and Gamma, and the spatial angles (radian measure) are summarized in Fig. 5. The angels are all very close to zero, and features belong to different emotion states are much alike.

The performance comparison of the four classifier implementations is summarized in Table 2. The results are shown in the form 'mean (SD)' (four subjects considered). No matter what kind of classifier is applied, the Beta wave and Gamma wave possess absolute advantage over the others. Also, HCNN and SAE are far better than SVM and KNN. The peak accuracies of Beta-classifier and Gamma-classifier is highlighted in

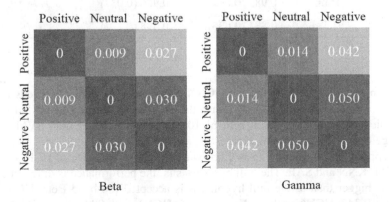

Fig. 5. The mean spatial angels for each pair of emotion-states (on Beta and Gamma).

Table 2. The performance of SVM, KNN, SAE and HCNN on five frequency bands.

Classifier	Wave band				
	Delta	Theta	Alpha	Beta	Gamma
SVM	0.597 (0.062)	0.501 (0.033)	0.595 (0.155)	0.732 (0.178)	0.744 (0.097)
KNN	0.533 (0.063)	0.429 (0.056)	0.587 (0.046)	0.697 (0.160)	0.755 (0.090)
SAE	0.491 (0.112)	0.407 (0.090)	0.671 (0.118)	0.783 (0.132)	0.854 (0.081)
HCNN	0.369 (0.032)	0.278 (0.106)	0.390 (0.091)	**0.862 (0.066)**	**0.882 (0.035)**

Table 3. The impact of HCNN training strategy on five frequency bands.

Wave band		Training strategy		
		A	B	C
Delta	Train	0.732 (0.040)	0.759 (0.013)	0.799 (0.042)
	Test	0.369 (0.032)	0.363 (0.023)	0.392 (0.031)
Theta	Train	0.726 (0.031)	0.759 (0.040)	0.741 (0.029)
	Test	0.278 (0.106)	0.421 (0.071)	0.449 (0.028)
Alpha	Train	0.767 (0.061)	0.773 (0.028)	0.849 (0.091)
	Test	0.390 (0.091)	0.344 (0.032)	0.372 (0.066)
Beta	Train	0.969 (0.017)	0.876 (0.036)	0.921 (0.028)
	Test	**0.862 (0.066)**	0.370 (0.019)	0.673 (0.076)
Gamma	Train	0.985 (0.017)	0.966 (0.037)	0.977 (0.036)
	Test	**0.882 (0.035)**	0.498 (0.117)	0.801 (0.096)

capital. On Beta, the performance of HCNN is around 86%, which exceeds the performance of SAE remarkably. On Gamma, the accuracy obtained by HCNN is around 88%, which beats KNN by a margin of 10%, and much better than SVM, yet the advantage over SAE is not remarkable.

We apply t-test to examine ($\alpha = 0.05$) whether the performance of HCNN is better than SVM, KNN and SAE. The null hypothesis is 'the performance is different', and if p-value is bigger than α, the null hypothesis is accepted (on band Beta, HCNN with SVM: p = 0.347; HCNN with KNN: p = 0.126; HCNN with SAE: p = 0.337. On band

Gamma, HCNN with SVM: $p = 0.059$; HCNN with KNN: $p = 0.059$; HCNN with SAE: $p = 0.556$).

The performance of HCNNs trained according to different strategies are summarized in Table 3. 'Train' refers to the accuracy on the training cases, and 'Test' refers to the accuracy obtained on the test samples. A, B, C are training strategies defined in Sect. 3.3. According to the results, if HCNN trained on other peoples is used directly on a new subject, the accuracy generally shows a downward cliff. On Beta, it is a surprising 50% decline, and on Gamma, a 30% decline occurs. When fine-tune method is applied on networks generated by B, the accuracy of Beta-classifier improves about 30%, but still much lower than that of the strategy A. The performance of Gamma-classifier under strategy A wins C by 8%. The superiority of strategy A over B and C is so obvious that hypothesis testing is not a necessary.

4   Discussion and Conclusion

The performance of HCNN classifier is better than SAE, which might be partly attributed to the way we organize the DE features. The two-dimensional maps contains extra spatial information for emotion recognition, and thus good for classifier training. Despite the training process demands more computational ability, HCNN is still a favorable tool to implement EEG-based emotion recognition system.

Deep models (HCNN and SAE) are better than the shallow models. HCNN is suitable, because the layer-wise convolution operations is efficient in feature synthesis and denoising. SAE is favorable, in that the representational ability acquired through goal-driven Back Propagation (BP) algorithm is strong. In this task, DL overbeats shallow models obviously. This phenomenon again shows the advantage of DL algorithm in complex data miming applications (when we evaluate the similarity of EEG features for different emotion states, we find it hard to discriminate them). The advantage of DL primarily lies in the powerful representational ability, which keeps growing as the models go deeper (quite similar to the human brain's working principle). Thus DL owns an insight into the data's internal features hidden deep in nonlinearity.

The results also demonstrate that 'complete transfer' method is not appropriate in EEG emotion recognition tasks, which means that the priori knowledge (now in the form of HCNN initial weights) learned from other peoples is not very useful to the present person. The initial weights learned on other peoples does not help the present HCNN converge faster, but on the contrary, their contribution cannot even match the random-assign method. This also tells us that the difference of EEG response patterns among different persons on the same task is huge, and the emotion-related BCI system for a certain customer should be individually designed to specially endow it with his (her) personal characteristics. However, previous studies [5] showed that for one single person, his (her) emotion-related EEG signal does not change much over time (at least for weeks), so the individually-designed HCNN emotion-reading system does not need frequent updates.

No matter how the features are organized and what kind of classifiers are applied, the frequency bands Beta and Gamma are always the best predictors of the emotion state. As a comparison, the accuracy obtained by the other bands of classifiers are poor and unstable. Such results further reveal the significance of high-frequency brain waves in task-evoked emotion-processing process. Our findings prove that Beta wave and Gamma wave are highly-involved in the reasoning and thinking activities of the brain. Therefore, we should focus on these two bands in the investigation of emotion. Simultaneously, the two bands are good basis for researchers to design more reliable emotion-related BCI systems.

In this paper, we analyze the EEG signal in the frequency domain, yet for each channel, the signal is a time series, which implies that autoregression and joint-regression relationship (between channels) should not be neglected. Therefore, for a further plan, we will introduce Recurrent Neural Networks (RNN), as well as Long-short Time Memory (LSTM) to the present study to conduct a more challenging time-frequency domain research concerning human's emotion.

Acknowledgement. This work was supported by National Natural Science Foundation of China (61271151, 91520202) and Youth Innovation Promotion Association CAS.

References

1. Kothe, C.A., Makeig, S.: Estimation of task workload from EEG data: new and current tools and perspectives. In: 2011 Annual International Conference of the IEEE Engineering in Medicine and Biology Society, pp. 6547–6551. IEEE (2011)
2. Shi, L.C., Lu, B.L.: EEG-based vigilance estimation using extreme learning machines. Neurocomputing **102**, 135–143 (2013)
3. Liu, Y., Sourina, O., Nguyen, M.K.: Real-time EEG-based emotion recognition and its applications. In: Gavrilova, M.L., Tan, C.J.K., Sourin, A., Sourina, O. (eds.). LNCS, vol. 6670, pp. 256–277Springer, Heidelberg (2011). doi:10.1007/978-3-642-22336-5_13
4. Ahern, G.L., Schwartz, G.E.: Differential lateralization for positive and negative emotion in the human brain: EEG spectral analysis. Neuropsychologia **23**(6), 745–755 (1985)
5. Zheng, W.L., Lu, B.L.: Investigating critical frequency bands and channels for EEG-based emotion recognition with deep neural networks. IEEE Trans. Auton. Mental Dev. **7**(3), 162–175 (2015)
6. Dash, M., Liu, H.: Feature selection for classification. Intell. Data Anal. **1**(3), 131–156 (1997)
7. Krizhevsky, A., Sutskever, I., Hinton, G.E.: Imagenet classification with deep convolutional neural networks. In: Advances in Neural Information Processing Systems, pp. 1097–1105 (2012)
8. Szegedy, C., Liu, W., Jia, Y., Sermanet, P., Reed, S., Anguelov, D., Rabinovich, A.: Going deeper with convolutions. In: Proceedings of the IEEE Conference on Computer Vision and Pattern Recognition, pp. 1–9 (2015)
9. Deselaers, T., Hasan, S., Bender, O., Ney, H.: A deep learning approach to machine transliteration. In: Proceedings of the Fourth Workshop on Statistical Machine Translation, pp. 233–241. Association for Computational Linguistics (2009)
10. Vincent, P., Larochelle, H., Lajoie, I., Bengio, Y., Manzagol, P.A.: Stacked denoising autoencoders: Learning useful representations in a deep network with a local denoising criterion. J. Mach. Learn. Res. 3371–3408 (2010)

11. Hinton, G.E.: Deep belief networks. Scholarpedia **4**(5), 5947 (2009)
12. Li, M., Lu, B.L.: Emotion classification based on gamma-band EEG. In: 2009 Annual International Conference of the IEEE Engineering in Medicine and Biology Society, pp. 1223–1226. IEEE (2009)
13. Hadjidimitriou, S.K., Hadjileontiadis, L.J.: EEG-based classification of music appraisal responses using time-frequency analysis and familiarity ratings. IEEE Trans. Affect. Comput. **4**(2), 161–172 (2013)
14. Li, Y., Luo, M.L., Li, K.: A multiwavelet-based time-varying model identification approach for time–frequency analysis of EEG signals. Neurocomputing **193**, 106–114 (2016)
15. Duan, R.N., Zhu, J.Y., Lu, B.L.: Differential entropy feature for EEG-based emotion classification. In: 2013 6th International IEEE/EMBS Conference on Neural Engineering (NER), pp. 81–84. IEEE (2013)
16. Philippot, P.: Inducing and assessing differentiated emotion-feeling states in the laboratory. Cogn. Emot. **7**(2), 171–193 (1993)

Can Machine Generate Traditional Chinese Poetry? A Feigenbaum Test

Qixin Wang[1,4], Tianyi Luo[1,3], and Dong Wang[1,2(✉)]

[1] CSLT, RIIT, Tsinghua University, Beijing, China
{wqx,lty}@cslt.riit.tsinghua.edu.cn, wangdong99@mails.tsinghua.edu.cn
[2] Tsinghua National Lab for Information Science and Technology, Beijing, China
[3] Huilan Limited, Beijing, China
[4] CIST, Beijing University of Posts and Telecommunications, Beijing, China

Abstract. Recent progress in neural learning demonstrated that machines can do well in regularized tasks, e.g., the game of Go. However, artistic activities such as poem generation are still widely regarded as human's special capability. In this paper, we demonstrate that a simple neural model can imitate human in some tasks of art generation. We particularly focus on traditional Chinese poetry, and show that machines can do as well as many contemporary poets and weakly pass the Feigenbaum Test, a variant of Turing test in professional domains.

Our method is based on an attention-based recurrent neural network, which accepts a set of keywords as the theme and generates poems by looking at each keyword during the generation. A number of techniques are proposed to improve the model, including character vector initialization, attention to input and hybrid-style training. Compared to existing poetry generation methods, our model can generate much more theme-consistent and semantic-rich poems.

1 Introduction

The classical Chinese poetry is a special cultural heritage with over 2,000 years of history and is still fascinating many contemporary poets. In history, Chinese poetry flourished in different genres at different time, including Tang poetry, Song iambics and Yuan songs. Different genres possess their own specific structure, rhythmical and tonal patterns. The structural pattern regulates how many lines and how many characters per line; the rhythmical pattern requires that the last characters of certain lines hold the same or similar vowels; and the tonal pattern requires characters in particular positions hold particular tones, i.e., 'Ping' (level tone), or 'Ze' (downward tone). A good poem should follow all these pattern regulations (in a descendant order of priority), and has to express

---

Q. Wang and T. Luo—The first two authors contributed equally.

D. Wang—RM 1-303, FIT BLDG, Tsinghua University, Beijing (100084), P.R. China. This work was supported by the National Science Foundation of China (NSFC) under the project NO. 61371136, and the MESTDC PhD Foundation Project No. 20130002120011. It was also supported by Huilan Ltd. and FreeNeb.

C.-L. Liu et al. (Eds.): BICS 2016, LNAI 10023, pp. 34–46, 2016.
DOI: 10.1007/978-3-319-49685-6_4

Table 1. An example of a quatrain. The rhyming characters are in boldface, and the tonal pattern is shown at the end of each line, where 'P' indicates level tone and 'Z' indicates downward tone, and '*' indicates the tone can be either.

> 塞下曲 Frontier Songs
>
> 月黑雁飞高，(*ZZPP) The wild goose flew high to the moon shaded by the cloud,
> 单于夜遁逃。(PPZZP) With the dark night's cover escaped the invaders crowd,
> 欲将轻骑逐，(*PPZZ) I was about to hunt after them with my cavalry,
> 大雪满弓刀。(*ZZPP) The snow already covered our bows and swords.

a consistent theme as well as a unique emotion. For this reason, it is widely admitted that traditional Chinese poetry generation is highly difficult.

Among all the genres of traditional Chinese poetry, perhaps the most popular is the quatrain, a special style with a strict structure (four lines with five or seven characters per line), a regulated rhythmical form (the last characters in the second and fourth lines must follow the same rhythm), and a required tonal pattern (tones of characters in some positions should satisfy some pre-defined regulations). This genre of poems flourished mostly in Tang Dynasty, so often called 'Tang poem'. An example of quatrain written by Lun Lu, a famous poet in Tang Dynasty [16], is shown in Table 1.

Due to the stringent restriction in rhythm and tone, it is not trivial to create a fully rule-compliant quatrain. More importantly, besides such strict regulations, a good quatrain should also read fluently, hold a consistent theme, and express a unique affection.

We are interested in machine poetry generation, not only because of its practical value in entertainment and education, but also because it demonstrates an important aspect of artificial intelligence: the creativity of machines. We hold the belief that poetry generation (and other artistic activities) is a pragmatic process and can be largely learned from past experience. In this paper, we focus on traditional Chinese poetry generation, and demonstrate that machines can do it as well as many human poets.

There have been some attempts in this direction, e.g., by machine translation models [6] and recurrent neural networks (RNN) [22]. These methods can generate traditional Chinese poems with different levels of quality, and can be used to assist people in poem generation. However, none of them can generate poems that are fluent and consistent enough, not to mention innovation.

In this paper, we propose a simple neural approach to traditional Chinese poetry generation based on the attention-based Gated Recurrent Unit (GRU) model. Specifically, we follow the sequence-to-sequence learning architecture that uses a GRU [3] to encode a set of keywords as the theme, and another GRU to generate quatrains character by character, where the keywords are looked back during the entire generation process. By this approach, the generation is regularized by the keywords so a global theme is assured. By enriching the set of keywords, the generation tends to be more 'innovative', resulting in more diverse poems. Our experiments demonstrated that the new approach can generate traditional Chinese poems pretty well and even pass the Feigenbaum Test.

2   Related Work

A multitude of methods have been proposed for poem automatic generation. The first approach is based on rules and templates. For example, [15,18] employed a phrase search approach for Japanese poem generation, and [11] proposed an approach based on word association norms. [12] and [13] used semantic and grammar templates for Spanish poem generation.

The second approach is built on various genetic algorithms. For example, [23] proposed to use a stochastic search algorithm to obtain the best matched sentences. The search algorithm is based on four standards proposed by [9]: fluency, meaningfulness, poeticness, and coherence.

The third approach involves various statistical machine translation (SMT) methods. This approach was used by [7] to generate Chinese couplets, a special regulated verses with only two lines. [6] extended this approach to Chinese quatrain generation, where each line of the poem is generated by translating the preceding line.

Another approach to poem generation is based on text summarization. For example, [19] proposed a method that retrieves high-ranking candidates of sentences from a large poem corpus, and then re-arranges them to generate rule-conformed new sentences.

More recently, deep learning methods gain much attention in poem generation. For example, [22] proposed an RNN-based approach that was reported to work well in quatrain generation [22]; however, the structure seems rather complicated (a CNN and two RNN components in total), preventing it from extending to other genres. Our model is a simple sequence-to-sequence structure, which is much simpler than the model proposed by [22] and can be easily extended to more complex genres such as Sonnet and Haiku without modification.

Finally, [17] proposed an attention-based model for Song Iambics generation. However, their model performed rather poor when was applied directly to quatrain generation using keywords input, possibly because quatrains are more condensed and more individually unique than iambics. Our approach follows the attention-based strategy in [17], but introduces several innovations. Firstly, the poems were generated through key words rather than the first sentence to provide more clear themes; Secondly, a single-word attention mechanism was used to improve the sensitivity to key words; Thirdly, a loop generation approach was proposed to improve the fluency and coherence of the attention-based model.

3   Method

In this section, we first present the attention-based Chinese poetry generation framework, and then describe the implementation of the encoder and decoder models that have been tailored for our task.

3.1   Attention-Based Chinese Poetry Generation

The attention-based sequence-to-sequence model proposed by [1] is a powerful framework for sequence generation. Specifically, the input sequence is converted by an 'encoder' to a sequence of hidden states to represent the semantic status at each position of the input, and these hidden states are used to regulate a 'decoder' that generates the target sequence. The important mechanism of the attention-based model is that at each generation step, the most relevant input units are discovered by comparing the 'current' status of the decoder with all the hidden states of the encoder, so that the generation is regulated by the fine structure of the input sequence.

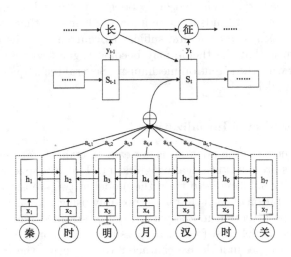

Fig. 1. The attention-based sequence-to-sequence framework for Chinese poetry generation.

The entire framework of the attention-based model applied to Chinese poetry generation is illustrated in Fig. 1. The encoder (a bi-directional RNN) converts the input keywords, a character sequence denoted by $(x_1, x_2, ...)$, into a sequence of hidden states $(h_1, h_2, ...)$. The decoder (another RNN) then generates the whole poem character by character, denoted by $(y_1, y_2, ...)$. At each step t, the prediction for the next character y_t is based on the 'current' status s_t of the decoder as well as all the hidden states $(h_1, h_2, ..., h_T)$ of the encoder. Each hidden state h_i contributes to the generation according to a relevant factor $\alpha_{t,i}$ that measures the similarity between s_t and h_i. To alleviate the problem that vanilla RNN tend to forget historical input quickly [21], we used GRU in every RNN in our model to provide a strong memory for theme.

3.2   Model Training

The goal of the training is to let the predicted character sequence match the original poem. We chose the cross entropy between the distributions over Chinese characters given by the decoder and the ground truth (essentially in a one-hot form) as the objective function. To speed up the training, the minibatch stochastic gradient descent (SGD) algorithm was adopted. The gradient was computed in sentences, and the AdaDelta algorithm was used to adjust the learning rate [21]. In the training phase, there are no keyword input, so we use the first line as the input to generate the entire poem.

4   Implementation

The basic attention model does not naturally work well for Chinese poetry generation. A particular problem is that every poem was created to express a special affection of the poet, so it tends to be 'unique'. This means that most valid (and often great) expressions can not find sufficient occurrence in the training data. Another problem is that the theme may become vague towards the end of the generation, even with the attention mechanism. Several techniques are presented to improve the model.

4.1   Character Vector Initialization

Since the uniqueness of each poem, it is not easy to train the attention model, as many expressions are not statistically significant. This is a special form of data sparsity. A possible solution is to train the model in two steps: firstly learn the semantic representation of each character, possibly using a large external corpus, and then train the attention model with these pre-trained representations. By this approach, the model most focuses on possible expressions and hence is easier to train. In practice, we first derive character vectors using the word2vec tool[1], and then use these character vectors to initialize the word embedding matrix in our model. Since part of the model (embedding matrix) has been pre-trained, the problem of data sparsity can be largely alleviated.

4.2   Input Reconstruction

Poets tend to express their feelings following an implicit theme, instead of an explicit reiteration. We found this implicit theme is not easy for machines to understand and learn, leading to possible theme drift at run-time. A simple solution is to force the model to reconstruct the input after it has generated the entire poem. More specifically, in the training phase, we use the first line of a training poem as the input, and based on this input to generate five lines sequentially: line 1-2-3-4-1. The last generation step for line 1 forces the model to keep the input in mind during the entire generation process, so learns how to focus on the theme.

---

[1] https://code.google.com/archive/p/word2vec/.

4.3 Input Vector Attention

The popular configuration of the attention model attends on hidden states. Since hidden states represent *accumulated* semantic meaning, this attention is good to form a global theme. However, as the semantic contents of individual keywords have been largely averaged, it is hard to generate diverse poems sensitive to each and different keywords.

We propose a multiple-attention solution that attends on both hidden states and input character vectors, so that both accumulated and individual semantics are considered during the generation. It has been found that this approach is highly effective for generating diverse and novel poems: just given sufficient keywords, new poems can be generated with high quality. Compared to other approaches such as noise injection or n-best inference, this approach can generate unlimited alternatives without any quality sacrifice. Interestingly, our experiments show that more keywords tend to generate more unexpected but highly impressive poems. Therefore, the multiple-attention approach can be regarded as an interesting way to promote innovation.

4.4 Hybrid-Style Training

Traditional Chinese quatrains are categorized into 5-char quatrains and 7-char quatrains that involve five and seven characters per line, respectively. These two categories follow different regulations, but also share the same words and similar semantics. We utilize the hybrid-style training method as [17] that trains the two types of quatrains using the same model, with a 'type indicator' derived from eigen vectors of a 200×200 dimensional random matrix, to notify the model the type of present training sample.

5 Experiments

We describe the experimental settings and results in this section. Firstly the datasets used in the experiments are presented, and then we report the evaluation in two phases: (1) the first phase focuses on searching for optimal configurations for the attention model; (2) the second phase compares the attention model with other methods; (3) the third phase is the Feigenbaum Test.

5.1 Datasets

Two datasets are used to conduct the experiments. Firstly a Chinese quatrain corpus was collected from Internet. This corpus consists of $13,299$ 5-char quatrains and $65,560$ 7-char quatrains. As far as we know, this covers most of the quatrains that are retained today. We filters out some poems which contain 100% low frequency words. Through corpus cleaning, a corpus which contains $9,195$ 5-char quatrains and $49,162$ 7-char quatrains was obtained. $9,000$ 5-char and $49,000$ 7-char quatrains are used to train the GRU model of the attention model and LSTM model of a comparative model based on RNN language models and the rest poems are used as the test datasets.

The second dataset was used to train and derive character vectors for attention model initialization. This dataset contains 284, 899 traditional Chinese poems in various genres, including Tang quatrains, Song iambics, Yuan Songs, Ming and Qing poems. This large amount data ensures a stable learning for semantic content of most characters.

5.2 Model Development

In the first evaluation, we intend to find the best configurations for the proposed attention-based model. The 'Bilingual Evaluation Understudy' (BLEU) [14] is used as the metric to determine which enhancement techniques are effective. BLEU was originally proposed to evaluate machine translation performance [14], and was used by [22] to evaluate quality of poem generation. We used BLEU in the development phase to determine which design option to choose, without the costly human evaluation.

The method proposed by [6] and employed by [22] was adopted to obtain reference poems. A slight difference is that the reference set was constructed for each *input keyword*, instead of each sentence as in [22]. This is because our attention model generates poems as an entire character sequence, while the vanilla RNN approach in [22] does that sentence by sentence. Additionally, we used 1-gram and 2-grams in the BLEU computation, according to the fact that semantic meaning is mostly represented by single characters and some character pairs in traditional Chinese.

Table 2 presents the results. The baseline model is trained with character initialization where the character vectors are trained using quatrains only. This is mostly the system in [17]. Then we use the large corpus that involves all traditional Chinese poems to enhance the character vectors, and the results demonstrated a noticeable performance improvement in fluency (from our human judgements) and a small improvement in BLEU (2nd row in Table 2). This is understandable since poems in different genres use similar languages, so involving more training data helps infer more reliable semantic content for each character. Additionally, we observe that reconstructing the input during model training

Table 2. BLEU scores with various enhancement techniques.

Model	BLEU	
	5-char	7-char
Basic model	0.259	0.464
+ All poem training	0.267	0.467
+ Input Reconstruction	0.268	0.500
+ Input Vector Attention	0.290	0.501
+ Hybrid training	**0.330**	**0.630**

improves the model (3rd row). This is probably due to the enhancement in theme consistence. What's more, attention to both input vectors and hidden states leads to additional performance gains (4th row). Finally, the hybrid-style training is employed to train a single model for the 5-char and 7-char quatrains. The BLEUs are tested on 5-char and 7-char quatrains respectively and the results are shown in the 5-th row of Table 2. Note that in the hybrid training, we stop the training before convergence in favor of a good BLEU.

From these results, we obtain the best configuration that involves character vector trained with extern training data, input reconstruction, input vector attention and hybrid training. In the reset of the paper, we will use this configuration to train the attention model (denoted by 'Attention') and compare it with the comparative methods.

5.3   Comparative Evaluation

In the second phase, we compare the attention model (with the best configuration) and three comparative models: the SMT model proposed by [6], the vanilla RNN poem generation (RNNPG) proposed by [22], and an RNN language model (RNNLM) that can be regarded as a simplified version (One-direction LSTM RNN neural network without attention mechanism) of the attention model [10].

Following the work of [22], we selected 30 subjects (e.g., falling flower, stone bridge, etc.) in the Shixuehanying taxonomy [8] as 30 themes. For each theme, several phrases belonging to the corresponding subject were selected as the input keywords. For the attention model, these keywords were used to generate the first line directly; For the other three models, however, the first line had to be constructed beforehand by an external model. We chose the method provided by [22] to generate the first lines for the SMT, vanilla RNN and LSTMLM approaches. A 5-char quatrain and a 7-char quatrain were generated for each theme by the four methods, and were evaluated by experts.

For reference, some poems written by ancient poets were also involved in the evaluation. To prevent the impact of prior knowledge of the experts, we deliberately chose the poems written by poets that are not very famous. The poems were chosen from [2,5,20]; and a 5-char quatrain and a 7-char quatrain were selected for each theme.

The evaluation was conducted by experts based on the following four metrics, in the scale from 0 to 5:

- Compliance: if the poem satisfies the regulation on tones and rhymes;
- Fluency: if the sentences read fluently and convey reasonable meaning;
- Consistence: if the poem adheres to a single theme;
- Aesthesis: if the poem stimulates any aesthetic feeling.

In the experiments, we invited 26 experts to conduct a series of scoring evaluations[2]. These experts were asked to rate the generation of our model and

---

[2] These experts are professors and their postgraduate students in the field of Chinese poetry research. Most of them are from the Chinese Academy of Social Sciences (CASS).

Table 3. Averaged ratings for Chinese quatrain generation with different methods. 'char-5' and 'char-7' represent 5-char and 7-char characters quatrains respectively in the evaluation.

Model	Compliance		Fluency		Consistence		Aesthesis		Overall	
	char-5	char-7	char-5	char-7	char-5	char-7	char-5	char-7	char-5	char-7
SMT	3.04	2.83	2.28	1.92	2.15	2.00	1.93	1.67	2.35	2.10
LSTMLM	3.00	3.71	2.39	3.10	2.19	2.88	2.00	2.66	2.39	3.08
RNNPG	2.90	2.60	2.05	1.70	1.97	1.70	1.70	1.45	2.15	1.86
Attention	**3.44**	**3.73**	2.85	3.13	2.77	2.98	2.38	2.87	2.86	3.17
Human	3.33	3.54	**3.37**	**3.33**	**3.45**	**3.26**	**3.05**	**2.96**	**3.30**	**3.27**

three comparative approaches: SMT, LSTMLM, and RNNPG. The SMT-based approach is available online[3] and we use this online service to obtain the generation. For RNNPG, we invited the authors to conduct the generation for us. The LSTMLM approach was implemented by ourselves, for which we used the GRU instead of the vanilla RNN to enhance long-distance memory, and used character vector initialization to improve model training.

Poems written by ancient poets are also involved in the test. For each method (including human-written), a 5-char quatrain and a 7-char quatrain were generated or selected for each of the 30 themes, amounting to 300 poems in total in the test. For each expert, 80 poems were randomly selected for evaluation.

Table 3 presents the results. It can be seen that our model outperforms all the comparative approaches in terms of all the four metrics. More interestingly, we find that the scores obtained by our model are approaching to those obtained by human poets, especially with 7-char poems. This is highly encouraging and indicates that our model can imitate human beings to a large extent, at least from the eyes of contemporary experts.

The second best approach is the LSTMLM approach. As we mentioned, LSTMLM can be regarded as a simplified version of our attention model, and shares the same strength in LSTM-based long-distance pattern learning and improved training strategy with character vector initialization. This demonstrated that a simple neural model with little engineering effort may learn artistic activities pretty good. Nevertheless, the comparative advantage of the attention model still demonstrated the importance of the attention mechanism.

The RNNPG and the SMT approaches perform equally worse, particularly RNNPG. A possible reason is that RNNPG requires an SMT model to enhance the performance but the SMT model was not used in this test[4]. In fact, even with the SMT model, RNNPG can hardly approach to human as the attention model does, as shown in the original paper [22]. The SMT approach, with a bunch of unknown optimizations by the Microsoft colleagues, can deliver reasonable

---

[3] http://duilian.msra.cn/jueju/.

[4] The author of RNNPG [22] could not find the SMT model in the reproduction, unfortunately.

quality, but the limitation of the model prevents it from approaching a human-level as our model does. The T-test results show that the difference between the attention LSTM model (ours) and the vanilla RNN and SMT are both significant ($p < 0.01$), though the difference between the attention LSTM model and LSTMLM is weakly significant ($p = 0.03$).

It is noticeable that the human ratings of human-written poems are lower than the ratings reported by [22]. We are not sure the experts that Zhang and Lapata invited, but the experts in our experiments are truly professional and critical: most of them are top-level experts on classical Chinese poetry education and criticism, and some of them are winners of national competitors in classic Chinese poetry writing.

Interestingly, in the metric of compliance, our attention model outperforms human. This is not surprising as computers can simply search vast candidate characters to ensure a rule-obeyed generation. In contrast, human artists put meaning and affection as the top priority, so sometimes break the rule.

Finally, we see that the quality of the 7-char poems generated by our model is very close to that of the human-written poems. This should be interpreted in two perspectives: On one hand, it indicates that our generation is rather successful; On the other hand, we should pay attention that the poems we selected are from infamous poets. Our intention was to avoid biased rating caused by experts' prior knowledge on the poems, but this may have limited the quality of the selected poems, although we have tried our best to choose good ones.

5.4 Feigenbaum Test

We design a Feigenbaum Test [4] to evaluate the quality of poems generated by our models. Feigenbaum test (FT) can be regarded as a generalized Turing test (TT), the most well-known method for evaluating AI systems. A particular shortcoming of TT is that it is only suitable for tasks involving interactive conversions. However, there are many professional domains where no conversations are involved but still require a simple method like TT to evaluate machines' intelligence. Feigenbaum Test follows the core idea of TT, but focuses on professional tasks that can be done only by domain experts. The basic idea of FT is that an intelligent system in a professional domain should behave as a human expert, and the behavior can not be *distinguished from* human experts, when *judged by* human experts in the same domain. We believe that this is highly important when evaluating AI systems on artistic activities, for which mimicking the behavior of human experts is an important indicator of its success.

In this section, we follow this idea and utilize FT to evaluate the poetry generation models. Specifically, we distributed the 30 themes to some experts in traditional Chinese poem generation[5]. We asked these experts to select one theme that they are most favor so that the quality can be ensured.

---

[5] These experts were nominated by professors in the field of traditional Chinese poetry research.

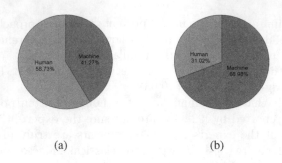

(a)   (b)

Fig. 2. Decision option for (a) human-written (b) machine-generated poems.

We received 144 submissions. To ensure the quality of the submission, we generated the same number of poems by our model and then asked a highly-professional expert in traditional Chinese poem criticism to give the first round filtering. After the filtering, 83 human-written poems (57.6%) and 180 computer-generated poems (86.5%) were remained, respectively. This indicates that human-generated poems are in a larger variance in quality, which is not very surprising as the knowledge and skill of people tend to vary significantly.

The remained 263 poems were distributed to 24 experts for evaluation[6]. The experts were asked to answer two questions: (1) if a poem was generated by people; (2) quality of a poem, rated from 0 to 5.

The results of the human-machine decision are presented in Fig. 2. For a clear representation, the minor proportions of zero scores are omitted in the figure. We observe that 41.27% of the human-written poems were identified as machine-generated, and 31% of the machine-generated poems were identified as human-written. This indicates that a large number of poems can not be correctly identified by people. According to the criterion of Turing Test (Actually, Feigenbaum Test can be regarded as domain specific "Turing Test"), our model has weakly passed[7]. Interestingly, among the top-5 high-ranked poems, the machine takes the position 1 and 2, and among the top 10, the machine takes the position 1, 2 and 7. This means that our model can generate better poems even than human poets, although in general it is still beat by human.

5.5   Generation Example

Finally we show a 7-char quatrain generated by the attention model. The theme of this poem is 'crab-apple flower' (Table 4).

---

[6] These experts again are mostly from CASS, part of them attended the previous test.

[7] The criterion is to fool people in more than 30% of the trials. Refer to https://en.wikipedia.org/wiki/Turing_test.

Table 4. A quatrain example generated by the attention model.

海棠花 Crab-apple Flower	
红霞淡艳媚妆水，	Like the rosy afterglows with light make-up being sexy,
万朵千峰映碧垂。	Among green leaves, thousands of crabapples blossoms make the branch droopy.
一夜东风吹雨过，	After a night of wind and shower,
满城春色在天辉。	With the bright sky, spring is all over the city.

6   Conclusion

This paper proposed an attention-based neural model for Chinese poetry generation. Compared to existing methods, the new approach is simple in model structure, strong in theme preservation, flexible to produce innovation, and easy to be extended to other genres. Our experiments show that it can generate traditional Chinese quatrains pretty well. A future work will employ more generative models, e.g. variational generative deep models, to achieve more natural innovation. We also plan to extend the work to other genres of traditional Chinese poetry, e.g., Yuan songs.

References

1. Bahdanau, D., Cho, K., Bengio, Y.: Neural machine translation by jointly learning to align and translate. arXiv preprint arXiv:1409.0473 (2014)
2. Chen, Y.: Jin Poetry Chronicle. Shanghai Chinese Classics Publishing House, Shanghai (2013)
3. Cho, K., Van Merriënboer, B., Gulcehre, C., Bahdanau, D., Bougares, F., Schwenk, H., Bengio, Y.: Learning phrase representations using RNN encoder-decoder for statistical machine translation. arXiv preprint arXiv:1406.1078 (2014)
4. Feigenbaum, E.A.: Some challenges and grand challenges for computational intelligence. J. ACM (JACM) **50**(1), 32–40 (2003)
5. Han, W.: Study on the Liao, Jin and Yuan Poetry and Music Theory. China Social Sciences Press, Beijing (2015)
6. He, J., Zhou, M., Jiang, L.: Generating Chinese classical poems with statistical machine translation models. In: Twenty-Sixth AAAI Conference on Artificial Intelligence (2012)
7. Jiang, L., Zhou, M.: Generating Chinese couplets using a statistical MT approach. In: Proceedings of the 22nd International Conference on Computational Linguistics, vol. 1, pp. 377–384. Association for Computational Linguistics (2008)
8. Liu, W.: ShiXueHanYing (1735)
9. Manurung, R., Ritchie, G., Thompson, H.: Using genetic algorithms to create meaningful poetic text. J. Exp. Theor. Artif. Intell. **24**(1), 43–64 (2012)
10. Mikolov, T., Karafiát, M., Burget, L., Cernocký, J., Khudanpur, S.: Recurrent neural network based language model. In: 11th Annual Conference of the International Speech Communication Association. INTERSPEECH 2010, Makuhari, 26–30 September 2010, pp. 1045–1048 (2010)

11. Netzer, Y., Gabay, D., Goldberg, Y., Elhadad, M.: Gaiku: generating haiku with word associations norms. In: Proceedings of the Workshop on Computational Approaches to Linguistic Creativity, pp. 32–39. Association for Computational Linguistics (2009)

12. Oliveira, H.: Automatic generation of poetry: an overview. Universidade de Coimbra (2009)

13. Oliveira, H.G.: PoeTryMe: a versatile platform for poetry generation. In: Proceedings of the ECAI 2012 Workshop on Computational Creativity, Concept Invention, and General Intelligence (2012)

14. Papineni, K., Roukos, S., Ward, T., Zhu, W.J.: BLEU: a method for automatic evaluation of machine translation. In: Proceedings of the 40th annual meeting on association for computational linguistics, pp. 311–318. Association for Computational Linguistics (2002)

15. Tosa, N., Obara, H., Minoh, M.: Hitch haiku: an interactive supporting system for composing haiku poem. In: Stevens, S.M., Saldamarco, S.J. (eds.) ICEC 2008. LNCS, vol. 5309, pp. 209–216. Springer, Heidelberg (2008). doi:10.1007/978-3-540-89222-9_26

16. Wang, L.: A Summary of Rhyming Constraints of Chinese Poems (Shi Ci Ge Lv Gai Yao). Beijing Press, Beijing (2002)

17. Wang, Q., Luo, T., Wang, D., Xing, C.: Chinese song iambics generation with neural attention-based model. In: IJCAI 2016 (2016)

18. Wu, X., Tosa, N., Nakatsu, R.: New hitch haiku: an interactive renku poem composition supporting tool applied for sightseeing navigation system. In: Natkin, S., Dupire, J. (eds.) ICEC 2009. LNCS, vol. 5709, pp. 191–196. Springer, Heidelberg (2009). doi:10.1007/978-3-642-04052-8_19

19. Yan, R., Jiang, H., Lapata, M., Lin, S.D., Lv, X., Li, X.: I, poet: automatic Chinese poetry composition through a generative summarization framework under constrained optimization. In: Proceedings of the Twenty-Third International Joint Conference on Artificial Intelligence, pp. 2197–2203. AAAI Press (2013)

20. Yoshikawa, K.: Gen Min shi gaisetsu. Iwanami Shoten Publishers, Tokyo (1963)

21. Zeiler, M.D.: AdaDelta: an adaptive learning rate method. arXiv preprint arXiv:1212.5701 (2012)

22. Zhang, X., Lapata, M.: Chinese poetry generation with recurrent neural networks. In: Proceedings of the 2014 Conference on Empirical Methods in Natural Language Processing (EMNLP), pp. 670–680 (2014)

23. Zhou, C.L., You, W., Ding, X.: Genetic algorithm and its implementation of automatic generation of Chinese songci. J. Softw. **21**(3), 427–437 (2010)

Decoding Visual Stimuli in Human Brain by Using Anatomical Pattern Analysis on fMRI Images

Muhammad Yousefnezhad and Daoqiang Zhang[(✉)]

College of Computer Science and Technology,
Nanjing University of Aeronautics and Astronautics, Nanjing, China
{myousefnezhad,dqzhang}@nuaa.edu.cn

Abstract. A universal unanswered question in neuroscience and machine learning is whether computers can decode the patterns of the human brain. Multi-Voxels Pattern Analysis (MVPA) is a critical tool for addressing this question. However, there are two challenges in the previous MVPA methods, which include decreasing sparsity and noises in the extracted features and increasing the performance of prediction. In overcoming mentioned challenges, this paper proposes Anatomical Pattern Analysis (APA) for decoding visual stimuli in the human brain. This framework develops a novel anatomical feature extraction method and a new imbalance AdaBoost algorithm for binary classification. Further, it utilizes an Error-Correcting Output Codes (ECOC) method for multi-class prediction. APA can automatically detect active regions for each category of the visual stimuli. Moreover, it enables us to combine homogeneous datasets for applying advanced classification. Experimental studies on 4 visual categories (words, consonants, objects and scrambled photos) demonstrate that the proposed approach achieves superior performance to state-of-the-art methods.

Keywords: Brain decoding · Multi-Voxel Pattern Analysis · Anatomical feature extraction · Visual Object Recognition · Imbalance classification

1 Introduction

One of the key challenges in neuroscience is how the human brain activities can be mapped to the different brain tasks. As a conjunction between neuroscience and computer science, Multi-Voxel Pattern Analysis (MVPA) [1] addresses this question by applying machine learning methods on task-based functional Magnetic Resonance Imaging (fMRI) datasets. Analyzing the patterns of visual objects is one of the most interesting topics in MVPA, which can enable us to understand how brain stores and processes the visual stimuli [2,3]. It can be used for finding novel treatments for mental diseases or even creating a new generation of the user interface in the future.

© Springer International Publishing AG 2016
C.-L. Liu et al. (Eds.): BICS 2016, LNAI 10023, pp. 47–57, 2016.
DOI: 10.1007/978-3-319-49685-6_5

Technically, there are two challenges in previous studies. The first challenge is decreasing sparsity and noise in preprocessed voxels. Since, most of the previous studies directly utilized voxels for predicting the stimuli, the trained features are mostly sparse, high-dimensional and noisy; and they contain trivial useful information [2–4]. The second challenge is increasing the performance of prediction. Most of the brain decoding problems employed binary classifiers especially by using a one-versus-all strategy [1,2,5–7]. In addition, multi-class predictors are even mostly based on the binary classifiers such as the Error-Correcting Output Codes (ECOC) methods [8]. Since task-based fMRI experiments are mostly imbalance, it is so hard to train an effective binary classifier in the brain decoding problems. For instance, consider collected data with 10 same size categories. Since this dataset is imbalance for one-versus-all binary classification, most of the classical algorithms cannot provide acceptable performance [2,5,9].

For facing mentioned problems, this paper proposes Anatomical Pattern Analysis (APA) as a general framework for decoding visual stimuli in the human brain. This framework employs a novel feature extraction method, which uses the brain anatomical regions for generating a normalized view. In practice, this view can enable us to combine homogeneous datasets. The feature extraction method also can automatically detect the active regions for each category of the visual stimuli. Indeed, it can decrease noise and sparsity and increase the performance of the final result. Further, this paper develops a modified version of imbalance AdaBoost algorithm for binary classification. This algorithm uses a supervised random sampling and penalty values, which are calculated by the correlation between different classes, for improving the performance of prediction. This binary classification will be used in a one-versus-all ECOC method as a multi-class approach for classifying the categories of the brain response.

The rest of this paper is organized as follows: In Sect. 2, this study briefly reviews some related works. Then, it introduces the proposed method in Sect. 3. Experimental results are reported in Sect. 4; and finally, this paper presents conclusion and pointed out some future works in Sect. 5.

2   Related Works

There are three different types of studies for decoding visual stimuli in the human brain. Pioneer studies just focused on the special regions of the human brain, such as the Fusiform Face Area (FFA) or Parahippocampal Place Area (PPA). They only proved that different stimuli can provide different responses in those regions, or found most effective locations based on different stimuli [2].

The next group of studies introduced different correlation techniques for understanding similarity or difference between responses to different visual stimuli. Haxby et al. recently showed that different visual stimuli, i.e. human faces, animals, etc., represent different responses in the brain [2]. Further, Rice et al. proved that not only the mentioned responses are different based on the categories of the stimuli, but also they are correlated based on different properties of the stimuli. They used GIST technique for extracting the properties of stimuli and calculated the correlations between these properties and the brain responses. They separately reported the correlation matrices for different human faces and different objects (houses, chairs, bottles, shoes) [12].

The last group of studies proposed the MVPA techniques for predicting the category of visual stimuli. Cox et al. utilized linear and non-linear versions of Support Vector Machine (SVM) algorithm [5]. Norman et al. argued for using SVM and Gaussian Naive Bayes classifiers [1]. Carroll et al. employed the Elastic Net for prediction and interpretation of distributed neural activity with sparse models [13]. Varoquaux et al. proposed a small-sample brain mapping by using sparse recovery on spatially correlated designs with randomization and clustering. Their method is applied on small sets of brain patterns for distinguishing different categories based on a one-versus-one strategy [14]. McMenamin et al. studied subsystems underlie abstract-category (AC) recognition and priming of objects (e.g., cat, piano) and specific-exemplar (SE) recognition and priming of objects (e.g., a calico cat, a different calico cat, a grand piano, etc.). Technically, they applied SVM on manually selected ROIs in the human brain for generating the visual stimuli predictors [6]. Mohr et al. compared four different classification methods, i.e. L1/2 regularized SVM, the Elastic Net, and the Graph Net, for predicting different responses in the human brain. They show that L1-regularization can improve classification performance while simultaneously providing highly specific and interpretable discriminative activation patterns [7]. Osher et al. proposed a network (graph) based approach by using anatomical regions of the human brain for representing and classifying the different visual stimuli responses (faces, objects, bodies, scenes) [3].

3   The Proposed Method

Blood Oxygen Level Dependent (BOLD) signals are used in fMRI techniques for representing the neural activates. Based on hyperalignment problem in the brain decoding [2], quantity values of the BOLD signals in the same experiment for the two subjects are usually different. Therefore, MVPA techniques use the correlation between different voxels as the pattern of the brain response [3,4]. As depicted in Fig. 1, each fMRI experiment includes a set of sessions (time series of 3D images), which can be captured by different subjects or just repeating the imaging procedure with a unique subject. Technically, each session can be partitioned into a set of visual stimuli categories. Indeed, an independent category denotes a set of homogeneous conditions, which are generated by using the same type of photos as the visual stimuli. For instance, if a subject watches 6 photos of cats and 5 photos of houses during a unique session, this 4D image includes 2 different categories and 11 conditions.

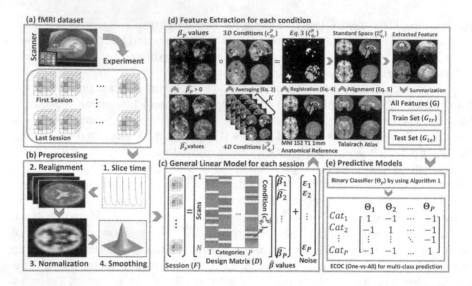

Fig. 1. Anatomical Pattern Analysis (APA) framework

3.1 Feature Extraction

Consider $F \in \mathbb{R}^{N \times X \times Y \times Z} = \{$number of scans $(N) \times$ 3D images$\}$ for each session of the experiment. F can be written as a general linear model: $F = D\beta + \varepsilon$, where $D = \{$number of scans (N) $\times$ P categories (regressors)$\}$ denotes the design matrix; ε is the noise (error of estimation); and also $\beta = \{$number of categories $(P) \times$ 3D images$\}$ denotes the set of correlations between voxels for the categories of the session. Design matrix can be calculated by convolution $(D(t) = (S * H)(t))$ of onsets (or time series $S(t)$) and the Hemodynamic Response Function (HRF) [4]. This paper uses Generalized Least Squares (GLS) approach for estimating optimized solution $(\hat{\beta} = (D^{\intercal}V^{-1}D)^{-1}D^{\intercal}V^{-1}F)$, where V is the covariance matrix of the noise $(Var(\varepsilon) = V\sigma^2 \neq \mathbb{I}\sigma^2)$ [2,4]. Now, this paper defines the positive correlation $\beta = \hat{\beta} > 0 = \{\hat{\beta}_1 > 0, \hat{\beta}_2 > 0, \ldots, \hat{\beta}_P > 0\} = \{\beta_1, \beta_2, \ldots, \beta_P\}$ for all categories as the active regions, where $\hat{\beta}$ denotes the estimated correlation, $\hat{\beta}_p$ and β_p are the correlation and *positive* correlation for the p-th category, respectively. Moreover, the data F is partitioned based on the conditions of the design matrix as follows:

$$\hat{C} = \{\hat{c}_1^1, \hat{c}_2^1, \ldots, \hat{c}_{Q_1}^1, \hat{c}_1^2, \hat{c}_2^2, \ldots, \hat{c}_{Q_2}^2, \ldots, \hat{c}_1^p, \hat{c}_2^P, \ldots, \hat{c}_{Q_R}^P\} \qquad (1)$$

where $\hat{C}$ denotes the set of all conditions in each session, P and Q_r are respectively the number of categories in each session and the number of conditions in each category. Further, $\hat{c}_{q_r}^p = \{$number of scans $(K_{q_r}^p) \times$ 3D images$\}$ denotes the 4D images for the p-th category and q_r-th condition in the design matrix. Now, this paper defines the sum of all images in a condition as follows:

$$C^p_{q_r} = \sum_K \hat{c}^p_{q_r} = \sum_{k=1}^{K^p_{q_r}} \hat{c}^p_{q_r}[k,:,:,:] \tag{2}$$

where $c^p_{q_r}[k,:,:,:]$ denotes all voxels in the k-th scan of q_r-th condition of p-th category; also $K^p_{q_r}$ is the number of scans in the given condition. $\zeta^p_{q_r}$ matrix is denoted for applying the correlation of voxels on the response of each condition as follows:

$$\zeta^p_{q_r} = \beta_p \circ C^p_{q_r} = \{\forall [x,y,z] \in C^p_{q_r} \implies (\zeta^p_{q_r})_{[x,y,z]} = (\beta_p)_{[x,y,z]} \times (C^p_{q_r})_{[x,y,z]}\} \tag{3}$$

where $\circ$ denotes Hadamard product; and $(C^p_{q_r})_{[x,y,z]}$ is the $[x,y,z]$-th voxel of the q_r-th condition of p-th category; and also, $(\beta_p)_{[x,y,z]}$ is the $[x,y,z]$-th voxel of the correlation matrix (β values) of the p-th category.

Since mapping 4D fMRI images to standard space decreases the performance of final results, most of the previous studies use the original images instead of the standard version. By considering 3D image $\zeta^p_{q_r}$ for each condition, this paper enables to map brain activities to a standard space. This mapping can provide normalized view for combing homogeneous datasets. For registering $\zeta^p_{q_r}$ to standard space, this paper utilizes the FLIRT algorithm [10], which minimizes the following cost function:

$$T^* = argmin_{T \in S_T}(NMI(Ref, \Xi^p_{q_r})) \tag{4}$$

where Ref denotes the reference image, S_T is the space of allowable transformations, the function NMI denotes the Normalized Mutual Information between two images, $\Xi^p_{q_r} = T(\zeta^p_{q_r})$ is the condition after registration (T denotes the transformation function) [10]. The performance of (4) will be analyzed in Sect. 4. Now, consider $Atlas = \{A_1, A_2, \ldots, A_L\}$, where $\cap_{l=1}^{L}\{A_l\} = \emptyset$, $\cup_{l=1}^{L}\{A_l\} = A$ and A_l denotes the set of indexes of voxels for the l-th region. The extracted feature for l-th region of q_r-th condition of p-th category is calculated as follows, where $a_v = [x_v, y_v, z_v]$ denotes the index of v-th voxel of l-th atlas region; and A_l is the set of indexes of voxels in the l-th region.

$$\forall a_v = [x_v, y_v, z_v] \in A_l \implies \Gamma^p_{q_r}(l) = \frac{1}{|A_l|} \sum_{v=1}^{|A_l|} (\Xi^p_{q_r})[a_v] = \frac{1}{|A_l|} \sum_{v=1}^{|A_l|} (\Xi^p_{q_r})[x_v, y_v, z_v] \tag{5}$$

3.2 Classification Algorithm

This paper randomly partitions the extracted features $G = \{[\Gamma^1_1(1) \ldots \Gamma^1_1(L)], \ldots, [\Gamma^1_{Q_1}(1) \ldots \Gamma^1_{Q_1}(L)], \ldots, [\Gamma^P_{Q_R}(1) \ldots \Gamma^P_{Q_R}(L)]\}$ to the train set (G_{tr}) and the test set (G_{te}). As a new branch of AdaBoost algorithm, Algorithm 1 employs G_{tr} for training binary classification. Then, G_{te} is utilized for estimating the performance of the classifier. As mentioned before, training binary classification for fMRI analysis is mostly imbalance, especially by using a one-versus-all strategy. As a result, the number of samples in one of these binary classes

---

Algorithm 1. The proposed binary classification algorithm

Input: Data set G_{tr} : is train set, I_{tr} : denotes real class labels of the train sets,
Output: Classifier E,
Method:

1. Partition $G_{tr} = \{G_{tr}^S, G_{tr}^L\}$, where G_{tr}^S, G_{tr}^L are Small and Large classes.
2. Calculate $J = Int(|\, G_{tr}^S \,|\,/\,|\, G_{tr}^L \,|)$ based on number of elements in classes.
3. Randomly sample the $G_{tr}^L = \{G_{tr}^L(1), \ldots, G_{tr}^L(J)\}$.
4. By considering $\bar{G}_1 = \bar{I}_1 = \emptyset$, generating $j = 1, \ldots, J+1$ classifiers:
5. Construct $G_j = \{G_{tr}^S, G_{tr}^L(j), \bar{G}_j\}$ and $I_j = \{I_{tr}^S, I_{tr}^L(j), \bar{I}_j\}$

6. Calculate $W_j = \{w_j\}_{|G_j|} = \begin{cases} 1 & \text{for instances of } G_{tr}^S \text{ or } \bar{G}_j \\ 1- |\, corr(G_{tr}^S, G_{tr}^L) \,| & \text{for instances of } G_{tr}^L(j) \end{cases}$

7. Train $\theta_j = Classifier(G_j, I_j, W_j)$.
8. Construct $\bar{G}_{j+1}$, $\bar{I}_{j+1}$ as the set of instances cannot truly trained in θ_j.
9. **If** $(j \leq J+1)$: go to line 5; **Else:** return $\Theta_p = \{\theta_1, \ldots, \theta_{J+1}\}$ as final classifier.

---

is smaller than the other class. This paper also exploits this concept. Indeed, Algorithm 1 firstly partitions the train data (G_{tr}) to small (G_{tr}^S) and large (G_{tr}^L) classes (groups) based on the class labels $(I_{tr} \in \{+1, -1\})$. Then, it calculates the scale (J) of existed elements between two classes; and employs this scale as the number of the ensemble iteration $(J+1)$. Here, $Int()$ denotes the floor function. In the next step, the large class is randomly partitioned to J parts. Now, train data (G_j) for each iteration is generated by all instances of the small class (G_{tr}^S), one of the partitioned parts of the large class $(G_{tr}^L(j))$ and the instances of the previous iteration $(\bar{G}_j)$, which cannot truly be trained. In this algorithm, $corr()$ function denotes the Pearson correlation $(corr(A, B) = cov(A, B)/\sigma_A \sigma_B)$; and $W_j \in [0, 1]$ is the train weight (penalty values), which is considered for the large class. Further, $Classifier()$ denotes any kind of weighted classification algorithm. This paper uses a simple classical decision tree as the individual classification algorithm (θ_j) [9].

Generally, there are two techniques for applying multi-class classification. The first approach directly creates the classification model such as multi-class support vector machine [5] or neural network [1]. In contrast, (indirect) decomposition design uses an array of binary classifiers for solving the multi-class problems. As one of the classical indirect methods, Error-Correcting Output Codes (ECOC) includes three components, i.e. base algorithm, encoding and decoding procedures [8]. As the based algorithm in the ECOC, this paper employs Algorithm 1 for generating the binary classifiers (Θ_p). Further, it uses a one-versus-all encoding strategy for training the ECOC method, where an independent category of the visual stimuli is compared with the rest of categories (see Fig. 1e). Indeed, the number of classifiers in this strategy is exactly equal to the number of categories. This method also assigns the brain response to the category with closest hamming distance in decoding stage.

4   Experiments

4.1   Extracted Features Analysis

This paper employs two datasets, shared by openfmri.org, for running empirical studies. As the first dataset, 'Visual Object Recognition' (DS105) includes 71 sessions (6 subjects). It also contains 8 categories of visual stimuli, i.e. gray-scale images of faces, houses, cats, bottles, scissors, shoes, chairs, and scrambled (nonsense) photos. This dataset is analyzed in high-level visual stimuli as the binary predictor, by considering all categories except scrambled photos as objects, and low-level visual stimuli in the multi-class prediction. Please see [2,5] for more information. As the second dataset, 'Word and Object Processing' (DS107) includes 98 sessions (49 subjects). It contains 4 categories of visual stimuli, i.e. words, objects, scrambles, consonants. Please see [11] for more information. These datasets are preprocessed by SPM 12 (www.fil.ion.ucl.ac.uk/spm/), i.e. slice timing, realignment, normalization, smoothing. Then, the beta values are calculated for each session. This paper employs the *MNI 152 T1 1 mm* (see Fig. 1d) as the reference image (Ref) in Eq. (4) for registering the extracted conditions (ζ) to the standard space (Ξ). In addition, this paper uses *Talairach* Atlas (contains $L = 1105$ regions) in Eq. (5) for extracting features (See Fig. 1d).

Figures 2a–c demonstrate examples of brain responses to different stimuli, i.e. (a) word, (b) object, and (c) scramble. Here, gray parts show the anatomical atlas, the colored parts (red, yellow and green) define the functional activities, and also the red rectangles illustrate the error areas after registration. Indeed, these errors can be formulated as the nonzero areas in the brain image which are located in the zero area of the anatomical atlas (the area without region number). The performance of objective function (4) on DS105, and DS107 data sets is analyzed in Fig. 2d by using different distance metrics, i.e. Woods function (W), Correlation Ratio (CR), Joint Entropy (JE), Mutual Information (MI), and Normalized Mutual Information (NMI) [10]. As depicted in this figure, the NMI generated better results in comparison with other metrics.

Figure 3a and c illustrate the correlation matrix of the DS105 and DS107 at the voxel level, respectively. Similarly, Fig. 3b and d show the correlation matrix the DS105 and DS107 in the feature level, respectively. Since, brain responses are sparse, high-dimensional and noisy at voxel level, it is so hard to discriminate between different categories in Fig. 2a and c. By contrast, Fig. 2b and d provide distinctive representation when the proposed method used the correlated patterns in each anatomical regions as the extracted features.

4.2   Classification Analysis

The performance of our framework is compared with state-of-the-art methods, i.e. Cox and Savoy [5], McMenamin et al. [6], Mohr et al. [7], and Osher et al. [3], by using leave-one-out cross validation in the subject level. Further, all of algorithms are implemented in the MATLAB R2016a (9.0) by authors in

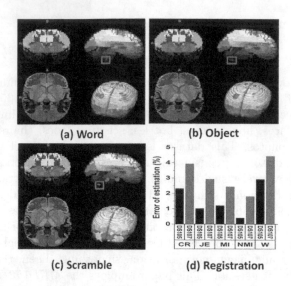

Fig. 2. Extracted features based on different stimuli, i.e. (a) word, (b) object, and (c) scramble. (d) The effect of different objective functions in (4) on the error of registration. (Color figure online)

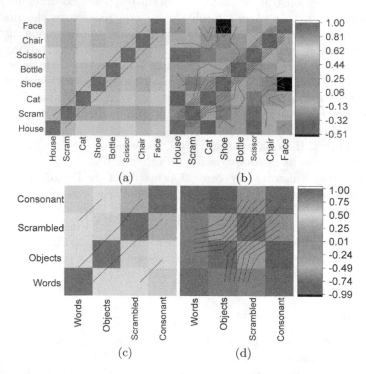

Fig. 3. The correlation matrices: (a) raw voxels and (b) extracted features of the DS105 dataset, (c) raw voxels and (d) extracted features of the DS107 dataset.

Table 1. Accuracy of binary predictors

Data sets	Cox & Savoy	McMenamin et al.	Mohr et al.	Osher et al.	Binary-APA
DS105-Objects	71.65 ± 0.97	83.06 ± 0.36	85.29 ± 0.49	90.82 ± 1.23	**98.37 ± 0.16**
DS107-Words	69.89 ± 1.02	89.62 ± 0.52	81.14 ± 0.91	94.21 ± 0.83	**97.67 ± 0.12**
DS107-Consonants	67.84 ± 0.82	87.82 ± 0.37	79.69 ± 0.69	95.54 ± 0.99	**98.73 ± 0.06**
DS107-Objects	65.32 ± 1.67	84.22 ± 0.44	75.32 ± 0.41	**95.62 ± 0.83**	95.06 ± 0.11
DS107-Scramble	67.96 ± 0.87	86.19 ± 0.26	78.45 ± 0.62	93.1 ± 0.78	**96.71 ± 0.18**

Table 2. Area Under the ROC Curve (AUC) of binary predictors

Data sets	Cox & Savoy	McMenamin et al.	Mohr et al.	Osher et al.	Binary-APA
DS105-Objects	68.37 ± 1.01	82.22 ± 0.42	80.91 ± 0.21	88.54 ± 0.71	**96.25 ± 0.92**
DS107-Words	67.76 ± 0.91	86.35 ± 0.39	78.23 ± 0.57	93.61 ± 0.62	**97.02 ± 0.2**
DS107-Consonants	63.84 ± 1.45	85.63 ± 0.61	77.41 ± 0.92	94.54 ± 0.31	**96.92 ± 0.14**
DS107-Objects	63.17 ± 0.59	81.54 ± 0.92	73.92 ± 0.28	94.23 ± 0.94	**95.17 ± 0.03**
DS107-Scramble	66.73 ± 0.92	85.79 ± 0.42	76.14 ± 0.47	92.23 ± 0.38	**96.08 ± 0.1**

Table 3. Accuracy of multi-class predictors

Data sets	Cox & Savoy	McMenamin et al.	Mohr et al.	Osher et al.	Multi-APA
DS105 (P = 8)	18.03 ± 4.07	38.34 ± 3.21	29.14 ± 2.25	50.61 ± 4.83	**57.93 ± 2.1**
DS107 (P = 4)	38.01 ± 2.56	71.55 ± 2.79	64.71 ± 3.14	89.69 ± 2.32	**94.21 ± 2.41**
ALL (P = 4)	32.93 ± 2.29	68.35 ± 3.07	63.16 ± 4	80.36 ± 3.04	**95.67 ± 1.25**

order to generate experimental results. Tables 1 and 2 respectively illustrate the classification Accuracy and Area Under the ROC Curve (AUC) for the binary predictors based on the category of the visual stimuli. All visual stimuli in the dataset DS105 except scrambled photos are considered as the object category for generating these experimental results. As depicted in the Tables 1 and 2, the proposed algorithm has achieved better performance in comparison with other methods because it provided a better representation of neural activities by exploiting the anatomical structure of the human brain. Table 3 illustrates the classification accuracy for multi-class predictors. In this table, 'DS105' includes 8 different categories (P = 8 classes) and 'DS107' contains 4 categories of the visual stimuli. As another 4 categories dataset, 'ALL' is generated by considering all visual stimuli in the dataset DS105 except scrambled photos as object category and combining them with the dataset DS107. In this dataset, the accuracy of the proposed method is improved by combining two datasets, whereas, the performances of other methods are significantly decreased. As mentioned before, it is the standard space registration problem in the 4D images. In addition, our framework employs the extracted features from the brain structural regions instead of using all or a subgroup of voxels, which can increase the performance of the predictive models by decreasing noise and sparsity.

5   Conclusion

This paper proposes Anatomical Pattern Analysis (APA) framework for decoding visual stimuli in the human brain. This framework uses an anatomical feature extraction method, which provides a normalized representation for combining homogeneous datasets. Further, a new binary imbalance AdaBoost algorithm is introduced. It can increase the performance of prediction by exploiting a supervised random sampling and the correlation between classes. In addition, this algorithm is utilized in an Error-Correcting Output Codes (ECOC) method for multi-class prediction of the brain responses. Empirical studies on 4 visual categories clearly show the superiority of our proposed method in comparison with the voxel-based approaches. In future, we plan to apply the proposed method to different brain tasks such as low-level visual stimuli, emotion and etc.

Acknowledgment. We thank the anonymous reviewers for comments. This work was supported in part by the National Natural Science Foundation of China (61422204 and 61473149), Jiangsu Natural Science Foundation for Distinguished Young Scholar (BK20130034) and NUAA Fundamental Research Funds (NE2013105).

References

1. Norman, K.A., Polyn, S.M., Detre, G.J., Haxby, J.V.: Beyond mind-reading: multi-voxel pattern analysis of fMRI data. Trends Cogn. Sci. **10**(9), 424–430 (2006)
2. Haxby, J.V., Connolly, A.C., Guntupalli, J.S.: Decoding neural representational spaces using multivariate pattern analysis. Annu. Rev. Neurosci. **37**, 435–456 (2014)
3. Osher, D.E., Saxe, R., Koldewyn, K., Gabrieli, J.D.E., Kanwisher, N., Saygin, Z.M.: Structural connectivity fingerprints predict cortical selectivity for multiple visual categories across cortex. Cereb. Cortex **26**(4), 1668–1683 (2016)
4. Friston, K.J., Ashburner, J.O.H.N., Heather, J.: Statistical parametric mapping. Neurosci. Databases Pract. Guide **1**(237), 1–74 (2003)
5. Cox, D., Savoy, R.L.: Functional magnetic resonance imaging (fMRI) 'brain reading': detecting and classifying distributed patterns of fMRI activity in human visual cortex. NeuroImage **19**(2), 261–270 (2003)
6. McMenamin, B.W., Deason, R.G., Steele, V.R., Koutstaal, W., Marsolek, C.J.: Separability of abstract-category and specific-exemplar visual object subsystems: evidence from fMRI pattern analysis. Brain Cogn. **93**, 54–64 (2015)
7. Mohr, H., Wolfensteller, U., Frimmel, S., Ruge, H.: Sparse regularization techniques provide novel insights into outcome integration processes. NeuroImage **104**, 163–176 (2015)
8. Escalera, S., Pujol, O., Petia, R.: Error-correcting output codes library. J. Mach. Learn. Res. **11**, 661–664 (2010)
9. Liu, X.Y., Wu, J., Zhou, Z.H.: Exploratory undersampling for class-imbalance learning. IEEE Trans. Cybern. **39**(2), 539–550 (2009)
10. Jenkinson, M., Bannister, P., Brady, M., Smith, S.: Improved optimization for the robust and accurate linear registration and motion correction of brain images. NeuroImage **17**(2), 825–841 (2002)

11. Duncan, K.J., Pattamadilok, C., Knierim, I., Devlin, J.T.: Consistency and variability in functional localisers. NeuroImage **46**(4), 1018–1026 (2009)
12. Rice, G.E., Watson, D.M., Hartley, T., Andrews, T.J.: Low-level image properties of visual objects predict patterns of neural response across category-selective regions of the ventral visual pathway. J. Neurosci. **34**(26), 8837–8844 (2014)
13. Carroll, M.K., Cecchi, G.A., Rish, I., Garg, R., Rao, A.R.: Prediction and interpretation of distributed neural activity with sparse models. NeuroImage **44**(1), 112–122 (2009)
14. Varoquaux, G., Gramfort, A., Thirion, B.: Small-sample brain mapping: sparse recovery on spatially correlated designs with randomization and clustering. In: International Conference on Machine Learning (2012)

An Investigation of Machine Learning and Neural Computation Paradigms in the Design of Clinical Decision Support Systems (CDSSs)

Summrina K. Wajid[1(✉)], Amir Hussain[1,2], Bin Luo[2], and Kaizhu Huang[3]

[1] Computing Science and Mathematics, School of Natural Sciences,
University of Stirling, Stirling, UK
skwl@cs.stir.ac.uk
[2] School of Computing Science and Technology, Anhui University,
Hefei, China
[3] Xi'an Jiaotong-Liverpool University, Suzhou, China

Abstract. This paper reviews the state of the art techniques for designing next generation CDSSs. CDSS can aid physicians and radiologists to better analyse and treat patients by combining their respective clinical expertise with complementary capabilities of the computers. CDSSs comprise many techniques from inter-desciplinary fields of medical image acquisition, image processing and pattern recognition, neural perception and pattern classifiers for medical data organization, and finally, analysis and optimization to enhance overall system performance. This paper discusses some of the current challenges in designing an efficient CDSS as well as some of the latest techniques that have been proposed to meet these challenges, primarily, by finding informative patterns in the medical dataset, analysing them and building a descriptive model of the object of interest, thus aiding in enhanced medical diagnosis.

Keywords: Neural computation · Clinical decision support systems (CDSS) · Image processing · Machine learning · Neural networks

1 Introduction

Recognition of the variable quality of medical care provided to patients has drawn attention to enhanced medical care for patients. CDSSs help improving medical care in diagnosis of the patients by analysing available data for pathophysiologic (medical condition combined with processes in the organism) explanation of the disease symptoms. For this it provides a diagnosis process - a replacement for the hectic (very busy) traditional process, which comprises a complete a set of inquiry questions to ask, prescribing tests, procedures and assessment of the results [1]. Clinical Decision Support Systems (CDSSs) help in detecting or diagnosing abnormal conditions in medical datasets that may consist of images or other disease-relevant information for multiple patients. It is vital to integrate validated clinical information and convert it into

© Springer International Publishing AG 2016
C.-L. Liu et al. (Eds.): BICS 2016, LNAI 10023, pp. 58–67, 2016.
DOI: 10.1007/978-3-319-49685-6_6

the knowledge that can be helpful in diagnosis, prognosis and treatment of a patient. This entails development of efficient CDSSs that can help health providers in providing medical health facilities [19].

This paper provides a brief survey of state-of-the-art techniques applied to design CDSSs in Sect. 2 and a conclusion and future prospects in Sect. 3.

2 Survey on Techniques in CDSSs Design

To meet the challenges of the latest health care requirements, CDSS design is making extensive use of the state-of-the-art image processing, neural computation, machine learning and data mining techniques which help in discovering and analysing hidden information patterns in medical datasets. Some of these techniques are reviewed in the following section keeping the medical images in perspective. Medical image processing may be applied on three levels as depicted in Fig. 1 and described below.

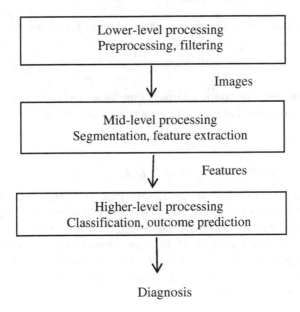

Fig. 1. Medical image processing system diagnosis model [2].

2.1 Medical Imaging Acquisition/Formation

Medical images of human organs, such as the heart, breast, lungs and brain aid medical diagnosis in radiology, psychiatry, cardiology and internal medicine. This is a rapidly advancing field and has resulted in the improvement of image quality and computerized image analysis. When integrated with patient clinical information, it enriches the analysis of a specific case. These images come in different modalities, namely X-rays, mammograms, magnetic resonance imaging (MRI), ultrasound (US) and so on.

2.2   Image Pre-processing Techniques

Loss of information can result from the introduction of artefacts by components of the image-capturing device. It is important to identify and erase the outer effects of these artefacts, as they can hamper the diagnosis procedure [3]. Pre-processing of medical images includes image orientation, label and artefact removal and image enhancement and de-noising. Extensive research has been conducted to solve these issues. Some of the frequently used techniques for medical enhancement are discussed below.

Histogram Equalization (HE) based Image Enhancement Techniques. It is a classical technique using a histogram of an image for contrast adjustment. It increases the contrast of low intensity areas in the image by spreading out the most frequent intensity values. For an image I with pixel intensity values ranging from 0 to $L-1$, where L being 256 here, a normalized histogram p with a bin for each possible intensity level, the probability of occurrence of intensity value k can be written as [21].

$$p(k) = \frac{number\ of\ pixels\ with\ intensity\ k}{total\ number\ of\ pixels\ in\ the\ image} = \frac{n_k}{n} k : 0\ to\ L-1 \tag{1}$$

The Cumulative Distribution Function corresponding to p is given as:

$$cdf(k) = \sum_{j=0}^{k} p(j)) \tag{1}$$

Then histogram equalization is an image transformation such that the transformed image has flat Cumulative Frequency Distribution (CDF) given as:

$$df(m) = i * m \tag{2}$$

where m is a contrast within the *range 0 to L−1.*

Contrast Limited Adaptive Histogram Equalization (CLAHE). The most common medical image enhancing technique, CLAHE applies histogram equalization (HE) to sub-regions of an image by dividing the image into contextual blocks (tiles) [4]. Sundaram et al. proposed a modified histogram equalization technique, named as (HM-LCE) Histogram Modified Local Contrast Enhancement. This technique allows controlling the level of contrast on an image by tuning the value of the contrast parameter where in case of classical HE, there is no such control provided [4].

Unsharped Masking (UM). It is a method that increases the contrast of an image by using blurring mask of the original image given as:

$$I_i' = I_i + f(I_i - s_i(\sigma)) \tag{3}$$

Where I_i' is the processed pixel, I_i is the original pixel at ith location and $s_i(\sigma)$ is the smoothed image pixel value and f is the function which determines the level of enhancement. Blurring is performed using Gaussian smoothing. Scale of smoothing function defines the limit of contrast enhancement. UM is capable of enhancing high frequency components of an image and that is why it is specifically used for micro calcification enhancement. Siddharth et al. [5] and Zhe Wu et al. [22] applied UM for enhancing mammogram images.

Fuzzy Set Theory. Fuzzy set theory has been applied to image processing for decades [6] Fuzzification of a certain set of elements maps the elements of a set into a real number [0, 1]. These numbers represent the degree of membership of an element to its set. The higher the degree, the stronger belonging to the set is [6, 7]. Gordon & Rangyan [23], Cheng et al. [6] and A. Hassanien et al. [24] applied fuzzy set based enhancement to enhance mammograms to further detect abnormalities from them.

Comparison of Image Pre-processing Techniques. The following Table 1 summarizes merits and demerits of difference enhancement techniques for medical images:

Some of the other image enhancement techniques found in literature are Contrast Stretching [25], Spatial Filters (Mean, Median, Tophat, Bottomhat) [21], contourlet transform filters [26], steerable filter [27] etc. It is also common to apply combination of techniques to improve medical images.

Table 1. Merits and demerits of difference pre-processing techniques for medical images.

Name	Merits	Demerits
Histogram Equalization based techniques	Simple and straightforward, Good for bright and dark areas, Intensity values are effectively spread out	Increases background noise. Can produce undesirable effects for low colour depth images
UM	Very simple method, sharpens the edges of the objects even in the presence of noise	Contrast in darker area enhanced more than contrast in lighter area. Also enhances the noise and digitised effects
Fuzzy methodologies	Good for detecting micro calcifications, can manage ambiguity and vagueness efficiently	Less effective for images with diverse features [8]

2.3   Image Segmentation

It is partitioning of an image into non-overlapping regions so that they are homogenous in certain respects, such as intensity, texture, shape etc. If I is an image, then segmentation is a process of determining image subsets $S_k \subset I$ so that their union is the whole image I, and their intersection is n empty set [9]. Image segmentation techniques fall into three major categories.

- Manual
- Automatic
- Semiautomatic

Manual Segmentation. It is the most common technique in which some image processing tool is used to trace the boundary of the region of interest (ROI) which is mostly an object like mass, lesion or an organ like breast, kidney etc. It involves an expert to outline the object boundary. State-of-the-art segmentation tools on computers help in drawing the outline, like completing the open contour etc. Tools like Slicer, ImageJ, ITK-SNAP [13].

Semi-automatic and Automatic Segmentation

Thresholding. It is the simplest method of segmentation in which one chooses a range of grey level values that represent an object to segment. The pixels in that range are retained while the rest of them are set to zero. For quantitative image analysis it is required that threshold is chosen objectively e.g. maximum pixel value in the image or some values based on image histogram analysis [13].

Region Growing. It is an interactive method, in which one can define the range of grey level values to represent a region or object of interest, and chose the pixel to be part of a region of interest called a seed point. Consequently, an outline is automatically drawn around the set of pixels defining the object of interest [13].

The methods that rely on grey levels are subject to grey level inhomogeneity and the partial volume effect means that same tissue may differ in the grey scale around the image or medical image pixel, voxel may be large to comprise more than one type of object. Or there is a possibility that the image is blurred and boundaries are not well defined [13].

Table 2. Merits and demerits of difference segmentation techniques for medical images.

Technique Name	Merits	Demerits
Manual segmentation	It is more accurate as it is easy to ensure segment boundary manually	Time-consuming method and results may not be scientifically reproducible [12]
Thresholding	It's a simple and fast algorithm with minimum computational cost [11]	Sensitive to noise, choosing an inappropriate value may lead to over or under segmentation. It can cause misleading edge detection [11]
Region Growing	Provides better results compared to other segmentation techniques as it is initialized with inner point as seed to grow to outer regions [11]	Incorrect choice of seed may lead to inappropriate segmentation and seed selection is manual. Similarly stopping criteria selection is a tedious job [11]
Active Contours and Snakes	Focuses on refining the boundary of the objects and thus generates closed contours [10]	Computationally expensive technique, which demands setting up multiple [10]

Active Contours and Snakes. It is a computational segmentation technique based on complex mathematics, which involves using an outline or contour to represent a region of interest. The outline, initially, starts at a certain position and then calculation is performed, to drive the contour towards points in the image, which satisfies predefined conditions based on known properties. The method requires understanding of the data and selection of suitable parameter values. Additional conditions can be applied to develop contour around the realistic shape. Among the most common variants of this method is the active shape model [13] Table 2.

2.4 Feature Extraction

Feature extraction is an essential step for medical image analysis, which is performed after the preprocessing stage. It is a process to retrieve highly significant information from a raw image so that extracted information defines the object of interest uniquely and precisely [14]. Feature extraction can be applied as global, block-based or region-based technique. These features represent the relevant shape in the image pattern so that it can be used to classify this pattern. It is also considered a form of dimensionality reduction, where the aim is to extract the most relevant information from the original image. And thus it transforms the information into feature vectors, which is a reduced representation of the image pattern of interest. These features can be categorized as [14]:

Shape Features. Shape features are commonly used for detecting malignancy of masses or nodules. They comprise geometric and morphological aspects of the mass or nodules depicted as area, perimeter, compactness, radial length, minimum and maximum axis, eccentricity, circularity, roughness, orientation, statistical mean, variance, moments of the ROI. Delogu et al. [15] extracted 16 different shape features, such as the mass perimeter, mass circularity, mean of the normalized radial length etc., from segmented masses and studied the different combinations of these features. The features were further selected using Feature Discriminating Power and Linear Correlation Interplay techniques and fed to a Multi-Layer Perceptron Neural Network for classification. The method achieved the classification accuracy of 97.8%.

Texture Features. Image texture is a set of matrices, used to define the spatial arrangement of colour and intensities inside an image [17]. There are multiple approaches to define texture features. Some common approaches are structural and statistical.

Grey Level First-Order Statistics (GLFOS). These features are calculated considering individual pixel values, giving no weight to neighborhood pixels. These features are the analysis of grey level distribution in the image. Most common of them are maximum intensity, minimum intensity, standard deviation, skewness, kurtosis etc.

Grey Level Co-occurrence Matrix (GLCM). One of the common statistical approaches is Grey Level Co-Occurrence Matrix (GLCM). It extracts second order statistical features from the image. GLCM is a matrix with a number of rows and columns equal to the grey levels in the image [16].

Multi-resolution Features. It is a powerful tool to analyse images. They comprise a broad range of algorithms like wavelet transform, contourlet, curvelet etc. Multi-resolution methods are of great interest to researchers in the image processing, analysis, biological and other fields.

Discussion. Different feature extraction techniques have their specific capabilities to highlight important aspects of information within the images. In general, shape features are mostly used to analyse masses. Texture features are used for both, masses and micro-calcifications detection and the same is the case with multi-resolution features. It is important to note that for micro-calcification, multi-resolution features perform better than any other feature extraction technique. Wavelet features also turned out to be excellent in discrimination among different types of abnormalities in mammograms. Other feature extraction methods found in the literature are intensity, morphological, grey level and temporal features etc.

2.5 Classification with Machine Learning and Neural Computation Techniques

Machine learning and neural computation play an important role in CDSSs for clinical data analysis. These systems can change their behaviour based on their experiences. They extract a general model from the dataset and use training data to elucidate patterns within the dataset. The dataset can be in the form of a one-dimensional record or two- or three-dimensional image (either a region of interest or the entire image). Some of the most common machine learning techniques to be applied in CDSSs are briefed below.

Probabilistic and Statistical Model. Probabilistic and statistical models incorporate regression analysis, discriminant analysis, time series analysis, and principal component analysis, among many other methods. The most famous probabilistic models, Bayesian models, are based on the probabilistic Bayesian framework, which calculates the probability of a sample belonging to a certain class given the data and prior assumptions. An example is the Naïve Bayes (NB) classifier, which assumes independence between features [18].

Neural Network based Classification. Several machine learning algorithms are inspired by biology. Neural networks imitate the human nervous system by representing information as nodes that are connected by weighted links (synapses). The learning algorithm adjusts the weights in the neural network so that it can predict the class of unseen examples correctly [18]. Neural networks are distinguished by their architecture, such as back-propagation or feed-forward. The most famous neural networks are self-organizing maps and Hopfield networks. Due to their predictive power, they are used for classification and clustering problems [18].

Symbolic Learning and Rule-induction Methods. These methods represent a model as a set of rules, and can be further categorized as learning by role, by being told, by analogy, by example and by discovery. Algorithms include decision-tree induction, the ID 3 decision tree building algorithm, C 4.5, CART and logic programming [3]. These algorithms search for the attributes that are best suited for dividing the dataset into classes by minimizing the entropy or information uncertainty. After classification, the results are represented as decision trees or production rules.

Instance-Based Methods. Instance-based methods do not extract a model, but instead use the full training dataset to classify new samples. Methods such as K-nearest neighbour (KNN), weighted regression and case-based reasoning come under this category [3]. Finally, kernel methods characterize each sample using a kernel function, which maps the samples from original space to high-dimensional feature space. Support vector machines (SVMs) are the most prominent example of this type of method [3].

Comparison of Classification Techniques. Abrief comparison of machine learning techniques is provided in the Table 3 below [20].

Table 3. Merits and demerits of difference segmentation techniques for medical images.

Technique Name	Merits	Demerits
Probabilistic and statistical model	Computational time for training is minimal	Less accurate compared to other classifiers
Neural Network Based Classification	Inherently parallel which can be used to speed up the computational process via parallel processing	Requires long learning time
Symbolic learning and rule-induction methods	Simple and fast. Easy to understand	Long training time
Instance-based methods	The most robust and accurate methods among all well-known classifiers	Requires large storage requirements

3 Conclusion and Future Work

Modern medicine relies on medical images, which contain complex patterns that are not easy to detect or discriminate by eye. There is thus a need for a learning paradigm that can understand the useful information in the image, interpret it and help make decisions on the basis of this information. Medical images come in different modalities, and there is an increasing need to understand, analyse and manipulate these different modalities; thus, the importance of machine learning and neural computation is growing day by day. Further challenges to be address in future are to provide better human computer interface (HCI) for these CDSSs for helping clinicians reduce errors like FP (false positive) as well as FN (false negative). Development of intelligent methods which can automatically summarize relevant information from patient data, collected from various resources and prioritize them as well as provide specialized recommendations is also part of our future endeavors [28].

The state-of-the-art machine learning and neural computational method can be employed in multiple stages of a CDSSs system, depending on the learning paradigm and thus can enhance system diagnosis performance. Due to shortage of space, it was unable to provide a detailed study of these and other recent techniques. These will be covered in our future research publications.

Acknowledgments. Professor A. Hussain was supported by the UK Engineering and Physical Sciences Research Council (EPSRC) grant no. EP/M026981/1, and the Digital Health & Care Institute (DHI) funded Exploratory project: PD2A. The authors are grateful to the anonymous reviewers for their insightful comments and suggestions, which helped improve the quality of this paper.

References

1. Musen, M.A., et al.: Biomedical informatics. In: Clinical Decision-Support Systems, 4 Edn. pp. 643–674 (2013)
2. Meyer-Bäse, A.: Introduction. In: Pattern Recognition in Medical Imaging, pp. 1–13. Academic Press, San Diego (2004)
3. Romero, E., González, F.: From biomedical image analysis to biomedical image understanding using machine learning. In: Biomedical Image Analysis and Machine Learning Technologies: Applications and Techniques, pp. 1–26. IGI Global (2010)
4. Sundaram, M., et al.: Histogram based contrast enhancement for mammogram images. In: 2011 International Conference on Signal Processing, Communication, Computing and Networking Technologies (ICSCCN), pp. 842–846 (2011)
5. Siddharth, Gupta, R., Bhateja, V.: A new unsharp masking algorithm for mammography using non-linear enhancement function. In: Satapathy, S.C., Avadhani, P.S., Abraham, A. (eds.) Proceedings of the InConINDIA 2012. AISC, vol. 132, pp. 779–786. Springer, Heidelberg (2012)
6. Cheng, H., et al.: A novel approach to microcalcification detection using fuzzy logic technique. IEEE Trans. Med. Imag. **17**(3), 442–450 (1998)
7. Sutton, M.A., Bezdek, J.: Enhancement and analysis of digital mammograms using fuzzy models. Proc. SPIE. **3240**, 179–190 (1997)
8. Leiner, B.J., et al.: Microcalcifications detection system through discrete wavelet analysis and contrast enhancement techniques. In: Electronics, Robotics and Automotive Mechanics Conference, CERMA 2008, vol. 272, p. 276 (2008)
9. Singh, S., et al.: Performance analysis of mammographic image enhancement techniques for early detection of breast cancer. Adv. Parallel Distrib. Comput. Commun. Comput. Inf. Sci. **203**, 439–448 (2011)
10. Weeratunga, S., Kamath, C.: An investigation of implicit active contours for scientific image segmentation. In: Video Communications and Image Processing, SPIE Electronic Imaging, San Jose (2004)
11. Khan, A.M., Ravi, S.: Image segmentation methods: a comparative study. Int. J. Soft Comput. Eng. (IJSCE) **3**, 2231–2307 (2013)
12. Taneja, A., et al.: A performance study of image segmentation techniques. In: 2015 4th International Conference on Reliability, Infocom Technologies and Optimization (ICRITO) (Trends and Future Directions), Noida, pp. 1–6 (2015)
13. Berry, E.: A Practical Approach to Medical Image Processing. CRC Press, Boca Raton (2007)
14. Kumar, G., Bhatia, P.K.: A detailed review of feature extraction in image processing systems. In: 2014 Fourth International Conference on Advanced Computing & Communication Technologies (ACCT), Rohtak, pp. 5–12 (2014)

15. Karahaliou, A.N., et al.: Breast cancer diagnosis: analyzing texture of tissue surrounding microcalcifications. IEEE Trans. Inf Technol. Biomed. **12**(6), 731–738 (2008)
16. Mingqiang, Y., et al.: A survey of shape feature extraction techniques. In: Yin, P.-Y. (ed.) Pattern Recognition Techniques, vol. 1, pp. 3–90. InTechOpen, Rijeka (2008)
17. Jain, R., et al.: Texture. Machine Vision. McGraw-Hill, Inc, New York (1995)
18. Li, Q.: Computer-Aided Detection and Diagnosis in Medical Imaging. CRC Press, Boca Raton (2015)
19. Castaneda, C., et al.: Clinical decision support systems for improving diagnostic accuracy and achieving precision Medicine. J. Clin. Bioinf. **5**, 1 (2015). 4. PMC. Accessed 3 Jul 2016
20. Bhavsar, H., Ganatra, A.: A comparative study of training algorithms for supervised machine learning. Int. J. Soft Comput. Eng. (IJSCE) **2**, 2231–2307 (2012)
21. Gonzalez, R.C., Woods, R.E.: Digital Image Processing, 2nd edn. Pearson Education, Upper Saddle River (2002). ISBN 0-201-18075-8
22. Wu, Z., et al.: Digital mammography image enhancement using improved unsharp masking approach. In: 2010 3rd International Congress on Image and Signal Processing (CISP), vol. 2 (2010)
23. Gordon, R., Rangayan, R.M.: Feature enhancement of Film mammograms using fixed and adaptive Neighborhoods. Appl. Opt. **23**, 560–564 (1984)
24. Hassanien, A., Badr, A.: A comparative study on digital mammography enhancement algorithms based on fuzzy theory. Stud. Inf. Contr. **12**, 21–31 (2003)
25. Davies, E.: Machine Vision: Theory, Algorithms and Practicalities, pp. 26–27, 79–99. Academic Press, New York (1990)
26. Candes, E.J., Donoho, D.L.: Curvelets: a surprisingly effective nonadaptive representation for objects with edges (2000). http://www.Curvelet.org/papers/Curve99.pdf
27. Freeman, W.T., Adelson, E.H.: The design and use of steerable filters. IEEE Trans. Pattern Anal. Mach. Intell. **13**(9), 891–906 (1991)
28. Sittig, D.F., Wright, A., Osheroff, J.A., Middleton, B., Teich, J.M., Ash, J.S., Campbell, E., Bates, D.W.: Grand challenges in clinical decision support. J. Biomed. Inf. **41**(2), 387–392 (2008)

A Retina Inspired Model for High Dynamic Range Image Rendering

Xian-Shi Zhang and Yong-Jie Li[(⊠)]

Key Laboratory for Neuroinformation of Ministry of Education,
Center for Information in BioMedicine, University of Electronic Science and
Technology of China, Chengdu, China
liyj@uestc.edu.cn

Abstract. We propose a new tone mapping model to render high dynamic range (HDR) images in limited dynamic range devices in this paper. This neural network model is inspired by the retinal information processing mechanisms of the biological visual system, including the adaptive gap junction between horizontal cells (HCs), the negative HC-cone feedback pathway, and the center-surround antagonistic receptive fields of bipolar cells (BCs). The key novelty of the proposed model lies in the adaptive adjustment of the receptive field size of HCs based on the local brightness, which simulates the dynamic gap junction between HCs. This enables the brightness of distinct regions to be recovered into clearly visible ranges while reducing halo artifacts common to other methods. The BCs serve to enhance the local contrast with their center-surround RF structure. By comparing with the state-of-the-art tone mapping methods qualitatively and quantitatively, our method shows competitive performance in term of improving details in both dark and bright areas.

1 Introduction

From starlight to sunlight, light intensity in natural scenes of real world has high dynamic range (HDR), which can be as high as in the ratio of 100, 000 to 1. However, the dynamic range of most display devices available to us is less than 100 to 1. When images captured from HDR scenes are directly displayed on these low dynamic range (LDR) devices, some parts of the images are too dark while some parts are too bright to be seen in details. To solve this problem, HDR images need be compressed, or 'Tone Mapped' (TM), to a proper dynamic range matching the display devices. The goal of TM is to reproduce the images visibly, so that the details in both the dark and bright areas are as faithfully visible as possible. This means that the resulting displayable images should preserve the characteristics, such as contrast, structure or color appearance, of the input HDR images [1].

To achieve this goal, various TM methods have been developed. Among others, Mai et al. [2] developed a statistical model to optimize the tone-curve. Inspired by dodging and burning in photographic practices, Reinhard et al. [3] mapped the whole image using a local averaging logarithmic operator and then convolved it with circular Gaussian filters at multiple scales to correct the bright and dark regions. Using a bilateral filter, an edge-preserving smoothing filter, Durand et al. [4] separated a HDR

© Springer International Publishing AG 2016
C.-L. Liu et al. (Eds.): BICS 2016, LNAI 10023, pp. 68–79, 2016.
DOI: 10.1007/978-3-319-49685-6_7

image into two layers, a base layer and a detail layer, and reduced the contrast in the base layer. Fattal et al. [5] compressed HDR images in the gradient field.

Along another line, a group of methods are inspired by the human visual system (HVS), which deals with its limited bandwidth in the visual pathways and allows us to perceive the details simultaneously in the darkest as well as the brightest areas of an HDR scene [1]. By signaling the absolute brightness and local contrast function of HVS, Ashikhmin constructed an automatic approach with only one parameter [6]. Imitating the human response to light, Drago et al. used adaptive logarithmic mapping to produce perceptually tuned images with high dynamic content [7]. Trying to replicate basic properties of the HVS, Ferradans et al. mimicked the retinal visual adaptation and cortical local contrast enhancement in two independent stages [8]. The attempts of Drago et al. [9], Rahman et al. [10], and Meylan et al. [11] are based on the famous Retinex theory, which approximates the spectral properties of object surfaces with the ratio of the reflected light in this area to others. Employing the model of photoreceptor adaptation, Ward [12], Tumblin et al. [13], and Reinhard et al. [14] proposed global tone reproduction operators for computational efficiency. Moreover, Van Hateren et al. [15] and Alleysson et al. [16] introduced the horizontal cells (HCs) feedback to adjust the photoreceptor responses.

Basically different with previous HVS inspired methods, especially the model of HCs, we take the gap junction between HCs into account inspired by physiological findings [17]. This is the main novelty of the proposed model. By sampling and sharing the responses of a large number of cones with relatively large receptive fields (RFs), which are resulted from their gap junctional coupling, HCs get the ambient illumination and feed this information back into the cones. Following this retinal non-linear signal processing mechanism, our proposed method is capable of locally adjusting a HDR image and enhancing its details while reducing the halos and artifacts. The main purpose of our method is to provide a faithful visual representation of HDR real-world scenes on LDR devices. The advantage of the proposed model lies in its ability of simultaneous dynamic range compressing and detail enhancing of a HDR image due to the specific mechanisms of different retinal sub-layers. The proposed model clearly enhances the biological details of the retinal processing that underlies most of the high-performing HDR tone-mapping techniques. In that sense, the contribution of this work is not only an efficient way to realize TM for computer vision applications, but also a possible computational description about the retinal mechanisms of dynamic range adjustment in biological vision.

2 Method

Visual information is not simply conveyed from the retina to the brain. Before it leaves the eye, many calculations have taken place. Basically, there are two types of streams for visual information processing in the retina: vertical pathways, from the photoreceptors to ganglion cells transmitted by bipolar cells (BCs), which are directly involved in sending signals to the brain, and lateral pathways, comprising the local feedback circuits from HCs back to photoreceptors and from amacrine cells to BCs, which mainly serve to optimize the signals in different stages of the vertical pathways by means of gain adjustment [18]. As shown in Fig. 1, our method takes both pathways into account, and takes the response of BCs as the final output of the proposed model. We will show that without the further processing by the amacrine cells and ganglion cells, which are thought to mainly execute more complicated processing like sparse coding and color constancy [17], our current model with only HCs and BCs can render high dynamic range images very well.

Retinal information processing begins with the sampling by photoreceptors. The red (R), green (G) and blue (B) components of the input color image are responded respectively by long-, medium-, and short-wavelength cone photoreceptors (i.e., L, M, and S cones) of retina, while the brightness of the dim regions in the input image is sensitively responded by rod photoreceptors [17]. When lights fall in their RFs, photoreceptors hyperpolarize and reduce the release of glutamate, which results in hyperpolarizing in HCs and OFF BCs and depolarizing in ON BCs. In the human retina, there are 11 different types of morphologically distinct BCs, which are arranged in a rod connected ON BC group and a cone connected ON and OFF BCs group [18]. Here we only consider the cones, HCs and ON midget BCs, which carry chromatic signals in high resolution because a BC of this type near the fovea receives direct input from just one cone and then transfers the signal to one midget ganglion cell.

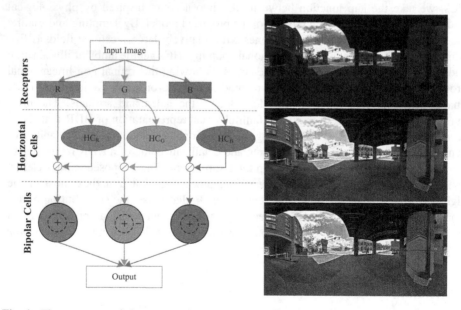

Fig. 1. The structure of the proposed model. The RGB components of the input image are respectively sent into the three cone photoreceptors. Then the outputs of cones are modulated by the feedback from horizontal cells (HCs), the receptive field of which is a dynamic Gaussian function simulating the junction coupling among HCs. The modulated cone signals are then sent to bipolar cells, the receptive field of which is structured as a difference of Gaussian (DOG) function. From top to bottom, the image patches listed on right side are respectively the input image, the output of the modulated cones, and the final output of bipolar cells.

HCs average the input from photoreceptors and then send feedback signals to photoreceptors. This feedback shifts the dynamic ranges of both pre- and post-synaptic neurons, serving to keep the gain of these synapses relatively high at different ambient light levels, remove redundancy from the cone output and assure adequate contrast sensitivity of the visual signal [18].

Given an input color image $f_c(x, y)$, $c \in \{R, G, B\}$, the three components are respectively sampled by three cone types. Then the HC output that will be feedbacked to cone signals is computed as

$$HCfeedback_c(x, y) = f_c(x, y) \otimes g(x, y; \sigma(x, y)) \tag{1}$$

where $\otimes$ is a convolution operator. $g(x, y; \sigma(x, y))$ is a two-dimensional (2D) Gaussian filter written as

$$g(x, y; \sigma(x, y)) = \frac{1}{2\pi\sigma(x, y)^2} \exp\left(-\frac{(x^2 + y^2)}{2\sigma(x, y)^2}\right) \tag{2}$$

where $\sigma(x, y)$ is the scale of the Gaussian shaped RF center, determined by the strength of local gap junctional coupling.

Benefited from the extensive gap junctional coupling, HCs have quite large RFs, which can be 25 times of the size of an individual cell's dendritic arbor [19]. This coupling is in general modulated by light [20]. Under dim starlight conditions, the conductance of the gap junctions is relatively low. In this condition, photoreceptors absorb photons of light sporadically and only neighboring HCs carry correlated signals. Such limited coupling prevents the signals from dissipating into a largely inactive network and thereby increases sensitivity at dim light. As the ambient background light increases to twilight condition, the conductance increases. The increased coupling removes part of the noise from signals by integrating over large areas. Under bright daylight condition, the conductance is reduced again. The decreased coupling limits lateral interactions among HCs, resulting in more local contrast detection for higher acuity, which is essential for daylight vision [21]. Such dependence of junctinal conductance of gap junction channel on transjunctional voltage can be well described by a two-state asymmetrical Boltzmann equation [20], as indicated by the black curve shown in Fig. 2. For computational efficiency, we simplify this light-induced coupling dependence as a piecewise linear function (the blue line in Fig. 2), which is described as

$$\sigma(x, y) = \begin{cases} sigma & m - s < f_c(x, y) < m + s \\ sigma * 3/5 & m - 2s < f_c(x, y) < m - s \ or \ m + s < f_c(x, y) < m + 2s \\ sigma * 2/5 & m - 3s < f_c(x, y) < m - 2s \ or \ m + 2s < f_c(x, y) < m + 3s \\ sigma/5 & f_c(x, y) < m - 3s \ or \ f_c(x, y) < m + 3s \end{cases} \tag{3}$$

where m is the mean of all pixel brightness across the whole input image, and s is the half of the standard deviation of the pixel brightness across the whole image. *Sigma* is a

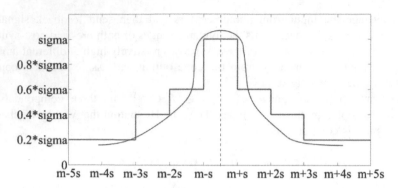

Fig. 2. The plot of junction coupling strength vs the local brightness. The blue line is the response curve of Eq. 3, which simply imitates the black curve that describes the true relationship between the junctional conductance and the transjunctional voltage (originally described by a two-state asymmetrical Boltzmann equation) [20]. (Color figure online)

parameter defining the max coupling strength of HCs, which is experimentally set to be 1.0 in this work.

Modulated by the HC feedback computed by Eq. 1 with spatially varying HC receptive field (described by Eqs. 2 and 3), the cone signals $f_c(x, y)$ (which will be sent into BCs) is then given by

$$BCinput_c(x, y) = \frac{f_c(x, y)}{a + HCfeedback_c(x, y)} \qquad (4)$$

where a is a user-defined HC feedback parameter, partially to avoid dividing by zero. We experimentally set $a = 0.2$ in this work for all the processed images, and its influence on the model's performance will be analyzed later.

The RF of most BCs consists of a smaller excitatory center and a lager inhibitory annular surround, which is commonly described by the "difference of Gaussian" (DOG) model [22]. This center-surround interaction reduces redundant information and improves the spatial resolution. Sufficient evidence supports that HCs mainly contribute to this surround antagonism [23]. We denote the output of BCs, the final output of our method, as $BC_c(x, y)$, $c \in \{R, G, B\}$, which is computed as

$$BCoutput_c(x, y) = BCinput_c(x, y) \otimes (g(x, y; \sigma_{cen}) - k \cdot g(x, y; \sigma_{sur})) \qquad (5)$$

where k is the sensitivity of the inhibitory surround, σ_{cen} and σ_{sur} are respectively the standard deviations of Gaussian shaped RF center and its surround, which are experimentally set to be 0.5 and 1.0, respectively, in this work.

3   Experimental Results and Comparisons

3.1   Light-Induced Coupling

The light-induced modulation of HC coupling (Eq. 3) can optimize the extraction of details in natural scenes [21]. With a fixated coupling, signal along the borders of the dark and light parts are distorted by the relatively strong interactions of HCs locating across the areas of different brightness. As shown inside the white circle of Fig. 3, the extra attenuation caused by the signals from HCs in the highlight bulb area results in a dark circle surround the bulb. The light-induced modulation of coupling can greatly decrease these interactions and hence prevent the distortion near the edges.

Fig. 3. Light induced Coupling of HCs. From top to bottom, the first row is the input of cones, and second row is the feedback from HCs to cones, and the third row is the input of BCs. The left column of the second and third rows correspond the processing with a fixated coupling, while the right column list the processing with light-induced coupling. The results of the local regions in the dotted white circles especially reveal the advantage of light-induced coupling.

3.2   Analysis of HC Feedback Parameter a

Among the free parameters of the proposed model, we experimentally found that the HC feedback parameter a in Eq. 4 has strong influence on the performance of our model. As shown in Fig. 4, the lower value of this parameter is, the brighter the dark area is, and the darker the brightness area is. But at the same time, the image loses more color information become gray. In contrast, a higher value of HC feedback parameter means higher color fidelity but lower dynamic range compression.

Fig. 4. Different results with varying values of the HC feedback parameter a. From left to right, the parameter values are 0.01, 0.1, 0.2, 0.3 and 0.4, respectively.

3.3   Results and Comparisons

All the results of our method in this part were calculated with the parameter setting as: $a = 0.2$, $sigma = 1$ and $k = 0.5$.

Figure 5 shows comparisons between the results of our method and Meylan's adaptive center-surround Retinex [11], which is claimed better than MSRCR of

Fig. 5. Comparison with Meylan's Retinex on several HDR images. From left to right, the three columns list the original images, the results of Meylan's Retinex, and the results of the proposed model, respectively.

Fig. 6. Comparison on the scenes of Hotel Room (HR) and Napa Valley (NV) selected from the set of MPII. For each scene, from top to bottom and left to right, the images are: (1) the original HDR image; the results of: (2) our model; (3) Ashikhmin; (4) Drago's adaptive logarithmic method; (5) Durand; (6) Fattal; (7) Reinhard; (8) Drago's Retinex; (9) Tumblin; and (10) Ward, respectively.

Table 1. Comparison of the metric HDR-VDP-2 on five images from MPII. The numbers marked by red, green and blue denote the first, second and third best scores, respectively.

Method	Ashikhmin	Drago	Durand	Fattal	Reinhard	Drago's Retinex	Tumblin	Ward	Proposed
AN	48.34	50.01	**51.91**	50.51	50.99	49.55	**54.66**	48.50	**51.90**
AM	**46.95**	46.06	41.03	37.60	**46.60**	39.33	45.14	44.19	**47.53**
M	43.00	43.06	**43.90**	37.77	42.54	42.08	**45.58**	40.86	**44.34**
HR	47.68	**50.45**	48.84	46.30	**50.65**	48.69	**53.37**	41.70	50.18
NV	47.14	50.49	**52.50**	43.70	**52.07**	51.92	**55.34**	47.85	51.97
Mean	46.62	48.01	47.64	43.18	**48.57**	46.31	**50.82**	44.62	**49.18**

Rahman et al. [10]. Note that the results of Meylan's method were obtained by running the original code from the authors. From the figure we can find that in those bright areas, e.g., the wall near the S relief and the ground, Meylan's Retinex loses meaningful details, which are well preserved, or even enhanced, by our method.

We also compared our method with eight typical methods [3–7, 9, 12, 13]. The results of these existing methods shown in Fig. 6 are directly cited from the MPII database (http://resources.mpi-inf.mpg.de/tmo/NewExperiment/TmoOverview.html). Generally speaking, our method not only lightens the dark regions, but also improves the contrast of the bright regions. The visibility of structures and color loyalty of our results are more natural as the scenes should be. We quantified this comparison with the metric of HDR-VDP-2 [24], and in general, a higher HDR-VDP-2 score means a better result. The results are listed in Table 1. This table also includes three extra scenes which are not graphically shown in this paper due to the space limitation. The last row of the table further shows the mean of the scores over all scenes for each method. On average, only worse than the method of Tumblin [13], our method obtains the second place in term of mean HDR-VDP-2 in this comparison.

Table 2. Comparison of the metric HDR-VDP-2 on multiple images from pfs. The numbers marked by red, green and blue denote the first, second and third best scores, respectively.

Method	Semour Park	Forest Path	MPI Atrium 1	MPI Atrium 3	MPI Office	NancyChurch1	NancyChurch2	NancyChurch3	Mean
Drago	**47.96**	54.62	50.91	48.99	**49.18**	48.89	52.31	**52.81**	50.71
Durand	44.11	**55.55**	**53.40**	**50.70**	43.55	47.66	49.83	**53.94**	49.84
Fattal	44.65	51.52	49.64	43.46	41.39	42.17	48.86	47.59	46.16
Ferradans	42.64	53.21	51.87	44.01	43.39	45.06	**54.21**	46.31	47.59
Mai	47.83	51.22	46.13	45.24	**48.72**	50.17	47.84	51.45	48.58
Mantiuk06	43.46	50.97	51.77	43.21	40.99	42.00	51.18	45.16	46.09
Mantiuk08	44.66	**55.95**	51.00	46.67	46.99	**50.29**	50.42	48.71	49.34
Pattanaik	44.07	50.17	**55.81**	44.33	45.70	45.47	**53.93**	47.29	48.35
Reinhard02	47.48	**55.29**	50.33	49.07	**53.87**	**53.06**	51.92	51.98	**51.63**
Reinhard05	**49.68**	54.02	**52.51**	**50.25**	48.33	48.76	51.52	51.77	**50.86**
Proposed	**49.97**	52.61	50.37	**49.88**	48.04	**50.92**	**52.78**	**54.10**	**51.08**

Fig. 7. Comparison on the scene of nancy_church_3 from pfs. In the first two rows, from top to bottom and left to right, the images are: (1) the original HDR image; (2) the results of ours; (3) Ferradans; (4) Mai; (5) Mantiuk's perceptual framework and (6) adaptive TM; (7) Pattanaik; and (8) Reinhard, respectively. In the same arrangement, the last two rows list the enlarged patches of the local region of window in the images of original size.

Table 2 further compares with some typical methods [2–5, 7, 8, 14, 25–27] on eight scenes from pfstools (http://pfstools.sourceforge.net/tmo_gallery/). It is clear that no method can always obtain the best (highest) HDR-VDP-2 score on all the scenes listed here. However, our model has larger chance to obtain the scores that are within the range of top three on various scenes, e.g., five out of eight scenes, and for the remaining three scenes (i.e., Forest Path, MPI Atrium1, and MPI Office), the scores by our model are quite competitive, in comparison to the best scores by other methods. The last column of Table 2 shows the average scores of all scenes for each method, which also indicate the competitive performance of the proposed method.

Figure 7 shows an example of one scene in Table 2 for multiple methods. It is clear that our result preserves more details in both bright and dark areas. In contrast, Ferradans' results [8] can keep the details in illuminated areas, which are too bright in Mai's [2] and Reinhard's [3] results, without clear improvement in dark areas. It seems that Mantiuk's perceptual framework [25] compresses the global contrast too much. Pattanaik's adaption [27] loses color information. Mantiuk's adaptive TM [26] works well in most places but fails in some quite bright areas, e.g., the window.

4 Conclusion

We proposed a tone mapping method inspired by the information processing mechanisms in the outer layers of the retina, including the HC light-induced gap coupling, the HCs' feedback to photoreceptors, and the DOG RF of BCs. Corresponding to the amazing ability of HVS to quickly achieve stable perception under varying natural light environments, our method provides a robust performance for various scenes. The proposed method was compared with the state-of-the-art methods qualitatively and quantitatively, showing quite competitive or even better results by our model. In particular, our method is capable of enhancing the visibility of both dark and bright regions while improving the local contrast, without sacrificing the color fidelity.

This simplified retinal method proposed here also provides valuable suggestions about some roles of the BC surround inhibition as well as the HC feedback in HVS. In our method, HC negative feedback shifts photoreceptor sensitivity in response to the spatial context of input illuminant, and the DOG RF of BCs, which filters the low spatial frequency elements, serves to obtain a fast removal of redundant information, so that retina can make optimal use of its limited bandwidth and only pass relevant information to the next stages, reducing the cost of neural activities. Different with the former HC feedback models [15, 16], the most important novelty of our model is to automatically regulate the feedback to RGB components by adaptively varying the RF size of HC based on the physiological evidence on the gap junction between HCs.

References

1. Reinhard, E., Heidrich, W., Debevec, P., et al.: High Dynamic Range Imaging: Acquisition, Display, and Image-Based Lighting. Morgan Kaufmann, San Francisco (2010)
2. Mai, Z., Mansour, H., Mantiuk, R., Nasiopoulos, P., Ward, R., Heidrich, W.: Optimizing a tone curve for backward-compatible high dynamic range image and video compression. IEEE Trans. Image Process. **20**, 1558–1571 (2011)
3. Reinhard, E., Stark, M., Shirley, P., Ferwerda, J.: Photographic tone reproduction for digital images. ACM Trans. Graph. (TOG) **21**(3), 267–276 (2002). ACM
4. Durand, F., Dorsey, J.: Fast bilateral filtering for the display of high-dynamic-range images. ACM Trans. Graph. (TOG) **21**, 257–266 (2002)

5. Fattal, R., Lischinski, D., Werman, M.: Gradient domain high dynamic range compression. ACM Trans. Graph. (TOG) **21**(3), 249–256 (2002). ACM

6. Ashikhmin, M.: A tone mapping algorithm for high contrast images. In: Proceedings of the 13th Eurographics Workshop on Rendering, pp. 145–156. Eurographics Association (2002)

7. Drago, F., Myszkowski, K., Annen, T., et al.: Adaptive logarithmic mapping for displaying high contrast scenes. In: Computer Graphics Forum, pp. 419–426. Wiley Library (2003)

8. Ferradans, S., Bertalmio, M., Provenzi, E., Caselles, V.: An analysis of visual adaptation and contrast perception for tone mapping. IEEE Trans. Pattern Anal. Mach. Intell. **33**, 2002–2012 (2011)

9. Drago, F., Martens, W., et al.: Design of a tone mapping operator for high-dynamic range images based upon psychophysical evaluation and preference mapping. In: Electronic Imaging 2003, pp. 321–331. International Society for Optics and Photonics (2003)

10. Rahman, Z.-U., Jobson, D.J., Woodell, G.A.: Retinex processing for automatic image enhancement. J. Electron. Imag. **13**, 100–110 (2004)

11. Meylan, L., Süsstrunk, S.: High dynamic range image rendering with a retinex-based adaptive filter. IEEE Trans. Image Process. **15**, 2820–2830 (2006)

12. Ward, G.: A Contrast-Based Scalefactor for Luminance Display, pp. 415–421. Graphics Gems IV (1994)

13. Tumblin, J., Hodgins, J.K., Guenter, B.K.: Two methods for display of high contrast images. ACM Trans. Graph. (TOG) **18**, 56–94 (1999)

14. Reinhard, E., Devlin, K.: Dynamic range reduction inspired by photoreceptor physiology. IEEE Trans. Visual. Comput. Graph. **11**, 13–24 (2005)

15. Van Hateren, J.: Encoding of high dynamic range video with a model of human cones. ACM Trans. Graph. (TOG) **25**, 1380–1399 (2006)

16. Alleysson, D., Meylan, L., Susstrunk, S.: HDR CFA image rendering. In: 14th European Signal Processing Conference, 2006, pp. 1–4. IEEE (2006)

17. Masland, R.H.: The neuronal organization of the retina. Neuron **76**, 266–280 (2012)

18. Joselevitch, C.: Human retinal circuitry and physiology. Psychol. Neurosci. **1**, 141–165 (2008)

19. Bloomfield, S.A., Xin, D., et al.: A comparison of receptive field and tracer coupling size of horizontal cells in the rabbit retina. Vis. Neurosci. **12**, 985–999 (1995)

20. Xin, D., Bloomfield, S.A.: Dark- and light- induced changes in coupling between horizontal cells in mammalian retina. J. Comp. Neurol. **405**, 75–87 (1999)

21. Bloomfield, S.A., Völgyi, B.: The diverse functional roles and regulation of neuronal gap junctions in the retina. Nat. Rev. Neurosci. **10**, 495–506 (2009)

22. Enroth-Cugell, C., Robson, J.G.: The contrast sensitivity of retinal ganglion cells of the cat. J. Physiol. **187**, 517–552 (1966)

23. Thoreson, W.B., Mangel, S.C.: Lateral interactions in the outer retina. Progr. Retinal Eye Res. **31**, 407–441 (2012)

24. Mantiuk, R., Kim, K.J., Rempel, A.G., Heidrich, W.: HDR-VDP-2: a calibrated visual metric for visibility and quality predictions in all luminance conditions. ACM Trans. Graph. (TOG) **30**, 40 (2011). ACM

25. Mantiuk, R., Myszkowski, K., Seidel, H.-P.: A perceptual framework for contrast processing of high dynamic range images. ACM Trans. Appl. Percept. (TAP) **3**, 286–308 (2006). ACM

26. Mantiuk, R., Daly, S., Kerofsky, L.: Display adaptive tone mapping. ACM Trans. Graph. (TOG) **27**(3), 68 (2008). ACM

27. Pattanaik, S.N., Tumblin, J., Yee, H. Greenberg, D.P.: Time-dependent visual adaptation for fast realistic image display. In: Proceedings of the 27th annual conference on Computer graphics and interactive techniques, pp. 47–54. ACM (2000)

Autoencoders with Drop Strategy

Cong Hu[1] and Xiao-Jun Wu[1,2(✉)]

[1] School of Digital Media, Jiangnan University, Wuxi, China
{wxhucong, xiaojun_wu_jnu}@163.com
[2] School of IoT Engineering, Jiangnan University, Wuxi, China

Abstract. In this paper, we propose a new approach for unsupervised learning using autoencoders with drop strategy (DrAE). Different from Explicit Regularized Autoencoders (ERAE), DrAE has no any additionally explicit regularization term to the cost function. A serial of drop strategies are exploited in the training phase of autoencoders for robust feature representation, such as dropout, dropConnect, denoising, winner-take-all, local winner-take-all. When training DrAE, subset of units or weights are set to zero. The results of our experiments on the MNIST dataset show that the performance of DrAE is better or comparative to ERAE.

Keywords: Autoencoders · Unsupervised learning · Drop strategy

1 Introduction

Recently, supervised learning has been successfully developed and used to produce representations that have enabled leaps forward in classification accuracy for several tasks [1]. However, the question that has remained unanswered is whether it is possible to learn powerful representations from unlabeled data without any supervision [2, 3].

The idea of autoencoder has been part of the historical landscape of neural networks for decades [4, 5]. It has been widely used in many scientific and industrial applications, solving mainly dimensionality reduction and unsupervised pre-training tasks.

Various autoencoders had been proposed, such as L2-norm regularized autoencoders, sparse autoencoders [6, 7] and contractive autoencoders [8]. These ERAEs use a cost function including an additional penalty term that encourages the model to have other properties besides the ability to copy its input to its output. These other properties include sparsity of the representation, smallness of the derivative of the representation. However, they all have to design carefully, and also some hyper-parameters need to be tuned. We propose an easy way to train autoencoders without any additional penalty term to the cost function. Instead, a series of drop strategies are used in the unsupervised feature learning for robust feature representation. Through dropping input units, connect weights, hidden units in the training phase, DrAE would train thousands of subnets of autoencoders network.

In this paper, we propose a method how to train DrAE with a series of drop strategies rather than ERAE with an additional penalty to the cost function. We compare and contrast ERAEs and DrAEs on the datasets MNIST and USPS, and DrAEs get better or comparative performance to ERAEs.

C.-L. Liu et al. (Eds.): BICS 2016, LNAI 10023, pp. 80–89, 2016.
DOI: 10.1007/978-3-319-49685-6_8

2 Background

2.1 The Basic Autoencoders

Autoencoder is based on the encoder-decoder paradigm, where an input is first transformed into a typically lower-dimensional space (encoder part) and then expanded to reproduce the initial data (decoder part). It is trained in unsupervised fashion allowing it to extract generally useful features from unlabeled data, to detect and remove input redundancies and to present essential aspects of analyzing data in robust and discriminative representations.

The basic autoencoders framework considered here starts from an encoding function f that maps an input $x \in R^{d_x}$ to hidden representation $h(x) \in R^{d_h}$.

It has the form:

$$h = f(x) = s(wx + b_h), \tag{1}$$

where s is the logistic sigmoid activation function $s(z) = \frac{1}{1+e^{-z}}$. The encoder is parametrized by a $d_h \times d_x$ weight matrix W, and a bias vector $b_h \in R^{d_h}$.

A decoder function g then maps hidden representation h back to a reconstruction y:

$$y = g(h) = s(W'h + b_y), \tag{2}$$

The decoder's parameters are a bias vector $b_h \in R^{d_h}$, in which $W' = W^T$.

Basic autoencoders training consists in finding parameters $\theta = \{W, b_h, b_y\}$ that minimize the reconstruction error on a training set of examples D_n, i.e. minimizing the following objective function:

$$J_{AE}(\theta) = \sum_{x \in s} L(x, g(f(x))), \tag{3}$$

where $L(t, r)$ is the reconstruction error between target t and reconstruction r (typically squared error or cross-entropy loss).

2.2 ERAE

Ideally, one could train any architecture of autoencoder successfully, choosing the code dimension and the capacity of the encoder and decoder based on the complexity of distribution to be modeled. Regularized autoencoders provide the ability to do so. Typically, L2-norm weights regularization is explicitly added to the reconstruction error:

$$J_{AE+wd}(\theta) = \sum_{x \in s} L(x, g(f(x))) + \lambda \sum_{i,j} W_{i,j}^2, \tag{4}$$

where g is the decoder output and we have f(x), the encoder output.

Sparse autoencoder is another autoencoder whose training criterion explicitly involves an additional sparse penalty on the hidden units. We can think of the sparse penalty simply as a regularized term in addition to the reconstruction error. Sparse penalty function proportional to the KL divergence between the hidden unit marginal $(\hat{\rho})$ and the target sparsity proportional (ρ) is added to the cost function:

$$J_{AE+sp}(\theta) = \sum_{x\in s} L(x, g(f(x))) + \beta \sum_{i,j} KL(\rho \| \hat{\rho}), \tag{5}$$

where,

$$KL(\rho \| \hat{\rho}) = \rho * \log \frac{\rho}{\hat{\rho}_j} + (1 - \rho) * \log \frac{1 - \rho}{1 - \hat{\rho}_j}, \tag{6}$$

$$\hat{\rho}_j = \frac{1}{N} \sum_{i=1}^{N} h_j(x^{(i)}). \tag{7}$$

3 DrAE

Rather than ERAE with an additional penalty term, DrAE have no any additional penalty:

$$J_{AE + "drop"}(\theta) = \sum_{x\in s} L(x, g(f(x))), \tag{8}$$

the cost function of DrAE have only one term. It is the same as the basic autoencoders, except the reconstruction error of denoising $L(x, g(f(\hat{x})))$, where $\hat{x}$ is the corrupted x.

Using some drop strategies to get robust feature representations can aim for any sparsity rate, robust for slightly change of the input and has no hyper-parameter to tune (except the drop rate). The training method of DrAE is the same as the basic autoencoders'. However, in the training phase, the activation values and reconstruction error only propagate through the none-zero units and weights. We analyze five kinds of drop strategies.

3.1 Dropout

Dropout [9] was proposed by Hinton et al. as a form of regularization for fully con-nected neural network layers. Each element of a layer's output is kept with probability p, otherwise being set to 0 with probability $(1-p)$. The activation values and reconstruction error only propagate through none-zero activation units. Extensive experiments show that Dropout improves the network's generalization ability, giving improved test performance. Dropout can be considered as a kind stochastic drop strategy on the activation.

3.2 DropConnect

DropConnect [10] was proposed by Li Wan et al. as the generalization of dropout in which each connection can be dropped with probability $1-p$. DropConnect is similar to Dropout as it introduces dynamic sparsity within the model, but differs in that the sparsity is on the weights W, rather than the output vectors of a layer. DropConnect can be considered as a kind stochastic drop on the weights. The activation values and reconstruction error propagate through none-zero connected weights.

3.3 Denoising

Denoising [11] was proposed by Vincent et al. as a kind of unsupervised representation learning based on the idea of making the learned representations robust to partial corruption of the input pattern. In this paper, we use binary mask as noise add to input layer. So the input values only propagate through none-zero input units.

3.4 WTA

Winner-Take-All [12] was proposed by Makhzani et al. as a method of learning hierarchical sparse representations. In the feedforward phase, after computing the hidden codes of the last layer of the encoder, rather than reconstructing the input from all of the hidden units, for each hidden unit, WTA keeping the k percent largest activation of that hidden unit across the mini-batch samples and setting the rest of activations of that hidden unit to zero. In the backpropagation phase, the error is only backpropagated through the k percent non-zero activations.

3.5 LWTA

Local Winner-Take-All (LWTA) [13] artificial multilayer NNs was proposed by Srivastava et al. as an activation function with local competition. During the forward propagation of inputs in LWTA networks, local competition between the neurons in each block turns off the activation of all neurons except the one with the highest activation. LWTA is considered as a kind of drop strategy with local competitive on the hidden units.

4   Experiments

We evaluate DrAE as a feature representation learner in handwritten digit recognition on MNIST and USPS datasets. The main parameters in the models are chosen by cross-validating on the training set or using the available validation set.

4.1   MNIST

We use the standard benchmark datasets MNIST. The MNIST handwritten digit classification task [14] consists of 28×28 black and white images, each containing a digit 0 to 9 (10-classes). There are 60, 000 training images and 10,000 test images. We randomly separate the training set into 50,000 training cases and 10,000 cases for validation. We scale the pixel values to the [0, 1] range before inputting to our models.

To empirically verify the advantage of the representation learnt using the DrAE for their discriminative power, we train autoencoders with different drop strategy and use these representations followed by a softmax classification layer, and we use sigmoid function as activation function. We train autoencoders and softmax classification for 100 epochs respectively. IRAE are also compared to ERAE, such as L2 regularized autoencoders (weights decay coefficient $\lambda = 0.01$) and sparse autoencoders with sparse penalty ($\rho = 0.05$), sparse penalty term coefficient $\beta = 0.1$.

For this experiment, a fully connected network is used consisting one 1000-units hidden layer. The first layer takes the image pixels as input, while the second layer's output is fed into a 10-class classification layer.

We use the validate error to choose the best hyper-parameter with the unsupervised learning methods. We show five explanatory experiments in Figs. 1, 2, 3, and 4. Figure 1 shows the effect of varying the drop rate p for DropConnect and Dropout. Both DropConnect and Dropout autoencoders give optimal performance in the vicinity of 0.5. Figure 2 shows the effect of varying the masked rate for Denoising. Denoising autoencoders gives optimal performance in the vicinity of 0.3. Figure 3 shows the

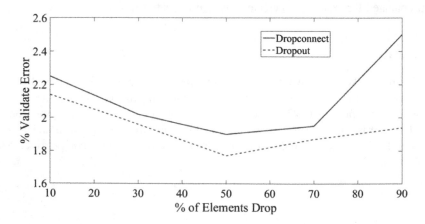

Fig. 1. Performance on varying the drop-rate of DropConnect and Dropout

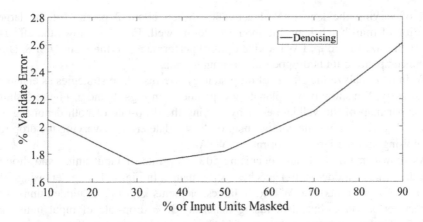

Fig. 2. Performance on varying the mask-rate of Denoising

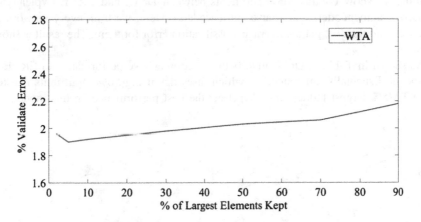

Fig. 3. Performance on varying the kept-rate of WTA

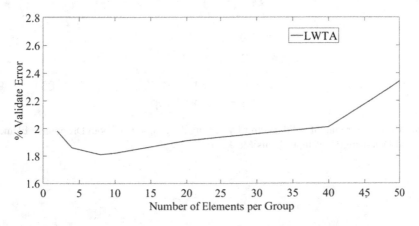

Fig. 4. Performance on varying the kept-rate of LWTA

effect of varying the kept rate of activation, when about 2 percent of the largest activation of mini-batch kept, the model performs well. Figure 4 shows the effect of varying the size of group, LWTA give optimal performance in the vicinity of 8, about 88% uncompetitive units dropped in the training phase.

To further analyze the effects of drop strategy, we fuse drop strategies as enhanced drop strategy. We show two explanatory experiments in Figs. 5 and 6. Figure 5 shows the contour map of the validate error by varying the drop-rate of both denoising and dropout. Figure 6 shows the contour map of the validate error by varying the drop-rate of denoising and the largest kept-rate of WTA.

As shown in Fig. 5, fusing denoising(50% drop-rate of input units) and dropout (10% drop-rate of hidden units) gets best performance. In Fig. 6, fusing denoising(50% drop-rate of input units) and WTA(5% largest elements kept-rate of hidden units) gets the best performance, but also, fusing denoising(30% drop-rate of input units) and WTA(50% largest elements kept-rate of hidden units) also gets excellent performance.

We use the test error to test different drop strategies with the unsupervised learning methods, we show contrastive experiments between DrAE and ERAE (typically L2 regularized autoencoders and sparse autoencoders). Here, we train every network for five times, and then we get the average classification error for them. The result is shown in Table 1.

As shown in Table 1, DrAE give better or comparative performance to ERAE on this model. Especially, autoencoders which fuses denoising(50% input units masked) and WTA(5% largest hidden units kept) get the best performance on this model.

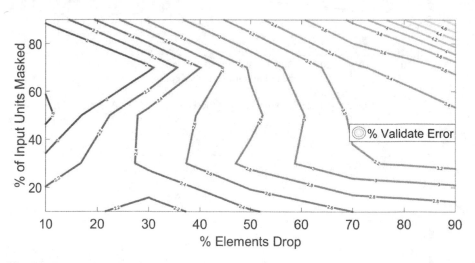

Fig. 5. The contour map of validate error by varying the drop-rate of both Dropout(% Elements Drop) and Denoising(% of input Units Masked)

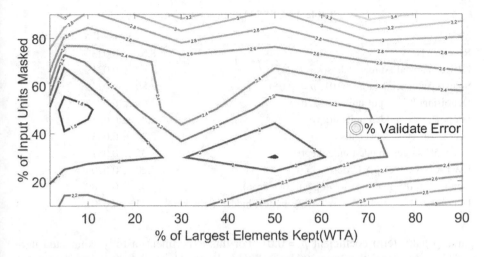

Fig. 6. The contour map of validate error by varying the drop-rate of both WTA(% of Largest Elements kept) and Denoising(% of input Units Masked)

Table 1. MNIST classification error.

Model	Test Error (five networks)
Raw pixels	7.40 ± 0.037%
L2 Regularized Autoencoders($\lambda = 0.01$)	1.89 ± 0.034%
Sparse Autoencoders($\beta = 0.1, \rho = 0.05$)	2.08 ± 0.026%
Denoising(30% input units masked)	1.73 ± 0.039%
Dropout(50% hidden units drop)	1.77 ± 0.045%
DropConnect(50% weights drop)	1.92 ± 0.057%
WTA(2% largest hidden units kept)	1.86 ± 0.038%
LWTA-8(Number per Group = 8)	1.81 ± 0.042%
Denoising(50% masked) + Dropout(10% drop)	1.74 ± 0.078%
Denoising(50% masked) + WTA(5% largest hidden units kept)	1.71 ± 0.084%

4.2   Usps

We also use the handwritten digit dataset USPS [15]. The USPS dataset consists of 16×16 black and white images, each containing a digit 0 to 9 (10-classes). There are 1, 100 images for every digit. We randomly choose 1,000 images of every digit for training set, others for test set. We randomly separate the training set into 9000 training cases and 1000 cases for validation and scale the pixel values to the [0, 1] range before inputting to our models.

We train autoencoders with different drop strategies and use these representations followed by a softmax classification layer, and sigmoid function is used as activation function. We train autoencoders and softmax classification for 500 epochs respectively. They are also compared to ERAE, such as L2 regularized autoencoders(weights decay coefficient $\lambda = 0.01$) and sparse autoencoders with sparse penalty ($\rho = 0.05$),

Table 2. USPS classification error.

Model	Test Error (five networks)
Raw pixels	8.55 ± 0.023%
L2 Regularized Autoencoders($\lambda = 0.01$)	3.60 ± 0.031%
Sparse Autoencoders($\beta = 0.01$, $\rho = 0.05$)	3.80 ± 0.024%
Denoising(20% input units masked)	2.60 ± 0.035%
Dropout(50% hidden units drop)	2.77 ± 0.025%
DropConnect(50% weights drop)	3.34 ± 0.053%
WTA(5% largest hidden units kept)	3.35 ± 0.057%
LWTA-2(Number per Group = 2)	3.20 ± 0.020%
Denoising(10% masked) + Dropout(50% drop)	3.46 ± 0.078%
Denoising(50% masked) + WTA(8% largest hidden units kept)	3.74 ± 0.030%

sparse penalty term coefficient $\beta = 0.01$. For this experiment, a fully connected network is used, consisting one 300-units hidden layer. The first layer takes the image pixels as input, while the second layer's output is fed into a 10-class classification layer. Here, we train every network for five times, and then we get the average classification error for them. The classification result is shown in Table 2.

As shown in Table 2, DrAE give better or comparative performance to ERAE on this model. Especially, autoencoders which denoising(20% input units masked) gets the best performance on this model.

5 Conclusion and Future Work

In this work, we have proposed a kind of autoencoder trained by a novel principle, called DrAE. The main contribution of this paper is that we can train autoencoders with a generalized drop strategy to get better or comparative performance to ERAE(typically L2 regularized autoencoders and sparse autoencoders).

This principle can be used to train stack autoencoders to initialize a deep neural network. In the future, we hope to explore more drop strategies for autoencoders.

Acknowledgments. This work was supported by National Natural Science Foundation of China under Grant No.61373055, Industry Project of Provincial Department of Education of Jiangsu Province (Grant No. JH10-28), and Industry Oriented Project of Jiangsu Provincial Department of Technology (Grant No. BY2012059).

References

1. Krizhevsky, A., Sutskever, I., Hinton, G.E.: Imagenet classification with deep convolutional neural networks. In: Advances in Neural Information Processing Systems, pp. 1097–1105 (2012)
2. Bengio, Y.: Learning deep architectures for AI. Found. Trends® Mach. Learn. **2**(1), 1–127 (2009)

3. Bengio, Y., Goodfellow, I.J., Courville, A.: Deep Learning. MIT Press, Cambridge (2015). http://www.iro.umontreal.ca/ ~ bengioy/dlbook

4. Bourlard, H., Kamp, Y.: Auto-association by multilayer perceptrons and singular value decomposition. Biol. Cybern. **59**(4–5), 291–294 (1988)

5. Hinton, G.E., Zemel, R.S.: Autoencoders, minimum description length, and Helmholtz free energy. Adv. Neural Inf. Process. Syst. 3 (1994)

6. Ng, A.: Sparse autoencoder. CS294A Lect. Notes **72**, 1–19 (2011)

7. Olshausen, B.A., Field, D.J.: Sparse coding with an overcomplete basis set: A strategy employed by V1? Vis. Res. **37**(23), 3311–3325 (1997)

8. Rifai, S., Vincent, P., Muller, X., et al.: Contractive auto-encoders: explicit invariance during feature extraction. In: Proceedings of the 28th International Conference on Machine Learning (ICML-2011), pp. 833–840 (2011)

9. Srivastava, N., Hinton, G., Krizhevsky, A., et al.: Dropout: a simple way to prevent neural networks from overfitting. J. Mach. Learn. Res. **15**(1), 1929–1958 (2014)

10. Wan, L., Zeiler, M., Zhang, S., et al.: Regularization of neural networks using DropConnect. In: Proceedings of the 30th International Conference on Machine Learning (ICML-2013), pp. 1058–1066 (2013)

11. Vincent, P., Larochelle, H., Bengio, Y., et al.: Extracting and composing robust features with denoising autoencoders. In: Proceedings of the 25th International Conference on Machine learning, pp. 1096–1103. ACM (2008)

12. Makhzani, A., Frey, B.J.: Winner-take-all autoencoders. In: Advances in Neural Information Processing Systems, pp. 2773–2781 (2015)

13. Srivastava, R.K., Masci, J., Kazerounian, S., et al.: Compete to compute. In: Advances in Neural Information Processing Systems, pp. 2310–2318 (2013)

14. LeCun, Y., Cortes, C., Burges, C.J.C.: The MNIST database of handwritten digits (1998)

15. http://www.cs.nyu.edu/ ~ roweis/data.html

Detecting Rare Visual and Auditory Events from EEG Using Pairwise-Comparison Neural Networks

Min Wang$^{(\boxtimes)}$, Hussein A. Abbass, Jiankun Hu, and Kathryn Merrick

School of Engineering and Information Technology, University of New South Wales,
Canberra, ACT 2600, Australia
min.wang@student.adfa.edu.au, {h.abbass,j.hu,k.merrick}@adfa.edu.au

Abstract. Detection of unanticipated and rare events refers to a process of identifying an occasional target (oddball) stimulus from a regular trail of standard stimuli based on brain wave signals. It is the premise of human event-related potential (ERP) applications, a significant research topic in brain computer interfaces. The focus of this paper is to investigate whether unanticipated and rare visual and auditory events are detectable from EEG signals. In order to achieve this, an exploratory experiment is conducted. A novel pairwise comparison neural network approach to detect those unanticipated and rare visual and auditory events from EEG signals is introduced. Results indicate that the change in EEG signals caused by unanticipated rare events is detectable; a piece of finding that opens opportunities for ERP-based applications.

Keywords: Electroencephalogram (EEG) · Pairwise-comparison neural networks · Event-related potential (ERP) · Unanticipated events

1 Introduction

Electrical potentials are continuously generated from the human brain. These potentials represent neural activities and can be measured from the scalp as electroencephalogram (EEG) [1]. An EEG signal as being discussed in this paper is a surface-level non-intrusive recording of cortical electrical activities. It offers promising non-invasive modalities for brain wave based applications; for example, in the research area of EEG biometrics has recently received substantial attention [2]. Ongoing EEG in humans is a continuous signal that can be acquired without intentional stimuli by an observer or analyst. However, the absence of intentional stimuli makes it more difficult to analyze research-wise. For many applications, it is unnecessary to infer users' intent from their ongoing EEG signals. Instead, it is more practical to rely on event detection techniques such as event related potential (ERP). In contrast to ongoing continuous EEG analysis, an ERP is a stimulus-averaged signal time-locked to the presentation of some event of interest [3]. For a particular type of events, an ERP is obtained by averaging signals over multiple trials. The assumption is that EEG responses

© Springer International Publishing AG 2016
C.-L. Liu et al. (Eds.): BICS 2016, LNAI 10023, pp. 90–101, 2016.
DOI: 10.1007/978-3-319-49685-6_9

to a stimulus would cause stronger spikes in the signal, while in the absence of these stimuli, the strength is less. This property allows for some control over the analysis of users' cognitive states, which is not possible with raw ongoing EEG signals as it is hard to isolate different functional processing within EEG signals.

ERPs recorded from the central nervous system have been demonstrated to be associated with the recognition of important events that are more cognitively determined than autonomic responses. Two ERP components, the auditory mismatch negativity (MMN) and visual mismatch negativity (vMMN) [4], are explored for automatic detection of the corresponding changes in outer auditory and visual stimuli [5]. Functional magnetic resonance imaging (fMRI) was used to provide access to brain data. In this paper, we based this study on EEG because it is much more applicable and cheaper for practical use. An endogenous ERP is the P300 wave, which is a large, distinct response potential elicited by a rare (oddball) target stimulus embedded in a sequence of more common stimuli. It is a positive deflection in voltage with a latency of 250 ms to 500 ms and is typically measured most strongly by the electrodes covering the parietal lobe. ERP has been an important topic for studying cognitive processes [6]. First, it is subject invariant; that is, it exists in all subjects. Second, it is associated with low variations in the measurement techniques that may help simplify interface designs and permit greater usability.

The main contribution of this paper is to offer a methodology to detect ERPs from single trials. A color varying oddball experiment and a pitch varying oddball experiment are the bases for the experimental protocol. We then introduce a pairwise comparison neural network approach, which demonstrates significant potential towards the goal of ERPs detection from a single trial. The successful detection of these unanticipated events forms the foundation of our current research on real-time detection of evoked potential for biometrics and the first step to design an ERP-based biometric.

In our experiment, two oddball event types were designed to trigger the P300, the visual oddball and the auditory oddball, where low-probability target items are mixed with high-probability standard items. Generally, ERP relies on averaging multiple trials to visually inspect the change in the signal. In this paper, however, we attempt to use a classifier to detect ERP from single trials. This will accelerate the process of detecting target events and open the possibility of using the technology for real-time applications, which is a leap-forward when compared to the current state-of-the-art literature that is based on averaging a large number of trials [7]. A straightforward classification method based on neural network was then applied, but the accuracy of the classifier was low. Consequently, we propose a pairwise comparison neural network approach to detect the unanticipated visual and auditory events from the EEG signals. The proposed approach, while still offering a lower accuracy than what we have hoped to reach, doubles the accuracy of detection.

The rest of the paper is organized as follows. Section 2 presents the details of the experimental protocol. Section 3 describes the methods for data collection and EEG signal processing. Results and analysis are shown and described in Sect. 4, followed by discussions in Sect. 5.

2   Experimental Protocol

Different external stimuli will trigger neurons in certain parts of the brain reacting in response to the stimuli. Among different types, stimulations through visual and auditory stimuli are the most basic and commonly used methods for triggering neuro-responses in laboratory settings. The objective of this experimental protocol is to detect and associate the changes of EEG signals with the unanticipated and rare visual and auditory events. To determine a suitable paradigm for this, two tasks were designed for the participants and two variations of oddballs were studied, namely visual oddballs and auditory oddballs.

Visual Task: At the start of each trial, participants were asked to focus on a big black dot shown in the center of the screen in front of them for two seconds. One of the small unlit rectangle bars close to the big black ball gets lit up for 500 ms, followed by the succeeding bar in the same direction until the last eighth bar is reached. During this process, participants were asked to focus their attention on the moving lit bar. The above procedure was periodically repeated for each trial and a selection out of the four basic directions (up, down, left, right) is chosen completely at random.

We designed a color varying oddball to form the visual oddball events, that is, during some trials (selected with a probability of 0.2) the color of the lit bar changes from the original black to red. An example of the color varying visual oddball experiment is shown in Fig. 1. Our hypothesis here is that, when participants respond to this color-varied oddball target stimulus embedded in a sequence of common color stimuli, there will be some detectable changes in the EEG signals triggered by this unanticipated and rare event.

Visual and Audio Task: The difference between this task and the previously described visual task is the addition of a piece of directional sound to visual stimuli. A spatial audio system implemented with MAYA 22USB is used to provide a sound source with directions and the participants are fitted with a set of headphones to perceive the direction of the sound. This sound file lasts for 4 s. Each audio signal has binary channels with a sampling rate of 44100 Hz and 16 bit quantization. In each trial, the same sound clip moves from the auditory perception center to one of the four basic directions, synchronized with the moving lit rectangular bars on the screen. For auditory oddball events, we designed a pitch varying oddball paradigm, which is achieved by changing the pitch of a random 500 ms fragment in the clip away from the standard directional sound during some selected trials. The software CoolEditPro 2.1 was used to achieve pitch shift while maintaining the same playback tempo or speed. To integrate the audio stimuli with visual stimuli, we made the duration of the directional sound clip equal to the synchronized moving lighted bars with matching direction in each trial. Besides, the pitch-varied auditory oddball events were restricted to synchronize to the color-varied visual oddball events.

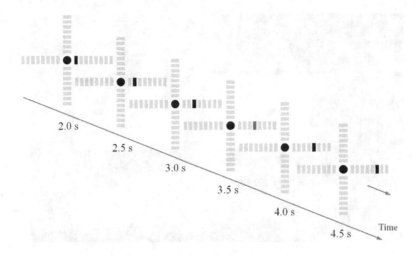

Fig. 1. Color varying visual oddball paradigm (Color figure online)

Each trial performs one of the two tasks and the sequence of different task trials is randomly generated. Four directions and two kinds of stimuli result in eight categories which will henceforth be referred to as 'VisualUp', 'VisualDown', 'VisualLeft', 'VisualRight' and 'AudioVisualUp', 'AudioVisualDown', 'AudioVisualLeft', 'AudioVisualRight'.

3 Methods

3.1 Procedure

Ten subjects (5 males, 5 females) volunteered in this experiment with an age range of 18–40. Each subject met with one investigator in a noise-controlled room for a 40 min session. We fitted the subjects with an electrode cap after brief introduction of the objective of the experiment and provided instructions for conducting tasks. A training session was provided for the subjects to get familiar with the tasks. The experiment started when the subject was comfortable with the tasks and clicked start button. During the performance period, subjects' EEG signals were collected and transferred to a computer for recording and further precessing. The experiment scenario is shown in Fig. 2.

Each trial takes 6 s which contains 2 s fixation at the central black dot and 4 s following the moving lighted bars (and the corresponding directional sound in visual and audio trials). A total of 120 trials were conducted for each subject. They were asked to remain as still as possible and refrain from blinking eyes during a trial, and to relax and blink during the interval between two trails.

Fig. 2. Experiment scenario

3.2 EEG Recording

EEG signals were collected from 21 active electrodes with a sampling rate of 2048 Hz using MindMedia Nexus-32 QEEG system. The 21 electrodes corresponds to positions Fp1, F7, T3, T5, Fp2, F8, T4, T6, F3, C3, P3, O1, F4, C4, P4, O2, Fz, Cz, Pz, A1 and A2 according to 10–20 system, and they were referenced to the average of the left and right mastoids (A1 and A2). During data acquisition, the EEG signal quality was monitored continuously in case certain electrodes lose signals due to poor contact. The signal quality monitor interface is shown in Fig. 3 with different color indicating the seven signal states. For example, the Blue color indicates the electrodes are inactive, the Green color indicates the electrodes are active while receiving high quality signal.

3.3 Feature Extraction

Effective EEG signals are mainly within the frequency band 1–42 Hz. Therefore Fast Fourier Transform (FFT) was conducted on EEG signals and a band pass filter was adopted to divide signals into several frequency bands for feature extraction in the frequency domain. We also applied Inverse Fast Fourier Transform (IFFT) on the EEG components within 1–42 Hz for signal visualization. The calculations of FFT and IFFT follow the following standard equations.

$$X_k = \sum_{n=0}^{N-1} x_n e^{-i2\pi k \frac{n}{N}} \quad k = 0, 1, ..., N-1. \tag{1}$$

$$x_n = \frac{1}{N} \sum_{k=0}^{N-1} X_k e^{i2\pi n \frac{k}{N}} \quad n = 0, 1, ..., N-1. \tag{2}$$

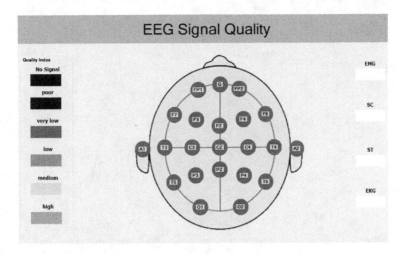

Fig. 3. Signal quality monitor interface and electrodes locations (Color figure online)

Table 1. EEG frequency bands

Band		Frequency (Hz)	Amplitude (microvolts)	Brian location
Delta		1-4	100-200	Frontal
Theta		4-7	5-10	Various
Alpha	Alpha Low	8-11	20-80	Posterior, both sides (higher on dominant side) Central sites at rest
	Alpha High	11-12		
Beta	Beta 1	13-16	1-5	Left and right side Symmetrical distribution Most evident frontally
	Beta 2	17-20		
	Beta 3	21-31		
Gamma		32-42	0.5-2	Somatosensory cortex

x_n presents a 500 ms EEG data, which has 1024 points with a sampling rate of 2048 Hz. X_k is the FFT result of x_n. Instead of this equation, we applied fast FFT algorithm to accelerate the speed of calculations. We define $N = 2048$ to make 2048×2 (real and imaginary) points FFT for all the data, obtaining a frequency resolution of 1 Hz. Band-pass filtering was used to extract signal components within the Delta, Theta, Alpha, Beta and Gamma band, respectively. We also divided Alpha and Beta band into Alpha Low and Alpha High, Beta 1, Beta 2 and Beta 3 respectively. Details of the band division are showed in Table 1.

Figure 4 shows the visualization results of two 500 ms pieces of EEG signals in a trial from the single electrode positioned on the left side of the frontal lobe (FP1) of a subject. The task category is 'VisualDown' therefore the oddball

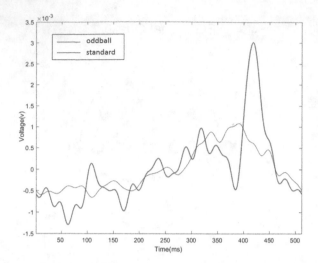

Fig. 4. Visualization results of two 500 ms pieces of EEG signals in a trial from FP1 electrode for subject 1. The undertaken task is 'VisualDown'. The oddball event here is triggered by color-varied stimulus. Red and Blue curves depict EEG reaction to oddball and standard stimuli respectively. (Color figure online)

event here is formed by color-varied visual stimulus. The red and blue curve in the figure depict the EEG reaction to the oddball event and a comparative standard event respectively. It is even possible to see a peak occurring between 400 ms to 450 ms after the unanticipated event happens, indicating that the detection of unanticipated visual and auditory events is feasible.

For data samples recorded from each channel, we calculated the average power Theta-Beta Ratio (TBR), the average peak-to-peak amplitude, the average voltage in time domain and the average power over each divided frequency band according to Table 1. Notice that redundant features can actually decrease the classification performance and increase the cost and running time of the following classification procedure; thus, the selection of the best discriminative feature set is of great importance. In this experiment, feature selection was based on a wrapper method, that is to feed all possible features into a classifier and use the classifier to select features. A J48 decision tree was built for feature selection, as a result we picked average power over divided and whole frequency bands from 11 channels (F3, Fz, F4, C3, Cz, C4, P3, Pz, P4, O1 and O2) as relevant features for detection of unanticipated visual and auditory events in this experiment. These channels show the most significant impact on the oddball events from our visualization results, which is consistent with previous results that the EEG reaction for a rare event mainly locates in the parietal areas [8].

3.4   Pairwise Comparison Classification

An artificial neural network (ANN) is a widely used machine learning method for classification of EEG related features [9]. In this study, we deployed a perceptron neural network, which is based on the back propagation algorithm and contains 10 hidden neurons, to detect unanticipated events based on some selected features. Each 4 s trial was divided into eight 500 ms epochs. A total of 9600 epoch samples were produced in this experiment from 10 subjects with each of them performing 120 trials and each trial containing 8 epochs. Each 500 ms EEG epoch consisted of 1024 points. Then six kinds of epochs were extracted as O, B, A, N1, N2, N3, where O represents the odd epoch with oddball stimuli, B and A represent the epoch occurring before and after the odd epoch respectively. N1, N2 and N3 represent three consecutive standard epochs with standard common stimuli.

'Independent and identically distributed (IID)' assumption underpins many classification dataset in classical classification algorithms. This assumption can be detrimental as it ignores the underlying relationship that may exist among features across different instances [10]. Among several factors breaking the IID assumption, dependency is a key factor and it usually results in coupling between values, relations, attributes, objects or methods. Therefore, in that situation, the instances in the dataset can be seen as pairs and the two instances within a pair share certain kind of dependency.

To uncover the hidden patterns existing between each pair of instances, the attribute values of the two instances should be considered simultaneously rather than individually. Therefore, a special classification approach, known as pairwise classification was introduced in [10]. The approach relies on simultaneous classification of two interdependent instances.

Since we are using artificial neural networks, we will implement a relaxed version of the approach by taking the difference between two or more instances. In our experiment, six kinds of epoch data were obtained, where B, O, A and N1, N2, N3 form two consecutive epoch sequences respectively. By making backward and forward subtraction of attribute values of these consecutive epochs, we can approximate gradient information in each pair and the changes in an attribute from one epoch to the next epoch. This process results in four classes (O-B, A-O, N2-N1, N3-N2), which may show more robustness against intra-trial variations. It is important to highlight that these classes are themselves interdependent. There are dependencies within (O-B, A-O) and (N2-N1, N3-N2). A pairwise comparison approach was proposed to form a two-class classification problem by linking (O-B, A-O) and (N2-N1, N3-N2) instances together as pairs, respectively. This is a process of comparing entities in pairs. Therefore if any of the O-B and A-O is classified as either O-B or A-O, an unanticipated rare event is identified. The whole dataset was divided into two parts, the visual part regarding those trials only containing visual stimuli and the audio visual part regarding the trials containing both the visual and auditory stimuli. 20% of the data were extracted to form a test set.

4   Results and Analysis

In order to detect the unanticipated and rare visual and auditory events, which are the odd epochs in our samples, three experiments were conducted.

Experiment 1. In the first experiment, the neural network was designed to classify three kinds of epochs, the odd epoch (O), the before-odd (B) and after-odd epoch (A). This is to test whether the odd epochs can be identified directly from two consecutive non-odd epochs by the features. So the data set was made of three kinds of samples, the odd, before-odd and after-odd. The number of samples for each kind was equal and the whole data set was divided into a training set containing 80% of the data and a testing set containing the rest 20%. The classification accuracy is 29% for visual part and 31% for audio visual part. Although the accuracy is relatively low, it provides the classification accuracy baseline for following experiment.

Experiment 2. Since each trial may have different magnitudes as the subjects getting tired during moving from one trial to another, it will add extra effects on the classification results. However these effects can be reduced by relying on the changes occurring in the features instead of the magnitude of features, which means combining the before-odd, odd and after-odd epoch by subtraction O-B and A-O. If the unanticipated rare visual and auditory stimuli successfully trigger a specific change in the EEG signals, then O-B and A-O is detectable from the differences between 3-consecutive standard epochs with no deviant stimuli inside. Therefore in the second experiment, we defined two classification targets O-B and A-O, representing the change from a standard epoch to a oddball epoch and the change coming back to a standard epoch respectively. For a control group, we randomly chose three consecutive standard epochs N1, N2 and N3 from a standard trial with the same moving direction and same kind of stimuli, then calculated N2-N1 and N3-N2. So now the data set was made of four kinds of samples, the O-B, A-O, N2-N1 and N3-N2. The classification objective was to identify O-B and A-O from N2-N1 and N3-N2. The number of samples for each kind was equal and the whole data set was divided into a training set containing 80% of the data and a testing set containing the rest 20%. We made five runs of training and testing, and each time the training and testing samples ware randomly selected from the whole data set. Tables 2 and 3 show the results of classification accuracy for visual samples and audio visual samples respectively. Although the accuracy is still not high, classification based on the changes between epochs is more reliable than based on the epoch samples themselves. This is because by calculating the differences between two consecutive piece of signals, many unexpected effects can be reduced from the EEG signals.

Experiment 3. In this experiment, a pairwise comparison approach is proposed to deal with the four targets O-B, A-O, N2-N1, N3-N2 designed in Experiment 2. It is a process of comparing entities in pairs to judge which entity pair

Table 2. Results of Experiment 2 (Visual). Classification accuracy as percentage. B = before-odd epoch, O = odd epoch, A = after-odd epoch, N1 N2 N3 = three consecutive standard epochs from a standard trial.

Class	Run1	Run2	Run3	Run4	Run5	Average
O-B	32	32	29	29	32	31
A-O	31	36	32	38	33	34
N2-N1	35	37	39	37	35	37
N3-N2	34	36	32	35	34	34
Overall	33	35	33	35	34	34

Table 3. Results of Experiment 2 (AudioVisual). Classification accuracy as percentage. B = before-odd epoch, O = odd epoch, A = after-odd epoch, N1 N2 N3 = three consecutive standard epochs from a standard trial.

Class	Run1	Run2	Run3	Run4	Run5	Average
O-B	27	29	26	26	27	27
A-O	28	27	29	27	30	28
N2-N1	31	30	29	29	26	29
N3-N2	28	28	31	33	33	31
Overall	28	28	29	28	29	28

is preferred, or has a greater amount of some quantitative property. An reverse mapping from pairwise comparison is adopted to form a two-class classification problem in Experiment 3 by linking O-B with A-O and N2-N1 with N3-N2. Therefore, an unanticipated rare event is identified if any of the O-B and A-O is classified as either O-B or A-O. In other words, while a class B-O being miss-classified as A-O is a wrong classification in the absolute sense, it is considered that the classifier has detected the odd epoch. The data set is the same as in experiment 2. We made five runs of training and testing, and each time the training and testing samples were randomly selected from the whole data set. Results of classification accuracy for visual samples and audio visual samples are showed in Tables 4 and 5 respectively. FN, TP, TN and FP represent false negative, true positive, true negative and false positive respectively. The classification accuracy improved to around 60% and the standard deviation of accuracy is 0.02 and 0.01, verifying that detection of unanticipated events based on EEG by a comparison neural network approach proposed in this study is applicable.

Experiment 4. In the last experiment, we made a comparison of detection accuracy between our proposed pairwise-comparison neural network method and three other classifiers. The three classifiers are based on random tree, logistic

Table 4. Result of Experiment 3 (Visual). Accuracy as percentage. FN = false negative, TP = true positive, TN = true negative, FP = false positive.

	Run1	Run2	Run3	Run4	Run5	Average
FN	16	17	18	15	16	16
TP	34	33	32	35	34	37
TN	26	31	27	26	26	27
FP	24	19	23	24	24	23
Accuracy	60	64	59	61	60	61

Table 5. Results of Experiment 3 (AudioVisual). Accuracy as percentage. FN = false negative, TP = true positive, TN = true negative, FP = false positive.

	Run1	Run2	Run3	Run4	Run5	Average
FN	18	18	25	21	26	22
TP	32	32	25	29	24	27
TN	24	24	32	24	32	27
FP	26	26	18	26	18	23
Accuracy	56	56	57	54	56	56

regression and support vector machine (SVM) respectively. The SVM was implemented with an RBF kernel as indicated by pilot work. Separate training and testing data sets were made for testing the four algorithms. We ran five times for each algorithm and each time we randomly selected 80% of the data for training and the rest of the data for testing. Table 6 shows the averaged accuracy and deviation of each classifier for visual samples and audio visual samples. It can be seen that the proposed pairwise-comparison neural network approach achieves better performance than the common methods. It also indicates that the changes in EEG signals caused by rare stimulation can be detected from single trial with proper methods, while the current approaches are based on averaging multiple trials.

Table 6. Comparison of odd epochs detection results with three other classifiers. Accuracy as percentage.

	Visual		Audio visual	
Classifier	% Accuracy	Deviation	% Accuracy	Deviation
Random Tree	32	0.03	30	0.03
Logistic Regression	48	0.01	45	0.02
SVM	51	0.01	47	0.01
Proposed Method	61	0.02	56	0.01

5   Discussion

This study explored the potential of detecting unanticipated and rare visual and auditory events based on a single trial event related potentials in EEG signals. An oddball paradigm experiment including 10 subjects is conducted. After pre-processing and feature extraction in frequency domain, a pairwise comparison neural network approach is proposed for classification and has been tested with a high number of EEG signal samples. The proposed approach, supported by the analysis and experiments has clearly indicated the potential for identifying unanticipated and rare visual and auditory stimuli based on brain electrical activities.

Verifying the feasibility of using deviant visual and auditory events to trigger specific changes in EEG signals is the first step for designing further EEG-based applications. One of our interests is to design ERP-based neural biometrics, as it is shown in some literature that the morphology of ERP exhibits individual variations [7]. We are currently working on improving the classification accuracy by designing more discriminatory features and testing more classification algorithms.

Acknowledgment. The authors wish to thank Ms Xuejie Liu for implementing the directional sound system. The Human Research Ethics Advisory Panel of University of New South Wales approved the experimental protocol under Approval HC15806.

References

1. Sanei, S., Chambers, J.A.: EEG Signal Processing. Wiley, New York (2013)
2. Campisi, P., La Rocca, D.: Brain waves for automatic biometric-based user recognition. IEEE Trans. Inf. Foren. Secur. **9**(5), 782–800 (2014)
3. Fabiani, M., Gratton, G., Coles, M.: Event-related brain potentials: methods, theory. In: Handbook of Psychophysiology, pp. 53–84 (2000)
4. Kimura, M., Schröger, E., Czigler, I.: Visual mismatch negativity and its importance in visual cognitive sciences. Neuroreport **22**(14), 669–673 (2011)
5. Cléry, H., Andersson, F., Fonlupt, P., Gomot, M.: Brain correlates of automatic visual change detection. Neuroimage **75**, 117–122 (2013)
6. Polich, J.: Neuropsychology of P300, In: Oxford Handbook of Event-Related Potential Components, pp. 159–188 (2012)
7. Ruiz-Blondet, M., Jin, Z., Laszlo, S.: CEREBRE: a novel method for very high accuracy event-related potential biometric identification (2016)
8. Sellers, E.W., Arbel, Y., Donchin, E., Wolpaw, J., Wolpaw, E.: BCIs that use P300 event-related potentials. Brain-Computer Interfaces: Principles and Practice, pp. 215–226 (2012)
9. Bashivan, P., Rish, I., Yeasin, M., Codella, N.: Learning representations from EEG with deep recurrent-convolutional neural networks. arXiv preprint arXiv:1511.06448 (2015)
10. Elfiki, H., Petraki, E., Abbass, H.: Pairwise comparative classification for translator stylometric analysis. ACM Trans. Asian Lang. Inf. Process. **16**(1) (2016)

Compressing Deep Neural Network for Facial Landmarks Detection

Dan Zeng[✉], Fan Zhao, and Yixin Bao

Key Laboratory of Specialty Fiber Optics and Optical Access Networks,
Shanghai University, Shanghai 200072, China
dzeng@shu.edu.cn, shu_zfan@i.shu.edu.cn, elaine.bao@foxmail.com

Abstract. State-of-the-art deep neural networks (DNNs) have greatly improved the performance of facial landmarks detection. However, DNN models usually have a large number of parameters, which leads to high computational complexity and memory cost. To address this problem, we propose a method to compress large deep neural networks, which includes three steps. (1) Importance-based neuron pruning: compared with traditional connection pruning, we introduce weights correlations to prune unimportant neurons, which can reduce index storage and inference computation costs. (2) Product quantization: further use of product quantization helps to enforce weights sharing, which stores fewer cluster indexes and codebooks than scalar quantization. (3) Network retraining: to reduce training difficulty and performance degradation, we iteratively retrain the network, compressing one layer at a time. Experiments of compressing a VGG-like model for facial landmarks detection demonstrate that the proposed method achieves 26x compression of the model with 1.5% performance degradation.

Keywords: Compression · Pruning · Product quantization · Facial landmarks detection

1 Introduction

Facial landmarks detection is a fundamental work in many face vision tasks, such as face detection [1], emotion recognition [2] and face verification [3,4]. A good detection method should not only be robust to deformation, expression and illumination, but also computational efficient. Recent years have witnessed the significant improvement in the performance of facial landmarks detection [5–7], mainly due to the development of deep neural networks (DNNs). Typically, larger models are always needed for more accurate facial landmarks detection, which results in greater number of parameters and greater storage demand. In order to reduce the size of detection models and make them well suited for mobile applications, model miniaturization methods are in great need.

In this paper, we address the problem by proposing an effective compression method based on the fusion of pruning and product quantization [8]. We first train a baseline model for 68 facial landmarks, which has a good performance,

© Springer International Publishing AG 2016
C.-L. Liu et al. (Eds.): BICS 2016, LNAI 10023, pp. 102–112, 2016.
DOI: 10.1007/978-3-319-49685-6_10

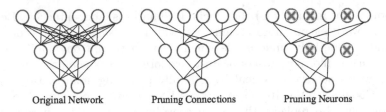

Fig. 1. An illustration of differences between pruning connections and neurons.

but with a large model size. Then we iteratively retrain the network, compressing one layer at a time. When compressing each layer, we prune unimportant neurons based on weights correlations and apply product quantization on the absolute value of remaining weights. Finally, we successfully achieve a 26x compression with only 1.5% performance loss.

Pruning aims at removing redundancy and constructing a sparser network. It shares some similarity with Dropout [11], which is used to avoid overfitting through randomly setting the neural output to zero. Pruning is a common method in dense network compression [12–14], and is usually used to prune connections between neurons. While this kind of pruning can reduce the model size and storage costs, it needs to reconstruct the sparse weights matrix during testing and the computation time and memory may still stay the same. Instead of pruning connections, we introduce the neurons-pruning method, which is equal to build a smaller net with less neurons, as shown in Fig. 1. Product quantization decomposes the original high-dimensional weights into several low-dimensional Cartesian product subspaces, which are then quantized separately. Compared with scalar quantization in [14], product quantization needs fewer cluster indexes and codebooks, which means a high compressing ratio can be obtained without noticeable accuracy loss. On the other hand, public datasets of facial landmarks detection do not provide enough training data. Even by combining several datasets, we have only obtained 4k images of 68 labeled landmarks, which means we must be careful to avoid overfitting. Fortunately, with the use of pruning and quantization, we no longer need to worry about the overfitting problem, and we can use a larger learning rate even without a dropout layer.

The rest of the paper is organized as follows. Section 2 briefly reviews the related work. Section 3 describes the three main parts of our method: neuron pruning, production quantization and network retaining. In Sect. 4, we first introduce our baseline model and then compress the network and evaluate its performance. Finally, the conclusion is given in Sect. 5.

2   Related Work

The most straightforward way to improve the performance of deep neural networks is by making it deeper and wider. However, this strategy makes the networks more prone to be overfitting. Larger amount of training data may solve this problem, but manually labeling facial landmarks is labor-intensive. Besides, a larger network means more parameters, which can slow down the detection speed and is especially undesirable when we wish to run on mobile devices. Therefore, more and more works begin to explore network compression.

Some works achieve this goal by carefully designing small network architectures. GoogLeNet-V3 [16] not only uses 1×1 convolution kernels to reduce dimension, but also replaces the $n \times n$ convolution with a $1 \times n$ convolution followed by a $n \times 1$ convolution. As a result, the amount of parameters reduces by $\frac{n}{2}$. Unlike this, Courbariaux et al. [17] train a binarized neural network with binary weights and activations, which drastically reduces memory consumption. Denil et al. [18] represent the weight matrix as a product of two low rank factors, during training, they fix one factor and only update the other factor. Similarly, Sainath et al. [20] use a low-rank matrix factorization to reduce parameters in the final weight layer. However, training a factorized representation network directly usually performs poorly. Recently, Scardapane et al. [19] design a new loss function to perform features selecting, network training and weights compression simultaneously, but their work is not suitable for convolutional network.

In addition to training small models directly, compressing a larger model into a smaller one is another popular choice. Denton et al. [21] first consider singular value decomposition (SVD) to compress parameters. Gong et al. [22] systematically explore quantization methods for compressing the dense connected layers of DNNs, including binarization, scalar quantization, product quantization and residual quantization. Their experiments show that product quantization is obviously superior to other methods. However, these methods have no network retraining schemes, which can inevitably cause performance degradation. In our method, we draw the strength of production quantization and use it in the retraining procedure so that we can get a high compression ratio with negligible performance loss.

Han et al. [14] compress the network by combining pruning, trained quantization and huffman coding, which is a popular work recently. Inspired by it, we not only prune neural connections but also prune neurons, which means we are able to spend less to store the sparse structure and inference on a smaller net. We also replace its scalar quantization with absolute product quantization and introduce an iterative way to retrain the network layer by layer, the details are shown in Sect. 3. In addition, Sun et al. [13] find that weight magnitude is not a good indicator to the importance of neural connections, so they prune the network based on correlation rather than the weight magnitude, we improve this method and bring it into our work.

3   Our Method

We first train a dense network as our baseline and then compress it with the following steps.

3.1   Neurons Pruning

Having a pre-trained dense network, we use a pruning ratio R $(R > 1)$ to control the number of neurons that will be pruned, e.g., if there are P neurons in the input of one layer, then P/R neurons are preserved after pruning. The only problem here is to decide which neurons will be kept. A fairly straightforward approach is to iteratively drop a neuron with minimum prediction error.

$$\Delta(y) = ||\hat{W}x - Wx||^2. \tag{1}$$

Where x is the input neurons, Δy is the error of output neurons, W and $\hat{W}$ are the original weights matrix and the pruned-weights matrix respectively, $\hat{W}$ is computed by setting the matrix column where the pruned neuron is located to 0. However, this greedy algorithm is inefficient, especially when there are too many neurons. Inspired by [13], we measure the importance of neuron based on the sum of connection correlation, which has two aspects:

(1) For fully-connected and locally-connected layers that have no weight-sharing, the correlation coefficient between neuron x_i and y_j is computed as follows:
$$r_{ij} = \frac{E[(x_i - u_{x_i})(y_j - u_{y_j})]}{\sigma_{x_i}\sigma_{y_j}}. \tag{2}$$

where μ_{x_i}, μ_{y_j}, σ_{x_i} and σ_{y_j} denote the mean and standard deviation of x_i and y_j, respectively. Then the importance of neuron x_i is:

$$I_i = \sum_{j=1} |r_{ij}|. \tag{3}$$

Then we keep the most important P/R neurons.
(2) For convolutional layers with weight-sharing, pruning neurons is difficult, especially for pooling operations. So we prune connections first, and then we randomly add or remove weights in order to make the number of weights in each row equal, as shown in Fig. 2. This step dramatically reduces the index storage and makes it easy to apply product quantization on the rest of the weights.

3.2   Product Quantization

We cannot only use neurons pruning to get a high compression ratio, which will dramatically impact the performance, therefore we utilize product quantization to compress further. Product quantization is a popular vector quantization method. With decomposing original high-dimensional space into several low-dimensional subspaces and taking quantization separately, product quantization is able to make a good description of space distribution with less centroid codes.

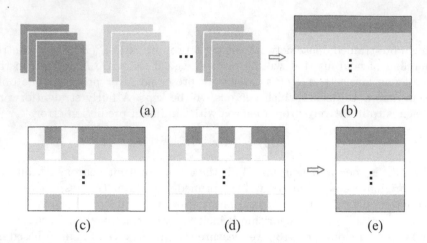

Fig. 2. (a) Convolutional kernels. (b)Weights matrix from reshaping and aligning all kernels. (c) Pruning connections using the method in [13], white squares mean the pruned connections (or weights). (d) Each row has same number of weights left after smoothing. (e)The remaining weights establish a new weights matrix, then product quantization can be applied on it directly.

Given the pruned weights matrix $\hat{W} \in R^{m \times n}$, we first record the positive or negative sign of each weight and substitute $\hat{W}$ for its absolute value. Then we split $\hat{W}$ column-wise into S submatrices

$$\hat{W} = [\hat{W}^1, \hat{W}^2, \ldots, \hat{W}^S]. \tag{4}$$

For each submatrix $\hat{W}^i \in R^{m \times (n/s)}, (i = 1, \ldots S)$, we run the K-Means clustering algorithm on it and get a sub-codebook C_i. The whole code space is therefore defined as the Cartesian product

$$C = C_1 \times C_2 \times \ldots \times C_S. \tag{5}$$

For each row $\hat{W}_r$ in $\hat{W}$, we can reconstruct it as

$$\hat{W}_r = [\hat{W}_r^1, \hat{W}_r^2, \ldots, \hat{W}_r^S], \qquad where\ \hat{W}_r^i \in C_i,\ r = 1, 2, \ldots, m. \tag{6}$$

Supposing that all submatrices have the same cluster number k, we can use $k \times S$ subcodes to generate a codebook with a large size of k^S. That is the reason why product quantization consumes less memory than scalar quantization. Suppose scalar quantization has the same kS clustering centers and the data format is float32, product quantization will yield a $(32kS + mn \log_2(kS))/(32kn + ms \log_2(k))$ compression ratio compared with the scalar quantization case.

3.3   Network Retraining

We compress the network layer by layer from backward to forward. For every iteration, we use the previously trained model to calculate correlated coefficients,

Index				Codes	Reconstruct weights			
-1	0	-2	0	1 0.01	-0.01	0	-0.16	0
0	0	-3	1	2 0.16	0	0	-0.07	0.01
+2	-4	0	0	3 0.07	0.16	-0.29	0	0
0	4	0	3	4 0.29	0	0.29	0	0.07

Fig. 3. Reconstructing weights with index and codes. Only if the index is nonzero, the corresponding weight will be recovered by looking up codes tables and adding a corresponding positive or negative sign.

and then prune and quantify one additional layer. To retrain the network, we use deep learning tools Caffe [23] and simply modify its convolutional and fully-connected layers by adding another two blobs to store index and codes. Each time before forward-propagation, we use index and codes to reconstruct the weights. Particularly, if the index is zero, it means the corresponding connection has been pruned, otherwise if the index is nonzero, we recover the corresponding weight by looking up tables and adding a positive or negative sign, as shown in Fig. 3. During back-propagation, we only update the centroids codes using the method describes in [14]. Layers after pruning and quantization become very sparse, therefore we no longer need the dropout layer before or after them, which can speed up training without suffering from overfitting.

4 Experiments

In this section, we first introduce our baseline VGG-like model, and compare its performance with SDM [10]. Then we compress the model, and compare the performance before and after compression. Finally, we discuss the impact of some parameters on the trade-off between accuracy and compression ratio.

4.1 Baseline Model

Our facial landmarks dataset contains 4025 images with 68 landmarks collected from LFPW, AFW, HELEN and 300W [24–27], and we randomly select 425 images as our test set. Then we augment the training set using mirror transform and geometric transform such as shifting, rotating. The baseline model is fine-tuned from VGG [9] net with the number of output of last fully-connected layer changing to 136 and the original softmax-loss layer replacing with Euclidean-loss layer. The architecture of our baseline model is shown as Table 1.

In order to measure the performance, we introduce two metrics:

(1) Mean normalized euclidean distance (MNED):

$$MNED = \frac{1}{M} \sum_{i=1}^{M} \frac{\sum_{j=1}^{68} (p_j - \hat{p}_j)^2}{d_i}. \tag{7}$$

Table 1. Structure of baseline model and configurations for compressed network

Layer	Weights	Params	Proportion	R	K	D
conv1+Maxpool	$3 \times 7 \times 7 \times 96$	14K	0.0001	-	-	-
conv2+Maxpool	$96 \times 5 \times 5 \times 256$	614K	0.0062	-	-	-
conv3	$256 \times 3 \times 3 \times 512$	1.18M	0.0119	-	128	4
conv4	$512 \times 3 \times 3 \times 512$	2.36M	0.0237	2	128	4
conv5+Maxpool	$512 \times 3 \times 3 \times 512$	2.36M	0.0237	4	128	4
fc6+dropout1	18432×4096	75.50M	0.7598	4	256	8
fc7+dropout2	4096×4096	16.78M	0.1689	2	128	4
fc8+loss	4096×136	557K	0.0056	2	64	4

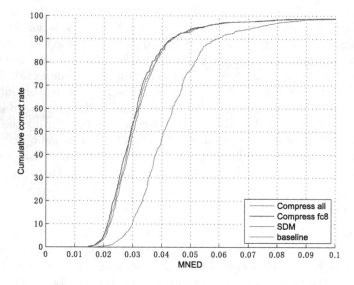

Fig. 4. Performance of the compressed network. The "Compress all" represents the compressed model with the configuration in Table 1. And the "Compress fc8" represents a same model with fc8 layer compressed alone.

where M is the number of images in the test set, d_i is the eye distance, p_j is the ground truth position of the specific facial landmark and $\hat{p}_j$ is the predicted position.

(2) A ROC-like curve, whose horizontal axis represents MNED and vertical axis denotes the percentage of images with error less than its MNED.

The MNED of our baseline model is 0.0329, while the MNED of SDM [10] is 0.0440, much larger than ours. The ROC-like curve is shown as Fig. 4.

4.2 Compressed Network

We compress the baseline network iteratively with the method described in Sect. 3. We directly remove the dropout layers before retraining the network, since they are unnecessary and will reduce retraining speed. The compressing configurations are shown as Table 1, where R indicates the ratio of pruning, D indicates dimensionality of subspace in product quantization and K indicates the cluster number in each subspace.

We prune neurons for fully connected layer and connections for convolutional layer respectively. For example, the size of left dense weights matrix in fc6 layer becomes 18432×2014 after pruning neurons in fc7 layer, and this matrix further becomes 4 times sparser after pruning connections in fc6 layer. Since the parameters in the fully connected layer are mostly redundant, a larger compression ratio is used. On the other hand, parameters in lower layers contribute a smaller part of the whole network and are harder to be reduced, so we take a smaller(or zero) compression ratio on them. As shown in Fig. 4, by making necessary trade-offs between performance and compression ratio, we achieve 26x compression of the baseline model with only 1.5% performance degradation. It is worth noting that, the black line in Fig. 4 represents a same model with fc8 layer compressed alone, whose performance is surprisingly better than baseline. We think some suitable sparseness will enhance generalization ability of DNNs models.

4.3 Discussion About Different Configurations

By now we know that quantization helps to reduce parameter size, while pruning can not only reduce parameter size, but also improve inference speed. It seems that we should heavily prune to get both high compression ratio and speed improvement. However, for facial landmarks detection, we find that a higher pruning ratio leads to significant performance degradation. Figure 5 shows the comparison of different pruning ratio on fully-connected layers, and the pruning method is described in [13]. The result shows the method [13] is not suitable for our facial landmarks detection, and pruning too many connections will severely degrade the performance.

In this case, we must be careful to prune neurons or connections and use product quantization to compress more parameters. We find that the performance of product quantization is positively correlated with the cluster number K in each subspace, and negatively correlated with the dimensionality D of subspace. To get a higher compression ratio, we obviously need a small K and a large D, but the performance will suffer from this. Fortunately, we find that applying product quantization on the absolute values can help, and the only extra expense is that we need one bit to record a positive or negative sign for each value. Figure 6 shows the comparison of taking product quantization on the absolute values for original values. The experiment of the weights of fc7 layer demonstrates that our method can use fewer quantization centroids with less error and compress the network further.

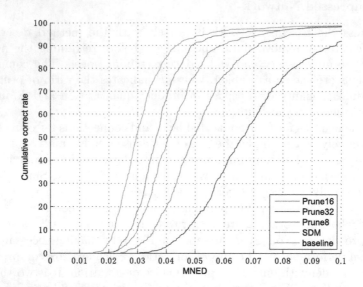

Fig. 5. Comparison of different pruning ratio on fully-connected layers, the pruning method is described in [13]. "PruneX" represents all fully-connected layers are pruned with a same pruning ratio X.

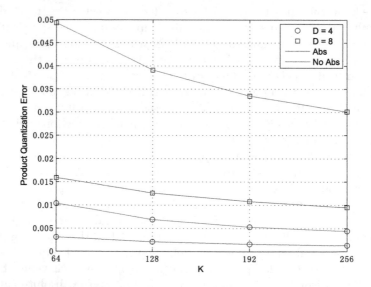

Fig. 6. Comparison of product quantization on absolute values or original values with different dimensionality D of subspace. It shows it is able to use fewer quantization centroids with less error on absolute values.

5 Conclusion

In this paper, we propose an efficient method to compress large DNN models. We fuse pruning and product quantization directly to reduce the time of compressing the whole network and the risk of overfitting. In addition, we prune unimportant neurons rather than connections, which not only reduces model size but also speeds up the computation. We also take product quantization on the absolute values of the remaining weights, so we use fewer quantization centroids and compress the network further.

In the experiment of facial landmarks detection with VGG-like model, we successfully achieve a 26x compression with only 1.5% performance degradation. In the future work, we will pay more attention to compression in convolution layers and acceleration on test phase.

References

1. Chen, D., Ren, S., Wei, Y., Cao, X., Sun, J.: Joint cascade face detection and alignment. In: Fleet, D., Pajdla, T., Schiele, B., Tuytelaars, T. (eds.) ECCV 2014. LNCS, vol. 8694, pp. 109–122. Springer, Heidelberg (2014). doi:10.1007/978-3-319-10599-4_8
2. Dhall, A., Goecke, R., Joshi, J., Sikka, K., Gedeon, T.: Emotion recognition in the wild challenge 2014: baseline, data and protocol. In: Proceedings of the 16th International Conference on Multimodal Interaction, pp. 461–466 (2014)
3. Taigman, Y., Yang, M., Ranzato, M.A., Wolf, L.: Web-scale training for face identification. In: Proceedings of the IEEE Conference on Computer Vision and Pattern Recognition, pp. 2746–2754 (2015)
4. Chen, J.C., Patel, V.M., Chellappa, R.: Unconstrained face verification using deep CNN features. In: 2016 IEEE Winter Conference on Applications of Computer Vision, pp. 1–9 (2016)
5. Sun, Y., Wang, X., Tang, X.: Deep convolutional network cascade for facial point detection. In: Proceedings of the IEEE Conference on Computer Vision and Pattern Recognition, pp. 3476–3483 (2013)
6. Zhang, Z., Luo, P., Loy, C.C., Tang, X.: Facial landmark detection by deep multi-task learning. In: Fleet, D., Pajdla, T., Schiele, B., Tuytelaars, T. (eds.) ECCV 2014. LNCS, vol. 8694, pp. 94–108. Springer, Heidelberg (2014). doi:10.1007/978-3-319-10599-4_7
7. Toshev, A., Szegedy, C.: DeepPose: human pose estimation via deep neural networks. In: Proceedings of the IEEE Conference on Computer Vision and Pattern Recognition, pp. 1653–1660 (2014)
8. Jegou, H., Douze, M., Schmid, C.: Product quantization for nearest neighbor search. IEEE Trans. Pattern Anal. Mach. Intell. **33**, 117–128 (2011)
9. Simonyan, K., Zisserman, A.: Very deep convolutional networks for large-scale image recognition. arXiv preprint arXiv:1409.1556 (2014)
10. Xiong, X., De la Torre, F.: Supervised descent method and its applications to face alignment. In: Proceedings of the IEEE Conference on Computer Vision and Pattern Recognition, pp. 532–539 (2013)
11. Hinton, G.E., Srivastava, N., Krizhevsky, A., Sutskever, I., Salakhutdinov, R.R.: Improving neural networks by preventing co-adaptation of feature detectors. arXiv preprint arXiv:1207.0580 (2012)

12. Han, S., Pool, J., Tran, J., Dally, W.: Learning both weights and connections for efficient neural network. In: Advances in Neural Information Processing Systems, pp. 1135–1143 (2015)
13. Sun, Y., Wang, X., Tang, X.: Sparsifying Reural Network Connections for Face Recognition. arXiv preprint arXiv:1512.01891 (2015)
14. Han, S., Mao, H., Dally, W.J.: Deep compression: compressing deep neural network with pruning, trained quantization and Huffman coding. CoRR, abs/1510.00149 (2015)
15. Krizhevsky, A., Sutskever, I., Hinton, G.E.: ImageNet classification with deep convolutional neural networks. In: Advances in Neural Information Processing Systems, pp. 1097–1105 (2012)
16. Szegedy, C., Vanhoucke, V., Ioffe, S., Shlens, J., Wojna, Z.: Rethinking the inception architecture for computer vision. arXiv preprint arXiv:1512.00567 (2015)
17. Courbariaux, M., Bengio, Y.: BinaryNet: training deep neural networks with weights and activations constrained to $+1$ or -1. arXiv preprint arXiv:1602.02830 (2016)
18. Denil, M., Shakibi, B., Dinh, L., de Freitas, N.: Predicting parameters in deep learning. In: Advances in Neural Information Processing Systems, pp. 2148–2156 (2013)
19. Scardapane, S., Comminiello, D., Hussain, A., Uncini, A.: Group sparse regularization for deep neural networks. arXiv preprint arXiv:1607.00485 (2016)
20. Sainath, T.N., Kingsbury, B., Sindhwani, V., Arisoy, E., Ramabhadran, B.: Low-rank matrix factorization for deep neural network training with high-dimensional output targets. In: 2013 IEEE International Conference on Acoustics, Speech and Signal Processing, pp. 6655–6659 (2013)
21. Denton, E.L., Zaremba, W., Bruna, J., LeCun, Y., Fergus, R.: Exploiting linear structure within convolutional networks for efficient evaluation. In: Advances in Neural Information Processing Systems, pp. 1269–1277 (2014)
22. Gong, Y., Liu, L., Yang, M., Bourdev, L.: Compressing deep convolutional networks using vector quantization. arXiv preprint arXiv:1412.6115 (2014)
23. Jia, Y., Shelhamer, E., Donahue, J., Karayev, S., Long, J., Girshick, R., Darrell, T.: Caffe: convolutional architecture for fast feature embedding. In: Proceedings of the 22nd ACM International Conference on Multimedia, pp. 675–678 (2014)
24. Belhumeur, P.N., Jacobs, D.W., Kriegman, D.J., Kumar, N.: Localizing parts of faces using a consensus of exemplars. IEEE Trans. Pattern Anal. Mach. Intell. **35**, 2930–2940 (2013)
25. Zhu, X., Ramanan, D.: Face detection, pose estimation, and landmark localization in the wild. In: Computer Vision and Pattern Recognition (CVPR), pp. 2879–2886 (2012)
26. Liang, L., Xiao, R., Wen, F., Sun, J.: Face alignment via component-based discriminative search. In: Forsyth, D., Torr, P., Zisserman, A. (eds.) ECCV 2008. LNCS, vol. 5303, pp. 72–85. Springer, Heidelberg (2008). doi:10.1007/978-3-540-88688-4_6
27. Sagonas, C., Tzimiropoulos, G., Zafeiriou, S., Pantic, M.: A semi-automatic methodology for facial landmark annotation. In: Proceedings of the IEEE Conference on Computer Vision and Pattern Recognition Workshops, pp. 896–903 (2013)

Learning Optimal Seeds for Salient Object Detection

Huiling Wang[1,2], Lixiang Xu[2], and Bin Luo[2(✉)]

[1] School of Computer and Information,
Fuyang Normal College, Fuyang, Anhui, China
wangsheng0417@sina.com
[2] School of Computer Science and Technology,
Anhui University, Hefei, Anhui, China
xulixianghf@163.com, luobin@ahu.edu.cn

Abstract. Visual saliency detection is useful for applications as object recognition, resizing and image segmentation. It is a challenge to detect the most important scene from the input image. In this paper, we present a new method to get saliency map. First, we evaluate the salience value of each region by global contrast based spatial and color feature. Second, the salience values of the first stage are used to optimize the background and foreground queries (seeds), and then manifold ranking is employed to compute two phase saliency maps. Finally, the final saliency map is got by combining the two saliency map. Experiment results on four datasets indicate the significantly improved accuracy of the proposed algorithm in comparison with eight state-of-the-art approaches.

Keywords: Saliency detection · Manifold ranking · Global region contrast · Superpixel segmentation · Optimal seeds

1 Introduction

Saliency detection aims to find the most outstanding parts from an image according to human visual attention. In the past decades, there are various vision applications, such as object recognition [1], image detection [2], image cropping/thumb-nailing [3], video compression [4] and video summarization [5].

In recent years significant progress has made in visual saliency models. Different methods based on different mathematical principles. One of the earliest saliency model was proposed by Itti et al. [11] defined image saliency using central-surrounded differences across multi-scale image features. However, the final saliency maps often emphasized small and local features.

In contrast, calculation methods had better application in computer vision. Some methods used low-level processing to determine the contrast of image region to their surroundings. We broadly classify the algorithms into local and global schemes. Local contrast methods are based on the rarity of image local (small) neighborhoods. Liu et al. [13] found multi-scale contrast by linearly combining in a Gaussian image pyramid. Gofermanet et al. [23] proposed a context-aware method, it modeled local low-level clues, visual organization and high-level features to highlight salient objects.

© Springer International Publishing AG 2016
C.-L. Liu et al. (Eds.): BICS 2016, LNAI 10023, pp. 113–124, 2016.
DOI: 10.1007/978-3-319-49685-6_11

Ma et al. [19] found rectangular saliency regions by fuzzy growth model to extend the significant analysis. However, such local methods tended to highlight the contours of the saliency object, rather than brightened the whole region.

Global methods utilized the contrast information of whole image and mid-level construction cue, and can uniform highlight the whole saliency object. Zhai et al. [8] defined pixel-level saliency based on a pixel's contrast to all other pixels. Cheng et al. [17] considered the global region contrast with respect to the entire image and spatial relationships to extract saliency map. Qing et al. [21] presented a hierarchical model by analyzing saliency cues from multi-levels structure. Global methods have their difficulty in distinguishing similar colors in both foreground and background.

A few recent methods based on graph model have high accuracy. Harel et al. [12] suggested a graph-based saliency model to extract saliency object through dissimilarity measurement. In the work of zhang et al. [16] performed saliency detection by integrating regional contrast, property and backgroundness descriptor. Jiang et al. [6] used absorbing Markov chain to detect saliency object. Yang et al. [20] got saliency map through manifold ranking (MR), which utilized the four boundaries of the original image as background seeds to extract final saliency map.

The experiment results in [20] showed that the MR algorithm outperforms most of the state-of-the-art methods. However, From Fig. 1 the first line and the second line, we notice that when saliency objects touch the image border to quite some extent, the algorithm is easy to fail. From line 3 in Fig. 1 shows, when the interior of the salient object is similar to boundary feature, easy to set it as background, and result in the whole significant object is not uniform. As a result, purely using image edge as the background seed point, the hypothesis is too ideal.

Inspired by the shortage, we reconsider fundamentally contrast approach to learn optimal seeds (queries), the method combines the global region contrast with manifold ranking. Our scheme can generate pixel-wised saliency maps, and uniformly highlight the whole salient regions.

The main contributions of this work are as follows:

(1) A spatial distances and color features-based global contrast propagation mechanism is presented for region saliency detection.

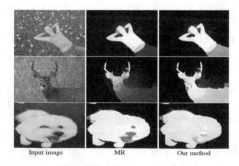

Input image   MR   Our method

Fig. 1. The saliency map from different saliency methods

(2) Exploit global region saliency results as a basis to improve the probability of selecting the correct seeds.

(3) We propose a new non-linear integration method to combine saliency maps, which achieves more favorable and uniformly results.

The rest of this paper is organized as follows. In Sect. 2, we review the principles of graph-based manifold ranking. In Sect. 3, we describe the details of the proposed bottom-up saliency algorithm. Section 4, experiment results are illustrated on the ASD, CSSD, SOD and ECSSD datasets with other state-of-the-art methods. Finally, the conclusion is made in Sect. 5.

2 Graph-Based Manifold Ranking

In this section, we provide a brief review of the manifold ranking model as preliminary knowledge.

In [20], given a set of point (such as image) $X = \{x_1, x_2 \ldots x_n\} \in R^{m \times n}$, some points are set to the queries and the rest is sorted according to its relevance to the query points. Let $y = [y_1, y_2 \ldots y_n]^T$ is an indicator vector, if x_i is a query, then $y_i = +1$, and $y_i = 0$ otherwise. Denote a ranking function $f : X \to R^n$ to estimate a ranking score f_i for each point x_i. Corresponding graph model G = (V,E) is defined on the dataset X, V is the nodes and E is edge set. Ranking score f is obtained by solving optimization problems by Eq. (1).

$$f^* = \arg\min_f \frac{1}{2} \left(\sum_{i,j=1}^n w_{ij} \left\| \frac{f_i}{\sqrt{d_{ii}}} - \frac{f_j}{\sqrt{d_{jj}}} \right\|^2 + u \sum_{i=1}^n \|f_i - y_i\|^2 \right) \tag{1}$$

where $\mathbf{W} = [w_{ij}]_{n \times n}$ denotes an affinity matrix which weight the edges E, in which $w_{ij} = \exp(-\frac{dist^2(x_i, x_j)}{\sigma^2})$, note that $w_{ii} = 0$ to avoid self-reinforcement. $\mathbf{D} = $ diag$(d_{11}, d_{22} \ldots d_{nn})$ is the degree matrix. u controls the balance of the smoothness constraint and the fitting constraint.

Computing derivative of Eq. (2), and makes result equal to zero to get the optimal solution. Sort function optimization results in the form of a matrix can be expressed as:

$$f^* = (\mathbf{I} - \alpha \mathbf{S})^{-1} y \tag{2}$$

See [9] for the rigorous proof. I is an identity matrix, $\alpha = 1/(1 + u), \mathbf{S} = \mathbf{D}^{-1/2} \mathbf{W} \mathbf{D}^{1/2}$ Saliency detection can be seen as an one-class classification problem, so we can use the unnormalized Laplacian matrix in Eq. (3):

$$f^* = (\mathbf{D} - \alpha \mathbf{W})^{-1} y \tag{3}$$

By comparison Eqs. (2) and (3), the latter can get better results. Hence we choose Eq. (3) in our implementation.

In [13], MR method have two-stage scheme for saliency detection using ranking with background and foreground. The first stage, selected the top, bottom, left and right image boundary as background seeds, compute the four saliency maps: $S_t(i)$, $S_b(i)$, $S_l(i)$, $S_r(i)$ by using $1 - \overline{f^*}(i)$, $\overline{f^*}$ denotes the normalized vector. The four saliency maps are integrated by the following process:

$$S_{bg}(i) = S_t(i) \times S_b(i) \times S_l(i) \times S_r(i) \tag{4}$$

The second stage, the saliency map of the first stage is binary segmented using an adaptive threshold, which facilitates selecting the nodes of the foreground salient object as queries. A foreground indicator vector was formed to compute the ranking vector f^* using Eq. (3), f^* was normalized to form the final saliency map.

3   Optimal Seeds for Object Saliency

In this section, we propose an algorithm to learning optimal seeds, by combining global region detection and manifold ranking. The proposed saliency detection algorithm is shown in Fig. 2, which consists of three major steps. The step one abstracts the input image into a set of super-pixels, which usually have more regular and compact shape with better boundary adherence. The step two generates saliency maps via global region contrast and manifold ranking. The step three combines the saliency results to calculate the pixel-wise saliency map.

3.1   Abstraction

In order to preserve relevant structure and better capture mid-level information of the image, super-pixel is more accord with human visual perception and contains less redundancy. We segment the original image into homogenization and compact super-pixels by SLIC [10] algorithm in the CIE LAB color space.

Given a dataset $X = \{x_1, x_2 \ldots x_n\} \in R^{m \times n}$, where X denotes the input image, n is the number of super-pixels. $x_i = \{L, a, b, x, y, num\} \in R^m$, where x_i denotes features of the ith segment, L, a, b is the three channels of LAB color space, x, y is the center coordinate of x_i, num is numbers of the pixels in x_i.

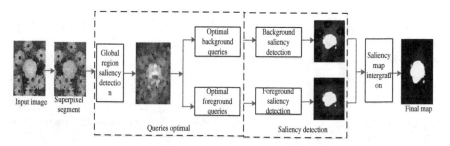

Fig. 2. Illustration of the main steps of our saliency detection algorithm

3.2 Optimal Seeds

In [13], only used the image boundary nodes as background seeds, the correctness of background seeds directly affects the follow-up stages. In order to get optimal seeds from an image, we combine global region contrast and manifold ranking. Our global method utilizes region contrast and spatial relationship between the super-pixels. On the basis of this, the large probability seeds are selected to get more accurate and more uniform saliency map. The proposed method is defined as:

$$S_g(x_i) = w_s(x_i) \sum_{j=1, x_i \neq x_j}^{n} \exp(D_s(x_i, x_j)/\varepsilon^2) w(x_i) D_c(x_i, x_j) \tag{5}$$

where $D_s(x_i, x_j)$ denotes the spatial Euclidean distance between regions x_i and x_j. $w(x_i)$ is the number of pixels in region x_i as a weight to emphasize bigger color contrast segments. $D_c(x_i, x_j)$ is the color distance between x_i and x_j in our experiment. We use $\varepsilon^2 = 2$ to controls the balance of spatial weight and color contrast, larger values of ε reduce the effect of spatial weighting, so that contrast to farther regions would contribute more to the saliency of the current region. $w_s(x_i)$ indicates that the inner region of the image is more likely to be a saliency object than the boundary.

$$w_s(x_i) = \exp\left(-9d_k^2\right) \tag{6}$$

where d_k is the average distance between x_i and the image center. The spatial distance between the two regions is defined as the Euclidean distance between the center of x_i and x_j.

In order to more accurately select the foreground and background seed points, the significant value calculated by the Eq. (5) is used as the basis for selecting query points. According to the Eq. (7), the foreground query points of the corresponding large probability are selected from the initial saliency results.

$$y_i = \begin{cases} 1 & if \quad S_g(x_i) \geq T_1 \\ 0 & if \quad S_g(x_i) < T_1 \end{cases} \tag{7}$$

Set a node as a foreground query which the saliency values are more than the adaptive threshold T_1. An indicator vector y_f is formed, by setting query segments is 1, the others is 0.

Similarly, the background seed points are chosen by two ways. One is similar to Eq. (7), by setting the super-pixels below the threshold T_2 for the background seed points. Another way is boundary priors. Based on the attention theories of early works for [20] visual saliency, assume that a narrow border of the image is the background region. So the nodes on the image boundary are also selected as the background seeds. Finally, obtain the background indicator vector y_b. From Fig. 3, we noticed that the seeds selected by our method are more accurate.

| Input image | The background seeds of MR(black) | The background seeds of our method (black) | The foreground seeds of MR(white) | The foreground seeds of our method (white) |

Fig. 3. The seeds compare of MR and our method

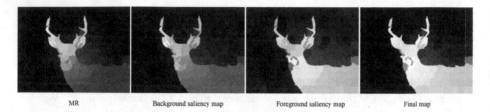

| MR | Background saliency map | Foreground saliency map | Final map |

Fig. 4. The saliency map of our method

3.3   Foreground and Background Saliency Cues

According to the indicator vector y_f and y_b, computing the ranking vector f^* using Eq. (3) respectively. Normalize ranking score $\overline{f^*}$ to from the background saliency map S_b and foreground saliency map S_f by Eq. (8).

$$S(i) = \overline{f^*}(i) \quad i = 1, 2 \ldots n \tag{8}$$

where i denotes super-pixel node on graph, n is the super-pixel numbers of original image. From Fig. 4, some background regions are mistakenly selected, but through choosing the foreground queries, the final saliency map can be better supplement.

3.4   Integration of Saliency Maps

According to above Eq. (8), the saliency measures based on background and foreground are complementary to each other. To get final saliency map, we propose a combination method by the following process:

$$S_{final} = 1 - \exp\left(-\delta \times S_b \times S_f\right) \tag{9}$$

where δ controls the brightness of the saliency map, the bigger the values of δ, the brighter the image. Due to foreground and background queries are selected according to the threshold, some pixels with the saliency regions may have low saliency, but by integrating two saliency maps, the significant part is uniformly highlighted, and meanwhile the background part is weakened. The main steps of the proposed are summarized in Algorithm 1.

Algorithm 1 Saliency detection via Global Region Contrast and Manifold Ranking

Input: An image and required parameters

1) Segment the input image into super-pixels by SLIC methods, construct graph G and compute degree matrix D and weight matrix W.

2) Compute global contrast saliency value by Eq. (5).

3) Choose the seeds by Eq. (7).

4) Integration of saliency maps by Eq. (9) to get the final saliency map.

Output: a final saliency map representing the saliency value of each pixel.

---

4 Experiment Results

In this section, we experiment with our saliency detection methods on four benchmark datasets, and qualitatively and quantitatively compare our method with several global methods: FT [7], CA [23], RC [17], SF [18], SR [15], and other methods BS [22], IM [14], MR [20]. For FT, CA, SF, SR, BS, SA, IM and MR, we run authors' codes. For RC, we use the implementation of [17]. In our Experiments, there are three parameters,They are empirically chosen: $\varepsilon^2 = 2$, $\alpha = 0.99$, $\delta = 2$.

The precision-recall curve is an objective evaluation criterion which is usually used. Precision indicates the proportion of correct detection results in the detection results. Recall corresponds to the proportion of correct detection in the ground truth. Often, neither Precision nor Recall can comprehensively evaluate the quality of a saliency map. The F-measure is estimated as a weighted harmonic mean of them with non-negative weight β^2:

$$F_\beta = \frac{(1 + \beta^2) Precision \times Recall}{\beta^2 Precision + Recall} \tag{10}$$

where we set $\beta^2 = 0.3$ in our experiments as suggested in [7].

4.1 Benchmark Datasets

ASD dataset: ASD dataset is the most popular dataset in the literature, which constructed with 1000 natural images from the MSRA-B containing 5000 highly unambiguous images. The dataset has only one significant object and clear background.

CSSD and ECSSD datasets: CSSD dataset includes 200 images which are collected from BSD dataset, PASCAL VOC and internet, each image of the dataset contains complex scene. It is expanded to the ECSSD dataset, which containing 1000 semantically meaningful but structurally complex images.

SOD dataset: SOD database consists of 300 images, which generally contain complex background and multiple salient objects with vague appearance. Some images have similar foreground and background features, and the others have not unified ground truths which are annotated by multiple subject. Consequently, it has been regards as the most challenging dataset for salient detection.

4.2 Qualitative Analysis

We evaluate the performance of our method against eight state-of-the-art bottom-up saliency algorithms. To reliably compare how well various saliency detection methods, we perform two different experiments.

In the first experiment, we get a binary segmentation to threshold the saliency map by varying the threshold from 0 to 255. The precision-recall curves in Fig. 5 show that the proposed methods significantly outperforms the FT [7], CA [23], RC [17], SF [18], SR [15] which are global saliency detection methods. In addition, our method also outperforms the MR model which is based on boundary priors and manifold ranking. Due to the complexity of the CSSD, ECSSD and SOD datasets, although the results are far less than the ASD database, but our method remains the highest accuracy. Our algorithm consistently produces results closer to ground truth at every threshold and for any given recall rate on four datasets.

In the second experiment we use the image-dependent adaptive threshold proposed by [2], which is defined as twice the mean saliency of the image:

$$T_a = \frac{1}{W \times H} \sum_{x=1}^{W} \sum_{y=1}^{H} S(x, y) \tag{11}$$

where W and H are the width and the height of the saliency map S, respectively. We also compute the precision, recall and F-measure with T_a. The Fig. 5(b) and Table 1 show that our method achieves the highest precision and F-measure values. The results also show that the proposed method outperforms above mentioned methods on ASD, CSSD, ECSSD and SOD datasets. Our scheme can handle complex images with different details, and can produce more accurate saliency maps.

4.3 Visual Contrast

Visual comparison of saliency maps obtained by the various methods can be seen in Fig. 6. These images contain a variety of different scenes, and some are more complex, such as significant region is not in the center of the image, or the background is similar to the foreground, or the significant object interior contains some regions that are similar to the boundary. According to the experimental results of several approaches, FT [7] method can highlight the special pixels of an image, but significant region is not complete. HC [17] can find high color contrast area, thus lead to part of high color contrast background region error identify as foreground. CA [23] is better to highlight the edge of the saliency region, however the saliency region interior cannot be fully highlighted. Although BS [22], SR [15] and MR [20] can get the whole prominent object, but the ability to restrain background is not ideal. our method unifies light up the significant objects, and better preserves the integrity of the saliency regions.

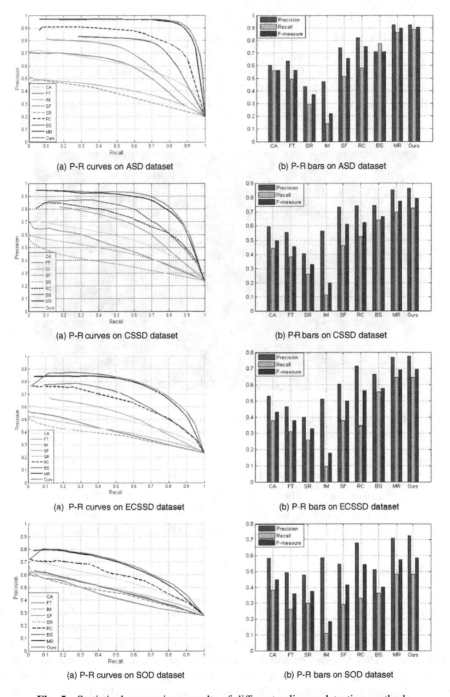

(a) P-R curves on ASD dataset

(b) P-R bars on ASD dataset

(a) P-R curves on CSSD dataset

(b) P-R bars on CSSD dataset

(a) P-R curves on ECSSD dataset

(b) P-R bars on ECSSD dataset

(a) P-R curves on SOD dataset

(b) P-R bars on SOD dataset

Fig. 5. Statistical comparison results of different saliency detection methods

Table 1. Comparison of F-measure on four datasets

Method	CA	FI	SR	IM	SF	RC	BS	MR	Ours
ASD	0.5618	0.5642	0.3703	0.2189	0.6557	0.7501	0.7091	0.7720	0.9048
CSSD	0.4967	0.4545	0.3265	0.1957	0.6117	0.6224	0.6648	0.8957	0.7931
ECSSD	0.4308	0.3787	0.3281	0.1760	0.4996	0.5651	0.5768	0.6906	0.6968
SOD	0.4489	0.3585	0.3705	0.1845	0.4161	0.5237	0.4023	0.5740	0.5862

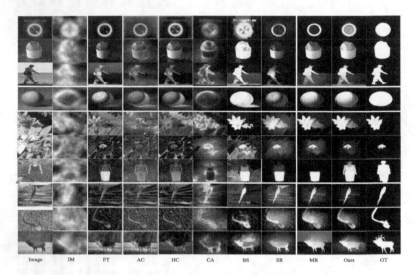

Fig. 6. Visual comparison of saliency detection methods on four datasets

Table 2. Comparison of average running times

Method	Ours	MR	RC	BS	FT	CA	IM
Time(s)	1. 134	0. 68	0. 14	259. 37	0. 19	53. 1	0. 991
Code	Matlab	Matlab	C++	Matlab	Matlab	Matlab	Matlab

4.4   RunTime

The experiments are carried out on a desktop with an Intel (R) Core (RM) i5-2410 M CPU and 4G RAM. In Table 2 we compare the average running time of our approach with other eight state-of-the-art on four benchmark images. Our method spends 0. 441 s (about 38%) on abstraction by SLIC, calculating the global saliency value costs 0.342 (about 31%), foreground saliency and background saliency computation costs 0. 276 s (about 24%), the others cost 0. 075 s. Ours algorithm increases the global saliency computation, so the cost of time is slightly longer than MR, FT, IM, RC algorithm, but significantly lower than BS, CA methods. Combined with the quantitative performance evaluation index, this method still has advantages.

5 Conclusion

In this paper, to improve the shortage that the idealistic background prior assumption is used in graph-based manifold ranking, we propose a saliency detection algorithm based on global regional contrast and manifold ranking. To combine the two saliency maps, we introduce a new nonlinear integration method to get the final saliency map. Extensive experiments on ASD and complex CSSD datasets demonstrates the effectiveness of the proposed method. The next work will consider using high-level information to improve image detection accuracy and completeness, such as the image contour, Semantic prior.

References

1. Li, W.T., Chang, H.S., Lien, K.C., Chang, H.T., Frank Wang, Y.C.: Exploring visual and motion saliency for automatic video object extraction. IEEE Trans. Image Process. **22**(7), 2600–2610 (2013)
2. Ren, Z., Gao, S., Chia, L.T., Tsang, I.: Region-based saliency detection and its application in object recognition. IEEE Trans. Circ. Syst. Video Technol. **24**(5), 769–779 (2014)
3. Borji, A., Cheng, M.M., Jiang, H., Li, J.: Saliency object detection: a survey. arXiv:1411. 5878 (2014)
4. Chen, D.Y., Luo, Y.S.: Preserving motion-tolerant contextual visual saliency for video resizing. IEEE Trans. Multimedia **15**(7), 1616–1627 (2013)
5. Lee, Y.J., Ghosh, J., Grauman, K.: Discovering important people and objects for egocentric video summarization. In: CVPR, pp. 1346–1353 (2013)
6. Jiang, B.W., Zhang, L.H., Lu, H.C.: Saliency detection via absorbing Markov chain. In: Proceedings of the IEEE International Conference on Computer Vision, Sydney, pp. 1665–1672 (2013)
7. Achanta, R., Hemami, S., Estrada, F.J., Süsstrunk, S.: Frequency-tuned salient region detection. In: CVPR, pp: 1597–1604 (2009)
8. Zhai, Y., Shan, M.: Visual attention detection in video sequences using spatiotemporal cues. ACM Multimedia **2006**, 815–824 (2006)
9. Cheng, X., Du, P., Guo, J.: Ranking on data manifold with sink points. IEEE Trans. Knowl. Data Eng. **25**(1), 177–191 (2013)
10. Achanta, R., Shaji, A., Smith, K., Lucchi, A., Fua, P., Süsstrunk, S.: SLIC super-pixels compared to state-of-the-art super-pixel methods. IEEE Trans. Pattern Anal. Mach. Intell. **34** (11), 2274–2282 (2012)
11. Itti, L., Koch, C., Niebur, E.: A model of saliency-based visual attention for rapid scene analysis. IEEE Trans. Pattern Anal. Mach. Intell. **20**(11), 1254–1259 (1998)
12. Harel, J., Koch, C., Perona, P.: Graph-based visual saliency. In: Advances in Neural Information Processing Systems, pp. 545–552 (2006)
13. Liu, T., Sun, J., Zheng, N., Tang, X., Shum, H.Y.: Learning to detect a salient object. In: CVPR, pp. 1–8 (2007)
14. Murray, N., Vanrell, M., Otazu, X., Parraga, C.A.: Saliency estimation using a non-parametric low-level vision model. In: IEEE CVPR 2011, pp: 433–440 (2011)
15. Hou, X., Zhang, L.: Saliency detection: a spectral residual approach. In: IEEE CVPR, pp. 1–8 (2007)
16. Jiang, P., Ling, H., Yu, J., Peng, J.: Salient region detection by UFO: uniqueness, focusness and objectness. In: ICCV (2013)

17. Cheng, M.M., Mitra, N.J., Huang, X., Torr, P.H.S., Hu, S.M.: Global contrast based salient region detection. IEEE TPAMI **37**(3), 569–582 (2015)
18. Perazzi, F., Krahenbuhl, P., Pritch, Y., Hornung, A.: Saliency filters: contrast based filtering for salient region detection. In: CVPR, pp. 733–740 (2012)
19. Ma, Y.F., Zhang, H.J.: Contrast-based image attention analysis by using fuzzy growing. In: ACM International Conference on Multimedia, pp. 374–381 (2003)
20. Yang, C., Zhang, L., Lu, H., Ruan, X., Yang, M.H.: Saliency detection via graph-based manifold ranking. In: CVPR, pp. 3166–3173 (2013)
21. Yan, Q., Xu, L., Shi, J.P., Jia, J.Y.: Hierarchical saliency detection. In: CVPR 2013, pp, 1155–1162 (2013)
22. Xie, Y.L., Lu, H.C., Yang, M.H.: Bayesian saliency via low and mid-level cues. IEEE Trans. Image Process. **5**(22), 1689–1698 (2013)
23. Goferman, S., Zelnik-Manor, L., Tal, A.: Context-aware saliency detection. IEEE Trans. Pattern Anal. Mach. Intell. **34**(10), 1915–1926 (2012)

A Spiking Neural Network Based Autonomous Reinforcement Learning Model and Its Application in Decision Making

Guixiang Wang[1,3], Yi Zeng[1,2,3(✉)], and Bo Xu[1,2,3]

[1] Institute of Automation, Chinese Academy of Science, Beijing, China
{guixiang.wang,yi.zeng}@ia.ac.cn
[2] Center for Excellence in Brain Science and Intelligence Technology, Chinese Academy of Sciences, Shanghai, China
[3] University of Chinese Academy of Sciences, Beijing, China

Abstract. Inspired by biological spike information processing and the multiple brain region coordination mechanism, we propose an autonomous spiking neural network model for decision making. The proposed model is an expansion of the basal ganglia circuitry with automatic environment perception. It automatically constructs environmental states from image inputs. Contributions of this investigation can be summarized as the following: (1) In our model, the simplified Hodgkin-Huxley computing model is developed to achieve calculation efficiency closed to the LIF model and is used to obtain and test the ionic level properties in cognition. (2) A spike based motion perception mechanism is proposed to extract key elements for learning process from raw pixels without large amount of training. We apply our model in the "flappy bird" game and after dozens of training times, it can automatically generate rules to play well in the game. Besides, our model simulates cognitive defects when blocking some of sodium or potassium ion channels in the Hodgkin-Huxley model and this can be considered as a computational exploration on the mechanisms of cognition deep into ionic level.

Keywords: Spiking neural network · Hodgkin-Huxley model · Autonomous reinforcement learning · Decision making · Basal Ganglia

1 Introduction

Human brains can handle complex tasks well, from visually observing the environment and situation to providing a plan. The brain can automatically analyze and understand the situation status and provide appropriate behavior output, while traditional artificial intelligence systems are short of automatic environmental status division and understanding. Algorithms inspired by brain structure and information processing mechanism may give a better solution to automatically understand and solve problems.

© Springer International Publishing AG 2016
C.-L. Liu et al. (Eds.): BICS 2016, LNAI 10023, pp. 125–137, 2016.
DOI: 10.1007/978-3-319-49685-6_12

In this paper, we build a spiking neural network that has the ability of autonomous reinforcement learning for decision making. We evaluate the proposed network model by testing its ability for wining in computer game "Flappy Bird". Taking raw images as inputs, the agent knows little about the environment at the beginning. After several times of detection, it can detect motions in the environment and avoid collision with objects. Knowing movement limitations and the environment, the agent will learn how to move to get better game scores.

Our motivation is to build a brain-inspired cognitive model for reinforcement learning and use it in decision making tasks, so that agents with this model will have autonomous learning ability without telling what the environment is. The agents can perceive the environment with proposed motion perception mechanism and calculate key elements for learning with a little prior knowledge. We hope that our work could give a step forward towards brain-inspired intelligence.

2   Related Work

2.1   The Basal Ganglia Model

The basal ganglia are one of the most important brain building block for cognition, especially for reinforcement learning and decision making.

The basal ganglia is composed of striatum, the STN, the GPe, and two output nuclei, the SNr and the GPi [3,5–8]. Other nuclei, including the SNc and the VTA, are also considered as part of the basal ganglia. In cognition process, the basal ganglia need to cooperate with other related brain regions to form the basal ganglia circuitry [4–6,8,25].

The cognitive research on the basal ganglia has produced a large number of models. Starting from the "box and arrow" model of the basal ganglia based on anatomical data of the brain [14,15], many computational models are proposed [5,7–10,13,15,16]. Most of the basal ganglia models are built using artificial neural networks [5,9,15], which are not really biological plausible. In addition, these models are used to do relatively simple action-selection experiments, rather than automatically solving complex cognitive tasks.

In this paper, we will build our autonomous learning model with more biological details based on the understanding of basal ganglia circuitry. Before describing our model, we need to introduce the mathematical model of the basal ganglia that gives us the inspiration.

2.2   A Spike Coding Model of the Basal Ganglia

Our work is related to a mathematical basal ganglia model for action selection [10] and its expanded spiking coding model [1,8].

We develop our autonomous reinforcement learning model based on the spike coding model with the following consideration: (1) The model has low computational complexity and keeps main biological features of the basal ganglia. (2) The model can deal with wide range of inputs with hundreds of dimensions [1].

The spike coding model's selection mechanism can be described as a linear equation [10]:

$$f(x_i) = \begin{cases} 0 & x_i < e_i \\ m(x_i - e_i) & e_i \leq x_i < 1/m + e_i \\ 1 & x_i > 1/m + e_i \end{cases} \tag{1}$$

where $f(x_i)$ is the output of a nucleus, and x_i is the input with $0 \leq x_i \leq 1$ as the value interval.

Each nucleus in the basal ganglia is represented by a group of biological neurons. It is generally believed that biological neurons carry information by producing complex spike sequences [1,11,18]. These spikes encode input stimulus as firing rates [17,18]. The coding and decoding process of this model can be find in [1,8,12].

2.3 The Hodgkin-Huxley Model

The Hodgkin-Huxley (H-H in short) model was proposed by Alan Lloyd Hodgkin and Andrew Fielding Huxley in 1952 [20]. They made this effort based on the understanding of squid giant axons. Many parameters in the model are fitted using the experimental data. The H-H model is regarded as the best one to describe action potential's dynamic properties in the ionic level. The model is written as four equations with I as the external current input [19–21].

The ionic current is composed of three components. Namely, the sodium (Na+) current with three activation gates and one inactivation gate, the potassium (K+) current with four activation gates, and the leak current carried primarily by chlorine (Cl−) [19,21].

In this paper, we use the H-H model to build the basal ganglia model following the spike coding method described above. It can simulate more biological effects related to cognition. And we will apply the model to real cognitive task to test the model's ionic property and simulate it's influence on learning performance.

3   Brain-Inspired Computational Model for Autonomous Reinforcement Learning

3.1 Simplified Computation for the Hodgkin-Huxley Model

We use the Hodgkin-Huxley equations to build the spiking neural network model of reinforcement learning. We use the H-H model here for two reasons. (1) The H-H model explains experimental results accurately and enables quantitatively voltage analysis on the nerve cell. (2) Sodium and potassium are associated to human cognition. The Changes on the computationally modeled ionic conductance in sodium or potassium channel will give us deeper understanding of their biological properties for cognition.

The basal ganglia model is usually built using the leaky integrate-and-fire (LIF) neuron. The reason is that LIF model has low computational complexity and is easy to control. While, LIF neuron has poor description on dynamic action potential and on ionic level activities. The H-H model does well deep into the ionic level.

Different from the LIF neuron, the H-H model is more elaborate. If LIF uses one step to climb up to fire a spike in 1 ms, the H-H model will spend hundreds of steps to reach the threshold in the same time period because of the ionic channels' dynamic properties. This phenomenon is determined by the H-H equations. If the LIF model runs in milliseconds, the H-H model runs in nanoseconds. This needs more simulations and costs more computational complexity, therefore, it is necessary to present simplified computing equations for the H-H model.

To achieve calculation efficiency closed to the LIF model, several changes are made in H-H equations in this paper. (1) The membrane capacitance C becomes smaller than the original value and is set to the value of 0.01–0.03 $\mu F/cm^2$. This will greatly increase the action potential in one step. And fewer steps are needed before reaching the threshold. (2) To ensure a large enough firing rate, the current input should be larger than 6–7 $\mu A/cm^2$, and greater current inputs can ensure better accuracy. According to our experiments, a value of 30 is a better choice for the current input. (3) There is no internal loop for action potential accumulation in the simulation of H-H equations. The first two changes gain enough voltage increment in one step. And one step simulation gets the same accuracy than before. (4) The H-H equations fire spikes automatically in some frequency. Therefore, to control H-H neuron's activity to encode different functions, intervention mechanisms are performed. We need to reset the voltage to zero after a spike and assign a refractory time period to the equations according to the function represented and the encoding process.

We rewrite the voltage equation of the H-H model as the following, with some improvement described above:

$$C\dot{V} = J(x) - \overbrace{\overline{g}_k n^4 (V - E_k)}^{I_k} - \overbrace{\overline{g}_{Na} m^3 h (V - E_{Na})}^{I_{Na}} - \overbrace{g_L (V - E_L)}^{I_L}$$
$$V = 0, \qquad\qquad if \quad V > 60\,mV \qquad\qquad (2)$$
$$J(x) = 30(ax + b), \qquad -1 < a, b < 1$$
$$C = 0.02\ \mu F/cm^2$$

where $J(x)$ is the current input, a linear function of the original input x, a and b are with random values for different neurons in the spike coding model. And 30 is a scale of the current input to guarantee enough firing rate of the H-H model. The peak voltage is about 80–100 mV.

Usually, the resting action potential is set as $V = V_{rest} = 0$ to simplify the calculation. Meanwhile, other potential and conductance parameters should be given the following values [19, 22, 24].

When the input current is larger than a specific value, which is about 6–7 $\mu A/cm^2$ in our simulations, regular spiking activity is observed [22]. If the spike interval is T, the average firing rate can be represented as $f = 1/T$, and it increases as the stimulus enhanced [22–24], as shown in Fig. 1.

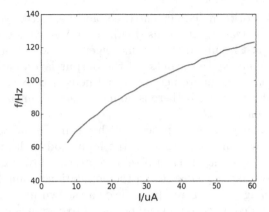

Fig. 1. Firing rate curve of the Hodgkin-Huxley model under various current inputs. In our experiments, the neuron starts to have stable regular spikes when the current input is larger than $7.5 \, \mu A/cm^2$. The resting potential is set to 0. The time constant is 0.01 ms. Simulation period is 1 s.

3.2 Spike Based Motion Perception

Eyes can detect the moving objects in the environment and the detection results will be used for cognitive tasks. In this paper, we build a neural network model as the eyes of agents. Agents with this model could percept and understand the environment to some extend. With a computational model of basal ganglia as the reinforcement learning model, agents will get the autonomous learning ability to do some complex cognitive task with image input rather than simple action selection.

The perception of an image is conducted in a multi-layer architecture, as shown in Fig. 2. It contains the input layer, the perceptive layer and the output layer. For an image input, Every pixel has a group of neurons to represent its value in the input layer. Population coding algorithm is used to change the pixel to spike sequences of a period of time. These spike sequences are the inputs of two special neurons in the perceptive layer. In this layer, two neurons represent

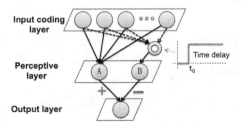

Fig. 2. Multi-layer structure of the motion perception model. The time delay here is used to keep the spike sequences of the last time. Therefore, the output layer will detect movements over time.

a pixel. Neuron A works in the current time, and neuron B works in the past with a constant time delay τ_0. It means that neuron A receives the current inputs and B receives the last inputs. If there is movement in the two neurons' position, they will have different spike outputs. In the output layer, each pixel has one neuron. The neuron's inputs are neuron A and neuron B. Neuron A is excited, and B has the contrary effect. If there is no movement, the neuron has no spike. Otherwise, it will release spikes.

The whole motion perception process is shown in Fig. 3. Each pixel in the image has its representing neurons from the input coding layer to the output layer. In the input coding layer, each pixel is represented by a group of neurons and converted into spike sequences using the population coding [26]. These neurons have overlapping gaussian receptive fields as shown in Fig. 3. The number of neurons and the encoding interval can be varied to obtain good coding results. With good parameters, the population coding can distinguish two similar values by different spike patterns. The experiment in the next section shows its good performance in pixel encoding.

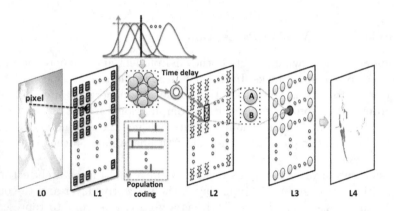

Fig. 3. The motion perception process for raw image inputs. L0 is the raw image, L1 is the input coding layer, L2 is the perception layer, L3 denotes the spike output layer, and L4 is the spike activity of the original image, showing the movement area. The population coding process is performed in L1. Every pixel is converted into a group of neurons' spiking sequence in L1.

In the population coding, suppose that $[I_{min}, I_{max}]$ is the encoding interval, and M is the number of neurons, the center of gaussian receptive field for each neuron can be calculated as [26]:

$$C_i = I_{min} + (i-1) \cdot \frac{I_{max} - I_{min}}{m - 2} \tag{3}$$

and the variance equation of each neuron is written as [26]:

$$\sigma_i = \beta \cdot \frac{I_{max} - I_{min}}{m - 2} \tag{4}$$

where the common values of β are at $[0, 2]$. The coding process will calculate a value's intersection with each gaussian receptive field and obtain spiking times for these gaussian neurons.

The output of the motion perception is an image with movement areas highlighted by spikes, as shown in L4 in Fig. 3. In the environment with less background variation, it's easy to get a object's moving direction and separate the moving area from other backgrounds. This is also useful for moving obstacle avoidance, which will be described in the next section.

3.3 Multiple Region Coordination and Spiking Neural Network Based Autonomous Reinforcement Learning Model

In this section, we will describe our whole autonomous reinforcement learning model. Our autonomous model is designed to interact with the environment and perform reinforcement learning to avoid moving obstacles without giving environment states. All the important model in this paper are built using the Hodgkin-Huxley model.

Our autonomous learning model is shown in Fig. 4. The model forms a Q learning loop to learn to interact with the environment. The motion perception model is used to detect moving objects from the image inputs and obtain new environment state function. The basal ganglia model takes the state function as input and performs action selection among all available actions every time step.

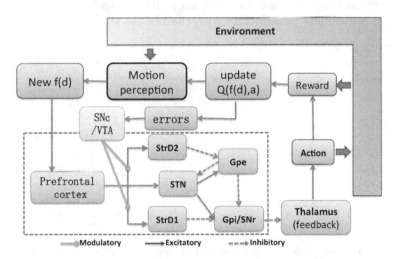

Fig. 4. The autonomous reinforcement learning model built using spiking neural network. The basal ganglia structure and their action selection function (in the rectangle) is referred from [1] and [2]. $f(d)$ is a function of distance d, named as the state function. The Q-value is a function of state function and action a. The environment status is calculated by the status function and not created manually. And the agent knows nothing except for several basic survival rules.

As introduced in Sect. 2, the basal ganglia model is built using methods in [1,2]. Learning in the basal ganglia circuitry is achieved by the updates of the synaptic connections between the basal ganglia and the prefrontal cortex. Learning will not finish until the basal ganglia obtains good action selections and the agent can interact well with the environment.

If the agent wants to survive in the environment, it has to follow two rules: (1) There should be no obstacles in agent's frontal direction. (2) The agent should be away from obstacles as far as possible if no other goals. The state function and rewards are calculated according to these two rules.

4   Experiments and Applications

In this section, we apply our model to the game called "flappy bird" to test our method's performance. In the following, we will firstly give experimental investigations for the simplified H-H model. And next, we will evaluate our model in the game of "flappy bird".

4.1   The Simplified Hodgkin-Huxley Model

We proposed our simplified H-H equations to reduce the computing complexity and keep their ionic properties at the same time. The experiments in Fig. 5 show the performance of our simplified H-H model. According to the experimental results, we can conclude that, the simplified H-H model has lower computing complexity and similar performance with the LIF model.

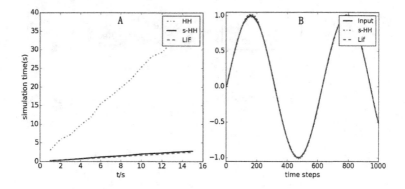

Fig. 5. The experiments for the simplified H-H equations. A: A comparative study on the simulation time between the original H-H model and its simplified model. B: The function tracking experiment for the simplified H-H model and the LIF model. The result shows that our simplified H-H model has similar function recover performance with the LIF model.

4.2 Autonomous Reinforcement Learning Model in the Game

Before playing the "flappy bird" game, we will explain how to calculate the environment status functions and rewards.

In the "flappy bird" game, the pipes move toward the bird, and the bird move up and down to adjust its position to try to pass through the pipes' gap without collision. According to the two surviving rules proposed above, the bird should avoid colliding with the pipes along their moving directions, and try to stay away from each pipe's terminal as far as possible.

The environment status is a key element that describes the environment. Without being specified in advance, it can be a function of distance to the center of the pipe's gap, written as $f(d)$. The bird gets the center of the pipes' gap using the motion perception model when a pair of pipes is coming. The environment status function $f(d)$ is calculated every time step according to the bird's position. For each value of state function, there are two actions the bird can take, which are up and down. The Q-value function of the Q learning process is represented by $f(d)$ and action a, written as $Q(f(d), a)$. Every time step the Q-value updates, the error is used for the autonomous model's learning.

The reward is important for learning. It can be calculated according to the motion perception results. If there are no pipes in the bird's forward direction, the rewards are positive. Otherwise, the rewards should be negative.

A. The Motion Perception. The proposed motion perception algorithm helps detect the obstacle's movement and key information such as status and reward could be calculated according to the spike results. The motion perception results is shown in Fig. 6.

The spike results shows a good input coding performance of the population coding algorithm. The coding process converts a pixel into spike sequences in

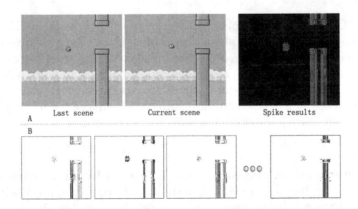

Fig. 6. The motion perception result for playing "flappy bird". A: The motion perception model takes the game scene as input in the current time step and gives the spike results in the next time step. B: The spike results of every population coding step.

a certain time interval. There are dozens of coding steps in this time interval. From Fig. 6B, we can see that, the motion perception process can detect the main moving areas even in single time step. The spike results in Fig. 6A is the result collection of all the coding time steps.

B. Playing the Game. We train our autonomous learning model in the "flappy bird" game. The experimental results are shown in Fig. 7. One can see from the Fig. 7. B that, at the beginning, the bird usually gets low scores before colliding pipes. After a couples of attempts, the bird has learned how to avoid the pipes and achieves more than 30 scores during its last attempts, and even larger scores if the game continues. This achievement can be compared with a good human player.

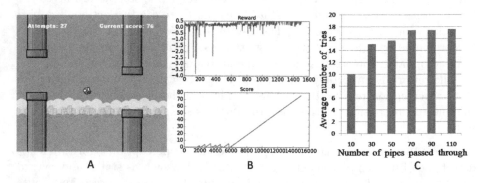

A   B   C

Fig. 7. The game playing results using our model. If the bird collides with the pipe, it costs one attempts. If the bird passes one pipe, 1 will be added to its score. A: the game scene. B: the score recording during the learning process. C: the average number of tries for passing through specific number of pipes using the proposed model.

In Fig. 7C, the average number of tries for passing through specific number of pipes using the proposed model are presented. Each of the average value for passing specific number of pipes are based on 20 successful tries. Note that after 10 times of training on average, the model can stably pass 10 pipes, while for 20 human players, the average training times for passing through 2 pipes is 12.1. In addition, when it is trained to have stable performance for passing through 70 pipes, passing through more pipes does not necessarily seem to require more training times.

C. Computational Validations on the Effects of Ions for Learning. The sodium and potassium ion are very important to the cognition process in biological brains[1]. Figure 8 shows some simulation results of the learning insufficiency

---

[1] Chris Eliasmith gave an invited keynote talk at the 2014 Computational Neuroscience Meeting (CNS 2014) on the effect of sodium channel for learning in SPAUN. This talk inspired our investigation introduced in this subsection.

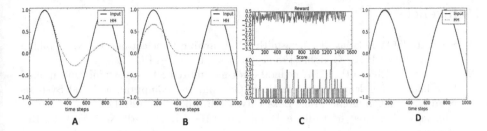

Fig. 8. The effects for learning under the condition of lacking of sodium and potassium ions. A: Learning without sodium ion. B: Learning without potassium ion. C: Reward and score for playing "flappy bird" without sodium ion. D: function tracking using normal H-H model.

under the condition of missing these two ions in the H-H model. The experiments show that, without sodium or potassium ions will lead to cognitive deficits for learning. Figure 8C shows that, the bird can only pass through a few pipes and can not get a higher score even with longer training time. Here we observe that the absence of potassium ion cause even worse case compared to the absence of sodium ion during online autonomous reinforcement learning.

5   Conclusion

This paper proposes an autonomous model for decision making based on spiking neural network and multiple brain region coordination mechanism. It can do autonomous reinforcement learning without predefined environment status.

In this paper, we propose the simplified Hodgkin-Huxley computing model to achieve calculation efficiency closed to the LIF model and keep the ionic level properties in cognition at the same time. To detect the moving objects in the environment, a spike based motion perception mechanism is developed to extract key elements from raw pixels without large amount of training. In the experiments section, we apply our model in the flappy bird game for evaluation, which shows good performance. Besides, our model simulates cognitive defects when blocking sodium or potassium ion channels in the Hodgkin-Huxley model and this is an exploration of cognition deep into the ionic level.

Although with these contributions, our model still has several limitations. It can not detect the moving object correctly when the background is changing over time. The model itself is still in its initial phase for high biological plausibility. In the near future, we will introduce more useful biological details to improve our model to get better cognitive performance.

Acknowledgements. This study was funded by the Strategic Priority Research Program of the Chinese Academy of Sciences (XDB02060007), and Beijing Municipal Commission of Science and Technology (Z151100000915070, Z161100000216124).

References

1. Stewart, T.C., Bekolay, T., Eliasmith, C.: Learning to select actions with spiking neurons in the Basal Ganglia. Front. Neurosci. **6**(2), 1–14 (2012)
2. Bekolay, T., Eliasmith, C.: A general error-modulated STDP learning rule applied to reinforcement learning in the Basal Ganglia. In: Computational and Systems Neuroscience Conference, Salt Lake City, Utah, pp. 24–27 (2011)
3. Eliasmith, C.: How to Build a Brain, pp. 121–171. Oxford, New York (2013). Reprint edition
4. Chakravarthy, V.S., Joseph, D., Bapi, R.S.: What do the Basal Ganglia do? Model. Perspect. Biol. Cybern. **103**(3), 237–253 (2010)
5. Frank, M.J.: Dynamic dopamine modulation in the Basal Ganglia: a neuro computational account of cognitive deficits in medicated and nonmedicated Parkinsonism. J. Cogn. Neurosci. **17**(1), 51–72 (2005)
6. Utter, A.A., Basso, M.A.: The Basal Ganglia: an overview of circuits and function. Neurosci. Biobehav. Rev. **32**(3), 333–342 (2008)
7. Redgrave, P., Rodriguez, M., Smith, Y., Rodriguez-Oroz, M.C., et al.: Goal-directed and habitual control in the Basal Ganglia: implications for Parkinson's disease. Nat. Rev. Neurosci. **11**, 760–772 (2011)
8. Stewart, T.C., Choo, X., Eliasmith, C.: Dynamic behavior of a spiking model of action selection in the Basal Ganglia. In: Proceedings of the 10th International Conference on Cognitive Modeling, pp. 5–8 (2010)
9. Frank, M.J.: Hold your horses: a dynamic computational role for the subthalamic nucleus in decision making. Neural Netw. **19**(8), 1120–1136 (2006)
10. Gurney, K., Prescott, T.J., Redgrave, P.: A computational model of action selection in the Basal Ganglia. Biol. Cybern. **84**(6), 401–410 (2001)
11. Stewart, T.C., Eliasmith, C.: Large-scale synthesis of functional spiking neural circuits. Proc. IEEE **102**(5), 881–898 (2014)
12. MacNeil, D., Eliasmith, C.: Fine-tuning and the stability of recurrent neural networks. Public Lib. Sci. (PLoS One) **6**(9), 1–16 (2011)
13. Gurney, K., Prescott, T.J., Wickens, J.R., Redgrave, P.: Computational models of the Basal Ganglia: from robots to membranes. Trends Neurosci. **27**(8), 453–459 (2004)
14. Albin, R.L., Young, A.B., Penney, J.B.: The functional anatomy of Basal Ganglia disorders. Trends Neurosci. **12**(10), 366–375 (1989)
15. Bar-Gad, I., Bergman, H.: Stepping out of the box: information processing in the neural networks of the Basal Ganglia. Curr. Opin. Neurobiol. **11**(6), 689–695 (2011)
16. Iqarashi, J., Shouno, O., Fukai, T., Tsujino, H.: Real-time simulation of a spiking neural network model of the Basal Ganglia circuitry using general purpose computing on graphics processing units. Neural Netw. **24**(9), 950–960 (2011)
17. Cessac, B., Paugam-Moisy, H., Viéville, T.: Overview of facts and issues about neural coding by spikes. J. Physiol. Paris **104**(1), 5–18 (2010)
18. Dayan, P., Abbott, L.F.: Computational and Mathematical Modeling of Neural Systems: Model Neurons I: Neuroelectronic. MIT Press, Cambridge (2003)
19. Izhikevich, E.M.: Dynamical Systems in Neuroscience: The Geometry of Excitability and Bursting. MIT Press, Cambridge (2004)
20. Hodgkin, A.L., Huxley, A.F.: A quantitative description of membrane current and its application to conduction and excitation in nerve. J. Physiol. **117**(4), 500–544 (1952)

21. Nelson, M.E.: Electrophysiological models. In: Databasing the Brain: From Data to Knowledge. Wiley, New York (2004)
22. Gerstner, W., Kistler, W.M.: Spiking Neuron Models. Single Neurons, Populations, Plasticity. Cambridge University Press, Cambridge (2002)
23. Wells, R.B.: Introduction to biological signal processing and computational neuroscience. Moscow (2010)
24. Long, L.N., Fang, G.L.: A review of biologically plausible neuron models for spiking neural networks. In: AIAA InfoTech Aerospace Conference, Atlanta, 20–22 April 2010
25. Weber, C., Elshaw, M., Wermter, S., Triesch, J., Willmot, C.: Reinforcement Learning: Theory and Applications: Reinforcement Learning Embedded in Brains and Robots. Austria (2008)
26. Bohte, S.M., Poutre, H.L., Kok, J.N.: Unsupervised clustering with spiking neurons by sparse temporal coding and multilayer RBF networks. IEEE Trans. Neural Netw. 13(2), 426–435 (2002)

Classification of Spatiotemporal Events
Based on Random Forest

Hongmin Li, Guoqi Li, and Luping Shi[✉]

Department of Precision Instrument, Center for Brain-Inspired Computing Research (CBICR),
Optical Memory National Engineering Research Center, Tsinghua University,
Beijing 100084, China
lpshi@tsinghua.edu.cn

Abstract. Classification of spatiotemporal events captured by neuromorphic vision sensors or event based cameras in which each pixel senses the luminance changes of related spatial location and produces a sequence of events, has been of great interest in recent years. In this paper, we find that the classification accuracy can be significantly improved by combing random forest (RF) classifier with pixel-wise features. RF is a statistical framework with high generalization accuracy and fast training time. We uncover that random forest could grow deep and tend to learn highly irregular patterns of spatiotemporal events with low bias, and thus it is more suitable for achieving the classification objective. The experimental results on MNIST-DVS dataset and AER Posture dataset show that the RF based classification approach in this work outperforms the state of art algorithms in both classification accuracy and computation time cost.

Keywords: Neuromorphic vision · Dynamic Vision Sensor (DVS) · Random forest · Bag of Events (BOE)

1 Introduction

Neuromorphic vision is inspired from the retinas and aims to develop a computing method to solve the event-based vision tasks. Event based cameras record the natural scenes in the form of spatiotemporal event streams like spike trains produced by biological retinas [1–3]. One of the most successful and widely used neuromorphic image sensors is dynamic vision sensor (DVS). Different from the traditional frame-based cameras, the DVS senses the transient in a dynamic scene and generates a series of events instead of capturing entire images at a fixed frame rate. DVSs use Address-Event Representation (AER) [4] to transmit events in response to local change in temporal or spatial contrast. Every event is a quadruple (x, y, t, p), where (x, y) denotes the position of the pixel, t denotes the time when the event is generated, and p denotes the polarity of the event. The polarity p = 1 denotes the increasing light intensity and p = −1 denotes the decreasing light intensity. Every stimulus onset makes DVS produce and output four AER events at the same time in a fairly random manner. In the case of static background and fixed DVS, the moving speed and direction of the object will influence the number of events. Figure 1(a) shows the structure of the DVS. Each firing element (FE) or pixel

© Springer International Publishing AG 2016
C.-L. Liu et al. (Eds.): BICS 2016, LNAI 10023, pp. 138–148, 2016.
DOI: 10.1007/978-3-319-49685-6_13

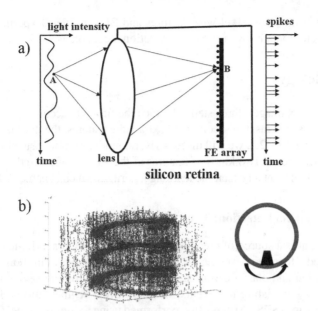

Fig. 1. (a) Dynamic vision sensor. The dynamic process of the point A in the light field is projected through lens to the FE B of the silicon retina which generates a series of spikes. (b) Spatiotemporal spike patterns of a rotating scene.

of the device produces spikes according the change of the light intensity of the relative spatial position. Figure 1(b) shows the spatiotemporal event streams generated by a rotating object.

Neuromorphic vision sensors have the advantages of high time resolution, low data redundancy and energy-saving [1, 2]. Many impressive visual processing systems have been proposed for the object recognition, real-time tracking, and other application fields [5–7]. However, in many applications, pattern recognition plays a critically important role. In this paper, we mainly focus on the problem of pattern recognition of spatiotemporal event process. There have been many works on the AER recognition systems [8–13]. Many of them are event-based feed-forward network architectures. Recently, a statistical learning method based on pixel-wise bag of events (BOE) feature and support vector machine (SVM) shows remarkably faster than others' methods in both feature extraction and training [8].

In this paper, we efficiently address the classification problem of AER images by combining the random forest (RF) classifier [15, 16] with two types of pixel-wise features i.e., BOE feature and firing rate feature. An ensemble of trees is grown and vote for the most popular class, which results in significant improvements in classification accuracy. The RF has been used in many classification tasks [17–20]. In [19], the RF outperforms the SVM in classification tasks of the Caltech-101 and Caltech-256 data sets. Advantages of RF includes: (i) its computation efficiency in both training and classification, (ii) the seamless handling of many kinds of visual features (e.g. color, depth, raw pixels etc.) [20], (iii) it can overcome the over-fitting problem when more trees are added [15]. In Sect. 2, we present the proposed methods: motion symbol detection based time slice, pixel-wise features and RF classifier. Experimental details, results and discussion are given in Sect. 3. Section 4 concludes.

2   Methodology

To classify the AER images, three steps of which the first is to accumulate the spatiotemporal events into segments, the second is to extract the features, the third is to make decision are needed. In Sect. 2.1, we will discuss several motion symbol detection methods. In Sect. 2.2, we will present two kinds of features of the AER images used in this paper. In Sect. 2.3, we will present an ensemble learning algorithm which is named RF classifier.

2.1   Motion Symbol Detection: Time Slice

Every AER event is a source of meaningful information. In general, the event streams are accumulated into multiple segments which represent a series of motion or recordings. Feature extraction and classification are performed based on the segments. There are two classes of accumulating the events, i.e., hard event segmentation (HES) and soft events segmentation (SES). SES is often performed using a single channel (i.e., synapse) LIF neuron. Each input event produce a postsynaptic potential (PSP) to the neuron. When the membrane potential exceeds a given threshold, the neuron fires a spike signal representing a new segment. In this case, there are two event channels, of which one is for accumulating events, and the other is for training and classification, which makes the system more complex. Besides, the LIF neuron will always wait for the input events and update the membrane potential, which increases the computational complexity.

In this paper, we employ the HES method which divides the event streams into segments using fixed time slices (e.g., 10 ms). In fact, the HES has a biological foundation. Michael H. Herzog et al. found that human percept the visual world in a discrete manner. In addition, HES reduces the system complexity because only a clock is needed. It also reduces the computational complexity because it need not accumulate the events and compare the accumulating value with the threshold.

2.2   Feature Representations

In this paper, pixel-wise BOE feature of spatiotemporal events is used to represent the motion segments. For the pixel-wise feature vector, the dimension is the number of the pixels of the AER images. In addition, we also apply the firing rate feature which counts the number of events on every pixel.

BOE [8] combines two measures of popularity and specificity. Let $X = \{x_1, x_2, \cdots, x_N\}$ be a collection of segments and $x_i = \{x_{i1}, x_{i2}, \cdots, x_{iM}\}$ is be the BOE feature vector, where N and M are the number of segments and the dimension of feature which is equal to the number of DVS pixels, respectively. Each segment x_i is represented by a joint probability distribution (JPD). The JPD can be represented mathematically as $x_i = p(e_1^i, e_2^i, \ldots, e_M^i)$. $p(e_j^i)$ is the event frequency of pixel j within the segment x_i. Event frequency is a kind of popularity measurement which assumes that the frequent events are important. In fact the frequent events are less discriminative at some times. As a speciality measurement, more weight is allocated to the infrequent events. The BOE can be represented as

$$x_{ij} = w_j p(e_j^i) \tag{1}$$

where w_j measures the speciality of e_j^i. Let n_j be the number of segments that contains e_j. The weight can be represented as

$$w_j = -\log \frac{N}{n_j} \tag{2}$$

Then by combining (1) and (2), BOE is defined as

$$x_{ij} = p(e_j^i) \log \frac{n_j}{N} \tag{3}$$

The speciality measurement w_j reflects the change in the amount of information after observing a specific event. By combining these two measurements, BOE features prove to be discriminative.

In addition, a Firing rate (FR) feature is also used to represent the segments. FR is calculated by counting the number of events of each pixel in a segment. For each segment, the firing rate feature is represented as $x = [c_1, c_2, \cdots, c_M]$, where c_j represent the firing rate of DVS pixel j in the segment.

2.3 Random Forest Classifier

For the given training set $\{X, C\}$, where $X \in R^{M \times N}$ is the input AER images with N samples, and C is the set of all classes for all the samples. K tree-structured classifiers $\{h_k(x, \Phi_k), k \cdots\}$ are generated in a RF classifier H. For the k-th tree in the forest, a random vector Φ_k is generated independently of the past random vectors $\Phi_1, \Phi_2, \cdots \Phi_{k-1}$ with the same distribution. A tree is grown using the training set and Φ_k, generating a classifier $h_k(x, \Phi_k)$. For a sample x, let $h_{k,l}(x)$ represent that x reaches the terminal node l in k-th tree. In the training process, the posterior probabilities $P(c|h_{k,l}(x))$ for each class $c \in C$ at each terminal node are found for each tree. The probabilities are calculated by the fraction of class c samples over all samples are assigned to terminal node l as

$$P(c|h_{k,l}(x)) = \frac{P(c, h_{k,l}(x))}{\sum_{c' \in C} P(c', h_{k,l}(x))} \tag{4}$$

For classification, a sample x is classified by considering the average of the probabilities $P(c|h_{k,l}(x))$:

$$H(x) = \arg\max_c \frac{1}{K} \sum_{k=1}^{K} P(c|h_{k,l}(x)). \tag{5}$$

The highest probability gives the class label of the x.

If the number of variables is M, m << M variables are selected at each node randomly out of the M to split the node. The value of m is a user-defined parameter and is held constant during the forest growing. The computational complexity of the algorithm can be reduced by limiting the number of the variables used for a split. In this paper, a selected such value is set to be the square root of the number of input variables [18]. Besides, the trees in RF are not pruned, which also reduces the computational complexity. Then, the RF classifier can handle high dimensional data. Breiman [16] shows that RF's computational time can be represented as aK$\sqrt{MN}$ log(N), where a is a constant.

Given the trees and training set drawn randomly from the distribution of the random vectors X, C, a margin function denoted as mg(.) is defined as

$$mg(X, C) = av_k I(h_k(X) = C) - \max_{j \neq C} av_k I(h_k(X) = j) \tag{6}$$

where I ($\bullet$) is the indicator function, and av_k represents average operation. The margin function measures how much the average number of votes at X, C for the right class exceeds the average vote for any other class.

3   Experiment and Discussion

In this section, we evaluate the RF method using two popular AER data sets in terms of classification accuracy and computation time cost. In addition, SVM is also used as a comparison to RF. SVM searches for the optimal separating hyper-plane that leaves the greatest margin between the two classes. The problem of maximizing the margin can be solved using Quadratic Programming optimization techniques. The data points which are termed as 'support vectors' and closest to the hyper-plane are used to measure the margin. Besides, kernel functions are often used to reduce the computational load of dealing with high dimensional feature space. The used RF classifier and SVM are based on a machine learning library [23]. The experiments were carried out on a PC with an Intel(R) Core(TM) i5-3317U-1.7 GHz CPU and 8-GB RAM.

3.1   Data Sets

Two DVS data sets were used to evaluate the proposed method, i.e., MNIST-DVS [9], human AER Posture [10]. The MNIST-DVS dataset has 10000 recording of spatiotemporal event streams which are captured from 10000 original 28 × 28 MNIST digit images. The chosen digit images were enlarged to three different scales (scale-4, scale-8, scale-16) by smoothing interpolation algorithms. The scaled images were displayed on a liquid crystal display with slow movements. A fixed AER DVS was used to capture the moving digit images. Because of the movement, noise, blur, and other factors, the MNIST-DVS is more challenging than the standard MNIST dataset. In this paper, we

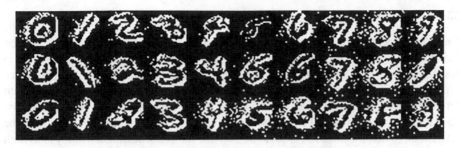

Fig. 2. Some reconstructed images from the used MNIST-DVS databases.

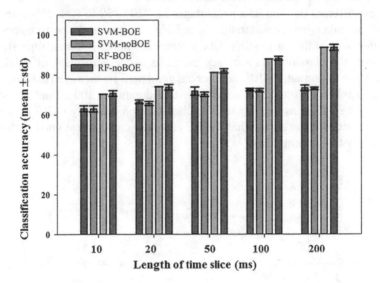

Fig. 3. Classification accuracy of RF classifier and SVM on the MNIST-DVS dataset with increasing length of time slice, where 90% samples are used for training.

only used the scale-4 DVS digit recordings (Fig. 2). Different time slices were used to detect the motion symbols. We evaluate five different durations, i.e., 10 ms, 20 ms, 50 ms, 100 ms, 200 ms, in our experiments. 90% were randomly selected as the training set and the others are used for testing. As expected, the classification accuracy increases when longer recordings are used.

The AER posture dataset was recorded by an AER image sensor. Three human actions, i.e., walking back and forth (WALK), bending to pick something (BEND), sitting down and standing up (SITSTAND) are contained in the dataset. The pixel array of the posture recording is 32×32. We randomly partition the data set into two parts, i.e., training set and testing set.

In the experiments, we randomly partition the data set into two parts for training and testing and repeat the experiment multiple times (e.g., 10 times) with different training and testing partitions. The mean accuracy is calculated as the classification accuracy.

3.2   Result and Discussion

Time slice and training data percentage. In this section, we compare the classification performance between RF classifier and SVM [21]. For the RF, 300 trees are grown in this experiment. The influence of length of the time slice to the recognition performance is considered. We compare the two classifiers on the two pixel-wise features with different length of time slice i.e., 10 ms, 20 ms, 50 ms, 100 ms, 200 ms. As Fig. 3 shows, the classification accuracy of RF classifier increases with the increasing duration of the time slices. When the duration is set to be 200 ms, the classification accuracy is as high as 93.08% which is state of art performance. Compared with SVM, RF classifier always has better performance under different time slices.

Besides, different training data percentages i.e., 20%, 30%, 40%, 50%, 60%, 70%, 80%, 90%, are taken into consideration as well. We evaluated the performance of the RF classifier with different training data percentages under different time slices. As Fig. 4 shows, the classification accuracy increases as the percentage of training data increases. More important, the RF classifier has good performance even the training data percentage is as low as 20%. For example, when the duration is 200 ms and 20% samples of data set are selected as training set, the classification accuracy of RF is as high as 89.62%. This experiment shows that the RF classifier can achieve good performance even with very few training data.

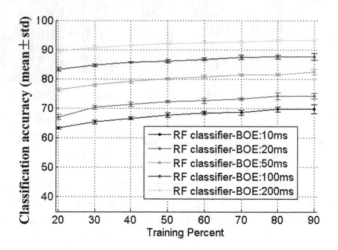

Fig. 4. Classification performance under different training data percentages.

From the result, we have three several observations. Firstly, the RF classifier can achieve good performance on the classification of spatiotemporal events. On both BOE feature and FR feature, the RF classifier show better performance than SVM classifier. Secondly, as the time slice or training data percentage increases, the classification accuracy of the RF classifier increases. Finally, the RF classifier method is robust to the training data percentage. While the training data percentage increases from 60% to 90%, the classification accuracy remains almost unchanged, slightly varying about 1.5%.

Computation time cost in training and classification. In this section, we compare the computation time cost in both the training process and the testing process. The RF and SVM are tested on the BOE feature. We choose different training data percentages i.e., 20%, 30%, 40%, 50%, 60%, 70%, 80%, 90%, as the hyper-parameter. In the RF, 300 trees are grown. We calculate the total training and testing time on the MINIST-DVS data set. As Fig. 5 shows, the training time of RF classifier is significantly reduced compared with SVM. For the computation time in classification, the time cost of RF is insignificant when compared with SVM as is shown in Fig. 6. As a matter of fact, SVM is computationally inefficient for huge data sets [22]. This experiment shows that the RF has the advantage of computation efficiency in both training and classification.

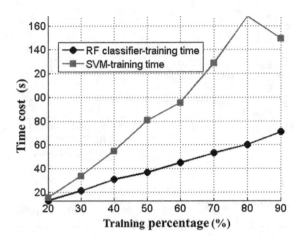

Fig. 5. Training time comparison between RF classifier and SVM under different training data percentages.

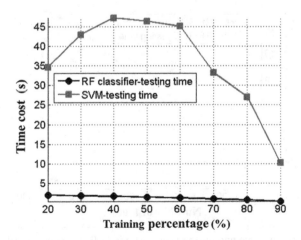

Fig. 6. Testing time comparison between RF classifier and SVM under different training data percentages.

Number of Trees in RF. The number of trees is an important parameter in RF which can influence the performance of the classifier. Different numbers of trees i.e., 50, 100, 200, 300, 400, 500, 600, 700, 800, 900, 1000, are considered in this paper. Figure 7 shows that the RF classifier is robust to the number of the trees. From 100 to 1000 trees in the forest, the classification accuracy fluctuates slightly with a range of about 1.5%. A relatively high accuracy can be achieved when the number of trees is set to be 500. But more trees will lead to more time cost in the training process and classification process as is shown in Fig. 8. Compared with computation time cost in testing, the time cost in training process is sensitive to the number of trees in RF. So the number of trees of RF is a trade-off between classification accuracy and computation efficiency.

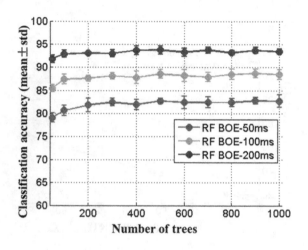

Fig. 7. Classification accuracy under different number of trees in RF.

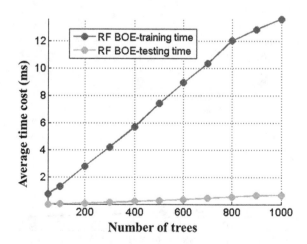

Fig. 8. Average training time and testing time cost per AER image under different numbers of trees in RF.

Table 1. Classification performance on the MNIST-DVS database.

Algorithms	Mean	std
RF classifier-BOE	**88.39 %**	1.54 %
RF classifier-FR	**88.26 %**	1.43 %
Peng's [8]	76.49 %	11.77 %
Zhao's [14]	75.52 %	11.17 %

Table 2. Recognition rate on the aer posture database. n denotes the number of segment

Algorithms	Mean	std	median	n
RF classifier-BOE	**98.90 %**	**0.21 %**	98.87 %	12000
RF classifier-FR	**98.82**	**0.24 %**	98.80 %	12000
Peng's [8]	98.66 %	0.23 %	98.65 %	24639
Zhao's [14]	95.61 %	0.46 %	95.50 %	17414

Comparison with the state of the art. We compare the RF classifier with two state of art methods, e.g., Peng's [8] and Zhao's [14]. Peng's method uses BOE feature and a linear support vector machine (SVM) as the classification system. Zhao's method extracts high-level features by passing Gabor features into the HMAX model and uses an event-driven tempotron classifier for classification. In our experiment, a RF classifier with 300 trees is used for the BOE feature. As the Tables 1 and 2 show, the proposed method achieves a good performance compared with state of art algorithms.

4   Conclusion

In this paper, RFs have been investigated for classification of spatiotemporal events streams, which is both a challenging and important classification problem in neuromorphic vision. We have demonstrated that combining RF classifier with pixel-wise features improves the recognition performance and reduces the training and testing time significantly as well, compared with the state of art algorithms by combining SVM classifier with BOE. In addition, RFs could overcome the over-fitting problem. Even with very few training data points, the RF algorithm also shows good performance. Furthermore, the RF classifier only requires two parameters to be set while the SVM classifier requires a number of user-defined parameters. The RFs also estimate the relative importance of different variables during the classification process which is of value for feature selection. The RF classifier can also be used for unsupervised learning for its capability for detecting outliers. With the combination of high classification accuracy and efficiency, the RF classifier is an ideal candidate for the recognition of neuromorphic vision.

References

1. Delbruck, T.: Frame-free dynamic digital vision. In: Proceedings of International Symposium on Secure-Life Electronics, Advanced Electronics for Quality Life and Society (2008)

2. Lichtsteiner, P., Posch, C., Delbruck, T.: A 128 × 128 120 dB 15 μs latency asynchronous temporal contrast vision sensor. IEEE J. Solid-State Circuits 43(2), 566–576 (2008)
3. Mahowald, M.: VLSI analogs of neuronal visual processing: a synthesis of form and function. California Institute of Technology (1992)
4. Lazzaro, J., Wawrzynek, J.: A multi-sender asynchronous extension to the AER protocol, pp. 158–171 (1995)
5. Conradt, J., Cook, M., Berner, R., et al.: A pencil balancing robot using a pair of AER dynamic vision sensors. In: 2009 IEEE International Symposium on Circuits and Systems, pp. 781–784. IEEE (2008)
6. Ni, Z., Pacoret, C., Benosman, R., et al.: Asynchronous event-based high speed vision for microparticle tracking. J. Microsc. 245(3), 236–244 (2012)
7. Ni, Z., Bolopion, A., Agnus, J., et al.: Asynchronous event-based visual shape tracking for stable haptic feedback in microrobotics. IEEE Trans. Robot. 28(5), 1081–1089 (2012)
8. Peng, X., Zhao, B., Yan, R., et al.: Bag of Events: an efficient probability-based feature extraction method for AER image sensors (2016)
9. Bichler, O., Querlioz, D., Thorpe, S.J., et al.: Extraction of temporally correlated features from dynamic vision sensors with spike-timing-dependent plasticity. Neural Netw. 32, 339–348 (2012)
10. Chen, S., Akselrod, P., Zhao, B., et al.: Efficient feedforward categorization of objects and human postures with address-event image sensors. IEEE Trans. Pattern Anal. Mach. Intell. 34(2), 302–314 (2012)
11. Pérez-Carrasco, J.A., Zhao, B., Serrano, C., et al.: Mapping from frame-driven to frame-free event-driven vision systems by low-rate rate coding and coincidence processing-application to Feedforward ConvNets. IEEE Trans. Pattern Anal. Mach. Intell. 35(11), 2706–2719 (2013)
12. O'Connor, P., Neil, D., Liu, S.C., et al.: Real-time classification and sensor fusion with a spiking deep belief network. Neuromorphic Eng. Syst. Appl., 61 (2015)
13. Serrano-Gotarredona, T., Linares-Barranco, B.: Poker-DVS and MNIST-DVS. Their history, how they were made, and other details. Front. Neurosci. 9, 1–10 (2015)
14. Zhao, B., Ding, R., Chen, S., Linares-Barranco, B., Tang, H.: Feedforward categorization on AER motion events using cortex-like features in a spiking neural network. IEEE Trans. Neural Netw. Learn. Syst. 26(9), 1963–1978 (2015)
15. Breiman, L.: Random forests. Mach. Learn. 40, 5–32 (2001)
16. Breiman, L.: RF/tools–A class of two eyed algorithms. In: SIAM Workshop (2013) http://oz.berkeley.edu/users/breiman/siamtalk2003.pdf
17. Liaw, A., Wiener, M.: Classification and regression by random forest. R News 2(3), 18–22 (2002)
18. Díaz-Uriarte, R., De Andres, S.A.: Gene selection and classification of microarray data using random forest. BMC Bioinform. (2006)
19. Bosch, A., Zisserman, A., Munoz, X.: Image classification using random forests and ferns. In: 2007 IEEE 11th International Conference on Computer Vision, pp. 1–8. IEEE (2007)
20. Schroff, F., Criminisi, A., Zisserman, A.: Object class segmentation using random forests. In: BMVC, pp. 1–10 (2008)
21. Sastry, P.: An introduction to support vector machines. Computing and Information Sciences: Recent Trends (2003)
22. Rogez, G., Rihan, J., Ramalingam, S., et al.: Randomized trees for human pose detection. In: IEEE Conference on Computer Vision and Pattern Recognition, CVPR 2008, pp. 1–8. IEEE (2008)
23. Pedregosa, F., et al.: Scikit-learn: machine learning in Python. JMLR 12, 2825–2830 (2011)

Visual Attention Model with a Novel Learning Strategy and Its Application to Target Detection from SAR Images

Fei Gao[1], Xiangshang Xue[1], Jun Wang[1(✉)], Jinping Sun[1],
Amir Hussain[2], and Erfu Yang[3]

[1] School of Electronic and Information Engineering, Beihang University,
Beijing 100191, China
{feigao2000, xuexiangshang}@163.com,
wangj203@buaa.edu.cn
[2] Cognitive Signal-Image and Control Processing Research Laboratory,
School of Natural Sciences, University of Stirling, Stirling FK9 4LA, UK
[3] Space Mechatronic Systems Technology Laboratory, Department of Design,
Manufacture and Engineering Management, University of Strathclyde,
Glasgow G1 1XJ, UK

Abstract. The selective visual attention mechanism in human visual system helps human to act efficiently when dealing with massive visual information. Over the last two decades, biologically inspired attention model has drawn lots of research attention and many models have been proposed. However, the top-down cues in human brain are still not fully understood, which makes top-down models not biologically plausible. This paper proposes an attention model containing both the bottom-up stage and top-down stage for the target detection from SAR (Synthetic Aperture Radar) images. The bottom-up stage is based on the biologically-inspired Itti model and is modified by taking fully into account the characteristic of SAR images. The top-down stage contains a novel learning strategy to make the full use of prior information. It is an extension of the bottom-up process and more biologically plausible. The experiments in this research aim to detect vehicles in different scenes to validate the proposed model by comparing with the well-known CFAR (constant false alarm rate) algorithm.

Keywords: Visual attention model · Object detection · Learning strategy · Synthetic Aperture Radar (SAR) images

This work was supported by the National Natural Science Foundation of China (61071139; 61471019; 61171122; 61501011), the Aeronautical Science Foundation of China (20142051022), the Pre-research Project (9140A07040515HK01009), the National Natural Science Foundation of China (NNSFC) under the RSE-NNSFC Joint Project (2012-2014) (61211130210) with Beihang University, and the RSE-NNSFC Joint Project (2012-2014) (61211130309) with Anhui University.

© Springer International Publishing AG 2016
C.-L. Liu et al. (Eds.): BICS 2016, LNAI 10023, pp. 149–160, 2016.
DOI: 10.1007/978-3-319-49685-6_14

1 Introduction

Human visual system possesses the astonishing ability to perceive the inputs from visual scenes. Whatever a visual scene is simple or complicated, humans can efficiently pick the most interesting part (weather it is free viewing or under the condition of a specific task), which is far beyond the development of the field of computer vision. Research has shown there are massive visual data (10^8–10^9 bits) entering the eyes every second [1]. Without the help of any effective mechanism, the real-time processing seems impossible. Luckily, there exists a localization ability called visual attention or selective attention which enables human to act effectively and precisely in complex environment. When dealing with a complex visual scene, humans tend to turn their attention to one or few more salient objects or areas, while ignoring those which are not salient enough.

As the human visual system has so much potentials, researchers began to model it into a mathematically computational system. Almost all the attention models can be dated back to the feature integration theory (FIT) proposed by Treisman and Gelade in 1980 [2]. This theory claims the visual input is first decomposed into a set of topographic feature maps and then feed in a bottom-up manner into a master map which depicts the local conspicuity of a visual scene. Koch and Ullman [3] then proposed a purely bottom-up model to combine the features and introduced the concept of saliency map [1]. But until 1998, the first fully implementation based on [3] was formally proposed by Itti and Koch [4]. The Itti model is believed to be biologically inspired because it imitates the early stages of human visual system [4]. Since then, this field has drawn lots of attention and various models have emerged. However, most of the existing visual attention models follow a basic framework of Itti's method to generate a topological saliency map. Indeed, attention is not merely caused by the visual scene's conspicuity, but other factors like knowledge, expectations, rewards and current goals also play important roles in the visual search, which is considered as a task-dependent top-down process [1]. Based on this phenomena, a lot of models combining both bottom-up cues and top-down cues have been proposed in recent years with specific application like car detection, face and pedestrian recognition and et al.

Top-down cues. Neurobiological and psychophysical evidences have shown that the top-down mechanisms exist in the human brain for visual processing [5, 6]. Although the top-down attention is essential and inevitable, the computational models for top-down attention are fewer than the bottom-up ones, because how prior knowledge influence attention is still not fully understood. The existing top-down models can be classified into two categories. One is related to combine the low-level features in a top-down manner. The revised guided search structure (GS2 model) is believed to be the earliest computational model proposed by Wolfe in 1996 [6, 7]. By maximizing the signal-to-noise ratio of the target versus the background, Navalpakkam and Itti [8] derived an optimal integration of bottom-up cues when detecting targets. Frintrop [9] proposed the VOCUS model with a top-down extension which includes a learning mode and a search mode. Armmanfard et al. [10] proposed a feature fusion technique which applied a weighted feature summation block whose weights are optimized by the genetic algorithm, instead of both across scale combination and normalization and linear combination block. In [11], Han et al. proposed a saliency map generated from the weighted features where the rough sets are used to assign the weights for every feature. But, the problem in the aforementioned work is that they don't make the full use of prior information, which matters a lot in the human brain. The other one involves the representation of the top-down cues using tools like conditional random field (CRF), fuzzy theory and et al. Tsotsos et al. proposed a hierarchical system and a new winner-takes-all (WTA) updating rule to match the current related knowledge [12]. In [13] there's a top-down model considering the visual memory which adopts a fuzzy adaptive resonance theory neural network with the learning function. Borji et al. [14] used evolutionary algorithms to search some parameters inside the basic saliency model as the top-down priors. Ban et al. [15] proposed a growing fuzzy topology adaptive resonance theory (GFTART) with two roles: one is to form the bottom-up features of arbitrary objects, and the other is to generate the top-down bias. Yang et al. [16] proposed a top-down saliency model that jointly learns a conditional random field (CRF) and a visual dictionary. The model has a three-layered structure from the bottom to the top: CRF, sparse coding, and a visual dictionary. Obviously, those methods are more mathematical rather than biologically plausible.

Application of visual attention. It is known that the visual information is interpreted in a need-manner in the brain to serve the task demands [17]. A lot of attention models can be put into one category of computer vision. Usually, these models are applied to detect or recognize targets like faces, cars, pedestrians and so on [1, 18–20] in the context of real-life visual scenes. But we want to address the application in the area of remote sensing in this work. The remote sensing images, for example, SAR images are quite different from the optical images due to the completely different mechanisms of imaging, it is not proper to directly apply the attention model to the SAR images. As a result, there is few research on understanding the remote sensing images using attention model.

In our paper, we propose a visual attention model specifically for the application of the vehicle targets detection from SAR images by integrating a bottom-up stage and a top-down stage. The bottom-up stage follows the procedure of the Itti model but with some simplification and modification in some aspects. The top-down stage also generates a saliency map similar to that in the bottom-up stage. During the top-down stage, two weighting parameters are learned from the training set to instruct how the feature maps are combined. A training set is used for two reasons: one is to get the best weighting coefficients for two conspicuity maps; the other one is to get targets' average length or size used as thresholds. The global saliency maps is then generated through the linear combination of bottom-up and top-down saliency maps. Finally, the detection result is acquired from the global saliency through binarization and thresholding processes.

2 Proposed Method

The proposed method has both the bottom-up and top-down computational process to mimic the human visual system. Our proposed method is based on the saliency map, which means that the computational process is restricted to generate saliency maps

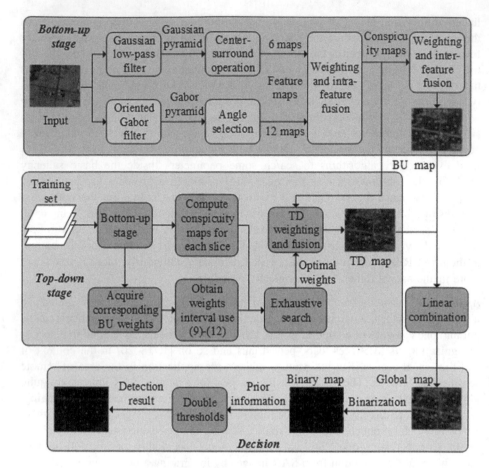

Fig. 1. Framework of the proposed method.

including a bottom-up saliency map, a top-down saliency map and a combined one. The framework of the proposed method is depicted in Fig. 1. The input is first processed by the bottom-up stage to generate a BU saliency map. Then after learning the optimal weights in the top-down stage, a TD saliency map is generated. At the decision stage, two saliency maps are combined into a single global map, and prior information are used as thresholds. The bottom-up saliency map is a modified version of Itti's and specifically tuned for SAR images. As for the top-down saliency map, it is generated from the intermediate bottom-up stage by applying a learning strategy. Then, the global map is computed from the two former saliency maps.

2.1   Bottom-up Attention

The bottom-up process in this paper is based on the well-known Itti model with some modifications in consideration of the characteristics of SAR images. For SAR images, there's no color information thus color channel in the Itti model can be ignored. Intensity and orientation channels are consistent with those in the Itti model, but possess some specific modifications. As can be seen from Fig. 1, the bottom-up saliency consists of a feature extraction stage, a weighting operation and a saliency map generating process. The detailed bottom-up saliency is described down below.

Feature Extraction

Intensity channel. For an intensity SAR image I, a five-scaled Gaussian pyramid is first created by applying a Gaussian filter and sub-sampling. The Gaussian image pyramid with five scales s_0–s_4 is further transformed into the feature maps by applying a center-surround operation. Unlike Itti's 9 scales, the image pyramid in our method has only 5 scales with almost the same function.

In Itti' model, the center-surround operation is implemented as the difference between the fine and coarse scales: the center is represented as scales $c \in \{2, 3, 4\}$, while the corresponding surround is at the scales $s = c + \delta$, where $\delta \in \{3, 4\}$. The across-scale difference is obtained by interpolating the coarse scale to the finer one and then point by point subtraction. However, we find that the operation has another alternative, and it needs only 5 scales. The detailed implantations are presented down below.

Step 1: Create five-scaled Gaussian pyramid I_σ, where $\sigma \in [0 \ldots 4]$ is the scale. The Gaussian low-pass filter is:

$$G(x, y, o) = \frac{1}{2\pi o^2} \exp(-\frac{x^2 + y^2}{2o^2}) \tag{1}$$

where x, y denote the coordinate of an arbitrary pixel and $o = 3$.

Step 2: Represent the surround of an arbitrary pixel.

For each pixel $I''_{\sigma=c}(x, y)$ in the center, its surround is represented as:

$$I''_{\sigma=c|\delta}(x, y) \frac{\sum (I_{s_i}(x - \delta, y - \delta) + \ldots I_{s_i}(x + \delta, y + \delta))}{\delta^2} \tag{2}$$

where $c \in \{2, 3, 4\}$ is the center, $\delta \in \{4, 8\}$ is the length of the side of neighborhood.

Step 3: Apply the center-surround operation and yield 6 feature maps $I''_{c,\delta}$.

The feature maps are defined as:

$$I''_{c,\delta} = I''_{\sigma=c} - I''_{\sigma=c|\delta} \tag{3}$$

Through these steps, 6 intensity maps are acquired and wait to be further processed.

Orientation channel. In SAR images, the targets for example vehicles are usually small, therefore the orientation information seems to matter only a little but still be indispensable. We accept the operation in [9] where only 5 scales are needed. The absence of the center-surround operation in orientation extraction is because the oriented center-surround difference is already determined implicitly by the Gabor filter

[9], and it can also prevent the images from getting blurred due to the center-surround mechanism. The oriented Gabor pyramid $O''_{\sigma,\theta}(x,y)$ is acquired by:

$$H(x,y,\sigma,\theta) = \frac{1}{\sigma^2}\exp(-\pi\frac{x^2+y^2}{\sigma^2})\{\exp[i2\pi(x\cos\theta + y\sin\theta)] - \exp(-\frac{\pi^2}{2})\} \quad (4)$$

where $\sigma \in \{2,3,4\}$ is the scale and $\theta \in \{0°,45°,90°,135°\}$ is the angle. Eventually, 12 raw orientation feature maps are yielded.

Weighting and normalization. After acquiring all the 6 intensity and 12 orientation feature maps, the feature maps should be normalized to the same scale and fused to form two conspicuity maps. In human visual systems, the fusion mechanism is quite complicated which is not clearly figured out even in a bottom up way let alone the high-level neural activity. Different features contribute differently to perceptual saliency [21] and the relevant feature fusion or weighting approaches are influenced by tasks, goals expectations et al. If the feature maps are combined in a purely straightforward way, they contribute equally [9]. To prevent this effect, we have to determine the most important maps and raise their influence. Therefore, a brand new weighting function is designed in this paper and somehow tested faithful. The weighting function is defined as:

$$W(X) = \frac{1}{\sqrt{2\pi}\sigma}e^{\frac{-(M-\overline{m})^2}{2\sigma^2}}\cdot\frac{\overline{m}}{\overline{r}}\cdot X \quad (5)$$

where M is the global maxima within a feature map, $\overline{m}$ is the expectation of local maxima, σ is the standard deviation of the feature map, $\overline{r}$ is the expectation of the rest of the feature map when taking out the local maxima.

$$I' = \bigoplus_{c,\delta} W(I''_{c,\delta}), \quad O' = \bigoplus_{\sigma,\theta} W(O''_{\sigma,\theta}) \quad (6)$$

where $\oplus$ indicates the point by point addition.

Bottom up saliency map. After acquiring the conspicuity map for each channel, the bottom-up saliency map is then computed by fusing the conspicuity maps together.

$$S_{BU} = W(I') + W(O') \quad (7)$$

Actually, saliency map is a topographic map which indicates the saliency or conspicuity of an area within the map.

2.2   Top-Down Attention

In SAR image with vehicle targets, even for human, it is very difficult to determine whether an object is a vehicle or not. Due to the mechanism of SAR imaging, the vehicles in SAR images are completely different with those in optical images, let alone the low-resolution of SAR images compared to optical images. But if observers are offered to watch some targets in advance, it then becomes very easy for observers to recognize it in a SAR scene. Apart from the vehicle's low-level characteristic like intensity and orientation, information like size, outline, texture play an important role in human's understanding process. So the use of this prior information provides a promising way to help detect vehicle targets.

In our proposed method, the top-down process is also based on the saliency map, but needs a learning process first.

Learning strategy. In the previous bottom-up saliency, two conspicuity maps are weighted and fused to generate the saliency map. But how can we know the weights computed from (5) are the perfect weights to generate the most accurate saliency map, what if there're other weights that outperform the former ones? The learning process is designed to make sure that the perfect weights are selected. Therefore, we need the following learning strategy.

The general process of the learning strategy is depicted in the middle of Fig. 1. A set of image slices with targets therein, is needed. For slice X_i, (i is the number of slices), two corresponding conspicuity maps I_i and O_i are computed with the afore-mentioned bottom-up stage. Instead of using the weighting function $W(\bullet)$ to form the saliency map, we obtain the most accurate weights by benchmarking the saliency maps generated from different weights. The F-measure is adopted to benchmark the most salient one. Below is the detailed steps.

Step 1: For each slice, compute the bottom-up weights of conspicuity maps: $w_{I\_i} = W(I_i'), w_{O\_i} = W(O_i')$;

Step 2: Determine the intervals of top-down weights $[w_{I\_min}, w_{I\_max}]$ and $[w_{O\_min}, w_{O\_max}]$. The interval is defined as:

$$w_{I\_min} = \min(w_{I\_i}) - \sigma_I, \ w_{I\_max} = \max(w_{I\_i}) + \sigma_I \tag{8}$$

$$w_{O\_min} = \min(w_{O\_i}) - \sigma_O, \ w_{O\_max} = \max(w_{O\_i}) + \sigma_O \tag{9}$$

where σ_I and σ_O are the standard deviation of w_{I_i} and w_{O_i}, respectively.

Step 3: Select 10 weights from every interval at a regular distance and compute 100 saliency maps for each target slice.

Step 4: Benchmark the 100 saliency maps and find the best one with its corresponding weights w_{I_i}' and w_{O_i}'. Here we use the Precision (P), Recall (R) and F-measure (F) as the benchmarks, defined as follows:

$$P = \sum (S \otimes A)/ \sum (S), \ R = \sum (S \otimes A)/ \sum (A) \tag{10}$$

$$F = \frac{(\alpha^2 + 1)P * R}{\alpha^2(P + R)} \tag{11}$$

where S is the saliency map, A is the segmentation map. Operator $\otimes$ is the point by point multiplication.

Step 5: The final weights are the means of the two set of weights.

$$w_I = mean(w'_{I\_i}), \; w_O = mean(w'_{O\_i}) \tag{12}$$

Top-down saliency map. After learning the weights, the top-down saliency map is generated from the two bottom-up conspicuity maps and the top-down weights.

$$S_{TD} = w_I \cdot I' + w_O \cdot O' \tag{13}$$

It should be noticed that, here we only compute the weights for the conspicuity maps. Actually, this approach is also suited to compute the weight for each raw feature map, but takes a lot of computing resource apparently.

2.3   Global Saliency Map and Decision

The global saliency map is then generated from the combination of the bottom-up and top-down maps. Parameter t determines how much the top-down process contribute to the global saliency map and it's usually set to 0.5.

$$S = S_{BU} + t * S_{TD} \tag{14}$$

Apart from the top-down weights learned from the target slices, the size and length of a specific type of vehicle also play important roles. In our model, the size represented by the number of pixels a vehicle possesses and the length used as two thresholds for the final decision stage. But first, we need to transform the saliency map to a binary map. Here we use the Ohtsu [22] method to create the threshold.

$$S_{bw}(x, y) = \begin{cases} 1 & S(x, y) > threshold \\ 0 & S(x, y) < threshold \end{cases} \tag{15}$$

For an arbitrary region in the binary map, it is determined whether it's a target or not by the size and length of the target.

$$R_i = \begin{cases} 1 & size \in [a, b] \& length \in [c, d] \\ 0 & size \notin [a, b] \| length \notin [c, d] \end{cases} \tag{16}$$

where R_i is the suspicious areas, 1 for target, 0 for not. The confidence intervals [a, b], [c, d] are computed from the segmentation maps in the learning stage.

3   Experiment

In this section, the experiments on the proposed method and the constant false alarm rate (CFAR) which is well an acknowledged method for SAR image detection in the literature are carried out. The result of the proposed method with only the bottom-up

 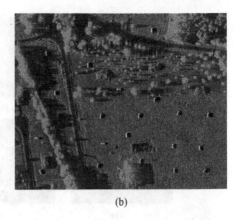

(a)   (b)

Fig. 2. SAR Images with 20 vehicles target inside. (a) Light cluttered SAR image; (b) Heavy cluttered SAR image.

process (is actually a modified Itti method, and is regarded as modified Itti hereafter) is also presented to demonstrate the effectiveness of our top-down strategy.

We picked up two cluttered image from the spotlight SAR images of ground vehicles in the moving and stationary target acquisition and recognition (MSTAR) database with the size of 1478×1784 pixels. Both images are added with 20 vehicles targets. One image has little distracters, whereas the other has much more. The images with the added targets are depicted in Fig. 2.

To evaluate the performance of the proposed method, we chose the Precision, Recall and F-measure as the benchmarks. They are defined as follows:

$$R = \frac{\text{Number of detected targets}}{\text{Total number of targets}}, \quad P = \frac{\text{Number of detected targets}}{\text{Number of detected units}} \quad (17)$$

$$F = \frac{(\alpha^2 + 1)P * R}{\alpha^2(P + R)} \quad (18)$$

Because of the learning strategy in the proposed method, a training set is needed. We selected 100 vehicle target slices from the MSTAR database as the training set. The training set is also used to determine the confidence interval mentioned in (16), calculated as [35.15, 46.40] and [420.30, 484.34] using (19). The interval [a, b] and [c, d] are defined as:

$$a = \overline{\mu_s} - \sigma_s, \, b = \overline{\mu_s} + \sigma_s$$
$$c = \overline{\mu_l} - \sigma_l, \, d = \overline{\mu_l} + \sigma_l \quad (19)$$

where $\overline{\mu_s}$ and $\overline{\mu_l}$ are the expectations of the size and length of each training target(the vehicle), σ_s and σ_l are the relevant standard deviations.

Figure 3 is the saliency maps of the two tested images. Top row are the saliency maps for the light cluttered image, bottom row is for the heavy cluttered one. From left

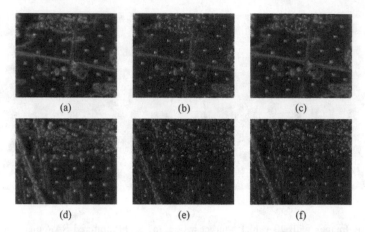

Fig. 3. Saliency maps for the tested SAR images.

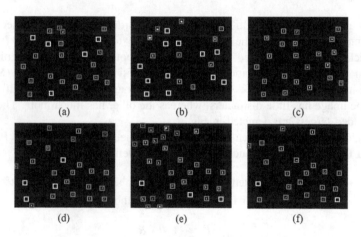

Fig. 4. Detection results from the tested images of the various methods.

to right, are the bottom-up maps, top-down and global maps respectively. Figure 4 depicts the detection results. Top row is for the light cluttered image and bottom row is for the other image. From left to right, the results of CFAR, modified Itti and the proposed method are depicted. The green rectangles mark the detected targets, while the red and white ones mark the false alarms and the undetected targets respectively.

From the light cluttered image, there are 2 false alarms generated and none undetected targets for the proposed method, whereas the CFAR has 5 targets undetected and generated 3 false alarms. As for the modified Itti method, the result seems unacceptable with 12 targets undetected and generated 2 false alarms.

When dealing with the heavy cluttered image, all the three methods didn't work as well as in the light cluttered one. But still, the proposed method outperforms the other two, with 2 false alarms and 2 undetected. CFAR generates 5 false alarms and misses 4 targets. The modified Itti method generates astonishing 11 false alarms and misses 3 targets.

Table 1. Quantitative measures obtained by various methods.

Methods	Image 1			Image 2		
	P	R	$F_{\alpha=1}$	P	R	$F_{\alpha=1}$
CFAR	83.33%	75.00%	78.95%	76.19%	80.00%	78.05%
Modified Itti	80.00%	40.00%	53.33%	60.71%	85.00%	70.83%
Proposed method	90.91%	100.0%	95.24%	90.00%	90.00%	90.00%

Table 1 shows the quantitative evaluation for the three methods. Taking into account the F-measure, the proposed method outperforms the CFAR method by 16.29% and 11.95% for the two images. And, the modified Itti method has 41.91% and 19.17% decreasing rates comparing with the proposed method for the two images which demonstrates the effectiveness of the top-down strategy.

4 Conclusion

In this paper a visual attention based approach has been presented for the underlying application in detecting targets from remote sensing images. The proposed method contains a bottom-up stage, which is a modified version of the Itti model, and specifically tuned for SAR images, as well as a top-down stage. The top-down process contains a novel time-consuming learning strategy, but it is a once-for-all job, because once the weights are learned it can be adapted to most of the scenes. The novelty of the method lies in the following three aspects. First, the brand new weighting function makes multi-target popping out possible. Second, the learning strategy selects the optimal weights from the training set. Last but not least, target's prior information like size and length are used as thresholds in the decision stage. Experiment results have demonstrated that the proposed method possesses greater ability in detecting vehicle targets in comparison with the CFAR. In addition, the results from the modified version of the original Itti method were presented, which were far inferior to that of the complete method, which further validated the effectiveness of the top-down strategy. However, the proposed method doesn't well in scenes where targets are covered with surroundings like trees and buildings, which will be an important issue in our future research work.

Though the proposed method was applied to the vehicle detection from SAR images, it can be adapted to other areas. For example, it can be potentially applied to detect other targets or applied to the optical images on fixation prediction. Our future work will explore these potentials by applying our method to other research fields.

References

1. Borji, A., Itti, L.: State-of-the-art in visual attention modeling. IEEE Trans. Pattern Anal. Mach. Intell. **35**, 185–207 (2013)
2. Treisman, A.M., Gelade, G.: A feature-integration theory of attention. Cogn. Psychol. **12**, 97–136 (1980)

3. Koch, C., Ullman, S.: Shifts in selective visual attention: towards the underlying neural circuitry. Hum. Neurobiol. **4**, 219–227 (1985)

4. Itti, L., Koch, C., Niebur, E.: A model of saliency-based visual attention for rapid scene analysis. IEEE Trans. Pattern Anal. Mach. Intell. **20**, 1254–1259 (1998)

5. Hopfinger, J.B., Buonocore, M.H., Mangun, G.R., Hopfinger, J.B., Buonocore, M.H., Mangun, G.R.: The neural mechanisms of top-down attentional control. Nat. Neurosci. **3**, 284–291 (2000)

6. Zhang, L., Lin, W.: Computational models for top-down visual attention. In: Selective Visual Attention: Computational Models and Applications, pp. 167–205. Wiley-IEEE Press (2013)

7. Wolfe, J.M.: Guided search 2.0 a revised model of visual search. Psychon. Bull. Rev. **1**, 202–238 (1994)

8. Navalpakkam, V., Itti, L.: An integrated model of top-down and bottom-up attention for optimizing detection speed. In: IEEE Computer Society Conference on Computer Vision and Pattern Recognition, CVPR 2006, pp. 2049–2056 (20116)

9. Frintrop, S.: VOCUS: A Visual Attention System for Object Detection and Goal-Directed Search. LNCS (LNAI), vol. 3899. Springer, Heidelberg (2006)

10. Armanfard, Z., Bahmani, H., Nasrabadi, A.M.: A novel feature fusion technique in saliency-based visual attention. In: International Conference on Advances in Computational Tools for Engineering Applications, ACTEA 2009, pp. 230–233 (2009)

11. Han, H., Tcheang, L., Walsh, V., Gao, X.: A novel feature combination methods for saliency-based visual attention. In: 2009 Fifth International Conference on Natural Computation, pp. 18–22 (2009)

12. Tsotsos, J.K., Culhane, S.M., Wai, W.Y.K., Lai, Y., Davis, N., Nuflo, F.: Modeling visual attention via selective tuning. Artif. Intell. **78**, 507–545 (1995)

13. Kim, B., Ban, S.W., Lee, M.: Growing fuzzy topology adaptive resonance theory models with a push–pull learning algorithm. Neurocomputing **74**, 646–655 (2011)

14. Borji, A., Ahmadabadi, M.N., Araabi, B.N.: Cost-sensitive learning of top-down modulation for attentional control. Mach. Vis. Appl. **22**, 61–76 (2011)

15. Sang-Woo, B., Bumhwi, K., Minho, L.: Top-down visual selective attention model combined with bottom-up saliency map for incremental object perception. In: The 2010 International Joint Conference on Neural Networks (IJCNN), pp. 1–8 (2010)

16. Yang, J., Yang, M.H.: Top-down visual saliency via joint CRF and dictionary learning. IEEE Trans. Pattern Anal. Mach. Intell. **PP**, 1 (2016)

17. Triesch, J., Ballard, D.H., Hayhoe, M.M., Sullivan, B.T.: What you see is what you need. IEEE Comput. Soc. **3**, 102 (2003)

18. Najemnik, J., Geisler, W.S.: Optimal eye movement strategies in visual search. Am. J. Ophthalmol. **434**, 387–391 (2005)

19. Felzenszwalb, P.F., Girshick, R.B., Mcallester, D., Ramanan, D.: Object detection with discriminatively trained part-based models. IEEE Trans. Pattern Anal. Mach. Intell. **32**, 1627–1645 (2010)

20. Viola, P., Jones, M.J.: Robust real-time face detection. Int. J. Comput. Vis. **57**, 137–154 (2004)

21. Itti, L., Koch, C.: Computational modelling of visual attention. Nat. Rev. Neurosci. **2**, 194–203 (2001)

22. Ohtsu, N.: A threshold selection method from gray-level histograms. IEEE Trans. Syst. Man Cybern. **9**, 62–66 (1979)

Modified Cat Swarm Optimization for Clustering

Saad Razzaq[1(✉)], Fahad Maqbool[1], and Amir Hussain[2,3]

[1] Department of Computer Science and Information Technology, University of Sargodha,
Sargodha, Pakistan
{saadrazzaq,fahadmaqbool}@uos.edu.pk
[2] Department of Computing Science and Maths, University of Stirling, Scotland, UK
[3] College of Computer Science and Engineering, Taibah University, Medina, Saudi Arabia
ahu@cs.stir.ac.uk

Abstract. Clustering is one of the most challenging optimization problems. Many Swarm Intelligence techniques including Ant Colony optimization (ACO), Particle Swarm Optimization (PSO), and Honey Bee Optimization (HBO) have been used to solve clustering. Cat Swarm Optimization (CSO) is one of the newly proposed heuristics in swarm intelligence, which is generated by observing the behavior of cats, and has been used for clustering and numerical function optimization. CSO based clustering is dependent on a pre-specified value of K i.e. Number of Clusters. In this paper we have proposed a "Modified Cat Swarm Optimization (MCSO)" heuristic to discover clusters based on the nature of data rather than user specified K. MCSO performs a data scan to determine the initial cluster centers. We have compared the results of MCSO with CSO to demonstrate the enhanced efficiency and accuracy of our proposed technique.

Keywords: Clustering · Cat Swarm Optimization · Swarm Intelligence

1 Introduction

This is a normal text. Through many years researchers have developed a lot of techniques to solve NP Hard problems. Due to the large solution set in such problems, it's hard to explore the complete solution space in reasonable (i.e. polynomial) time. Heuristics were developed for such problems. Heuristics provide good solutions in polynomial time while avoiding exhaustive search in solution space.

Traditional problem solving techniques requires clear understanding and formulation of the problem. The problem should be well defined, solvable in polynomial time, and well predictable. On the other hand, Swarm Intelligence (SI) techniques don't have a predefined path to solve the problem. SI systems emerge by interacting with each other and with the environment. So the individual behaviors as well as their interactions should be carefully modeled for the success of a SI system.

There are different swarm intelligence algorithm used for finding the solutions for optimization problems. Here is the brief description of them. Particle Swarm Optimization (PSO) was proposed by Kennedy and Eberhart used for solving optimization problems. PSO has been used in the training of neural network for the classification

© Springer International Publishing AG 2016
C.-L. Liu et al. (Eds.): BICS 2016, LNAI 10023, pp. 161–170, 2016.
DOI: 10.1007/978-3-319-49685-6_15

related problems. PSO algorithms can achieve global optimal solutions with high probability [1, 2].

Ant colony optimization (ACO) proposed by Dorgo [3]. It is a meta heuristic that is population-based and is used to find approximate solution for various hard and discrete optimization problems. Ant colony optimization mimics the behavior of ants. ACO has applications in communication networks and in the stochastic version of famous combinatorial optimization problem like TSP and JSSP [4].

Cat Swarm optimization (CSO) is used to solve optimization problems. CSO is based on cats behavior which itself is comprised of two behavior modes. It is consisted of two sub-models by replicating the cats' behavior. These are called "seeking mode" and "tracing mode". These two modes collectively improve CSO performance [5].

Swarm intelligence based algorithms are used for solving clustering problems and its applications in image processing, marketing, data mining and information retrieval. Recently, algorithm introduced by nature is being utilized for clustering. These algorithm have preferences in numerous perspectives, for example, self-association, adaptability, strength, no requirement of prior data, and decentralization [5].

Santosa et al. [6] used CSO for solving the clustering problem. There are three things which are used in CSO clustering: population of data, number of cluster k, and number of duplicate. The algorithm was used on four separate datasets: Iris, Soybean, Glass, and Balance Scale, taken from machine learning data repository. Clustering done through CSO has good accuracy over the clustering data with small number of clusters but having more computational time.

Sadeghi et al. used ACO for the finding the solution for clustering problems. In this model the number of ants and the quantity of clusters should be same. All data objects and ants area unit spread randomly on the grid. On a grid, data objects are represented in 2D-space. Each ant contains a load list that is initialized with a random object initially. Ants search the grid and take a look to gather the similar data in their load list. Result shown higher performance than k-means algorithm and the LF model of ant clustering. In comparison to k-mean's algorithm it doesn't fall in local minima. ACO is also having limitation on the number of clusters being informed in advance [7].

Karaboga et al. examined the implementation of Artificial Bee Colony (ABC) in resolving clustering problems [8]. The ABC performance is analyzed with Particle Swarm optimization algorithms and some other known clustering algorithms. Experimental results shown that ABC algorithm can be successfully used for clustering problems.

We have proposed a Modified Cat Swarm Optimization (MCSO) technique for clustering. The technique works in two steps. In the first step Cats discover the number of clusters and initial cluster centers. In the second step Cats improves the clusters to get the optimal centroids.

Orouskhani et al. presented the improved Cat Swarm optimization. They added an adaptive inertia weight to velocity update equation in order to facilitate the global and local search ability. They also used an adaptive formula for updating the acceleration coefficient. Experimental results showed that improved CSO performed well against different bench mark datasets [9].

Sharafi et al. presented a new algorithm based on Cat Swarm optimization. Binary Cat Swarm optimization (BCSO) is a binary version of CSO generated by observing the behaviors of cats. As in CSO, BCSO consists of 2 modes of operation: tracing mode and seeking mode. The distinction between the BCSO and CSO is that the parameters of BCSO will take the values of zero and one, this makes the algorithm entirely distinction. Binary Cat Swarm optimization (BCSO) is implemented on a number of Benchmark issues and zero-one knapsack problem. The result reflects BCSO outperforms BPSO and GA in accuracy and speed of convergence [10].

2 Preliminaries

Here are some of the basic concepts

2.1 Seeking Memory Pool (SMP)

SMP is used to describe the range of seeking memory for every cat. SMP decides the neighborhood that a cat can explore in it surrounding. Higher SMP means more neighbors to explore.

2.2 Seeking Range of Selected Dimension (SRD)

SRD declares the mutative ratio for the selected dimensions. In seeking mode, if a dimension is selected to mutate, the difference between the new value and the old one will not be out of the range.

2.3 Sum of Squared Error (SSE)/Objective Function

Sum of Squared Error is calculated using Eq. 1 given below. Objective of clustering is to get minimum SSE value by choosing optimal centroids.

$$SSE = \sum_{l=1}^{K} \sum_{j=1}^{N} \left\| x_j - m_i \right\|^2 \tag{1}$$

Here x_j represents the data points available. m_i represents the cluster center to which the data point belongs.

2.4 Cluster Membership (CM)

Cluster Membership (CM) is used to check if a new data point x' has the potential to be part of an existing cluster C' having N' data points. x_c and x_e belongs to the cluster C'. CM can be calculated using Eq. 2.

$$CM = \frac{N'x\left|SMP_{x'} \cap SMP_{x_c}\right|}{\left|SMP_{x_e} \cap SMP_{x_c}\right|} \tag{2}$$

The numerator of the fraction finds the common neighbors in SMP of x' and SMP of cluster data points. While the denominator finds the common neighbors between SMP of the Cluster's data points.

3   Modified Cat Swarm Optimization (MCSO) for Clustering

MCSO for clustering comprises of two steps. In first step cats look for the initial cluster centroids while in the second step cats work to improve the clusters and reduces cluster error. Both of the steps are discussed in detail in the following sub sections.

3.1   Initial Cluster Centroid

In the first step cats are initialized randomly to some data points. Each of these data points will be a separate cluster initially. The number of cats should be sufficiently large. Cats find the SMP of the current data point by looking all the data points that are within SRD range. These neighboring data points would become the SMP of the current data point. Each data point will have varying number of elements in SMP. For each element in SMP we will check Cluster membership. If Cluster Membership satisfies a certain threshold then that SMP element will become the part of the cluster. Figure 1 shows the algorithm.

---

1. Initialize M cats. Assign each cat c_m to a random object o_p
2. Each of these random object o_p would be considered as a cluster C_p at the start.
3. Find the objects N_m within SRD range from c_m. N_m would act as the SMP of o_m and also known as the neighborhood of o_m
4. Add objects of N_m to E, which is the set of objects to be explored.
5. Remove each o_i in E
   a. Find the objects N_i within SRD range from c_i
   b. Add objects of N_i to E
   c. If CM value is greater than threshold then add $_{oi}$ to the cluster C_p
6. Calculate Centroid for each cluster C_p

Fig. 1. First pass to find initial cluster centroids

3.2   Cluster Optimization

In this second step we reinitialize the cats. Cats work very similar to the CSO [6]. Few cats work in seeking mode while rest of the cats work in the tracing mode (Fig. 2).

Second pass to optimize clusters

1. Group Data into clusters by their closeness with cluster center and calculate SSE.
2. Initialize seeking mode parameters: SMP, SRD, SPC
3. For i=1 to K Centroids   /* SEEKING MODE*/
   a. Create m copies of Centroid i to create SMP
   b. For j=1 to m SMP
      i. Calculate   shifting   value $SV_{i,j}$ (SRD*$Centroid_i$)
      ii. Create a new Centroid $SMP_{i,j}$ by randomly adding or subtracting $Centroid_i$ from $SV_{i,j}$
      iii. Use $SMP_{i,j}$ in place of $Centroid_i$ and calculate SSE
   c. Use roulette wheel selection to select a centroid from $SMP_{i,j}$
   d. If seeking SSE is better than initial SSE then use new centroid
4. For i=1 to K Centroids   /* TRACING MODE*/
   a. Update Velocity of $Centroid_i$
   b. Update position to get new Centroid C_i^t
5. Calculate SSE based on new Centroids C_i^t
6. If tracing SSE is better than earlier SSE then use new Centroids C_i^t
7. Display best Cluster Centroids along with SSE

Fig. 2.   Second pass improves the clusters and reduces SSE.

In this phase each cat randomly chooses either seeking or tracing mode. In seeking mode each cat looks around new positions for being new potential centroid. If any of the new point is better in reducing SSE value then cat moves to the new point. The movement replaces the old centroid with new centroid. In case the new point doesn't improves SSE, then cat rejects the new points and there is no change in SSE. Tracing mode help avoid getting stuck in local optima. Tracing cat may look for far away points in search of a better centroid, hence improving SSE value.

4   Experiments

In this section experimental results of Modified Cat Swarm Optimization for solving clustering problem is discussed. We also compared the results with Cat Swarm optimization for the same dataset.

We have used two datasets for clustering optimization taken from UCI [11]. The Iris data set contains 150 instances, 04 attributes 3 classes of 50 instances each, where each class refers to a type of iris plant. Balance scale data set contains the 625 instances, 04 attributes and three classes.

The experiment are carried out by using 125 different combinations of values of parameters. There are 3 parameters that affect the algorithm execution i.e. SMP having values (2, 4, 6, 8, and 10), SRD values(0.2, 0.4, 0.6, 0.8, and 0.9) and C set values (0.1, 0.3, 0.5,0.7, 0.9).

Firstly we shows the results of balance scale data set according to SRD and SMP. Figures 3 and 4 shows the results calculated by CSO and MCSO respectively.

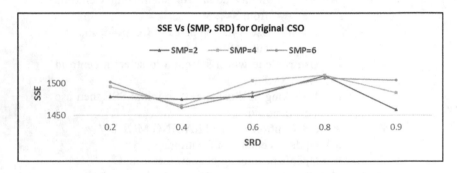

Fig. 3.   SSE compared to SRD at different SMP in CSO (BalanceSc)

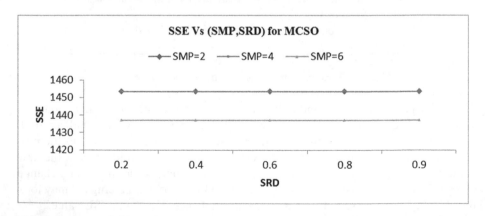

Fig. 4.   SSE compared to SRD at different SMP in MCSO (BalanceSc)

Figure 3 shows that when we increase the value of SRD it also increase the SSE. Against different values of SMP, there is varying effect on SSE.

In MCSO there is no effect on SSE while we change the SRD but, SSE gets effected by changing values of SMP from 2 to 4. SSE will remain same for the SMP 4 and 6.

Figures 5 and 6 shows the time comparison of CSO and MCSO for SRD parameter.

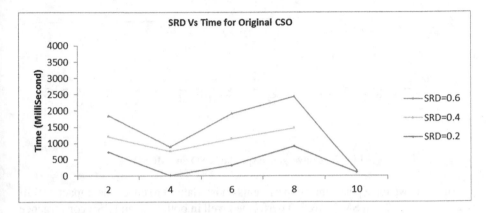

Fig. 5. Time consumed in CSO at varying SMP & SRD (BalanceSc)

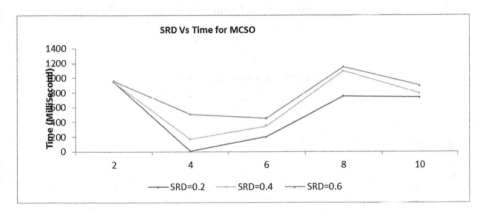

Fig. 6. Time consumed in MCSO at varying SMP & SRD (BalanceSc)

Figure 6 shows that MCSO take less time as compared to CSO for balance scale dataset. We also performed comparison for SMP parameter against time, but due to space limitations unable to present here.

Figure 7 shows the comparison for the SSE against the number of iterations for both CSO and MCSO. Results reflect that MCSO generates lower values of SSE against the performed iterations.

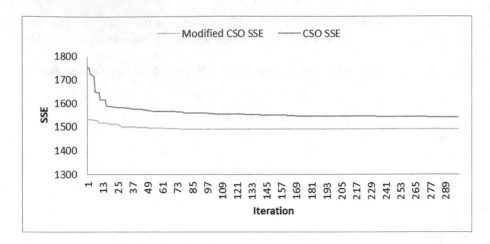

Fig. 7. Convergence speed of CSO and MCSO

Similarly we have performed experiments on iris dataset to check the impact of SSE by changing SRD and SMP. MCSO performed well in both time and SSE convergence as comparison as compared to CSO.

Figures 8 and 9 reflects the time comparison against SMP for CSO and MCSO. Results show that MCSO performs well in finding the cluster solution as compared to CSO.

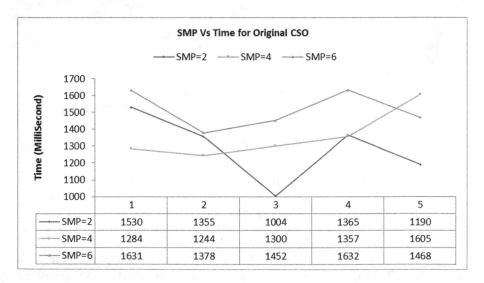

Fig. 8. Time consumed in CSO at varying SMP and SRD

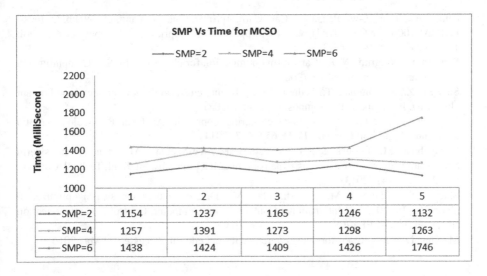

Fig. 9. Time consumed in MCSO at varying SMP and SRD

5   Conclusion

In this study, we present a variation of CSO, Modified Cat Swarm Optimization, through modeling the behaviors of cat to solve the optimization problems. We have adapted MCSO algorithm for solving the problem of clustering. We tested our methodology on two real life data sets i.e. (iris, and balance scale). We tried different values of SMP, SRD and C and study the results. We also note the effect of number of iterations on our methodology. From our results we concluded that Higher or lower values of SMP has no effect on clustering errors. In earlier iterations there is a quick reduction in clustering error which reduces gradually as the number of iteration increases. On average there is less clustering error for lower values of SRD and SMP. While for higher values of SMP this does not holds true. Results also reflect that MCSO is more effective in reducing the SSE as compared to CSO.

References

1. Eberhart, R., Kennedy, J.: A new optimizer using particle swarm theory. In: proceedings of the Sixth International Symposium on Micro machine Human Science, pp. 39–43. IEEE Press (1995)
2. Kennedy, J., Eberhart, R.: Particle swarm optimization. In: Proceedings of IEEE International Conference on Neural Networks, pp. 1942–1948 (1995)
3. Dorigo, M., Gambardella, L.M.: Ant colony system: a cooperative learning approach to the traveling salesman problem. IEEE Trans. Evol. Comput. **1**, 53–66 (1997)
4. Chu, S.C., Roddick, J.F., Pan, J.S.: Ant colony system with communication strategies. Inf. Sci. **167**, 63–76 (2004)

5. Chu, S.-C., Tsai, P.-w., Pan, J.-S.: Cat swarm optimization. In: Yang, Q., Webb, G. (eds.) PRICAI 2006. LNCS (LNAI), vol. 4099, pp. 854–858. Springer, Heidelberg (2006). doi: 10.1007/978-3-540-36668-3_94

6. Santosa, B., Ningrum, M.K.: Cat swarm optimization for clustering. In: Soft Computing and Pattern Recognition, pp. 54–59 (2009)

7. Sadeghi, Z., Mohammad, T., Pedram, M.M.: K-ants clustering-a new strategy based on ant clustering. In: Scope of the Symposium, p. 45 (2008)

8. Karaboga, D., Ozturk, C.: A novel clustering approach: Artificial Bee Colony (ABC) algorithm. Appl. Soft Comput. 11(1), 652–657 (2011)

9. Orouskhani, M., Orouskhani, Y., Mansouri, M., Teshnehlab, M.: A novel cat swarm optimization algorithm for unconstrained optimization problems. Int. J. Inf. Technol. Comput. Sci. 5(11), 32–41 (2013)

10. Sharafi, Y., Khanesar, M.A., Teshnehlab, M.: Discrete binary cat swarm optimization algorithm. In: 2013 3rd International Conference on Computer, Control & Communication (IC4), pp. 1–6. IEEE (2013)

11. Machine Learning Repository. https://archive.ics.uci.edu/ml. Accessed 24 May 2016

Deep and Sparse Learning in Speech and Language Processing: An Overview

Dong Wang[1,2(✉)], Qiang Zhou[1,2], and Amir Hussain[3]

[1] CSLT, RIIT, Tsinghua University, Beijing 100084, China
wangdong99@mails.tsinghua.eud.cn, zq-lxd@mail.tsinghua.edu.cn
[2] Tsinghua National Lab for Information Science and Technology, Beijing, China
[3] University of Stirling, Scotland FK9 4LA, UK
hussain.doctor@gmail.com

Abstract. Large-scale deep neural models, e.g., deep neural networks (DNN) and recurrent neural networks (RNN), have demonstrated significant success in solving various challenging tasks of speech and language processing (SLP), including speech recognition, speech synthesis, document classification and question answering. This growing impact corroborates the neurobiological evidence concerning the presence of layer-wise deep processing in the human brain. On the other hand, sparse coding representation has also gained similar success in SLP, particularly in signal processing, demonstrating sparsity as another important neurobiological characteristic. Recently, research in these two directions is leading to increasing cross-fertilisation of ideas, thus a unified Sparse Deep or Deep Sparse learning framework warrants much attention. This paper aims to provide an overview of growing interest in this unified framework, and also outlines future research possibilities in this multi-disciplinary area.

Keywords: Deep learning · Sparse coding · Speech processing · Language processing

1 Introduction

How the human brain processes information so effectively and efficiently is a long-standing mystery. Although still far from a full understanding, physiological studies seem to support two hypotheses: a sparse coding scheme that can represent information succinctly, redundantly and robustly, and a layer-wise hierarchical processing pipeline, gradually forming high-level abstraction with clear and rich semantic meaning [43,51]. This section summarizes findings from research on mammal neural systems, relating to sparse and hierarchical characteristics, and will then review the machine learning research inspired by each. Finally we will discuss the concept of combining these two characteristics.

1.1 Sparsity and Hierarchy in the Brain

The sparse information representation in the human brain has been recognized by researchers for a long time [4,17,46]. By scrutinizing cellular recordings physiologists found that neurons represent external stimuli in a rather sparse way.

© Springer International Publishing AG 2016
C.-L. Liu et al. (Eds.): BICS 2016, LNAI 10023, pp. 171–183, 2016.
DOI: 10.1007/978-3-319-49685-6_16

Specifically, many stimuli may activate the same neuron, and each stimulus is represented by only a few neurons [43]. This suggests a sparse coding scheme in our brain, where each stimulus is represented by a distribution of the activity it triggers over the neurons, and the number of activated neurons is small. In other words, stimuli are represented by *sparse codes* in our brain.

The layer-wised hierarchical structure, or the deep architecture, is another basic assumption for the neural system since early research on connectionist models [16]. The key advantage of this architecture is that high-level abstraction can be learned layer-by-layer. The high-level abstraction is assumed to be a key ingredient in perception and cognition [60]. Interestingly, the mammal brain was found to be organized in a deep architecture [51], where a given input is processed at multiple levels, and each level corresponds to a different area of cortex.

1.2   Sparsity and Hierarchy in Machine Learning

Both sparse representations and hierarchical architectures have attracted much attention in machine learning and artificial intelligence (AI) research. On the sparse coding part, researchers usually cast the sparse coding problem to a constrained optimization problem for over-complete linear equations, and developed numerous optimization approaches to solve the problem.

On the hierarchical architecture part, researchers in machine learning have demonstrated the brilliant success of deep learning methods over the past decade. A key point of deep learning is the layer-wised information processing within the hierarchical architecture [7], for example the deep neural network (DNN) and its convolutional and recurrent variants, i.e., convolutional neural networks (CNN) and recurrent neural networks (RNN). Deep learning has delivered remarkable performance on numerous machine learning tasks, including speech processing [5, 13, 14, 40, 73] and language processing [11]. A high-level summary was recently published in Nature [29], and more details can be found in the review papers written by Bengio [6, 7].

1.3   Deep Sparse or Sparse Deep Models?

Both sparsity and hierarchy are important properties of the brain and play fundamental roles in perception, cognition and other functions that comprise human intelligence. An interesting question is: How these two properties are integrated together to support these fundamental functions? A simple picture is that sparse coding provides efficient and robust codes, while the hierarchical architecture offers a constrained structure where the sparse codes are processed. Although not fully confirmed by physiological studies, machine learning researchers are investigating in this direction and have achieved some promising results, e.g., [21, 28, 32, 34, 50]. In this paper, we give a quick review for the recent development of deep *and* sparse models, and describe some applications of this new technique in speech and language processing. Note that the sparse models we are concerned with are not limited to sparse coding, but any models with sparsity regularization. Additionally, we distinguish deep sparse models and sparse deep models: the former refers to sparse models that are stacked to form a deep structure, while the later refers to deep models (usually neural networks) that involve sparsity regularization. Our review covers both categories, but sparse deep models are clearly dominant at present.

The paper is organized as follows: Sect. 2 describes sparse deep models, and Sect. 3 describes deep sparse models. Their application in speech and language processing is presented in Sect. 4, and some ideas for future research are presented in Sect. 5.

2   Sparse Deep Models

Sparse deep models refer to deep models (e.g., DNNs) that involve certain sparsity regularization. This regularization can be applied to various components of the deep model, e.g., units, weights, or gradients. It is often in the form of sparsity-oriented norms (e.g., ℓ-0 or ℓ-1), as well as special activation functions (e.g., rectifier) and some pre-training procedure.

2.1   Unit Sparsity by Norms

The deep model with unit sparsity is closely related to sparse coding, and can be regarded as a deep and non-linear extension to the conversional sparse coding model. The most straightforward way to produce sparse units is to impose certain sparse-oriented norms on the hidden units and add the norms into the objective function. Although ℓ-0 is the most ideal, l-1 is used more often due to its smoothness. For example, Olshausen et al. [46] used ℓ-1 to generate sparse units to model activities of the retina in mammals [28]. Another commonly used sparse-oriented regularization is the ℓ-1/ℓ-2 norm, which often leads to group sparsity [33,37].

An early work from Ranzato and colleagues [49] employed a sparse regularization in the form $\sum_i^M log(1 + z_i^2)$ on the hidden units when training deep encoder-decoding models, where z_i is the nonlinear-transformed activation of the i-th hidden unit, and M is the number of hidden units. The main purpose of this sparsity regularization was to limit the input space where the energy surface has a low value, which is a cheap approximation to the partition function and leads to an efficient training algorithm for deep models.

Another work presented by Lee et al. [31] imposed sparsity regularization when training RBMs, where the sparsity regularization was defined as follows:

$$\sum_{j=1}^n |p - \frac{1}{m} \sum_{l=1}^m \mathbb{E}[h_j^{(l)}|\mathbf{v}^{(l)}]|^2$$

where $\mathbf{v}^{(l)}$ represents the observed variables of the l-th example, $h_j^{(l)}$ denotes the j-th hidden variable of the l-th example. The authors found that the sparse RBM components can be stacked to form a sparse deep belief net (DBN). Particularly, they found a two-layer sparse DBN can model the cell receptive fields of the visual area V1 and V2. Note that similar sparsity regularization was also employed in the discriminative or semi-supervised RBM framework, as proposed by Larochelle et al. [28].

Luo et al. [37] proposed to use the $\ell 1/\ell 2$ mix norm to yield sparse units in RBMs. This norm is formulated as follows:

$$\sum_k \sqrt{\sum_{m \in G_k} P(h_m = 1|x^{(l)})^2}$$

where G_k is the k-th group of the hidden units. It can be seen that the regularization on the groups is ℓ-1, while the regularization on the hidden units (within a particular group) is ℓ-2. This leads to group-level sparsity, while keeping the firing probability of the units within one group equally small. The authors stacked the group-level sparse RMBs to construct sparse deep Boltzmann machines (DBMs). Experiments on letter recognition tasks with the MNIST and OCR databases confirmed that the sparse DBM can learn reasonable hierarchical features and provide good pre-training for DNNs. The ℓ-1/ℓ-2 norm was also used by Li et al. [33] to construct deep stacking networks (DSN). Experiments conducted on image classification confirmed the efficiency of their model.

The popular ℓ-1 regularization is equal to a Laplace prior distribution over the hidden units. Another sparsity-oriented prior is the spike-and-slab prior recently proposed by Goodfellow et al. [20]. Experiments on image pattern learning and classification tasks demonstrated that this prior can lead to better sparse representations.

2.2 Unit Sparsity by Activation Functions

The second approach to deriving sparse units is through special activation functions. Perhaps the most popular sparsity-deriving activation function is the rectifier function $g(x) = max(0, x)$, which suppresses the negative part of the activation to zero. Interestingly, this function was found to resemble the true activation function of human neurons, according to the leaky integrate-and-fire (LIF) model [15]. Xaiver et al. [18] presented an empirical study for deep neural networks with the rectifier activation function and found several merits associated with this function, particularly that the training is much easier, as the segment linearity of this activation avoids the notorious gradient vanishing and explosion problem. They found that with the rectifier activation, competitive performance can be obtained even without pre-training.

Poultney et al. [48] studied another sparse-oriented activation function called 'sparsifying logistic'. They found that with this type of activation function, simple and complex cell receptive fields can be derived, leading to a topographic layout of the filters, which is reminiscent of the topographic maps found in area V1 of the visual cortex.

Another sparse-oriented activation function called 'win-take-all' was proposed by Makhzani et al. [39]. This function applies to the convolutional layers of a CNN model and retains the largest activation while setting others to zero.

This approach was tested on the MNIST image classification task and obtained competitive performance.

2.3   Unit Sparsity by Pre-training

Recently, Li et al. [32] presented an interesting analysis and showed that various pre-training methods lead to sparse units, where the sparsity is measured by the ℓ-1 norm. They identified a sufficient condition and demonstrated theoretically and empirically that if the condition is satisfied, some popular pre-training approaches lead to sparse hidden units, including the pre-training methods based on denoising auto-encoders (DAEs) and RMBs. They also argued that pre-training improves DNN training because of the sparsenes. This argument seems to explain why pre-training is less important for DNNs with the rectifier activation function: the units have been sufficiently sparse already with this type of activation function so the sparsity contributed by the pre-training is less useful.

2.4   Weight Sparsity and Pruning

The sparsity regularization can also be applied to weights. This is not directly related to sparse coding, but it does help to learn prominent patterns, and can significantly reduce redundant parameters. This reduction of parameters leads to improved efficiency in terms of both statistics and computation.

Weight decay [27] and the variants (e.g., [52]) employ ℓ-2 norm to encourage weights of small values, while a true sparsity-oriented regularization is based on the ℓ-1 norm [34]. Connection pruning is a more efficient process for obtaining weight sparsity. The simplest pruning approach is to remove connections with small weights [74]; a more sophisticated approach considers the impact of the removal on the cost function, e.g., the optimal brain damage (OBD) method [12, 35]. The primary advantage of the pruning approach is that it can yield very compact models. For example, it was reported by Liu et al. [35] that 90% of connections can be removed with a 1.5% frame accuracy reduction in a speech recognition task. A particular problem with the compact model is that on modern CPUs the operations on sparse matrices are generally much slower than the operations on dense matrices. Recently, Liu et al. [34] presented an interesting approach that can speed up sparse matrix multiplication.

2.5   Gradient Sparsity

Another interesting approach related to sparse deep neural models is the contractive auto-encoder (CAE) proposed by Rifai et al. [50]. In this, the Frobenius norm of the Jacobian of the hidden units is used as a regularization. This 'contraction' penalty is imposed on the gradients and ensures robustness against minor change in the input. This is related to sparse coding, since if the activation function is sigmoid, the contraction penalty tends to drive the hidden unit activations to either zero or one where the gradient is zero.

Alain et al. [1] showed that the DAE model [61] is closely related to the CAE model, except that the contractive penalty for DAE is imposed on the Jacobian of the output units. Arpit et al. [2] presented a further study and showed that under certain conditions, deep neural models encourage sparse representations. Some popular models including DAE and CAE satisfy these conditions and therefore tend to produce sparse representations.

3   Deep Sparse Models

The sparse deep models described in the previous section focus on deep neural models with sparse regularization. In contrast, deep sparse models focus on sparse models, whilst borrowing the idea of hierarchical processing from deep learning and constructing multi-level sparse models.

For example, Yu et al. [75] presented a two-level sparse coding approach. In the first layer, sparse codes are derived from raw bits of an input image. Covariance matrices of the sparse codes are then computed for neighbouring patches. The second-level sparse codes are then derived from the diagonal vectors of the covariance matrices. These set-level codes are used as features for image classification. By using two-level sparse coding, features are extracted in a hierarchical way, leading to additional abstraction that can represent features of a larger scope.

He et al. [21] presented a similar multi-layer sparse coding framework. An innovation is that each sparse coding component is followed by a dense code conversion layer. This framework ensures that higher-level features cover larger scopes of the input than lower-level features, and the neighboring patches are placed close to each other in the dense code space. The entire framework is purely supervised. After the feature learning, a classifier is trained to conduct object recognition.

An interesting work presented by Kavukcuoglu [24,25] employs neural models to learn sparse codes. This predicted sparse decomposition (PSD) method is much more efficient at run-time and inherits most of the advantages of the conventional sparse coding method.

4   Application in Speech and Language Processing

Both sparse coding and deep learning have been widely employed in speech and language processing, however thorough investigation of deep sparse or sparse deep models is still limited. We start by summarizing the work in sparse coding and deep learning, and then present some recent studies which combine these two models.

Sparse Coding. Sparse coding has been widely employed in a wide range of speech processing tasks, including but not limited to speech coding [26,44], speech enhancement [38,53,68], source separation [45,70], music coding, classification and retrieval [8,42,47], speech recognition [54,62,63,66,67], overlap detection [64], voice activity detection [59], and sound localization [3].

Sparse coding is also applied to language processing. For example, Zhu et al. [79] presented a sparse topic model by introducing ℓ-1 regularization on both the document and word representations. This was later extended to an online version [77]. Note that sparse topic models can be extended to a hierarchical structure [79]. The probabilistic formulation was later changed to a non-probabilistic formulation that can effectively control the sparsity [77]. The idea of sparse topic models was also presented in [69], where ℓ-1 regularization was introduced to the conventional latent semantic analysis (LSA). Recently, Liu et al. [36] presented a document summary approach using two-level sparse representation.

The application of sparse coding in language processing is far from extensive, when compared to speech processing. A particular reason is that the vanilla sparse coding approach assumes a Gaussian residual, whereas language processing often uses discrete representations that are generally not Gaussian distributed. To solve this problem, Lee [30] extended the conventional Gaussian sparse coding to an exponential family sparse coding. This approach was successfully applied to text classification.

Deep Learning. Deep learning has obtained exceptional results in both speech and language processing, including speech recognition [13,73], speech synthesis [76], speech enhancement [71,78], speech separation [22], language modeling [41], semantic parsing [9], paraphrase detection [56], machine translation [10], and sentiment prediction [57]. There are numerous papers on deep learning methods for speech and language processing. Readers are referred to the recent book from Goodfellow et al. [19] and the deep learning website http://deeplearning.net.

Deep and Parse Models. Just very recently, deep sparse or sparse deep models were employed in speech and language processing. For example, Sivaram et al. [55] proposed a regularization in the form $log(1 + v^2)$ in DNN model training, where v is the activation of the unit to regularize. This regularization, is equivalent to a student-t prior on v, was found to deliver better performance in phone recognition [55]. Yogatam [72] introduced a hierarchical group sparse regularization to derive sparse word vectors. They reported better performance with the group-sparsity in a text classification task. Sun et al. [58] proposed an ℓ-1 regularized word embedding algorithm and found that sparsity leads to better performance on a bunch of analogy tasks, and the resulting embedding is more expressive and interpretable. Vyas et al. [65] recently presented a sparse bilingual word representation approach for cross-lingual lexical entailment, i.e., detect whether the meaning of a word in one language can be inferred from the meaning of a word in another language.

It should be emphasized that the studies mentioned are just a part of the contemporary work towards deep sparse and sparse deep learning. There may be some interesting research missed in our review, but generally the work in this direction is rather limited.

5   Conclusions and Future Directions

We gave a quick review of sparse and deep learning methods in machine learning. Both approaches can find strong physiological support and have demonstrated success in a wide range of machine learning tasks. It has been commonly adopted that sparse models can learn prominent patterns and are highly robust due to the redundancy in the code. Deep learning, on the other hand, has an advantage as it can learn high-level abstraction, which is more invariant and transferable across conditions and domains.

A particularly interesting question is how sparsity and hierarchy interact and complement each other to support the complex functions of human brains. It seems natural to believe that sparse coding plays the role of robust information representation, while the hierarchical structure plays the role of knowledge deduction and induction. However, how the two ingredients are integrated in a biological neural system and the mechanism driving hierarchical sparse information processing is far from known and requires further investigation.

Although the physiological mechanism remains unclear for machine learning researchers, pioneering work has been conducted in several groups, with the aim to leverage the respective advantages of deep and sparse models, as discussed in our paper. Interestingly, these studies demonstrate that both sparse deep models and deep sparse models are highly promising: in the former case, sparse regularizations encourage more plausible local patterns, while in the later case, deep structures yield large-scope representations.

It seems that most of the successful deep and sparse research resides in the unsupervised learning paradigm, e.g., with (stacked) RBMs or DAEs. Investigations into how the patterns can be learned with explicit supervision seem interesting and can be demonstrated in a semi-supervised framework, as shown in Larochelle's work [28]. Additionally, it is reasonable to hypothesize that different types of sparse regularization may contribute to the neural system in different but collaborative ways. For example, it is possible that the code sparsity and weight sparsity collaborate together to determine the characteristics of the human neural system. More investigation should be conducted on the impact of multiple sparse regularizations. Another interesting question is how sparsity functions differently at different layers in a deep structure. It is known that in deep neural models, the responses at high-level layers are more sparse than at low-level layers. This sparsity is mainly attributed to the layer-wised information disentanglement [7]. It is then interesting to know if sparse coding still contributes to form representations at high levels. If the answer is 'yes', the challenge is to understand how the sparsity is derived from the two forces, i.e., sparse-oriented regularization and the nature of high-level abstraction.

We also reviewed some papers on speech and language processing that employ deep sparse or sparse deep models. For speech processing, there are numerous studies on both sparse and deep models, however we didn't find much literature combining the two techniques. It is common practice for speech researchers to try ℓ-1 or ℓ-2 regularization when training deep neural models, but little work treats sparse representations seriously in the deep architecture. For language processing, neither sparse nor deep models were widely studied until very recently. One reason is that traditional language processing methods focus on symbolic representations, e.g., words, phrases, tags. These representations are discrete and are not amiable to both sparse and deep models. Thanks to the embedding technique, continuous representations (e.g., word vectors) have become popular, which in turn have motivated the investigation and application of deep and sparse learning in language processing, as already discussed in the paper.

We expect that more interesting findings will be obtained for speech and language processing, through novel combinations of sparse and deep models. In the past, researchers hoped to learn acoustic or semantic patterns by either sparse coding or deep learning, and both directions seem fruitful, e.g., [8, 23]. However, knowledge is still limited on how the patterns learned by the two very different methods differ from each other and which approach delivers more 'plausible' patterns. Importantly, can we combine the two approaches together to better learn patterns? If we accept the argument that the two mechanisms function in a collaborative way in our brain, then we posit exploiting them in a unified framework to decipher the complex information in human speech and language, as our brain seamlessly does every day.

Acknowledgments. This research was supported by the RSE-NSFC joint project (No. 61411130162), the National Science Foundation of China (NSFC) under the project No. 61371136, the UK Engineering and Physical Sciences Research Council Grant (EPSRC) Grant No. EP/M026981/1, and the MESTDC PhD Foundation Project No. 20130002120011. It is also supported by Huilan Ltd., Tongfang Corp., and FreeNeb.

References

1. Alain, G., Bengio, Y.: What regularized auto-encoders learn from the data-generating distribution. J. Mach. Learn. Res. **15**(1), 3563–3593 (2014)
2. Arpit, D., Zhou, Y., Ngo, H., Govindaraju, V.: Why regularized auto-encoders learn sparse representation? arXiv preprint arXiv:1505.05561 (2015)
3. Asaei, A., Taghizadeh, M.J., Haghighatshoar, S., Raj, B., Bourlard, H., Cevher, V.: Binary sparse coding of convolutive mixtures for sound localization and separation via spatialization. IEEE Trans. Signal Proces. **64**(3), 567–579 (2016)
4. Barlow, H.: Single units and sensation: a neuron doctrine for perceptual psychology? Perception **1**, 371–394 (1972)
5. Benesty, J.: Springer Handbook of Speech Processing. Springer, Heidelberg (2008)
6. Bengio, Y.: Learning deep architectures for AI. Found. Trends® in Mach. Learn. **2**(1), 1–127 (2009)
7. Bengio, Y.: Deep learning of representations for unsupervised and transfer learning. In: ICML Unsupervised and Transfer Learning (2012)
8. Blumensath, T., Davies, M.: Sparse and shift-invariant representations of music. IEEE Trans. Audio Speech Lang. Proces. **14**(1), 50–57 (2006)
9. Bordes, A., Glorot, X., Weston, J.: Joint learning of words and meaning representations for open-text semantic parsing. In: International Conference on Artificial Intelligence and Statistics (2012)

10. Cho, K., Merrienboer, B.V., Gulcehre, C., Bahdanau, D., Bougares, F., Schwenk, H., Bengio, Y.: Learning phrase representations using RNN encoder-decoder for statistical machine translation. Computer Science (2014)
11. Collobert, R., Weston, J.: A unified architecture for natural language processing: deep neural networks with multitask learning. In: Proceedings of the 25th International Conference on Machine Learning, pp. 160–167. ACM (2008)
12. Cun, Y.L., Denker, J.S., Solla, S.A.: Optimal brain damage. In: Proceedings of NIPS 1990 (1990)
13. Dahl, G.E., Yu, D., Deng, L., Acero, A.: Large vocabulary continuous speech recognition with context-dependent DBN-HMMs. In: Proceedings of IEEE International Conference on Acoustics, Speech and Signal Processing (ICASSP), pp. 4688–4691 (2011)
14. Dahl, G.E., Yu, D., Deng, L., Acero, A.: Context-dependent pre-trained deep neural networks for large-vocabulary speech recognition. IEEE Trans. Audio Speech Lang. Proces. **20**(1), 30–42 (2012)
15. Dayan, P., Abbott, L.F.: Theoretical Neuroscience: Computational and Mathematical Modeling of Neural Systems. MIT press, Cambridge (2001)
16. Fahlman, S.E., Hinton, G.E.: Connectionist architectures for artificial intelligence. Computer **20**(1), 100–109 (1987). (United States)
17. Földiák, P., Young, M.P.: Sparse coding in the primate cortex. In: The Handbook of Brain Theory and Neural Networks, vol. 1, pp. 1064–1068 (1995)
18. Glorot, X., Bordes, A., Bengio, Y.: Deep sparse rectifier neural networks. In: Proceedings of the 14th International Conference on Artificial Intelligence and Statistics (AISTATS), pp. 315–323 (2011)
19. Goodfellow, I., Bengio, Y., Courville, A.: Deep learning (2016). http://www.deeplearningbook.org. Book in preparation for MIT Press
20. Goodfellow, I., Courville, A., Bengio, Y.: Large-scale feature learning with spike-and-slab sparse coding. In: International Conference on Machine Learning, pp. 1439–1446 (2012)
21. He, Y., Kavukcuoglu, K., Wang, Y., Szlam, A., Qi, Y.: Unsupervised feature learning by deep sparse coding. arXiv preprint arXiv:1312.5783 (2013)
22. Huang, P., Kim, M., Hasegawajohnson, M., Smaragdis, P.: Deep learning for monaural speech separation. In: ICASSP 2014 (2014)
23. Jaitly, N.: Exploring deep learning methods for discovering features in speech signals. Ph.D. thesis, University of Toronto (2014)
24. Kavukcuoglu, K., Fergus, R., LeCun, Y., et al.: Learning invariant features through topographic filter maps. In: IEEE Conference on Computer Vision and Pattern Recognition, CVPR 2009, pp. 1605–1612. IEEE (2009)
25. Kavukcuoglu, K., Ranzato, M., LeCun, Y.: Fast inference in sparse coding algorithms with applications to object recognition. arXiv preprint arXiv:1010.3467 (2010)
26. Klein, D.J., König, P., Körding, K.P.: Sparse spectrotemporal coding of sounds. EURASIP J. Adv. Signal Proces. **2003**(7), 1–9 (2003)
27. Krogh, A., Hertz, J.A.: A simple weight decay can improve generalization. Adv. Neural Inf. Process. Syst. (NIPS) **4**, 950–957 (1992)
28. Larochelle, H., Bengio, Y.: Classification using discriminative restricted Boltzmann machines. In: Proceedings of the 25th International Conference on Machine Learning, pp. 536–543. ACM (2008)
29. LeCun, Y., Bengio, Y., Hinton, G.: Deep learning. Nature **521**(7553), 436–444 (2015)

30. Lee, H.: Unsupervised feature learning via sparse hierarchical representations. Ph.D. thesis, Stanford University (2010)
31. Lee, H., Ekanadham, C., Ng, A.Y.: Sparse deep belief net model for visual area V2. In: Advances in Neural Information Processing Systems, pp. 873–880 (2008)
32. Li, J., Zhang, T., Luo, W., Yang, J., Yuan, X.T., Zhang, J.: Sparseness analysis in the pretraining of deep neural networks. IEEE Trans. Neural Netw. Learn. Syst. **PP**(99), 1–14 (2016)
33. Li, J., Chang, H., Yang, J.: Sparse deep stacking network for image classification. arXiv preprint arXiv:1501.00777 (2015)
34. Liu, B., Wang, M., Foroosh, H., Tappen, M., Pensky, M.: Sparse convolutional neural networks. In: Proceedings of the IEEE Conference on Computer Vision and Pattern Recognition, pp. 806–814 (2015)
35. Liu, C., Zhang, Z., Wang, D.: Pruning deep neural networks by optimal brain damage. In: Interspeech 2014 (2014)
36. Liu, H., Yu, H., Deng, Z.: Multi-document summarization based on two-level sparse representation model. In: National Conference on Artificial Intelligence (2015)
37. Luo, H., Shen, R., Niu, C.: Sparse group restricted Boltzmann machines. arXiv preprint arXiv:1008.4988 (2010)
38. Luo, Y., Bao, G., Xu, Y., Ye, Z.: Supervised monaural speech enhancement using complementary joint sparse representations. IEEE Signal Process. Lett. **23**(2), 237–241 (2016)
39. Makhzani, A., Frey, B.: A winner-take-all method for training sparse convolutional autoencoders. In: NIPS Deep Learning Workshop (2014)
40. Martin, J.H., Jurafsky, D.: Speech and Language Processing. International Edition (2000)
41. Mikolov, T.: Statistical language models based on neural networks. Ph.D. thesis, Brno University of Technology (2012)
42. Nam, J., Herrera, J., Slaney, M., Smith, J.O.: Learning sparse feature representations for music annotation and retrieval. In: ISMIR, pp. 565–570 (2012)
43. Northoff, G.: Unlocking the Brain. Coding, vol. 1. Oxford, New York (2014)
44. Ogrady, P.D., Pearlmutter, B.A.: Discovering speech phones using convolutive nonnegative matrix factorisation with a sparseness constraint. Neurocomputing **72**(1), 88–101 (2008)
45. O'Grady, P.D., Pearlmutter, B.A., Rickard, S.T.: Survey of sparse and non-sparse methods in source separation. Int. J. Imaging Syst. Technol. **15**(1), 18–33 (2005)
46. Olshausen, B.A., Field, D.J.: Sparse coding with an overcomplete basis set: a strategy employed by V1? Vis. Res. **37**(23), 3311–3325 (1997)
47. Plumbley, M.D., Blumensath, T., Daudet, L., Gribonval, R., Davies, M.E.: Sparse representations in audio and music: from coding to source separation. Proc. IEEE **98**(6), 995–1005 (2010)
48. Poultney, C., Chopra, S., Cun, Y.L., et al.: Efficient learning of sparse representations with an energy-based model. In: Advances in Neural Information Processing Systems, pp. 1137–1144 (2006)
49. Ranzato, M.A., Boureau, Y.L., Cun, Y.L.: Sparse feature learning for deep belief networks. In: Platt, J.C., Koller, D., Singer, Y., Roweis, S.T. (eds.) Advances in Neural Information Processing Systems, vol. 20, pp. 1185–1192. Curran Associates, Inc. (2008). http://papers.nips.cc/paper/3363-sparse-feature-learning-for-deep-belief-networks.pdf
50. Rifai, S., Vincent, P., Muller, X., Glorot, X., Bengio, Y.: Contractive autoencoders: explicit invariance during feature extraction. In: International Conference on Machine Learning (2011)

51. Serre, T., Kreiman, G., Kouh, M., Cadieu, C., Knoblich, U., Poggio, T.: A quantitative theory of immediate visual recognition. Prog. Brain Res. **165**, 33–56 (2007)
52. Setiono, R.: A penalty function approach for prunning feedforward neural networks. Neural Comput. **9**(1), 185–204 (1994)
53. Sigg, C.D., Dikk, T., Buhmann, J.M.: Speech enhancement with sparse coding in learned dictionaries. In: 2010 IEEE International Conference on Acoustics, Speech and Signal Processing, pp. 4758–4761. IEEE (2010)
54. Sivaram, G., Nemala, S.K., Elhilali, M., Tran, T.D., Hermansky, H.: Sparse coding for speech recognition. In: 2010 IEEE International Conference on Acoustics, Speech and Signal Processing, pp. 4346–4349, March 2010
55. Sivaram, G.S., Hermansky, H.: Multilayer perceptron with sparse hidden outputs for phoneme recognition. In: 2011 IEEE International Conference on Acoustics, Speech and Signal Processing (ICASSP), pp. 5336–5339. IEEE (2011)
56. Socher, R., Huang, E.H., Pennington, J., Ng, A.Y., Manning, C.D.: Dynamic pooling and unfolding recursive autoencoders for paraphrase detection. Adv. Neural Inf. Process. Syst. **24**, 801–809 (2011)
57. Socher, R., Pennington, J., Huang, E.H., Ng, A.Y., Manning, C.D.: Semi-supervised recursive autoencoders for predicting sentiment distributions. In: Conference on Empirical Methods in Natural Language Processing, EMNLP 2011, 27–31 July 2011, John Mcintyre Conference Centre, Edinburgh, A Meeting of Sigdat, A Special Interest Group of the ACL, pp. 151–161 (2011)
58. Sun, F., Guo, J., Lan, Y., Xu, J., Cheng, X.: Sparse word embeddings using $\ell 1$ regularized online learning. In: IJCAI 2016, pp. 2915–2921 (2016)
59. Teng, P., Jia, Y.: Voice activity detection using convolutive non-negative sparse coding. In: 2013 IEEE International Conference on Acoustics, Speech and Signal Processing, pp. 7373–7377. IEEE (2013)
60. Utgoff, P.E., Stracuzzi, D.J.: Many-layered learning. Neural Comput. **14**(10), 2497–2529 (2002)
61. Vincent, P., Larochelle, H., Lajoie, I., Bengio, Y., Manzagol, P.A.: Stacked denoising autoencoders: learning useful representations in a deep network with a local denoising criterion. J. Mach. Learn. Res. **11**(Dec), 3371–3408 (2010)
62. Vinyals, O., Deng, L.: Are sparse representations rich enough for acoustic modeling? In: INTERSPEECH, pp. 2570–2573 (2012)
63. Vipperla, R., Bozonnet, S., Wang, D., Evans, N.: Robust speech recognition in multi-source noise environments using convolutive non-negative matrix factorization. In: Proceedings of CHiME, pp. 74–79 (2011)
64. Vipperla, R., Geiger, J.T., Bozonnet, S., Wang, D., Evans, N., Schuller, B., Rigoll, G.: Speech overlap detection and attribution using convolutive non-negative sparse coding. In: 2012 IEEE International Conference on Acoustics, Speech and Signal Processing (ICASSP), pp. 4181–4184. IEEE (2012)
65. Vyas, Y., Carpuat, M.: Sparse bilingual word representations for cross-lingual lexical entailment. In: NAACL 2016, pp. 1187–1197 (2016)
66. Wang, D., Tejedor, J.: Heterogeneous convolutive non-negative sparse coding. In: INTERSPEECH, pp. 2150–2153 (2012)
67. Wang, D., Vipperla, R., Evans, N., Zheng, T.F.: Online non-negative convolutive pattern learning for speech signals. IEEE Trans. Signal Process. **61**(1), 44–56 (2013)
68. Wang, D., Vipperla, R., Evans, N.W.: Online pattern learning for non-negative convolutive sparse coding. In: INTERSPEECH, pp. 65–68 (2011)

69. Wu, C., Yang, H., Zhu, J., Zhang, J., King, I., Lyu, M.R.: Sparse Poisson coding for high dimensional document clustering. In: IEEE International Conference on Big Data (2013)
70. Xu, T., Wang, W., Dai, W.: Sparse coding with adaptive dictionary learning for underdetermined blind speech separation. Speech Commun. **55**(3), 432–450 (2013)
71. Xu, Y., Du, J., Dai, L., Lee, C.: A regression approach to speech enhancement based on deep neural networks. IEEE Trans. Audio Speech Lang. Process. **23**(1), 7–19 (2015)
72. Yogatama, D.: Sparse models of natural language text. Ph.D. thesis, Carnegie Mellon University (2015)
73. Yu, D., Deng, L.: Automatic Speech Recognition: A Deep Learning Approach. Springer, London (2014). Incorporated
74. Yu, D., Seide, F., Li, G., Deng, L.: Exploiting sparseness in deep neural networks for large vocabulary speech recognition. In: Proceedings of ICASSP 2012 (2012)
75. Yu, K., Lin, Y., Lafferty, J.: Learning image representations from the pixel level via hierarchical sparse coding. In: 2011 IEEE Conference on Computer Vision and Pattern Recognition (CVPR), pp. 1713–1720. IEEE (2011)
76. Zen, H., Senior, A.W., Schuster, M.: Statistical parametric speech synthesis using deep neural networks. In: ICASSP2013 (2013)
77. Zhang, A., Zhu, J., Zhang, B.: Sparse online topic models. In: WWW 2013 (2013)
78. Zhao, M., Wang, D., Zhang, Z., Zhang, X.: Music removal by denoising autoencoder in speech recognition. In: APSIPA 2015 (2015)
79. Zhu, J., Xing, E.P: Sparse topical coding. In: UAI 2012 (2012)

Time-Course EEG Spectrum Evidence for Music Key Perception and Emotional Effects

Hongjian Bo[1], Haifeng Li[1(✉)], Lin Ma[1], and Bo Yu[1,2]

[1] School of Computer Science and Technology, Harbin Institute of Technology, Harbin, China
{bohongjian,lihaifeng}@hit.edu.cn
[2] Software College, Harbin University of Science and Technology, Harbin, China

Abstract. Being one of the most direct expressions of human feelings, music becomes the best tool for investigating the relationship between emotion and cognition. This paper investigated the long-term spectrum evidence of electroencephalogram (EEG) activities elicited by music keys. The EEG signals were recorded in 21 healthy adults during the entire process of music listening. There were two major music episodes and two minor ones, each lasted two minutes. Considering the spectral characteristics: (1) During two minutes of music listening, the alpha band activities recovered rapidly, which were more obvious under major music; (2) while, in the high-frequency gamma band, the activities declined gradually which were more obvious under minor music. Taken together, these results give clear evidence for the time-course difference in the music key perception.

Keywords: Time-course analysis · Music key perception · Electroencephalogram · Affective computing · Brain-computer interaction

1 Introduction

For centuries, music is one of the most infectious expressions of human feelings and emotions. The relation between tempo, mode, and emotional responses during music listening has been investigated for decades [1]. It is believed that music is the best tool for investigating the relationship between emotion and cognition. While music is widely understood to evoke an emotional response in the listener, the neural mechanism correlates are not yet fully explored.

Recently, the research on brain mechanism of music-evoked emotion has become a hot issue in the fields of cognitive neuroscience and psychology. Being familiar to western listeners, western music has two main classifications: the major and minor keys (melodies), which indicate the scale of a given composition is derived [2]. Early on 1935, a clear emotional discrimination has consistently been found at the behavioral level for listening major to minor keys [3]. Music using a major key tends to be perceived as relatively happy, or bright, whereas music using a minor key tends to be perceived as sad, or dark. It is believed that the organization of pitch intervals is the main difference between major and minor keys [4].

With the help of electromagnetic techniques, such as electroencephalography (EEG), magnetoencephalography (MEG) and functional magnetic resonance imaging (fMRI), the influence of music keys on the brain activities and the neural pathway have been studied. The changes of brain activities have been elicited by music in limbic brain structures known to be involved in emotional processing [5,6]. Both of musicians and nonmusicians had the ability to discriminate major and minor keys [7]. An fMRI study using natural continuous music found that minor melodies were evaluated as sadder than major melodies [8]. Moreover, brain responses to short discrete sounds have been studied intensively using the event-related potential (ERP) method, in which the EEG signals were divided into epochs time-locked to stimuli of interest. The study [9] indicated that the processes of underlying mismatch negativity (MMN) were able to make discriminations between major and minor keys. Poikonen and his partners [10] developed a novel paradigm based on ERP method in the research of neural correlates of continuous natural stimuli. The key of music was believed as the most important factor in emotion elicitation [11]. The study in 2014 [12] also indicated that the spectral power of EEG could be used in interpreting music-induced emotion. Also, human emotional states have a strong effect on their cognitive process. Menon and Levitin [13] reported that listening to pleasant music strongly modulated reward-processing networks.

Most of the previous studies focus on understanding the neural processing of separated artificial music clips designed to suit to the specification of each particular experiment. Although EEG has been used to study processing of emotional states in music, it remains unclear whether all of EEG bands are specific to music key perception during the entire process of music listening. Thus, this study investigates three questions: (a) How do different brain regions react to music key perception? (b) How can the electrophysiological basis of EEG band spectrum of music key perception be measured? and (c) whether the difference of EEG band spectrum (SP) could be elicited by the major and minor keys during the entire process of music listening?

In this study, we aim at uncovering stable relationships between different electrophysiological brain activities evoked by real musical stimuli. An experimental paradigm has been created to reveal music-evoked brain responses from continuous musical pieces. The neural correlates of music keys and evoked emotions have been examined. A time-course EEG spectrum analysis method has been investigated. The results of this study on brain activity patterns of emotional states could allow us to interpret and predict human emotional states. Research on music-evoked emotion perception could not only improve our understanding of the theoretical description of harmonic music but also offer us a window into the neural mechanism of the emotions.

2   Experiment Design

In this part, the stimuli have been given firstly and then an experimental paradigm has been created to reveal music-induced brain responses from continuous musical pieces.

2.1   Participants

Twenty-one healthy nonmusicians right-handed Chinese adults (nine females) took part in this study. The mean age was 24.5 years and ranged between 22 and 28 years. Participants had not received any professional training in music and had no auditory or visual impairments. An informed consent was signed by each participant before the EEG experiment, and participants were compensated after testing.

2.2   Materials

The stimuli used in the experiment were selected in two steps. First, we selected two typical major music episodes and two typical minor music episodes, which were all piano sonata and recorded from commercially available CDs. Then, an about two minutes highlight part was intercepted manually for each music episode (Table 1).

Table 1. The selected music list.

Name of music episode	Tone category	Pianist
Beethoven No.15, op.28 'pastorale'	in D major	Paavali Jumppanen
Beethoven No.17, Op.31 No.2 'Tempest'	in D minor	Stefano Ligoratti
Mozart K576 Sonata	in D major	Samuil Feinberg
Mozart: Fantasia K397	in D minor	Claudio Arrau

2.3   Procedure

Each subject was asked to sit in an armchair, throughout the duration of the experiment, in a quiet room at shaded daylight. Before the experiment, each participant signed a consent form and filled out a questionnaire. Then, they were given a set of instructions of the experiment protocol and the meaning of the different scales used for self-assessment. The discrete 9-point Self-Assessment-Manikin (SAM) Scales was used for rating valence, arousal and dominance [14]. The valence scale ranged from sad to happy. The arousal scale ranged from calm to excited. The dominance scale ranged from submissive to dominant. After the sensors had been placed and their signals had been checked, the participants performed a practice trial to familiar themselves with the system. There were four trials and each of them included three steps:

(a) A 15 s of the spontaneous recording;
(b) The 2 min of the music clips, during which central visual fixation was requested to reduce eyes movement;
(c) At the end of each trial, participants performed a self-assessment of valence, arousal and dominant.

For the presentation of the stimuli, the Presentation software by Neurobehavioral Systems was used.

2.4 Data Acquisition

The EEG signals were continuously recorded by a 64-channel EEG system (Neuroscan Synamp2 Amplifier) with electrode impedances less than $10\,k\Omega$ and a sampling rate of 512 Hz. An ElectroCap with 64 Ag/AgCl electrodes was used, which used the international 10–20 system and referred to the left mastoid. Electro-Oculogram (EOG) were recorded simultaneously from electrodes placed above and below the left eye. The experimenter checked the quality of the signals and the electrodes placement at the half of the test.

3   EEG Spectrum Analysis Method

In this part, we firstly investigated the grand average changes of band power during the entire process. Then, a time-course EEG spectrum analysis method has been studied to check the neural correlates of music keys and evoked emotions. There were several steps showed in Fig. 1.

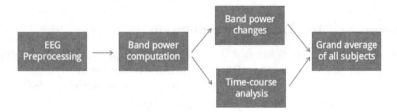

Fig. 1. EEG spectrum analysis flow chart.

3.1 Data Preprocessing

EEG data usually contains unwanted noises and artifacts which compromise the quality of the signal. To alleviate the influences of these sources, we firstly applied a band-pass filter (0.5 – 48 Hz) to obtain the desired frequency range and remove the electrical line noise at the same time, which was present due to insufficient shielding from electrical sources. Then, because the left mastoid

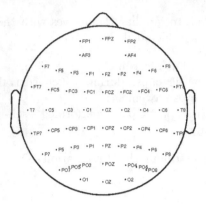

Fig. 2. The electrode locations.

electrode was used as the reference in the experiment, the transformation of the reference was necessary.

In a finite length sequence $x(n)$, $x_n^{(i)}$ is EEG signal of electrode i. M_1 is the left mastoid electrode and M_2 is the right one, the formula for re-referencing to both mastoids is given by

$$x_n^{(i)} = x_n^{(i)} - \frac{1}{2}(x_n^{M_1} + x_n^{M_2}) = x_n^{(i)} - \frac{1}{2}x_n^{M_2} \tag{1}$$

The EEG signals were re-referenced to both mastoid electrodes, which were usually used as the reference in the auditory electrophysiological experiment. Then, the eye blinks and muscular artifacts were excluded by artifact rejection using independent component analysis (ICA). After EOG (HEO, VEO) and mastoid electrodes were removed, 60 scalp electrodes were left for the EEG signal analysis, showed in Fig. 2.

3.2 Power Spectral Density Computation

As we know, brain rhythms are fast, but EEG could capture these rapid dynamics. The power spectral density (PSD) is advantageous for studying neurocognitive processes because that it directly measure neural activity. PSD of each electrode (60 electrodes) for each subject (21 subjects) was estimated using the Welch's estimation method.

Welch's method [15] is used for estimating the power of a signal at different frequencies. The sequence $X(n)$ of length N is divided into K segments. Its Welch's estimate is given by

$$PSD(w) = \frac{1}{K}\sum_{i=1}^{K}(\frac{1}{LV}\left|\sum_{n=1}^{L} w(n)x_i(n)e^{-jwn}\right|^2) \tag{2}$$

Where L is the length of each segment. V is the power of the window $w(n)$: $V = \frac{1}{L}\sum_{n=1}^{L}|w(n)|^2$. Compared with traditional spectrum estimate technique,

Welch's method is an improvement method, which increases the number of segments by allowing the overlap between segments. Therefore, it reduces noise in the estimated power spectra.

For each electrode, PSD values were estimated and then grouped into the following five bands: Delta (0.5 – 4 Hz), Theta (4 – 8 Hz), Alpha (8 – 13 Hz), Beta (13 – 20 Hz), and Gamma (30 – 48 Hz) according to their frequencies. To remove the drift of EEG signal, the relative value of band power has been used. The changes of band power given by

$$BP\_Changes_j = \frac{lg(PSD_j(music)) - lg(PSD_j(rest))}{lg(PSD_j(rest))} \tag{3}$$

Where j is the index of the frequency band which mentioned above. $PSD_j(rest)$ is the band power from the 15 s recording of spontaneous before music. $PSD_j(music)$ is the band power from 2 min recording of music clip.

Then, we obtained a series of normalized power values for each band (totally 5 bands), channel (totally 60 channels), music (totally 4 clips) and subject (totally 21 subjects). For each of the above EEG bands, a scalp field power spectral topographic map was interpolated from the above 60 channels and has been plotted on a 2D cortical model, showed in Fig. 5.

3.3 Time-Course Band Power Analysis

It is known that music perception is a dynamic brain processing. The grand band power analysis could not reveal the mechanisms of neural oscillations. To capture cognitive dynamics in the time frame, a time-course band power analysis is necessary. A sliding window was applied to capture the band power changes during the entire process of music listening. A window of four seconds length and the overlap of one second length have been applied. For each electrode and

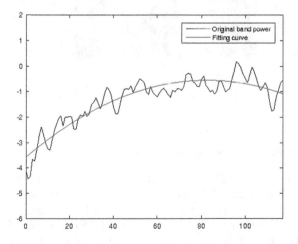

Fig. 3. The dynamic changes of alpha band power on Pz electrode. (Color figure online)

each key, the dynamic topographic distribution of power have been calculated, showed in Fig. 6.

Moreover, for a specific electrode, the dynamic curve of power could be calculated. To compare the curves, quadratic polynomial fitting was applied to get a smooth curve showed in Fig. 3. The black curve was the original alpha band power of Pz electrode during the entire two minutes of music listening. The red curve was the result of quadratic polynomial fitting.

4   Experimental Results

4.1   Behavioral Results

From the behavioral results, the average value of valence ratings was 6.3 for major stimuli (on a 9-point scale ranging from 1 to 9), while it was 4.9 for the minor stimuli. The difference between ratings was significant ($t = 2.1, p = 0.045 < 0.05$, t-test). Subjects rated the major stimuli as pleasant and the minor ones as unpleasant. But arousal ($p = 0.15$) and dominance ($p = 0.75$) were not rated significantly showed in Fig. 4.

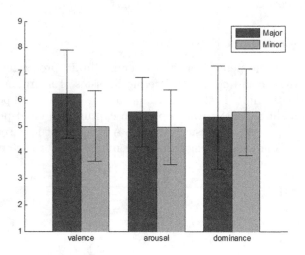

Fig. 4. The average ratings of valence, arousal and dominance.

4.2   Band Power Changes Comparison

In this section, the grand differences between major and minor keys were investigated by the SP changes of EEG band activities. In the awake adult, there were almost no delta and theta waves, which could be recorded in the state of extreme fatigue and lethargy. However, several differences were found from the spectral characteristics of their other band activities. First of all, a comparison of

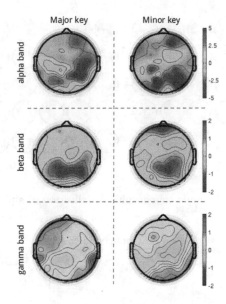

Fig. 5. Topographic spectral mappings of the band power changes in both major and minor keys.

the SP changes was examined during the music listening. Here, the 15 s recording of spontaneous were used as the baseline. From both of major and minor keys, there was a great decrease of the spectral power of alpha band during the music listening. (For major key, $t = 2.88, p = 0.013 < 0.05$; for minor key, $t = 3.16, p = 0.008 < 0.01$). While, for high-frequency gamma band, there was a slight increase of the spectral power during the music listening. (For major key, $t = 2.38, p = 0.035 < 0.05$; for minor key, $t = 2.75, p = 0.018 < 0.05$)

Additionally, two-way ANOVA was used for examining the influence of music keys and brain areas. The dominant spectral power changes of the alpha band were found at the posterior area, which was much eminent of the minor scale than the major scale, showed in Fig. 5. ($F = 2.4, p = 0.04 < 0.05$).

4.3 Time-Course Comparison

In this section, the cognitive dynamics in the time frame were compared between the major key and minor in different locations. As mentioned above, a sliding window of four seconds length was applied to capture the band power changes during the entire process of music listening. To see the results clearly, we plotted the time course topographic distribution every three seconds. Firstly, during two minutes of music listening, the alpha band activities augmented rapidly, which were more obvious under major music. Compared with minor music, they only reduced more slightly and recovered more quickly, showed in Fig. 6.

What's more, on the specific Fz and Pz electrodes, the dynamic curves of power were calculated among different EEG bands, showed in Fig. 7. Different

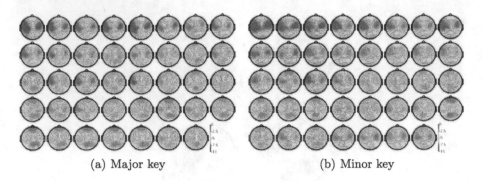

(a) Major key   (b) Minor key

Fig. 6. The dynamic topographic distribution of alpha power.

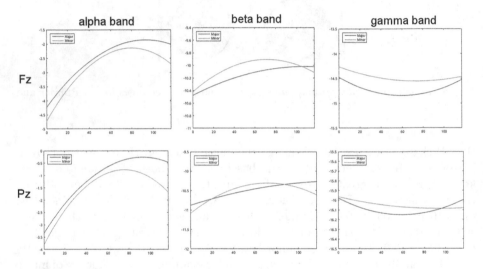

Fig. 7. Time-course spectral analysis of major and minor music. Black curve is from major music and red curve is from minor music (Color figure online)

from the alpha band, the activities in the high-frequency gamma band declined gradually which were more obvious under the minor key.

4.4   Music Evoked Emotion Classification

In this section, the spectral characteristics were tested in a two-category classification. As mentioned above, time-course based features have been calculated. For totally five bands, 60 electrodes and 117 frames, there were 35100 features. To reduce the feature dimension and improve the correct identification rate, Spearman rank correlation coefficient, was used for feature selection. It assessed

Table 2. The confusion matrix of two-category classification.

n=84	predicted major	predicted minor
actual major	28	14
actual minor	26	16

how well the relationship between valence ratings and the EEG features. For a sample of size s, and raw scores X_i, Y_i were converted to ranks x_i, y_i, and ρ was computed from:

$$\rho = \frac{\sum_i (x_i - \overline{x})(y_i - \overline{y})}{\sqrt{\sum_i (x_i - \overline{x})^2 \sum_i (y_i - \overline{y})^2}} \tag{4}$$

Finally, 23 features whose correlation was significant ($\rho < .05$) were selected. Because of the small sample size (84 samples, totally 21 subjects and 4 clips), support vector machines (SVM) has been employed for pattern classification [16]. After testing different kernels, the polynomial kernel has been used to maximize the separation margin between two classes. To ensure the accuracy, the leave-one-out cross-validation method has been used. The classification rate has reached 64.3% in a two-category classification of major and minor keys. The confusion matrix was showed in Table 2.

5   Discussion

The present study investigated the differences of music evoked emotions between major and minor keys by time-course based EEG spectral analysis. As we expected, several differences were found from the spectral characteristics of their EEG activities. First of all, the alpha band power reduced in a large brain area, especially at the occipital area, which spread over a larger area in the minor key than the major key. Then, the high-frequency gamma band was obviously different from that of the alpha band, which reduced gradually during the music listening process. Moreover, we investigated the cognitive dynamics in the time frame and found that the alpha band activities augmented rapidly during two minutes of music listening, while the brain activities declined gradually in the high-frequency gamma band.

Alpha band is considered to be inversely related to cortical activation. According to the Iwaki's study [17], alpha band activity was negatively correlated with the brain activity. The higher alpha band power, the lower degree of brain activity. In our study, the alpha band power of the major key only reduced slightly and recovered more quickly, which related to low brain activity. It suggested that major music made mental relax and the minor music gave a feeling of intense.

The high-frequency beta band (14 – 30 Hz) was usually considered to be related to the integration of information, such as math computing, language processing and other cognitive activities [18]. Gamma band (30 Hz above), also known as binding, which was generated by a number of cell clusters, was the integration of information found in visual stimulation, automatic processing, memory integration and other tasks [19].

What's more, the results showed that the difference existed among the subjects. The reason was that emotions evoked by music were not only related to music stimuli themselves, but also modulated by personality variables [20]. These differences caused the low classification rate.

6   Conclusions

In this study, we proposed a time-course based spectral analysis method on the EEG activities during the entire process of music listening. From the spectral characteristics of EEG signals, we found the differences between major key and minor key. The alpha band activities reduced at the beginning, and then augmented rapidly during music listening process. While the high-frequency gamma band was obviously different which reduced gradually during the music listening process. This study showed that the emotions evoked by music keys were clearly different on EEG signals. It was just the beginning. We aimed at providing an attractive framework for uncovering the neural correlates of music and emotion. Overall, this research could help us understand the influence of the emotional states on brain activity patterns, which might allow us to provide the user with more ways of controlling the affective BCI.

Acknowledgements. Our thanks to supports from the National Natural Science Foundation of China (61171186, 61271345, 61671187), Fundamental Research Project of Shenzhen (JCYJ20150929143955341), Key Laboratory Opening Funding of MOE-Microsoft Key Laboratory of Natural Language Processing and Speech (HIT.KLOF.20150xx, HIT.KLOF.20160xx), and the Fundamental Research Funds for the Central Universities (HIT.NSRIF.2012047). The authors are grateful for the anonymous reviewers who made constructive comments.

References

1. Gabrielsson, A., Lindström, E.: The role of structure in the musical expression of emotions. In: Juslin, P.N. (ed.) Handbook of Music and Emotion: Theory, Research, Applications, pp. 367–400. Oxford University Press, New York (2010)
2. Steblin, R.: A History of Key Characteristics in the Eighteenth and Early Nineteenth Centuries. University of Rochester Press, Rochester (2002)
3. Hevner, K.: The affective character of the major and minor modes in music. Am. J. Psychol. **47**(1), 103–118 (1935)
4. Krumhansl, C.L., Kessler, E.J.: Tracing the dynamic changes in perceived tonal organization in a spatial representation of musical keys. Psychol. Rev. **89**(4), 334 (1982)
5. Blood, A.J., Zatorre, R.J., Bermudez, P., Evans, A.C.: Emotional responses to pleasant and unpleasant music correlate with activity in paralimbic brain regions. Nat. Neurosci. **2**(4), 382–387 (1999)

6. Koelsch, S., Fritz, T., Müller, K., Friederici, A.D., et al.: Investigating emotion with music: an fMRI study. Hum. Brain Mapp. **27**(3), 239–250 (2006)
7. Halpern, A.R., Martin, J.S., Reed, T.D.: An ERP study of major-minor classification in melodies. MUSIC PERCEPT. INTERDISC. J. **25**(3), 181–191 (2008)
8. Green, A.C., Bærentsen, K.B., Stødkilde-Jørgensen, H., Wallentin, M., Roepstorff, A., Vuust, P.: Music in minor activates limbic structures: a relationship with dissonance? Neuroreport **19**(7), 711–715 (2008)
9. Virtala, P., Berg, V., Kivioja, M., Purhonen, J., Salmenkivi, M., Paavilainen, P., Tervaniemi, M.: The preattentive processing of major vs. minor chords in the human brain: an event-related potential study. Neurosci. Lett. **487**(3), 406–410 (2011)
10. Poikonen, H., Alluri, V., Brattico, E., Lartillot, O., Tervaniemi, M., Huotilainen, M.: Event-related brain responses while listening to entire pieces of music. Neuroscience **312**, 58–73 (2016)
11. Peretz, I., Zatorre, R.J.: Brain organization for music processing. Annu. Rev. Psychol. **56**, 89–114 (2005)
12. Mao, M., Rau, P.-L.P.: EEG-based measurement of emotion induced by mode, rhythm, and MV of Chinese pop music. In: Rau, P.L.P. (ed.) CCD 2014. LNCS, vol. 8528, pp. 89–100. Springer, Heidelberg (2014). doi:10.1007/978-3-319-07308-8_9
13. Menon, V., Levitin, D.J.: The rewards of music listening: response and physiological connectivity of the mesolimbic system. Neuroimage **28**(1), 175–184 (2005)
14. Morris, J.D.: Observations: Sam: the self-assessment manikin an efficient cross-cultural measurement of emotional response. J. Advertising Res. **35**(6), 63–68 (1995)
15. Welch, P.: The use of fast fourier transform for the estimation of power spectra: a method based on time averaging over short, modified periodograms. IEEE Trans. Audio Electroacoust. **15**(2), 70–73 (1967)
16. Lin, Y.P., Wang, C.H., Wu, T.L., Jeng, S.K., Chen, J.H.: Support vector machine for EEG signal classification during listening to emotional music. In: 2008 IEEE 10th Workshop on Multimedia Signal Processing, pp. 127–130. IEEE (2008)
17. Iwaki, T., Hayashi, M., Hori, T.: Changes in alpha band EEC activity in the frontal area after stimulation with music of different affective content. Percept. Motor Skills **84**(2), 515–526 (1997)
18. Schack, B., Chen, A.C., Mescha, S., Witte, H.: Instantaneous EEG coherence analysis during the stroop task. Clin. Neurophysiol. **110**(8), 1410–1426 (1999)
19. Fitzgibbon, S.P., Pope, K.J., Mackenzie, L., Clark, C.R., Willoughby, J.O.: Cognitive tasks augment gamma EEG power. Clin. Neurophysiol. **115**(8), 1802–1809 (2004)
20. Collins, T., Tillmann, B., Barrett, F.S., Delbé, C., Janata, P.: A combined model of sensory and cognitive representations underlying tonal expectations in music: from audio signals to behavior. Psychol. Rev. **121**(1), 33 (2014)

A Possible Neural Circuit for Decision Making and Its Learning Process

Hui Wei[✉], Yijie Bu, and Dawei Dai

Laboratory of Cognitive Modeling and Algorithms,
Shanghai Key Laboratory of Data Science, Department of Computer Science,
Fudan University, Shanghai, China
{weihui,yjbu15,dwdai14}@fudan.edu.cn

Abstract. To adapt to the environment and survive, most animals can control their behaviors by making decisions. The process of decision making and responding according to changes in the environment is stable, sustainable, and learnable. Understanding how behaviors are regulated by neural circuits, and the encoding and decoding mechanisms from stimuli to responses, are important goals in neuroscience. A biologically plausible decision circuit consisting of computational neuron and synapse models and its learning mechanism are designed in this paper. The learning mechanism is based on two parts: first, effect of the punishment from the environment on the temporal correlations of neuron firings; second, spike timing dependent plasticity (STDP) of synapse. The decision circuit was used successfully to simulate the behavior of Drosophila exhibited in real experiments. In this paper, we place focus on the connections and interactions among excitatory and inhibitory neurons and try to give an explanation at a micro level (i.e. neurons and neural circuit) of how the observable decision making behavior is acquired and achieved.

Keywords: Action potential · Neural circuit · Synaptic plasticity · Learning mechanism · Behavior · Decision making · Simulation

1 Introduction and Motivation

Most animals can accurately control their behaviors to pursue benefits, or avoid harm. For example, many insects have the ability to navigate by sunlight, accurately maintaining a fixed angle between flight and lighting direction. This behavior is highly stable and sustainable and must be regulated by an internal control system. This system is similar to a feedback control system in automatic control theory, making decisions based on sensory input, to carry out correct movements. Such decision-making behavior is more complex than a reflex and is usually achieved by the nervous system.

The choice behavior of Drosophila facing visual cues has been studied previously [15,19]. In one experiment, flies were fixed in the center of a flight simulator and were only able to rotate in place. Two different color cues in the environment were presented to flies, green and blue, with blue cues associated with a heat

© Springer International Publishing AG 2016
C.-L. Liu et al. (Eds.): BICS 2016, LNAI 10023, pp. 196–206, 2016.
DOI: 10.1007/978-3-319-49685-6_18

punishment. In the training session, flies were punished whenever the blue cue entered the frontal 90° sector of their visual field. The time the flies spent in different flight directions was recorded. Flies showed no color preference before the training session, but exhibited preference for the green cues, which were not associated with a heat punishment, after the training session. This result shows that flies can adjust their flight behavior depending on visual input stimuli, suggesting they can make decisions based on perceived color cues, rather than random reflexes. We can make a reasonable assumption that, underlying this behavior, a neural circuit for decision making exists, which determines the direction of rotation based on perceived color cues, clockwise or counterclockwise. The significant change of color preference before and after the training session suggests that a new decision-making neural circuit is formed. The behavior experiment described above raises several questions. First, in the case of Drosophila, what kind of neural circuit in central complex is likely to dominate this behavior? Second, this neural circuit changed before and after the training session, so how was it corrected? Around these questions, this paper attempts to explain the structure of the decision-making neural circuit and its learning process in the behavior experiment of Drosophila, based on the existing computational model of biological neuron and synaptic plasticity.

Previous related studies on the construction of neural circuits can be roughly divided into four categories. First, there are artificial neural network models in engineering that focus on functionality and are not consistent with the anatomical and electrophysiological evidence of the biological nervous system. These do not reflect the actual workings of the nervous system. Second, there are recurrent network models [17] to explain the process of decision making, however, changes of decision making or learning process, which is exemplified by the Drosophila experiment described above, were not considered in these models. Third, some large scale neural simulations [1,9,11,16] "seek 'computer simulations that are very closely linked to the detailed anatomical and physiological structure' of the brain, in hopes of 'generating unanticipated functional insights based on emergent properties of neuronal structure"' [5]. These simulations do not demonstrate the connection between the working mechanisms of neural circuits and specific observable behaviors [6]. Finally, some neural circuits [4,6,7,13,20] were built using biological neuron models to solve application problems. However, ideas that are not biologically plausible were introduced from artificial neural networks, external learning signals as indicator of errors were artificially imposed in their learning mechanisms and not integrated in circuits.

A learnable neural circuit for decision making, comprising different types of biological neurons, is presented in this paper. And changes in decision making process resulting from punishment signals was investigated, with consideration of biophysical characteristics of neurons. The neural circuit was related to the behavior of Drosophila in real experiments [15,19] and the simulation results are consistent with relevant experiment results.

2   Neuron Model and Synaptic Plasticity

Spiking neuron model proposed by Izhikevich [10] is used in this paper, see Eqs. (1, 2, 3). Three spiking patterns are used: Regular Spiking (RS), Chattering (CH), and Low-Threshold Spiking (LTS), as shown in Fig. 1. The RS and CH patterns are exhibited in excitatory neurons and the LTS pattern is exhibited in inhibitory neurons. When presented with a prolonged stimulus, RS type of neurons "fire a few spikes with short interspike period and then the period increases" [10]. They are used as input neurons in this paper, receiving stimuli and converting stimuli into spike trains. Neurons with CH pattern "fire stereotypical bursts of closely spaced spikes" [10]. They are used as control and output neurons in this paper because a burst of spikes can provide more stimuli in a short time period. LTS type of neuron is similar to RS type, and is used as interneuron.

$$v' = 0.04v^2 + 5v + 140 - u + I. \tag{1}$$

$$u' = a(bv - u). \tag{2}$$

$$\text{if } v \geq 30 \ mV, \text{ then } \begin{cases} v \leftarrow c \\ u \leftarrow u + d. \end{cases} \tag{3}$$

Synaptic plasticity is an important foundation of learning and memory. The intensity and timing of stimuli decided by synaptic connections can also affect the transmission of information in a circuit. In keeping with previous studies [4,13], multiple synaptic connections with different time delays and connection

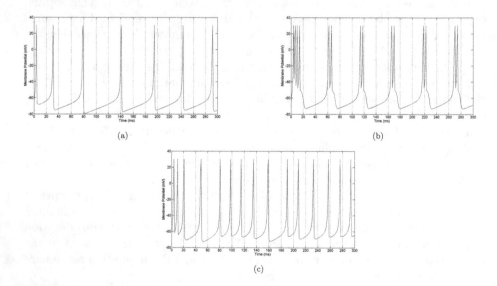

(a)   (b)

(c)

Fig. 1. Three types of spiking pattern, (A) Regular Spiking, (B) Chattering, (C) Low-Threshold Spiking.

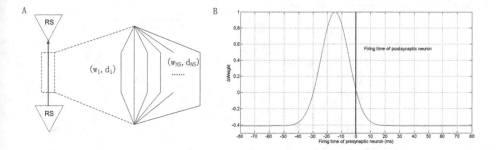

Fig. 2. (A) Multiple synaptic connections with different strengths and delays between a pair of neurons. (B) The STDP curve used in this paper. When the postsynaptic neuron fires a few milliseconds after the presynaptic neuron fires, the connection is strengthened.

strengths are used between a pair of neurons in this paper, as shown in Fig. 2(A). Stimuli received by neuron j from all pre-synaptic neurons i at time t is shown as Eqs. (4, 5), w_{ijk} and d_{ijk} is the strength and delay of the kth synapse from neuron i to j, t_i is the firing time of neuron i, $PSP(t)$ is a postsynaptic potential function as in [4], τ is set as 5.0.

$$I_j^t = \sum_i \sum_k w_{ijk} * PSP(t - t_i - d_{ijk}). \tag{4}$$

$$PSP(t) = \frac{t}{\tau}e^{1-t/\tau}. \tag{5}$$

Adjustment of the strength of synaptic connections in this paper is based on spike-timing-dependent plasticity (STDP) [2,3,8,12], which adjusts the connection strengths according to the relative timing of spikes of presynaptic and post-synaptic neurons. We use an alternative curve [4,13], see Eq. 6 ($b = -0.21, c = -12.7, \beta = 13.61$ in this paper) and Fig. 2(B), to the traditional STDP curve [3]. If the postsynaptic neuron fires a few milliseconds after the presynaptic neuron, connection between the neurons is strengthened; firing too early or late will weaken the connection [14,18].

$$L(\Delta t) = (1 - b)e^{-(\Delta t - c)^2/\beta^2} + b. \tag{6}$$

3   Neural Circuit and Its Learning Process

The architecture of the neural circuit designed in this study to simulate the behavior of Drosophila in real experiments [15,19] is shown in Fig. 3.

3.1   Input and Output of the Decision Circuit

Input stimuli from the color-sensing circuit are simulated by constant current, which are applied to different RS neurons according to the color and position

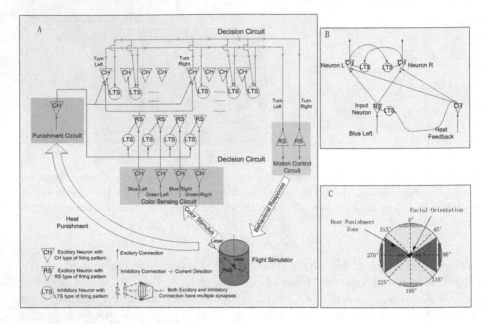

Fig. 3. (A) Architecture of the neural circuit in this study. Some neurons and connections are omitted for clarity. (B) A basic decision unit in the circuit. (C) Diagram of simulated environment. (Color figure online)

of the perceived cue. For example, when a blue cue appears on the left of the fly, constant current stimuli are applied to particular RS neurons in the decision circuit ("Blue Left" label in Fig. 3) as input. Output neurons are divided into two groups; the firing of one group of neurons indicates a left turn instruction with the other group indicating a right turn instruction. If a left turn instruction is emitted, the fly will turn left by a constant degree.

3.2 Punishment Feedback

In a previously described experimental setting [15,19], flies are punished by laser whenever the blue cue enters the front sector of their visual field during training sessions. Output spikes of the punishment circuit are projected into the decision circuit as feedback signals. These spikes can affect the firing of neurons in the decision circuit, and affect the temporal correlation of neurons' firing. Figure 3 (red lines) shows how punishment circuit output is projected into our decision circuit: at the interneurons near the input neurons and at the output neurons. If the punishment circuit is active, input neurons are inhibited and output neurons are excited.

3.3   Core of the Decision Circuit

The decision behavior of this circuit depends on which group of output neurons fire, when provided with a specific pattern of input stimuli. Each input neuron is connected to both the output neurons indicating left turn instruction and those indicating right turn instruction. This design is to ensure that each input neuron has the ability to produce two different decisions, which is crucial for decision reverse in learning process. There is a "winner-take-all" competition among output neurons achieved by interneurons' inhibitory effect. When an output neuron fires, it will inhibit other output neurons by exciting the nearby inhibitory neurons, relieving the inhibitory effect it receives. Only a portion of output neurons indicating the same instruction fire when the circuit is stable. So when the decision is stable, the circuit is in a biophysical balance state, and reverse the decision in learning process is to move the circuit into another biophysical balance state.

3.4   Learning Process

The synaptic connections of the decision circuit might be unsuitable, which will lead to wrong decisions. Therefore, a learning mechanism should be introduced to adjust the synaptic connections according to environmental feedback (i.e., heat punishment in this paper). The learning mechanism is based on the STDP rule. When there is no heat punishment, i.e. current decision is not bad, output neuron firing is caused by input neuron firing. According to the STDP rule, synaptic connections are strengthened. Because of the consolidation of connections, when the same input stimuli is presented, the same portion of output neurons are easier to fire, meaning that the decision is consolidated.

The decision circuit may not always emit the right instruction because of the dynamic property of the environment. When punishment happened, the decision circuit should be adjusted. The key question is to decide which part of the circuit is responsible to the current punishment, which is similar as the credit assignment problem in reward-based reinforcement learning. The solution in this paper is based on the biophysical characteristics of biological neurons. If the decision circuit emits a wrong instruction, the punishment circuit will receive stimuli and be activated. Input neurons in the decision circuit are then inhibited, but output neurons are excited by the spikes from the punishment circuit. Remember that there is a "winner-take-all" mechanism among output neurons, and the winners will not change because of the accumulated inhibitory effects on other output neurons (i.e. losers). So the output neurons who are responsible to the current punishment (i.e. the winners) are still firing, but the tight firing temporal correlations between the output and input neurons are lost, then synaptic connections are weakened according to the STDP rule, meaning that the wrong decision is weakened. Whenever a wrong instruction is emitted, producing a heat punishment, the decision is weakened. Remember that each input neuron has the ability to produce two different decisions, once the trace under wrong decision is weakened a few times, a correct decision is made. The correct decision is increasingly consolidated the more it is made, as no heat punishment occurs; logic in this decision circuit is reversed.

4   Experiments and Results

The learning capability of the decision circuit was investigated in two experiments. In the first experiment, the ability of a basic decision unit (Fig. 3(B)) to reverse decision output depending on whether there are punishment feedback signals was investigated and related to synaptic connections and plasticity. The whole circuit was used to control a simulated fly in experiment 2 to simulate the behavior in real experiments [15,19].

4.1   Learning of Correct Decision

A basic decision unit is shown in Fig. 3(B), only the situation where the blue cue appears on the left was considered. Spiking activity of the two output neurons in the learning process is shown in Fig. 4. Synaptic connections between the input neuron and the two output neurons are shown in Fig. 5. Initially, the connections from input neuron to output neurons were randomly set. The synaptic connections were not the same for the two output neurons, resulting in different stimulus accumulating speed. The output neuron which accumulated stimuli faster (i.e. neuron L) fired earlier and became the winner until the heat punishment occurred. The heat feedback neuron was then activated; neuron L was still firing, but the input neuron had stopped firing, then synaptic connections were weakened due to STDP rule, as expected in Sect. 3.4. Connections between neuron R and input neuron were not weakened because both two neurons did not fire during punishment. After the punishment stopped, re-stimulate the input neuron led to firings of output neuron R. For testing purposes, the heat feedback neuron was activated again, and the circuit output reversed again, meaning the designed basic decision unit can reverse the output depending on punishment feedback.

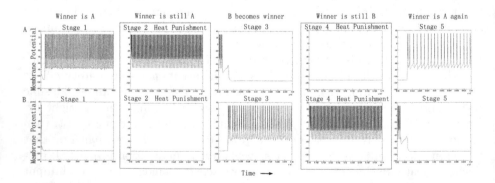

Fig. 4. Spiking activities of (A) neuron L, (B) neuron R.

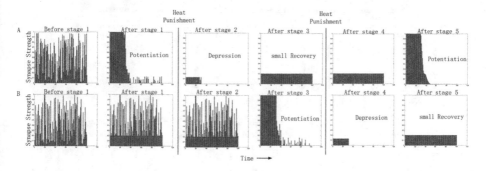

Fig. 5. Strength of synaptic connections between input neuron and (A) neuron L, (B) neuron R at different stages. 100 synaptic connections with different time delay (1 ms–100 ms) were set between each output neuron and input neuron. The size of the time delay is represented on the x-axis and the strength of the connection in that time delay is represented on the y-axis. Connection strength was randomly set at the start. Noticed that a little amount of connection recovery was set to ensure that input neuron and output neurons were always connected.

4.2   Simulation of the Behavior of Drosophila

The choice behavior of Drosophila facing color cues, as previously described in the literature [15,19], was simulated. The simulated environment is shown in Fig. 3(C). There were two types of color cue in the environment: green and blue bars. The fly was assumed to be fixed in the center of the environment, and could only rotate. The red sectors shown in Fig. 3(C) are heat punishment zones. In training sessions, the fly received punishment feedback whenever it rotated into the heat punishment zone, which would persist until the fly left the punishment zone.

The architecture of the decision circuit used in this simulation is shown in Fig. 3. Different input neurons in the decision circuit were stimulated according to the color and relative position of the perceived cue. Four situations were considered: blue cue on the left (BL), green cue on the left (GL), blue cue on the right (BR), and green cue on the right (GR). According to the current orientation of the fly, each situation had a probability to occur. For example, when orientation of the fly is in the range of $22.5° - 67.5°$ (see Fig. 3(C)), there is 0.5 probability that the fly will perceive the green cue on the left, and 0.5 probability it will perceive the blue cue on the right. Initial connections in the decision circuit were set so that simulated fly tended to rotate to the cue currently perceived.

The simulated fly rotated to the left or right according to the output of the decision circuit. The simulated trajectories and histograms of the time spent by the simulated fly in different directions are shown in Fig. 6. For illustrative purposes, the distance between the fly and the center of the environment is set proportional to time. However, flies in [15,19] only rotated in the same place. Figure 6 demonstrates that flight time of simulated fly in different directions was

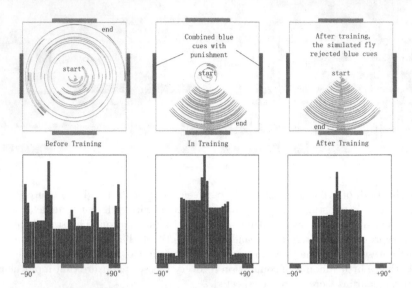

Fig. 6. Flight trajectories and histograms of the time spent in different directions. (Color figure online)

almost equal before the training session, with no color preference. The fly then exhibited preference for green cues and avoided blue cues, which were associated with a heat punishment. The behavior of simulated fly was consistent with previous experimental results [15,19].

5   Conclusion

This paper has presented the architecture and learning mechanism of a decision circuit comprising two typical types of neuron, excitatory and inhibitory. The neuron model proposed by Izhikevich [10] was used and the learning mechanism was based on environmental punishment feedback and its effect on synaptic plasticity in the decision circuit. Through the proper connection and combination of excitatory and inhibitory neurons, the decision circuit implements the process of information coding and transmission from stimuli input to decision output. In a sensor-actor behavior mode, the decision circuit can learn to respond appropriately to environmental stimuli. This learning process can be achieved under biological constraints, with environmental feedback. The decision circuit has been used successfully to simulate the behavior of Drosophila in real experiments [15,19]. Construction of the decision circuit in this paper assists in understanding how animal behaviors are regulated by neural circuits, and in understanding the underlying encoding and decoding mechanisms from stimulus to response.

Acknowledgments. This work was supported by NSFC project (Project No.61375122), and in part by Shanghai Science and Technology Development Funds (13dz2260200, 13511504300). We thank LetPub (www.letpub.com) for its linguistic assistance during the preparation of this manuscript.

References

1. Ananthanarayanan, R., Modha, D.S.: Anatomy of a cortical simulator. In: Proceedings of the 2007 ACM/IEEE Conference on Supercomputing, p. 3. ACM (2007)
2. Bell, C.C., Han, V.Z., Sugawara, Y., Grant, K.: Synaptic plasticity in a cerebellum-like structure depends on temporal order. Nature **387**(6630), 278–281 (1997)
3. Bi, G.-Q., Poo, M.-M.: Synaptic modifications in cultured hippocampal neurons: dependence on spike timing, synaptic strength, and postsynaptic cell type. J. Neurosci. **18**(24), 10464–10472 (1998)
4. Bohte, S.M., Poutré, H.L., Kok, J.N.: Unsupervised clustering with spiking neurons by sparse temporal coding and multilayer RBF networks. IEEE Trans. Neural Netw. **13**(2), 426–435 (2002)
5. Carandini, M.: From circuits to behavior: a bridge too far? Nat. Neurosci. **15**(4), 507–509 (2012)
6. Eliasmith, C., Stewart, T.C., Choo, X., Bekolay, T., DeWolf, T., Tang, Y., Rasmussen, D.: A large-scale model of the functioning brain. Science **338**(6111), 1202–1205 (2012)
7. Foderaro, G., Henriquez, C., Ferrari, S.: Indirect training of a spiking neural network for flight control via spike-timing-dependent synaptic plasticity. In: 2010 49th IEEE Conference on Decision and Control (CDC), pp. 911–917. IEEE (2010)
8. Gerstner, W., Kempter, R., van Hemmen, J.L., Wagner, H.: A neuronal learning rule for sub-millisecond temporal coding. Nature **383**, 76–78 (1996). (LCN-ARTICLE-1996-002)
9. Izhikevich, E.M., Edelman, G.M.: Large-scale model of mammalian thalamocortical systems. Proc. Nat. Acad. Sci. **105**(9), 3593–3598 (2008)
10. Izhikevich, E.M., et al.: Simple model of spiking neurons. IEEE Trans. Neural Netw. **14**(6), 1569–1572 (2003)
11. Markram, H.: The blue brain project. Nat. Rev. Neurosci. **7**(2), 153–160 (2006)
12. Markram, H., Lübke, J., Frotscher, M., Sakmann, B.: Regulation of synaptic efficacy by coincidence of postsynaptic APS and EPSPS. Science **275**(5297), 213–215 (1997)
13. Natschläger, T., Ruf, B.: Spatial and temporal pattern analysis via spiking neurons. Netw. Comput. Neural Syst. **9**(3), 319–332 (1998)
14. Nishiyama, M., Hong, K., Mikoshiba, K., Poo, M.-M., Kato, K.: Calcium stores regulate the polarity and input specificity of synaptic modification. Nature **408**(6812), 584–588 (2000)
15. Tang, S., Guo, A.: Choice behavior of Drosophila facing contradictory visual cues. Science **294**(5546), 1543–1547 (2001)
16. Waldrop, M.M.: Computer modelling: brain in a box. Nature **482**(7386), 456–458 (2012)
17. Wang, X.-J.: Probabilistic decision making by slow reverberation in cortical circuits. Neuron **36**(5), 955–968 (2002)
18. Wittenberg, G.M., Wang, S.S.-H.: Malleability of spike-timing-dependent plasticity at the ca3-ca1 synapse. J. Neurosci. **26**(24), 6610–6617 (2006)

19. Zhang, K., Guo, J.Z., Peng, Y., Xi, W., Guo, A.: Dopamine-mushroom body circuit regulates saliency-based decision-making in Drosophila. Science **316**(5833), 1901–1904 (2007)
20. Zhang, X., Xu, Z., Henriquez, C., Ferrari, S.: Spike-based indirect training of a spiking neural network-controlled virtual insect. In: 2013 IEEE 52nd Annual Conference on Decision and Control (CDC), pp. 6798–6805. IEEE (2013)

A SVM-Based EEG Signal Analysis:
An Auxiliary Therapy for Tinnitus

Pei-Zhen Li[1,2], Juan-Hui Li[1,2], and Chang-Dong Wang[1,2(✉)]

[1] School of Data and Computer Science, Sun Yat-sen University, Guangzhou, China
changdongwang@hotmail.com
[2] Guangdong Key Laboratory of Information Security Technology,
Guangzhou, China

Abstract. Tinnitus is a kind of auditory disease characterized by an ongoing conscious perception of a sound in the absence of any external sound source. It is a common symptom for which no effective treatment exists. Though many non-invasive functional imaging modalities have been rapidly developed and applied to this field, yet, whether the EEG signal can be utilized to distinguish tinnitus patients from normal populations has not been investigated. In the present study, we perform a binary classification based on EEG signal to distinguish tinnitus patients from normal populations. In this study, 22 subjects are involved in the experiment with 15 of them being tinnitus patients and the others being normal controls. The collected EEG signals are preprocessed in frequency domain and well represented as features that depict each subject. Then the linear support vector machine is applied to classify the subjects. Satisfactory results have been achieved, where the accuracy of the classification could reach 90.91% in spite of the undeniable fact that the collected EEG signals contain noises. Accordingly, the present study reveals that the EEG signals can be utilized to distinguish tinnitus patients from normal populations, which could be regarded as an auxiliary therapy in tinnitus.

Keywords: Tinnitus · EEG signal · Binary classification · Support Vector Machine · Auxiliary therapy

1 Introduction

Tinnitus is a kind of auditory disease characterized by an ongoing conscious perception of a sound in the absence of any physical sound source, which is perceived continuously by 5–15% of the adult population. But so far there is no effective treatment for it, though several studies have shown that focal stimulation of the temporal cortex by repetitive transcranial magnetic stimulation (rTMS) [1–3] can suppress tinnitus perception, but the maximal amount of tinnitus suppression by rTMS decreases with time [1–4]. With the rapid development and widespread application of non-invasive functional modalities, such as electroencephalogram (EEG), magnetoencephalogram (MEG), and functional

© Springer International Publishing AG 2016
C.-L. Liu et al. (Eds.): BICS 2016, LNAI 10023, pp. 207–219, 2016.
DOI: 10.1007/978-3-319-49685-6_19

magnetic resonance imaging (fMRI), such non-invasive methods make it possible to observe the central nervous system (CNS) in vivo. In particular, EEG is used most frequently in tinnitus since EEG signal is closely related with neural electric activity and has extremely high temporal resolution as well as spatial definition at the level of the scalp compared with other modalities. On the one hand, the notorious tinnitus is in an urgent need for treatment, on the other hand, the non-invasive functional modalities are rapidly developed. It becomes necessary to apply those advanced modalities to the therapies for tinnitus, in particular, it requires some effective and applicable methods to analyze and deal with medical data generated from such non-invasive devices.

To this end, the present study proposes a simple but effective method to analyze the EEG signals. We utilize the well-known machine learning algorithm, namely support vector machine (SVM) to perform a linear classification based on the features extracted from EEG signals, which works well in distinguishing tinnitus patients from normal controls. Extensive experiments have been conducted to confirm the accuracy of our method in the binary classification. This new finding can be regarded as an auxiliary therapy in tinnitus and has great significance in accelerating the clinical therapies of tinnitus especially when the tinnitus is no longer uncommon in populations while the medical resources is limited.

2 The Method

2.1 Support Vector Machine

Support vector machine (SVM) is a classical supervised machine learning model with associated learning algorithm based on statistical learning theorem, which is widely used for classification. Given a set of training samples, each marked for belonging to one of two categories, the SVM training algorithm constructs a non-probabilistic binary linear classifier to assign new testing samples into one category or the other. In the SVM model, each sample is represented by a point in a high-dimensional space, where a hyperplane separates the samples into two categories. New samples will be mapped to the same space and tagged as one category according to which side of the hyperplane they fall on. A good classifier is obtained by a hyperplane that has the largest functional margin making a least generalization error. SVM aims to improve the generalization ability of the learning via seeking for a structural risk minimization, which makes it perform well in spite of the small sample size. This is why we choose SVM for classification due to a small number of subjects and large quantities of features [5]. Figure 1 demonstrates the main idea of SVM in the case of 2-dimensional space.

2.2 Feature Selection

Feature selection is a vital step for classification. An appropriate feature selection leads to an accurate classifier since the feature vector plays an important role in

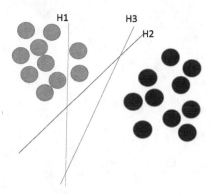

Fig. 1. SVM in 2-dimensional space. H1, H2, H3 are 3 hyperplanes, where H1 can not separate this two classes, while H2 and H3 can. H3 is the best choice with the maximum margin.

finding the "maximum-margin hyperplane" that divides the subjects represented by points in high-dimensional space. In the present study, each subject is mapped to a point represented by a feature vector with 129 features extracted from the corresponding 129 EEG signals collected from 129 electrodes.

According to the signal processing theorem, the EEG signals can be analyzed both in time domain and frequency domain. We propose to analyze in frequency domain due to the fact that EEG signals are often characterized and distinguished by their frequency bands: delta (1–4 Hz), theta (4–8 Hz), alpha (8–12 Hz), beta (12–30 Hz), and gamma (30–45 Hz) [6]. Therefore, the collected EEG signals are transformed into frequency domain after fast fourier transformation (FFT), where the number of FFT data points is equal to the sampled EEG data points. We compute the frequency spectrum for every EEG signals. As shown in Fig. 2, it is clear that each frequency spectrum consists of one primary tone at certain frequency point with the biggest absolute value in amplitude plus lots of other weak tones with small absolute value in amplitude. The primary tone is no wonder the most representative tone for this EEG signal, thus, the phase is calculated and the value is assigned to the feature vector after being mapped via a nonlinear cosine function, that is, the 129-element feature vector is composed of the strongest, cosine mapped component of the corresponding EEG signals. This is a technique to reduce the dimension of the feature vector and the disturbance in the sampled EEG data.

The cosine mapping can be viewed as a strategy aiming at recovering the essence of the signal while removing the strength or amplitude information. It makes sense in view of the large variability existing among individuals. Here, the phase and strength(amplitude) components are separated from one signal, where the signal strength(amplitude) varies much more from one subject to another due to many personal factors such as age, gender, emotion, etc. It may be more consistent when only signal phase is taken into consideration. To emphasize the function of this cosine mapping, we also perform the binary classification directly based on the extracted 129 phases as a contrast.

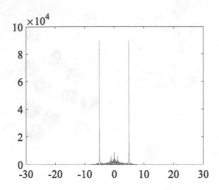

Fig. 2. The frequency-domain EEG signal of one electrode.

2.3   The Application of SVM

The linear support vector machine is applied to perform the classification due to a small number of subjects and large quantities of features [5]. During the process of classification, part of the subjects are used to train a SVM classifier, then all the subjects are used as testing data. The linear SVM is supplied by MATLAB toolbox. The performance of the classification is evaluated by accuracy, false positive rate (FPR) or Sensitivity (measuring the hit rate in tinnitus group) and false negative rate (FNR) or Specificity (measuring the hit rate in normal group), where the normal controls are labeled as 1 and tinnitus patients are labeled as −1. The formulas are displayed as follows:

$$Accuracy = \frac{TP + TN}{TP + TN + FP + FN} \tag{1}$$

$$FPR = \frac{FP}{FP + TN} \tag{2}$$

$$Sensitivity = \frac{TN}{FP + TN} \tag{3}$$

$$FNR = \frac{FN}{FN + TP} \tag{4}$$

$$Specificity = \frac{TP}{FN + TP} \tag{5}$$

where TP stands for the number of normal controls who were correctly classified; TN stands for the number of tinnitus patients who were correctly classified; FP stands for the number of tinnitus patients who were misjudged to be normal controls; and FN stands for the number of normal controls who were misjudged to be tinnitus patients.

3 Experiment

3.1 Subjects

22 subjects participate in this study, and they involve two groups: 15 patients (tinnitus group) and 7 healthy control subjects (control group). Table 1 shows the demographic information of the subjects. All the participants are recruited from the second affiliated hospital of Sun Yat-sen university. The patients are diagnosed by expert clinicians via a series of test routines. After filling in the tinnitus handicap inventory, the score (THI value) will be recorded as a partition criterion to the tinnitus severity level in the tinnitus group. None of the employed patients use medications that is expected to influence the EEG signals. All subjects involved in this study have normal or corrected-to-normal visual acuity, and no color blindness. Informed written consent is obtained from all the subjects before conducting the experiment.

Table 1. Demographic information of subjects participated in the study (THI, i.e. tinnitus handicap inventory, a measure to the tinnitus degree).

Index	Type	Gender	Age	THI
No.1	tinnitus	male	29	60
No.2	tinnitus	female	26	34
No.3	tinnitus	male	42	82
No.4	tinnitus	male	61	62
No.5	tinnitus	female	37	58
No.6	tinnitus	male	26	24
No.7	tinnitus	male	39	66
No.8	tinnitus	male	35	54
No.9	tinnitus	N/A	N/A	N/A
No.10	tinnitus	male	22	40
No.11	tinnitus	male	28	54
No.12	tinnitus	female	59	52
No.13	tinnitus	female	47	78
No.14	tinnitus	female	47	88
No.15	tinnitus	male	N/A	N/A
No.16	normal	female	42	–
No.17	normal	female	27	–
No.18	normal	N/A	N/A	–
No.29	normal	N/A	N/A	–
No.20	normal	N/A	N/A	–
No.21	normal	N/A	N/A	–
No.22	normal	N/A	N/A	–

3.2 EEG Data Collection and Preprocessing

The resting state EEG signals are used in this study. All the subjects are requested to calm down and sit upright on a comfortable chair with eye opened in a fully lighted room, wearing an electrode cap with 129 electrodes positioned according to the 10–10 international electrode placement system. The 2-dimensional position is shown in Fig. 3. Continuous EEG data are recorded from 129 scalp sites using the EEG acquisition system. During the whole 4 min data acquisition process, the impedance of each electrode is kept below 40 KΩ. The raw EEG signals are divided into 2-second epochs, by which we can get 120 epochs in total(the sampling rate of the EEG acquisition system is 1000 Hz). All episodic artifacts including eye blinks, eye movements, teeth clenching, body movement and ECG artifacts are removed from the original EEG signals. The signals are bandpass filtered with the accepted frequency band ranging from 0.1 to 60 Hz. Here, sampled EEG signals in time domain are shown in Fig. 4(a) and (b) for tinnitus patient and normal control respectively.

The overall process of the experiment is summarized in Fig. 5.

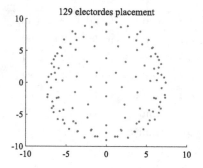

Fig. 3. The 2-dimensional placement for 129 EEG electrodes.

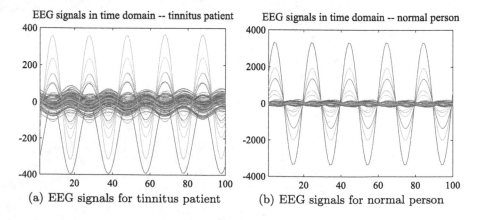

Fig. 4. Time domain EEG signals.

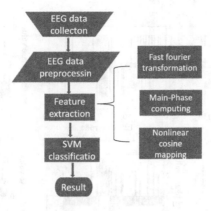

Fig. 5. The overall flow diagram for the experiment.

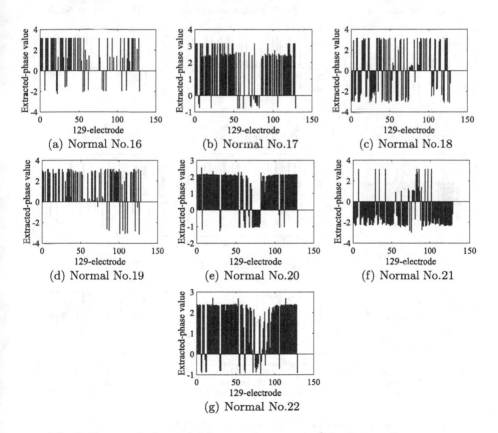

(a) Normal No.16   (b) Normal No.17   (c) Normal No.18

(d) Normal No.19   (e) Normal No.20   (f) Normal No.21

(g) Normal No.22

Fig. 6. Extracted phases (without cosine mapping) for 7 normal persons.

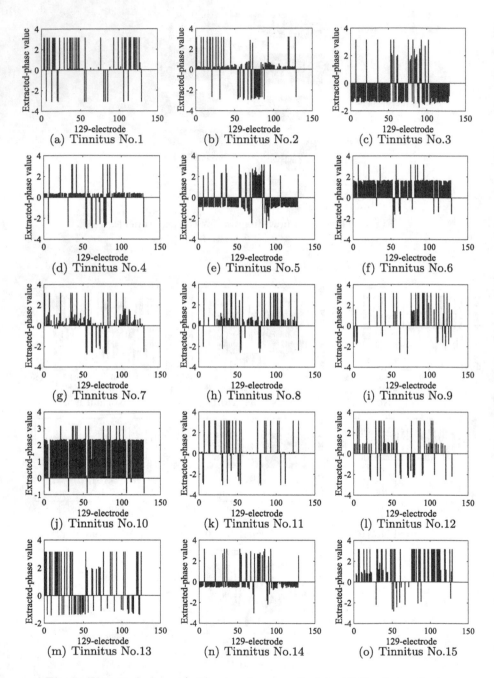

Fig. 7. Extracted phases (without cosine mapping) for 15 tinnitus patients.

Table 2. Part1: classification result without cosine mapping.

	Number of normal controls	Number of tinnitus patients
Ground truth	7	15
Results	9	13

Table 3. Part1: evaluation for the classification.

Performance	Value
Accuracy	81.82%
FPR	20.00%
Sensitivity	80.00%
FNR	14.29%
Specificity	85.71%

3.3   Result

Part1: Classification without Cosine Mapping. Figures 6 and 7 report the extracted phases for the 22 subjects (7 normal controls, 15 tinnitus patients).

From these figures, we can see that the phase distribution in the normal group turns out to be denser and tidier than tinnitus group, though the collected data contains noise in view of the fact that some subjects may be distracted in the process of EEG data collection. When the classifier is trained to be good enough, we are sure to get a satisfied result.

Tables 2 and 3 report the results in terms of accuracy, FPR, FNR, sensitivity and specificity. The results are quite satisfactory with accuracy higher than 80%, sensitivity being 80% and specificity reaching up to 85.71%, which indicates an anti-noise classifier in classifying EEG data with unavoidable personal disturbance. But still, we try another method in order to magnify the differences between two groups. The even better results are reported in the next part.

Part2: Classification with Cosine Mapping. Figures 8 and 9 report the cosine mapped features for the 22 subjects (7 normal controls, 15 tinnitus patients).

From these figures, we can see that there exist obvious differences in the distribution of cosine mapped values for tinnitus group and normal group, specifically,

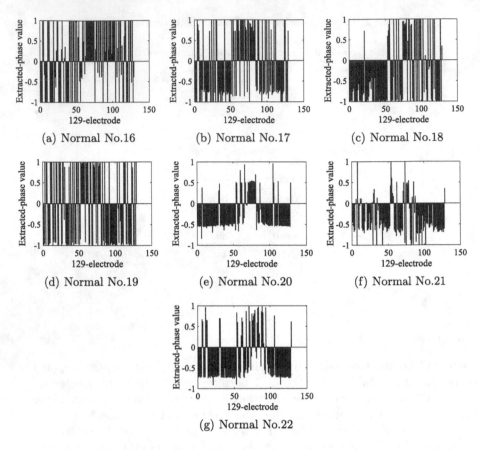

(a) Normal No.16   (b) Normal No.17   (c) Normal No.18

(d) Normal No.19   (e) Normal No.20   (f) Normal No.21

(g) Normal No.22

Fig. 8. Extracted phases (with cosine mapping) for 7 normal persons.

the negative part turns out to be much denser in tinnitus group than normal group, which is a difference-magnified version of classification in the previous part and may account for the better result in this part.

Tables 4 and 5 report the results in terms of accuracy, FPR, FNR, sensitivity and specificity. In this case where cosine mapping is applied to classification, only 2 tinnitus patients are misjudged to be normal controls and the specificity reaches up to 100%.

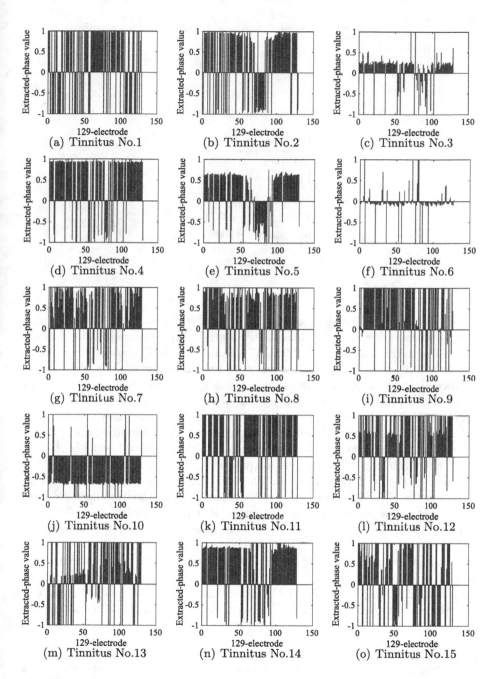

Fig. 9. Extracted phases (with cosine mapping) for 15 tinnitus patients.

Table 4. Part2: classification result with cosine mapping.

	Number of normal controls	Number of tinnitus patients
Ground truth	7	15
Results	9	13

Table 5. Part2: evaluation for the classification.

Performance	Value
Accuracy	90.91%
FPR	13.33%
Sensitivity	86.67%
FNR	0.00%
Specificity	100%

4   Conclusion

In this study, we utilize the machine learning algorithm, SVM, to distinguish tinnitus patients from normal controls, where the features corresponding to each subject are extracted from the 129 EEG signals. The EEG signals are carefully analyzed and preprocessed in frequency domain in order to fully express the variance between different groups (i.e., tinnitus group and normal group) and to be qualified as features in the vital process of classification. The main finding of this study is that the machine learning algorithm, SVM, can be utilized to deal with the EEG signals, and it works well in distinguishing tinnitus patients from normal controls in terms of the classification results. This new finding is of great significance from the following perspectives: first, it made much progress in the treatment of the mysterious tinnitus. The well trained classifier can help doctors to analyze the EEG data in an efficient way, particularly, the misjudged subjects may reflect more information, for example, if a person claims to suffer from tinnitus but only to be classified to the normal group, we would conclude that this is a patient with slight tinnitus. Therefore, the binary classifier could also play an important role in categorizing different tinnitus patients. In this sense, the new finding can be regarded as an auxiliary therapy in tinnitus. Secondly, this is a good attempt of applying ML algorithm to deal with medical data. The satisfied combination is bound to inspire more studies in this direction in the future.

Acknowledgment. This work was supported by NSFC (No. 61502543), Guangdong Natural Science Funds for Distinguished Young Scholar (2016A030306014), the PhD Start-up Fund of Natural Science Foundation of Guangdong Province, China (2014A030310180), the Fundamental Research Funds for the Central Universities (16lgzd15).

References

1. De Ridder, D., Verstraeten, E., Van der Kelen, K., De Mulder, G., Sunaert, S., Verlooy, J., Van de Heyning, P., Moller, A.: Transcranial magnetic stimulation for tinnitus: influence of tinnitus duration on stimulation parameter choice and maximal tinnitus suppression. Otol. Neurotol. **26**(4), 616–619 (2005)
2. Kleinjung, T., Steffens, T., Londero, A., Langguth, B.: Transcranial magnetic stimulation (TMS) for treatment of chronic tinnitus: clinical effects. Prog. Brain Res. **166**, 359–551 (2007)
3. Plewnia, C., Reimold, M., Najib, A., Brehm, B., Reischl, G., Plontke, S.K., Gerloff, C.: Dose-dependent attenuation of auditory phantom perception (tinnitus) by pet-guided repetitive transcranial magnetic stimulation. Hum. Brain Mapp. **28**(3), 238–246 (2007)
4. Khedr, E., Rothwell, J., Ahmed, M., El-Atar, A.: Effect of daily repetitive transcranial magnetic stimulation for treatment of tinnitus: comparison of different stimulus frequencies. J. Neurol. Neurosurg. Psychiatry **79**(2), 212–215 (2008)
5. He, Z., Xiao, B., Liu, F., Wu, H., Yang, Y., Xiao, S., Wang, C., Russell, T.P., Cao, Y.: Single-junction polymer solar cells with high efficiency and photovoltage. Nat. Photonics **9**(3), 174–179 (2015)
6. Knyazev, G.G., Volf, N.V., Belousova, L.V.: Age-related differences in electroencephalogram connectivity and network topology. Neurobiol. Aging **36**(5), 1849–1859 (2015)

Passive BCI Based on Sustained Attention Detection: An fNIRS Study

Zhen Zhang, Xuejun Jiao$^{(\boxtimes)}$, Jin Jiang, Jinjin Pan, Yong Cao, Hanjun Yang, and Fenggang Xu

National Key Laboratory of Human Factors Engineering,
China Astronaut Research and Training Center, Beijing 100094, China
18801969650@126.com

Abstract. Passive brain-computer interface (BCI) can monitor cognitive function through physiological signals in human-machine system. This paper established a passive BCI based on functional near-infrared spectroscopy (fNIRS) to detect the sustained attentional load. Three levels of attentional load were adjusted by modifying the number of stimulate in feature-absence Continuous Performance Test (CPT) tasks. 15 healthy subjects were recruited in total, and 10 channels were measured in prefrontal cortex (PFC). Performance and NASA-TLX scales were also recorded as reference. The mean value of oxyhemoglobin and deoxyhemoglobin, signal slope, power spectrum and approximate entropy in 0–10 s were extracted from raw fNIRS signal for support vector machine (SVM) classification. The best performance features were selected by SVM-RFE algorithm. In conclusion over 80% average accuracy was achived between easy and hard attentional load, which demonstrated fNIRS can be a proposed method to detect sustained attention load for a passive BCI.

1 Introduction

Brain-Computer Interface (BCI) can be divided into three modes according to trigger ways, including active BCI, reactive BCI and passive BCI [1]. In detail, active BCI conveyed control commands through consciousness directly, such as motor imagery based BCI, music imagery based BCI. Reactive BCI conveyed control commands through brain activity induced by external stimulants, such as P300 speller. Passive BCI need not special ways to stimulate brain activities, conversely, it monitored humans cognitive activities, such as human mental workload evaluation, drowsiness detection, mood detector, fatigue detection, etc.

In Human-machine system, it was important to obtain the operator's cognitive functions. The Human-machine system was more secure when operator in the appropriate mental workload, while worse performance and accidents may happen when operator was in uncomfortable state like overloaded, depression and fatigue.

BCI system usually consisted of five parts, including cerebral signal acquisition, signal preprocessing, feature extraction, classification and application.

© Springer International Publishing AG 2016
C.-L. Liu et al. (Eds.): BICS 2016, LNAI 10023, pp. 220–227, 2016.
DOI: 10.1007/978-3-319-49685-6_20

The means of cerebral signal acquisition including electroencephalography (EEG), magnetoencephalography (MEG), functional magnetic resonance imaging (fMRI) and functional near-infrared spectroscopy (fNIRS). FNIRS was a relatively new method for physiological measurements, which based on the effect of near-infrared light (650–1000 nm) absorbed by oxyhemoglobin and deoxyhemoglobin. Therefore, it was possible to detect changes of hemoglobin in cerebral functional areas and reflects cognitive activities indirectly. Compared with other methods, fNIRS was less sensitive to motion. Compared with fMRI, fNIRS was more portable and cheaper. Compared with EEG and MEG, fNIRS was hardly interfered by external electromagnetic. Therefore, researches about fNIRS was gradually increasing.

Sustained attention was the ability of maintaining attention and alertness when the human was stimulated for a long time. Thus sustained attention played an important role in Human-machine systems, such as, military reconnaissance, air traffic control, driving, etc. but humans attention resources were limited, when the attention load was too high, operators may be overloaded and miss alarm events. While when the task was too simple, operators may be fall into the state of out of loop [2]. Billings [3] thought that human-centered system should ensure that the operator is not in a too simple or too difficult task load. It was significant to keep humans in appropriate cognitive loads through allocate human machine tasks dynamically according to the operators cognitive state, and improve performance and reliability of human-machine system.

The study about cerebral oxygenation for sustained attention focused on the characteristics of oxygenation and the sensitive brain regions in sustained attention task, while a few studies were about the detection of sustained attention load [4]. The right hemisphere lateralization was proved consistently [5,6]. Besides, Helton noted that laterality of oxygen saturation was related to the difficulty of attention task, which can be used as the feature for distinction of attention load [7].

Many paradigms were used to study sustained attention in lab, of which the most widely used one was continuous performance test (CPT), CPT can be used to detect the ability of humans attention in neuroscience [8,9]. Various improved versions of the CPT were produced nowadays, for instance, Shalev designed a new conjunctive CPT task by taking shape and color as target characteristics, which was proved to obtain a more pure sustained attention component [10]. As a reference, we combined numbers and colors as target feature.

Attention load was related to the numbers and frequency of targets, Catanzaro found that the ability to detect absence-feature target will decrease with the target increase [11]. Therefore, we designed three levels of attention load by adjusting the number of targets from modified CCPT. Support vector machines (SVM) was used to establish sustained attention task load model according to the cerebral oxygenation.

2   Method

2.1   Participants

15 subjects in total were recruited from China Astronaut Research and Training Centre and China Agricultural University. All of the participants had normal or correct-ed-to-normal vision and were right-handed. They ranged in age from 19 to 37 years (M = 26.0, SD = 4.7).

2.2   Experimental Paradigms

The subject kept approximately 50 cm away from 50 * 30 cm2 LCD screen and adjusted to look directly at the central position of the screen. The target was 2 cm* 1 cm, Calibri font, target was exposed for 200 ms, and intervals between two stimulations was 1000 ms–2000 ms. The stimulation included 9 numbers (0,1,29), colored in red, green or blue, and the target stimulus was 3 in red. When no target appeared on the screen, subject should press the left key. Stimulation appeared in five positions, including 3,6,9,12 and center of screen. The probability for target of each level were 45%.

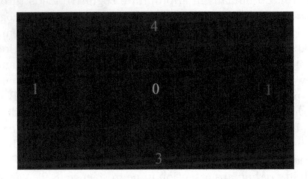

Fig. 1. Interface for modified CPT task for difficult task (Color figure online)

Three levels of attention load were set by the target numbers. For easy task, stimulation only appeared in the central location; for medium difficult task, stimulation appeared in the 6, 12 o'clock and central position; for difficult task, stimulation appeared in all of five positions. Experimental interface for difficult level was shown in Fig. 1. For each subject, the three levels of task appeared in random order, task time was 15 min in total with 5 min for each task. The subjects rested 2 min at the start and the end of each task as the baseline state.

2.3   Data Acquisition

Artinis Oxymon fNIRS equipment was used in this study with the wavelength of 765 nm and 856 nm. A total of 10 channels were placed in the prefrontal cortex

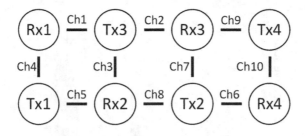

Fig. 2. Channel location of prefrontal region

(PFC) (1–10Ch) including four light source (Tx) and four detectors (Rx), as shown in Fig. 2, the sampling rate is 25 Hz. Before and after each task, the subjects need scale the Mental Demands, Physical Demands, Temporal Demands, Own Performance, Effort and Frustration in NASA-TLX scale, and each item was 10 points.

2.4 Data Processing

In this study, a band-pass filter (0.05–0.5 Hz) was used to remove cardiac interference and high frequency noise. The means of oxyhemoglobin change (ΔHBo) and deoxyhemoglobin change (ΔHB), the slope of ΔHBo, the power spectrum and the approximate entropy were extracted from 0–10 s fNIRS signal. The means of ΔHBo can reflected the active level of brain activity. The slope was obtained from the linear fit for ΔHBo. The power spectrum ranged from 0.1 Hz to 0.75 Hz. Approximate entropy described the degree of ordering for random signal. Note that fNIRS signal was also random signals.

3 Results

3.1 Subjective Evaluation Results

Overall workload scores were based on average of ratings on six subscales. The score of subjective scale for the simple task (M = 1.75, SD = 0.92); for the medium difficult task (M = 3.8, SD = 1.15); for the difficult tasks (M − 6.56, SD = 2.31) as showed in Fig. 3.

The ANOVA results showed significant difference between the three levels of the task ($F_{(2, 42)}$ = 61.84, $p < 0.001$), then the Post-hoc tests also showed significant difference between two levels: simple task and medium difficult task ($p = 0.03 < 0.05$); medium difficult task and difficult task ($p = 0.01 < 0.05$); simple task and difficult task ($p < 0.001$) (Fig. 4).

3.2 Behavioral Results

The correct rate and false alarm rate were extracted from performance data. For the correct rate: simple task (M = 0.77, SD = 0.05), medium difficult task

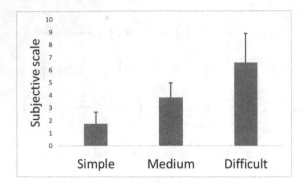

Fig. 3. Subjective scales for three levels tasks

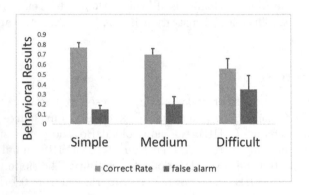

Fig. 4. Behavioral results for three levels tasks

(M = 0.70, SD = 0.06), difficult task (M = 0.56, SD = 0.10). The ANOVA results showed significant difference among the three levels of the tasks (F (2, 42) = 33.11, p < 0.001), then the Post-hoc tests also showed significant difference: simple task and medium difficult task (p = 0.02); medium difficult task and difficult task (p = <0.001); simple task and difficult task (p < 0.001).

For the false alarm rate: simple task (M = 0.15, SD = 0.04), medium difficult task(M = 0.20, SD = 0.08), difficult task M = 0.35, SD = 0.14, The ANOVA results showed significant difference between the three levels of the task (F (2,42) = 33.11, p < 0.001), then the Post-hoc tests also show significant difference besides simple task and medium difficult task (p = 0.06), and the medium difficult task and difficult task(p < 0.001); simple task and difficult task (p < 0.001).

3.3 fNIRS Data Processing Results

We extracted features from fNIRS signal from average all 10 channels, ANOVA-Test showed that the means, slope and approximate entropy of were different

Table 1. Classification accuracies of all subjects for 3 levels of attention load

Participant	3-class	Easy vs Medium	Medium vs Hard	Easy vs Hard
01	47.37	62.35	64.49	78.48
02	52.63	73.78	70.63	81.53
03	45.85	61.91	61.77	70.73
04	44.81	64.81	74.56	69.39
05	55.51	77.37	83.44	70.75
06	64.98	58.65	88.22	78.19
07	59.76	78.66	77.03	85.78
08	56.71	66.24	80.05	84.82
09	65.71	72.81	79.75	86.51
10	54.99	68.88	68.18	78.66
11	56.15	64.15	79.75	82.27
12	64.24	79.46	64.79	89.55
13	65.37	82.86	68.18	86.82
14	67.21	75.22	67.49	94.93
15	54.37	70.13	77.96	84.47
Mean accuracy	57.04	70.49	73.49	81.53

significantly among three tasks ($P < 0.05$), while power spectrum did not show a significant difference ($P > 0.05$)

SVM-RFE algorithm were used to order the features to get the highest classification accuracy for each subject, the highest accuracy rates of each subjects were shown in Table 1.

Average classification accuracy reaches 57.04% for the 3-classes classifier, 70.49% for the easy and medium difficult task classifier, 73.49% for the medium difficult and hard task and 81.53% for the easy and difficult classifier.

4 Discussion

For three levels of CPT tasks, subjective scales were significant different, which mean the subjects need more mental resource in the multi-target stimuli task, and performance also declined, such results are consistent with studies before [11].

It should be noted that False Alarm Rate was not significant different between simple and medium difficult task. The reason may be that the state of mental load was in the normal range, and high task load cant reduce the performance immediately, which was also decided by subjective efforts or other factors, but it was impossible to maintain performance in high task load state for a long time, which was also the shortcomings to assess humans functional state through performance.

From the physiological response, the means, slope and approximate entropy were sensitive to attention load. Specifically, for means of oxyhemoglobin, more active cerebration in attention task have been proved in many articles [5,7]; For the slope, the more active cerebration was corresponding to the larger slope [13]. Entropy has been applied in the near infrared studies [12], but the physiological significance was not obvious as the means and slope. Entropy reflected the activity of the brain from the complexity of the fNIRS signal.

The classification results showed that simple tasks and difficult tasks achieve the best classification accuracy of 80% compared with other 2-classes, which was consistent with the results of the subjective evaluation and performance between this two tasks. The discrimination for subjective rating between simple tasks and medium difficult task was the least, so the classification accuracy is lower than other 2-classes classifier.

In conclusion, attention load model was established from the classic CPT tasks, and we will continue to study the monitor task in a real environment and increase classification accuracy.

Acknowledgments. This research was supported in part by National Natural Science Foundation of China (grant no. 81671861), Advance Research Project of China Aerospace Medical Engineering (grant no. YJGF151204) and independent subject of National Key Laboratory of Human Factors Engineering, China Astronaut Research and training center, Beijing, China (grant no. SYFD150051805).

References

1. Zander, T.O., Kothe, C.: Towards passive brain-computer interfaces: applying brain-computer interface technology to human-machine systems in general. J. Neural Eng. **8**(2), 025005 (2011)
2. Young, L.R.: On adaptive manual control. Ergonomics **12**(4), 635–674 (1969)
3. Billings, C.E.: Aviation Automation: The Search for a Human-Centered Approach (1997)
4. Gaume, A., Abbasi, M.A., Dreyfus, G., et al.: Towards cognitive BCI: neural correlates of sustained attention in a continuous performance task. In: Proceedings of International IEEE EMBS Neural Engineering (2015)
5. Stroobant, N., Vingerhoets, G.: Transcranial doppler ultrasonography monitoring of cerebral hemodynamics during performance of cognitive tasks: a review. Neuropsychol. Rev. **10**(4), 213–231 (2000)
6. Warm, J.S., Matthews, G., Parasuraman, R.: Cerebral hemodynamics and vigilance performance. Mil. Psychol. **21**(1), 75–100 (2009)
7. Helton, W.S., Warm, J.S., Tripp, L.D., et al.: Cerebral lateralization of vigilance: a function of task difficulty. Neuropsychologia **48**(6), 1683–1688 (2010)
8. Cornblatt, B., Risch, N.J., Faris, G., Friedman, D., Erlenmeyer-Kimling, L.: The continuous performance test, identical pairs version (CPT-IP): I. New findings about sustained attention in normal families. Psychiatry Res. **29**, 65–68 (1988)
9. Adler, C.M., Sax, K.W., Holland, S.K., Schmithorst, V., Rosenberg, L., Strakowski, S.M.: Changes in neuronal activation with increasing attention demanding healthy volunteers: an fMRI study. Synapse **42**, 266–272 (2001)

10. Shalev, L., Ben-Simon, A., Mevorach, C., et al.: Conjunctive continuous performance task (CCPT) a pure measure of sustained attention. Neuropsychologia **49**(9), 2584–2591 (2011)
11. Catanzaro, J.M., Scerbo, M.W.: Searching for the presence and absence of features in vigilance: the decrement persists. Hum. Factors Ergon. Soc. Annu. Meet. Proc. **43**(23), 1285–1288 (1999)
12. Khan, M.J., Hong, K.S.: Passive BCI based on drowsiness detection: an fNIRS study. Biomed. Opt. Express **6**(10), 4063–4078 (2015)
13. Jiao, X., Bai, J., Chen, S., et al.: Monitoring mental fatigue in analog space environment using optical brain imaging. Engineering **05**(5), 53–57 (2014)

Incremental Learning Vector Quantization for Character Recognition with Local Style Consistency

Yuan-Yuan Shen[1,3] and Cheng-Lin Liu[1,2,3,4(✉)]

[1] Research Center for Brain-Inspired Intelligence,
Institute of Automation of Chinese Academy of Sciences, Beijing 100190, China
[2] National Laboratory of Pattern Recognition,
Institute of Automation of Chinese Academy of Sciences, Beijing, China
`liucl@nlpr.ia.ac.cn`
[3] University of Chinese Academy of Sciences (UCAS), Beijing, China
[4] CAS Center for Excellence in Brain Science and Intelligence Technology,
CAS, Beijing, China

Abstract. Incremental learning is a way relevant to human learning that utilizes samples in online sequence. In the paper, we propose an incremental learning method called Incremental Adaptive Learning Vector Quantization (IALVQ) which aims at classifying characters appearing in an online sequence with style consistency in local time periods. Such local consistency is present commonly in document images, in that the characters in a paragraph or text line are printed in the same font or written by the same person. Our IALVQ method updates the prototypes (parameters of classifier) incrementally to adapt to drifted concepts globally while utilize the style consistency locally. For style adaptation, a style transfer mapping (STM) matrix is calculated on a batch of samples of assumed same style. The STM matrix can be used both in training for prototypes updating and in testing for labels prediction. We consider supervised incremental learning and active incremental learning. In the latter way, class labels are attached only to samples that are assigned low confidence by the classifier. In our experiments on handwritten digits in the NIST Special Database 19, we evaluated the classification performance of IALVQ in two scenarios, interleaved test-then-train and style-specific classification. The results show that utilizing local style consistency can improve the accuracies of both two test scenarios, and for both supervised and active incremental learning modes.

Keywords: Incremental learning · Style transfer mapping · Local style consistency · Incremental Adaptive Learning Vector Quantization

1 Introduction

The size of real-world database has increased dynamically, therefore it is necessary to update existing models based on continuously acquired data instead of

© Springer International Publishing AG 2016
C.-L. Liu et al. (Eds.): BICS 2016, LNAI 10023, pp. 228–239, 2016.
DOI: 10.1007/978-3-319-49685-6_21

re-training them. Incremental learning is a branch of machine learning method centered on solving such problems. Classical incremental learning has been intensively studied in the machine learning research area [1–3]. The learning algorithm observes instances in a sequential manner (i.e., instances usually appear one-by-one, or batch-by-batch). In addition, incremental learning algorithms are always accompanied by distribution change (concept drift).

Various incremental learning algorithms have been developed for different pattern recognition applications. However, when it comes to incremental character recognition, there are some new characteristics to consider. First, character patterns are presented as groups frequently, which means we can utilize the local style consistency, i.e., patterns in a time period have the same style. For example, characters in a paragraph or a text line are usually printed in the same font or written by a same person. Second, the distribution change is ubiquitous. Characters from different sources (pages in different fonts or written by different persons) have different styles. Such style variation results in distribution change in the feature space. Last but not least, for the practical application of character recognition, we hope that the incremental learning can not only adapt to the changing styles in learning from sequence of patterns, but also remember all the styles in the previously learned patterns, because in application, the learned classifier will face test patterns of all possible styles.

To cope with the characteristics stated above in incremental character recognition, we propose incremental adaptive learning vector quantization (IALVQ). IALVQ can classify patterns appear in an online sequence with style consistency in local time periods. Learning vector quantization (LVQ) is a learning method for prototype classifier, which is akin to human learning in that prototypes (templates) are memorized in the brain to recognize new patterns and the prototypes can be learned by both generative and discriminative way. We use style transfer mapping (STM) [4] to compute the style matrix in consideration of local style consistency. After getting the style matrix, a pattern from feature space with changing style can be mapped into a style-free space. In order to adapt different styles, we bring in the forget mechanism in the way that old data are discarded or weakened to ensure that style transfer matrix is learned from the latest data. Prototype learning in style-free space is very helpful for the test-then-train scenario. However, we also hope the learned prototypes can memorize all the styles in the past data to enhance the performance of multi-style classification. To do this, we learn style-conscious prototypes as done in traditional Increment Learning Vector Quantization (ILVQ) simultaneously. In summarize, our proposed IALVQ is a new method which combines STM and ILVQ to realize incremental character learning and recognition.

The human learning of characters occasionally interacts with a teacher (i.e., inquire a teacher for the label when we face an un-known character). Inspired by this, we also introduce the active incremental learning mode of IALVQ. In this case, we attach labels to the training samples only when the confidence assigned by the classifier is low. Our experimental results show that in the case of active incremental learning, utilizing local style consistency by STM is also efficient to improve the classification performance.

The rest of this paper is organized as follows. Section 2 reviews related works. Section 3 presents the proposed IALVQ method in detail. Section 4 presents our experimental results and analysis. Section 5 is the conclusion of this paper, and a discussion of future directions is also provided.

2   Related Work

Our work is mainly related to previous works of incremental learning and style consistent learning. Some representative works are reviewed as follows.

Incremental learning has been extensively studied in recent years. Unlike traditional machine learning which assumes that all the training patterns are available before training, incremental learning is more relevant to practical environments where patterns appear in an sequential manner, and the pattern distribution may change over time. So, how to update classifier model (adapt pre-model into latest data) is the vital issue in incremental learning. One classical approach is the Perceptron algorithm [5] proposed in 1950s. Perceptron adopts a simple adaptive strategy for updating the weights of single-layer neural network when an incoming pattern is misclassified. Incremental prototype-based classifier [6,7] is another typical model which adapts newest data by updating two nearest prototypes from the genuine class and the rival class of input pattern. By using covariance matrix as confidence information of different dimensions, some second-order incremental algorithms [8,9] have been proposed. In [10] three guildlines about incremental learning for large-scale visual recognition were proposed. A comprehensive survey on incremental learning with concept drift can be found in [11].

In character learning and recognition, characters appearing together usually originates from the same source of consistent style. Such local consistency is commonly present in document images where the characters in a paragraph or text line are printed in the same font or written by the same person. Previous works have shown that exploiting style consistency can promote the performance of character recognition. Sarkar and Nagy [12] proposed an optimal style constrained classifier which processes entire fields of characters rendered in a consistent style. Veeramachaneni and Nagy [13,14] proposed a Gaussian quadratic discriminant filed classifier for field classification. In [15], Huang et al. learned a writer-specific LDA transformation matrix with the new labeled data in an incremental handwriting recognition. By learning a style transfer mapping (STM) matrix, Zhang and Liu [4] proposed a writer-specific adaptation method.

Although both incremental learning and style consistency have been actively studied, to the best of our knowledge, the combination of incremental learning and style consistency has been considered before. The closest methods to the work presented here are [15,16], which are to adapt an well-learned classifier to writer-specific data.

3   Proposed Methods

In this section, we first introduce the incremental adaptive LVQ, then extend to active incremental adaptive LVQ. At Last, we will outline two paradigms for evaluating the classification performance of incremental learning methods.

3.1   Incremental Adaptive Learning Vector Quantization

For M-class classification, prototype learning is to design a set of prototype vectors $m_{ij}(i = 1, 2, ..., M, j = 1, ..., n_i$. n_i is the number of prototypes in class i), usually by minimizing the empirical loss on a training set. An input pattern $x \in \mathbb{R}^d$ is classified to the class of the nearest prototype:

$$k = \arg \min_{i=1}^{M} \min_{j=1}^{n_i} \|x - m_{ij}\|_2^2 = G(x, m), \tag{1}$$

There are many variations of LVQ algorithm [17–19]. In this paper, we use the one of LOG-likelihood of Margin (LOGM) [19].

In our proposed method, we learn two types of prototypes for each class: one is style-conscious prototypes $m_{il_1}(i = 1, ..., M, l_1 = 1, 2, ..., L_1)$ which are completely the same with conventional ILVQ; the other is style-free prototypes $m_{il_2}(i = 1, ..., M, l_2 = 1, 2, ..., L_2)$, which are irrelevant to specific style. However, the learning of two types of prototypes is mutually independent.

For the learning of style-conscious prototypes, given that m_1 and m_2 are the nearest prototype to pattern x from the positive class and the one from the rival class, the posterior probability of x belonging to genuine class i (i.e., the probability of correct classification) can be approximated by the sigmoid function:

$$P(C_i|x) = \sigma(\xi(\|x - m_2\|^2 - \|x - m_1\|^2)), \tag{2}$$

where $\xi(\xi > 0)$ is a constant for tuning the smoothness of sigmoid function and the conditional log-likelihood loss of pattern x is $\phi(x) = -\log P(C_i|x)$.

As each pattern x is arriving in incremental setting, ILVQ updates two prototypes m_1 and m_2 by stochastic gradient descent [20]:

$$\begin{aligned} m_1 &= m_1 - \eta \frac{\partial \phi(x)}{\partial m_1}, \\ m_2 &= m_2 - \eta \frac{\partial \phi(x)}{\partial m_2}. \end{aligned} \tag{3}$$

The style-free prototypes are learned in a similar manner, as detailed in the following section.

In incremental setting, we assume that adjacent patterns share the same style. So, the style transfer matrix which maps pattern from style-conscious space to style-free space for current pattern can be computed from several latest past patterns approximately. The objective function of learning style transfer matrix is composed of three parts. The first part is from the past patterns, the second part is from the current patterns, and the last part is for regularization. So the objective function of STM is:

$$F(t) = DecayWeight * F(t-1) + \triangle F(t) + \beta \|A - I\|_F^2, \tag{4}$$

where $F(0) = 0$, $DecayWeight$ is the decay parameter, I is the identity matrix, the hyperparameter β controls the trade-off between style transfer and non-transfer. For every moment, in order to reduce the influence caused by the past patterns we decay the relative item.

Suppose that $X = \{x_i | i = 1, ..., b\}$ is a small batch of patterns arriving at time t, the second part is computed as:

$$\triangle F(t) = \sum_{i=1}^{b} \|Ax_i - \hat{t}\|_2^2, \tag{5}$$

where b is the batch size, A is style transfer matrix, x_i is a training pattern, $\hat{t}$ is the nearest style-free prototype from the genuine class from x_i.

Let

$$\begin{aligned} S(t) &= DecayWeight * S(t-1) + \triangle S, \\ s.t. \quad \triangle S &= xx^T, S(0) = 0, \\ T(t) &= DecayWeight * T(t-1) + \triangle T, \\ s.t. \quad \triangle T &= \hat{t}x^T, T(0) = 0, \end{aligned} \tag{6}$$

then the computation of A has a closed-form solution:

$$\begin{aligned} A &= QP^{-1}, \\ Q &= T(t) + \beta I, \\ P &= S(t) + \beta I. \end{aligned} \tag{7}$$

Please refer to [4] for more details.

With the mapping matrix A, we can map pattern x into a style-free space by:

$$\hat{x} = Ax. \tag{8}$$

And then, we update the style-free prototypes as follows similar to Eq. (3):

$$\begin{aligned} m_1 &= m_1 - \eta \frac{\partial \phi(\hat{x})}{\partial m_1}, \\ m_2 &= m_2 - \eta \frac{\partial \phi(\hat{x})}{\partial m_2}. \end{aligned} \tag{9}$$

We summarize the process of learning style-free prototypes in Algorithm 1.

3.2   Active Incremental Adaptive Learning Vector Quantization

In character recognition, active incremental learning is very helpful. By partial interaction between the learner and the environment we can label for patterns

---

Algorithm 1. Learning of style-free prototypes

Input: Prototypes m_{il_2}
Output: Prototypes m_{il_2}
  1: Initial style matrix $A = I$
  2: **while** Receive new patterns X **do**
  3:    Compute style-free patterns for each pattern in X by Eq. (8)
  4:    Update style-free prototypes m_{il_2} by Eq. (9)
  5:    Compute new style matrix A by Eq. (7)
  6: **end while**
  7: **return** m_{il_2}

---

that are assigned low confidence by the classifier. Due to the important effect of patterns that are assigned low confidence, active learning can boost the performance of classifier by requiring rare patterns.

In active incremental learning, how to evaluate the confidence for coming pattern is a vital problem. We use a simple but effective strategy that the confidence f for pattern x is calculated by Eq. (2) (posterior probability). Because of the unknown information of genuine class, we compute two nearest prototypes from the top two classes instead of the positive class and the rival class. Only when the confidence f is smaller than a predefined threshold p, the input pattern requests a label. Obviously, the larger the predefined threshold p is, the more are the required labels. For pattern x the conditional log-likelihood loss in active ILVQ and active IALVQ is computed as $\phi(x) = -f \log P(C_i|x)$. The active incremental adaptive learning vector quantization is summarized as Algorithm 2.

Algorithm 2. Active Incremental Adaptive Learning Vector Quantization

---

Input: Prototypes m_{ij}, Predefined threshold p
Output: Prototypes m_{ij}
  1: initial style matrix $A = I$
  2: **while** receive new patterns X **do**
  3:    **for** each pattern x in X **do**
  4:       Compute confidence f by Eq. (2)
  5:       Decide whether to query the label ($Z = 1$) or not ($Z = 0$)
  6:       **if** $Z = 1$ **then**
  7:          Query label y
  8:          Set confidence $f = 1$
  9:       **end if**
 10:       Update style-conscious prototypes m_{il_1} using pattern x by Eq. (3)
 11:       Compute style-free pattern $\hat{x}$ by Eq. (8)
 12:       Update style-free prototypes m_{il_2} using style-free pattern $\hat{x}$ by Eq. (9)
 13:    **end for**
 14:    Compute new style matrix A by Eq. (7)
 15: **end while**
 16: **return** m_{ij}

3.3   Evaluation

We evaluate our proposed algorithm in two scenarios: interleaved test-then-train and style-specific classification.

Interleaved Test-Then-Train. Each pattern is used to test the classifier before it's used for training, so the classifier is always being tested on patterns it has not seen before. This evaluation method can make maximum use of the available data.

Style-Specific Classification. After training an incremental classifier, we test the generalization performance of the classifier. During test time, a batch of b patterns with the same style are given once. The process of testing is reported in Algorithm 3. Note that we use style-conscious prototypes for first-round classification for obtaining the initial labels of patterns. Then in style adaptive classification, style-free prototypes are used because the patterns are mapped toward style-free space.

Algorithm 3. Style-Specific Classification

Input: Prototypes m_{ij}
         Style-specific unlabeled data $\{x_k\}_{k=1}^{b}$
Output: Predicted labels $\hat{y}_k, k = 1...b$
1: Initial style matrix $A = I$
2: **for** k=1:b **do**
3:     Compute label $\overline{y}_k = G(x_k, m_{il_1})$ using Eq. (1)
4:     Find nearest prototype $d_k = \arg\min_{l_2=1}^{L_2} \|x_k - m_{\overline{y}_k l_2}\|_2^2$
5: **end for**
6: **for** iter = 1:iterNum **do**
7:     Learn matrix style A using Eq. (7)
8:     **for** k=1:b **do**
9:        Predict label $\hat{y}_k = G(Ax_k, m_{il_2})$ using Eq. (1)
10:       Find nearest prototype $\hat{t}_k = \arg\min_{l_2=1}^{L_2} \|Ax_k - m_{\hat{y}_k l_2}\|_2^2$
11:     **end for**
12: **end for**

---

4   Experiments and Results

We evaluate the performance of the proposed IALVQ method on NIST hand-written digit data. Two learning modes were considered:

(i) supervised incremental learning;
(ii) active incremental learning.

Table 1. Handwritten numeral datasets

	Writers	Number of samples
SD3-Train	No.0-No.399 (400)	42969
SD7-Train	No.2100-No.2199 (100)	11585
SD3-Test	No.400-No.799 (399)	42821
SD7-Test	No.2200-No.2299 (100)	11660

4.1 Database

To test our proposed method on realistic data, we experimented with the datasets
SD3 and SD7, which are contained in the NIST Special Database SD19 [21]. The
datasets contain patterns of handwritten numerals labeled by writer and class.
From SD3, we use samples of 400 writers for training and 399 writers for testing,
and from SD7, samples of 100 writers for training and 100 writers for testing.
The patterns of each writer are assumed to have the same writing style. The
statistics of patterns for SD3 and SD7 are listed in Table 1. The patterns from
some writers are shown in Fig. 1. Our choice of data is similar to that of [13] for
adaptive classification.

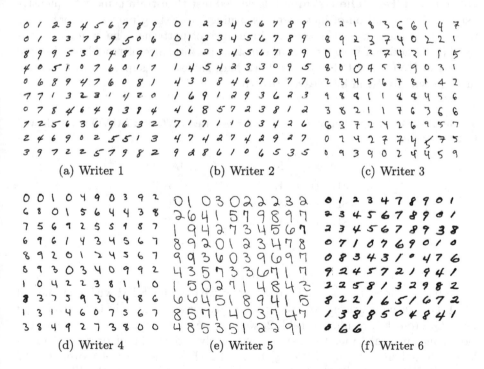

Fig. 1. Samples of handwritten digits from 6 different writers.

4.2 Experimental Setting

All these patterns are arranged by writer order and patterns are permuted randomly within one writer. We extracted 100 blurred directional (chain-code) features from each pattern [22]. A small number of patterns are used to construct the initial prototypes. After getting initial classifier, new coming patterns are used for both prototypes updating and estimating style transfer matrix. The classification performance are evaluated using interleaved test-then-train and style-specific classification.

For all the datasets, we use very small portion patterns (200 patterns) for initialization. The trade-off parameter β in style adaptation is set as in [4]: $\beta = \hat{\beta}\frac{1}{d}Tr(\sum_{i=1}^{n} x_i x_i^T)$, where n is the total number of patterns that have been seen in model and $\hat{\beta}$ is set as 3 in our experiments. The smoothing parameter ξ is initialized as $2/cov$ like [19], where cov is the average covariance estimated from training data. The initial rate of gradient descent is set as 1 and the learning rate of the n-th pattern is calculated by adagrad algorithm [23]. The batch size b is set as 5 and $delayParam$ is set as 0.9.

4.3 Results and Discussions

Interleaved Test-Then-Train. Interleaved test-then-train is most frequently-used in the evaluation of incremental learning. By testing pattern before being used for training, we can make maximum use of patterns. The result assessed by this method can better reflect the instant performance of model. We list the results of ILVQ and IALVQ in Table 2 and Table 3 for supervised and active mode, respectively, in interleaved test-then-train.

Table 2. Error rates on four datasets using supervised ILVQ and IALVQ in interleaved test-then-train.

Dataset	Incremental LVQ	IALVQ
SD3-Train	1.66 %	1.31 %
SD7-Train	4.17 %	3.45 %
SD3-Test	1.37 %	1.25 %
SD7-Test	3.68 %	3.25 %

When considering local style consistency, we combine STM with incremental LVQ. For fair comparison, we use 3 prototypes for every class in both ILVQ and IALVQ. From the results in Table 2, we can see that compared to the conventional incremental LVQ, IALVQ can effectively reduce the error rate of interleaved test-then-train, by utilizing the local style consistency of writer-specific samples. This can be attributed to better class separability resulted in via feature transformation from STM. From the results in Table 3, we can see that due to the availability of only small proportion of samples, active ILVQ yields higher

Table 3. Error rates on four datasets using active ILVQ and IALVQ in interleaved test-then-train.

Dataset	Active ILVQ	# of used patterns	Active IALVQ	# of used patterns
SD3-Train	1.93 %	1497/42969	1.77 %	1366/42969
SD7-Train	4.38 %	1043/11585	4.17 %	942/11585
SD3-Test	1.67 %	1571/42821	1.46 %	1391/42821
SD7-Test	3.90 %	1133/11660	3.63 %	981/11660

error rate than supervised ILVQ (in Table 2). Active IALVQ also yields higher error rate than the supervised IALVQ. However, compared to active ILVQ, active IALVQ results in reduced error rate due to the effect of local style consistency utilization via STM.

Style-Specific Classification. In order to evaluate the generalization performance of our proposed method, we compare 4 different supervised methods and 2 different active methods with our method. Tables 4 and 5 show the classification error rates for supervised and active mode, respectively. A/B represents that A is adopted in training stage and B is adopted in testing stage. In testing stage, NN is classified based on the nearest prototype without considering style consistency, while STM utilizes style consistency of writer-specific data. For fair comparison, we use the best prototypes parameters respectively, that is, 5 prototypes are used in ILVQ while 5 style-conscious prototypes and 2 style-free prototypes are used in IALVQ.

Table 4. Error rates using supervised ILVQ and IALVQ in style-specific classification.

Training set	Test set	LVQ/NN	LVQ/STM	ILVQ/NN	ILVQ/STM	IALVQ/STM
SD3-Train	SD3-Test	1.02 %	0.79 %	1.58 %	1.12 %	0.99 %
SD3-Train	SD7-Test	4.19 %	3.21 %	5.96 %	4.49 %	4.26 %
SD7-Train	SD3-Test	1.79 %	1.30 %	2.70 %	2.01 %	1.80 %
SD7-Train	SD7-Test	2.34 %	1.87 %	3.55 %	2.82 %	2.51 %

In the active incremental learning setting, the number of labeled patterns in SD3-Train is 1441 for ILVQ (1556 for IALVQ), which accounts for about only 3 % of total data, and 1114 for ILVQ (1001 for IALVQ) in SD7-Train, which accounts for about 10 % of total data. The results in Table 4 show that when evaluating generalized classification performance using NN without considering style consistency, the incremental LVQ results in higher error rate than supervised LVQ which treats all training samples iteratively. Style-specific classification by STM reduces the error rate of both LVQ and ILVQ considerably.

Table 5. Error rates using active ILVQ and IALVQ in style-specific classification.

Training set	Test set	Active-ILVQ/NN	Active-ILVQ/STM	Active-(IALVQ)/STM
SD3-Train	SD3-Test	1.52 %	1.13 %	0.99 %
SD3-Train	SD7-Test	5.87 %	4.67 %	4.65 %
SD7-Train	SD3-Test	3.90 %	2.60 %	2.34 %
SD7-Train	SD7-Test	4.09 %	3.15 %	2.86 %

This observation conforms with previous results in [4]. When comparing ILVQ/STM and IALVQ/STM, we can see that the proposed IALVQ method can further reduce the error rate of ILVQ even when style consistency is considered in testing. The results in Table 5 confirms that style-specific classification with STM can also reduces the error rate of active ILVQ. Comparing active IALVQ with active ILVQ, again the proposed active IALVQ can reduce the error rate of active ILVQ when style consistency is considered in testing.

5   Conclusion

In this paper, we propose an incremental learning method utilizing local style consistency of samples for improving the classification performance of character recognition. Experimental results have shown that the proposed method is effective in both supervised incremental learning and active incremental learning. Active incremental learning is akin to human learning which occasionally interacts with a teacher for inquiring labels for unknown patterns. In our experiments, however, the proportion of inquired samples is considerable and implies high cost of interactive learning. In the future, we will seek to realize efficient unsupervised incremental learning or interactive learning with very small number of samples inquired.

Acknowledgments. This work has been supported in part by the National Basic Research Program of China (973 Program) under Grant 2012CB316302 and the Strategic Priority Research Program of the CAS under Grant XDB02060009.

References

1. Syed, N., Liu, H., Sung, K.: Incremental learning with support vector machines. In: International Joint Conference on Artificial Intelligence, pp. 352–356. Morgan Kaufmann Publishers, Sweden (1999)
2. Hoi, S.C.H., Wang, J., Zhao, P.: LIBOL: a library for online learning algorithms. J. Mach. Learn. Res. **15**(1), 495–499 (2014)
3. Zhao, P., Hoi, S.C.: OTL: a framework of online transfer learning. In: Proceedings of the 27th International Conference on Machine Learning, pp. 1231–1238 (2010)
4. Zhang, X.Y., Liu, C.L.: Writer adaptation with style transfer mapping. IEEE Trans. Pattern Anal. Mach. Intell. **35**(7), 1773–1787 (2013)

5. Rosenblatt, F.: The perceptron: a probabilistic model for information storage and organization in the brain. Psychol. Rev. **65**(6), 386–408 (1958)
6. Kirstein, S., Wersing, H., Körner, E.: A biologically motivated visual memory architecture for online learning of objects. Neural Netw. **21**(1), 65–77 (2008)
7. Xu, Y., Shen, F., Zhao, J.: An incremental learning vector quantization algorithm for pattern classification. Neural Comput. Appl. **21**(6), 1205–1215 (2012)
8. Cesa-Bianchi, N., Conconi, A., Gentile, C.: A second-order perceptron algorithm. SIAM J. Comput. **34**(3), 640–668 (2005)
9. Crammer, K., Dredze, M., Kulesza, A.: Multi-class confidence weighted algorithms. In: Proceedings of the Conference on Empirical Methods in Natural Language Processing, pp. 496–504 (2009)
10. Ushiku, Y., Hidaka, M., Harada, T.: Three guidelines of online learning for large-scale visual recognition. In: Proceedings of the IEEE Conference on Computer Vision and Pattern Recognition, pp. 3574–3581 (2014)
11. Gama, J., Žliobaitèl, B.A., Pechenizkiy, M., Bouchachia, A.: A survey on concept drift adaptation. ACM Comput. Surv. (CSUR) **46**(4) (2014)
12. Sarkar, P., Nagy, G.: Style consistent classification of isogenous patterns. IEEE Trans. Pattern Anal. Mach. Intell. **27**(1), 88–98 (2005)
13. Veeramachaneni, S., Nagy, G.: Adaptive classifiers for multisource OCR. Doc. Anal. Recognit. **6**(3), 154–166 (2003)
14. Veeramachaneni, S., Nagy, G.: Style context with second-order statistics. IEEE Trans. Pattern Anal. Mach. Intell. **27**(1), 14–22 (2005)
15. Huang, Z., Ding, K., Jin, L., et al.: Writer adaptive online handwriting recognition using incremental linear discriminant analysis. In: Proceedings of the Conference on Document Analysis and Recognition, pp. 91–95. IEEE (2009)
16. Ding, K., Jin, L.: Incremental MQDF learning for writer adaptive handwriting recognition. In: Proceedings of the Conference on Frontiers in Handwriting Recognition (ICFHR), pp. 559–564 (2010)
17. Kohonen, T., Hynninen, J., Kangas, J., Laaksonen, J., Torkkola, K.: LVQ PAK: the learning vector quantization program package. Technical report, Helsinki University of Technology (1995)
18. Kuncheva, L.I., Bezdek, J.C.: Nearest prototype classification: clustering, genetic algorithms, or random search? IEEE Trans. Syst. Man Cybern. Part C (Appl. Rev.) **28**(1), 160–164 (1998)
19. Jin, X.B., Liu, C.L., Hou, X.: Regularized margin-based conditional log-likelihood loss for prototype learning. Pattern Recognit. **43**(7), 2428–2438 (2010)
20. Bishop, C.M.: Pattern recognition and Machine Learning. Springer, New York (2006)
21. Grother, P.: Handprinted forms and character database, NIST special database 19. Technical report and CDROM (1995)
22. Liu, C.L., Sako, H., Fujisawa, H.: Performance evaluation of pattern classifiers for handwritten character recognition. Int. J. Doc. Anal. Recognit. **4**(3), 191–204 (2002)
23. Duchi, J., Hazan, E., Singer, Y.: Adaptive subgradient methods for online learning and stochastic optimization. J. Mach. Learn. Res. **12**, 2121–2159 (2011)

A Novel Fully Automated Liver and HCC Tumor Segmentation System Using Morphological Operations

Liaqat Ali[1(✉)], Amir Hussain[1], Jingpeng Li[1], Newton Howard[2],
Amir A. Shah[3], Unnam Sudhakar[3], Moiz Ali Shah[4],
and Zain U. Hussain[5]

[1] School of Natural Sciences, University of Stirling, Stirling, UK
{lal,ahu,jli}@cs.stir.ac.uk
[2] Medical Sciences Division, Nuffield Department of Surgical Sciences,
University of Oxford, Oxford, UK
newton.howard@nds.ox.ac.uk
[3] University Hospital Crosshouse, Kilmarnock, UK
{amir.shah,s.unnam}@aaaht.scot.nhs.uk
[4] University of Glasgow, Glasgow, UK
moiz95@googlemail.com
[5] University of St. Andrews, St. Andrews, UK
zuah@st-andrews.ac.uk

Abstract. Early detection and diagnosis of Hepatocellular Carcinoma (HCC) is the most discriminating step in liver cancer management. Image processing is primarily used, where fast and accurate Computed Tomography (CT) liver image segmentation is required for effective clinical studies and treatment plans. The purpose of this research is to develop an automated HCC detection and diagnosis system, able to work with HCC lesions from liver CT images, with maximum sensitivity and minimum specificity.

Our proposed system carried out automated segmentation of HCC lesions from 3D liver CT images. First, based on chosen histogram thresholds, we create a mask to predict the segmentation area by exploiting prior knowledge of the location and shape. Next, we obtain a 3D HCC lesion using an appropriate combination of cancer area pixel density calculations, histogram analysis and morphological processing. To demonstrate the feasibility of our approach, we carried out a series of experiments using 31 CT cases, comprised of 18 HCC lesions and 13 non HCC lesions. The acquired CT images (in DICOM format) had 128 channels of 512×512 pixels, each with pixel space varying between 0.54 and 0.85.

Simulation results showed 92.68% accuracy and a false positive incidence of 9.75%. These were also compared and validated against manual segmentation carried out by a radiologist and other widely used image segmentation methods.

Fully automated HCC detection can be efficiently used to aid medical professionals in diagnosing HCC. A limitation of this research is that the performance was evaluated on a small dataset, which does not allow us to confirm robustness of this system. For future work, we will collect additional clinical and CT image data to ensure comprehensive evaluation and clinical validation. We also intend to apply this automated HCC detection and diagnosis system to Positron Emission Tomography (PET) and Magnetic Resonance Imaging

© Springer International Publishing AG 2016
C.-L. Liu et al. (Eds.): BICS 2016, LNAI 10023, pp. 240–250, 2016.
DOI: 10.1007/978-3-319-49685-6_22

(MRI) datasets, as well as adapting it for diagnosing different liver diseases using state-of-the-art feature extraction and selection, and machine learning classification techniques.

Keywords: HCC · Lesion · Detection · Segmentation · CT

1 Introduction

Hepatocellular Carcinoma (HCC) is the 5th most common type of cancer and the 2nd highest cause of cancer related deaths [1]. Diagnosis of this condition is made using 3-Dimensional Computed Tomography (CT), a non-invasive diagnostic imaging technique [2] which utilizes both X-rays and computer technology to produce horizontal or axial images (often called slices) of the body. A CT scan demonstrates detailed images of any part of the body, including the bones, muscles, fat, and internal organs. The early detection and diagnosis of HCC, especially small lesions less than 2 cm [3] is a labour intensive operation, requiring repetitive manual intervention. Additionally, HCC lesion detection is a challenging task due to irregular shapes, sizes, densities and the large number of slices to be processed in 3D CT scans. To tackle these challenges we proposed a fully automated, efficient and cost effective intelligent system to detect and diagnose HCC.

2 State of the Art

Fast and accurate CT liver image segmentation is very important in detection, diagnosis, clinical studies and treatment planning of HCC. Our main objective is to develop an automatic HCC segmentation system that can accurately detect and segment HCC from liver CT images. Canny Edge Detector [4] was introduced to approximate and optimize the edge-searching problem. In order to make the edges more prominent, two-dimensional Gaussian, Magnitude and Direction of the gradient are computed at each pixel level [4] presenting a new algorithm for segmentation of intensity images. This is robust, rapid, and free of tuning parameters but requires the input of a number of seeds, either individual pixels or regions, which will control the formation of regions into which the image is segmented. Region Growing [5] was used firstly to obtain homogeneous seeds via histogram analysis. The histogram of each band was analyzed to obtain a set of representative pixel values, then seeds generated with all the image pixels with representative grey values. Secondly, a modified seeded region growing algorithm was applied to perform the segmentation. This algorithm made use of instance based learning as similarity criteria. K-means clustering [5] and a priori knowledge to find and identify liver and non-liver pixels, which were use "object" and "background" seeds, respectively. Optimizing Fast Fuzzy C-Means [6] by utilizing the Particle Swarm Optimization method (PSOFFCM) [7] which showed higher values for jaccard index and dice coefficient on Liver CT images, and higher similarity with the ground truth presented. Furthermore to evaluate performance, ANOVA analysis and PSOFFCM were also applied, showing better results in terms of box and whisker plots. Different approaches to automatic liver tumour detection and semi-automatic segmentation from CT liver images were also proposed [4] by utilizing the kernel based extreme learning machine but it showed promising segmentation and detection performance in CT scans of 7 patients with total 20 tumours. An automated segmentation technique was also presented [8]. Their work was based on the liver region and likelihood intensity range of CT image data (determined by the histogram analysis, cell density and morphological operations). Graph Cut [9] was applied to detect and segment hepatic tumours using shape and enhancement constrains. Furthermore, tumour Burdon was computed from the segmented liver and tumour. The paper also reported that image registration computation was very expensive, with running time for one case between 50–60 min, including approximately 30–35 min for the initial liver segmentation, 20–25 min for liver segmentation correction and a couple of additional minutes for tumour analysis. The region growing [10] method applied, that automatically segments the liver by combining more phases of the contrast-enhanced CT examination. Also, morphological analysis and geometric feature methods were applied [11] to segment liver lesions automatically, but with inconclusive results. From previous literature it can be seen that there are very few methods which can automatically detect and segment liver tumours accurately. Furthermore, many studies were restricted to specific types of lesion or required certain types of images, some of which were slow in computation. In light of the above issues, there is a great requirement for a robust, state of art and fully automated system that can accurately detect and segment liver and HCC lesion.

3   Proposed Method

3.1   Automatic HCC Detection System

The aim of our research is to develop a robust, real time, and computationally efficient automated liver HCC detection and segmentation system. The proposed system consists of two steps: automatic liver segmentation and automatic HCC lesion detection, as shown in Figure 1. The novelty of the proposed fully automated liver and its lesion segmentation system is: (a) we have introduced a fully automated liver and lesion segmentation based on morphological operations with 3-D CT scan images, (b) the proposed system is fully integrated with the segmentation of the liver and its lesion, (c) it requires minimal computational power, (d) is cost effective, (e) it reduces the work load for the clinical experts, and (f) it can be configured with ease in clinical laboratories for further evaluation.

3.2   Automatic Liver and Lesion Segmentation

Automatic liver and lesion segmentation was carried out as follows:

(a)   Applied masking and prediction to visualize maximum area of liver.
(b)   Define and calculate liver area based on the shape and prior knowledge.
(c)   Morphological operations, as in [12], are carried out to segment the liver from rest of organs [13], which are removed by morphological erosion and result in an isolated liver region.

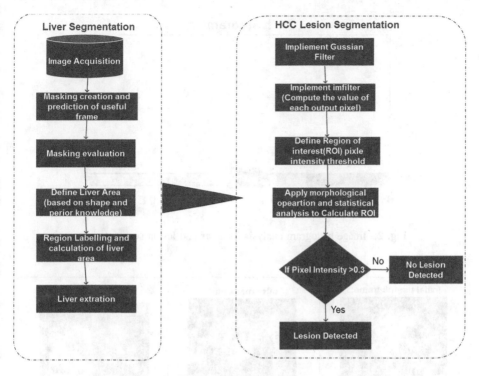

Fig. 1. Proposed system

(d) Applied Gaussian filter [10] to remove noise and preserve the edges.

(e) Defined pixel intensity threshold value using trial and error to find out the normal image surface and lesion surface.

(f) In its final state use histogram analysis, and other morphological operations, to detect HCC lesion.

Specifically, the following steps were followed for automatic liver segmentation from an abdominal CT image:

- First acquired and loaded all frames of the abdominal CT image
- Applied masking to predict the useful frame (where all organs clearly shown)
- Converted matrix image into an intensity image by scaling it between 0 and 1
- Found and determined threshold value of image pixel using a trial and error approach as in [5].

  (a) If image pixel intensity > 0.3 then threshold = 1, otherwise 0

- Applied morphological operations, following [5, 10, 14] listed below:

  (a) Applied disk structuring element to include true pixels and exclude false areas in the morphological computation, within a radius of 2 cm
  (b) Applied Erode function to erode the image
  (c) Removed other organs surrounding liver using the bwareaopen function.

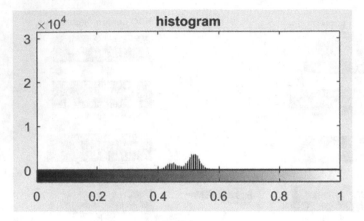

Fig. 2. Image histogram analysis for liver and lesion segmentation

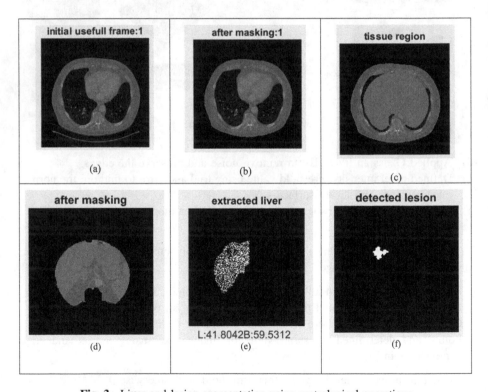

Fig. 3. Liver and lesion segmentation using metrological operations

(d) Used imdilate function to add pixels to the boundaries of objects in image
(e) Filled a hole of background pixels that cannot be reached by filling in the background from the edge of the image.

(f) Calculated average mask to determine the Region of Interest area(RIO)- cancer area

(g) Applied the histogram to show the liver area pixels in Fig. 2

(h) Finally showed the liver area in the window shown in Fig. 3

Applied rotationally symmetric Gaussian low pass filter of hsize 5 with standard deviation sigma = 5 to remove noise, and preserve high frequency edges. Mathematically Gaussian Filter can expressed in following equation [15]

$$G(x, y) = \frac{1}{\sqrt{2\pi}\sigma} \mathrm{EXP}\left(-\left(x^2 + y^2\right)/2\sigma^2\right) \qquad (1)$$

where x is the distance from the origin in the horizontal axis, y is the distance from the origin in the vertical axis and σ^2 represent the variance which determine the amount of smoothing.

- Applied threshold if ROI image pixel intensity >0.3.
- Applied morphological operations to find the threshold value and if ROI = 1 and row array is empty, then calculate the area of lesion by using the formula below: Pixel intensity = MAX(row) – Min(row) and Max(column) – Min(column) then calculation of array dimension = (row) If Pixel Intensity >0.3 then detected lesion else no lesion detection.

4 Comparative Studies

We compared proposed segmentation method with other widely used segmentation method, namely region growing, but results are compromised and computational performance is very low as shown in Fig. 4.

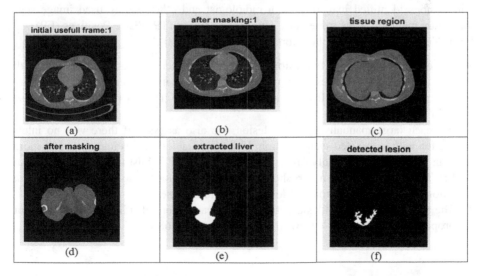

Fig. 4. Liver and lesion segmentation results using region growing method

5   Results and Discussion

A total of 31 CT images were obtained from Crosshouse Hospital, Glasgow, UK. The images were in the DICOM format, and had 128 channels of 512×512 pixels, each with pixel space varying between 0.54 and 0.85. A Liver and its lesion segmentation process, from a patient's abdominal CT scan, is shown in Fig. 3(a) shows the initial most suitable frame, by use of a masking method. Figure 3(b) shows bone masking along with elliptical masking. Figure 3(c) shows the tissue region. Figure 3(d) shows the shape of the abdomen in the frame. Figure 3(e) shows the extracted liver. Figure 3 (f) shows the detected lesion and its segmentation. Figure 2 is a histogram showing a liver lesion's minimum and maximum intensity, which aids in correctly and automatically identifying a lesion and its region. We performed morphological erosion on the abdominal CT, which removed the organs around the liver [4] and isolated it, as shown in Fig. 3(e). Gaussian filtering was then used to remove noise, preserve high frequency edges and determine pixel intensity threshold values. If the pixel intensity >0.3, then a lesion is present and has been detected, as shown in Fig. 3(f). The results showed successful automated liver and lesion segmentation in each frame of the 31 cases. We have compared the performance of our proposed automatic segmentation system, against manual segmentation by a radiologist for the same cases, as shown in Table 1, and obtained 92.68% accuracy. The false positive incidence was only 9.75%. Further, we also compared proposed method with widely used segment method region growing shown in Fig. 4 but results were compromising and computation performance very low. In Fig. 4 (e) showed, the region growing method was not correctly detected and segmented liver and lesion.

5.1   Performance Measure

The proposed automated segmentation was carried out on all data sets and compared with lesions identified manually by a radiologist and other widely used image segmentation method for the same data. The True Positives (TP), False Positives (FP) and False Negatives (FN) were then computed as follows [10]:

- For each manually detected lesion, we assessed if there was any intersection with the automated system lesion and checked whether it was intersection with any automatic detect lesion. If there was intersection, the TP was increased, otherwise the FN was increased.
- For each large manually detected lesion, we also assessed if there was no intersection with automated system lesion. If this manual lesion was intersected by more than one (automated), only one is considered as a TP, whilst the rest contribute to FP. Table 1 and Figs. 5 and 6 shows the TP and FP for results obtained from both automated system, and manual lesions, for the 31 cases.
- The results show that all lesions from the 31 cases were identified correctly by our proposed automated system, with an accuracy of 92.68%.

Table 1. Manual V/S automatic segmentation performance evaluation

Case	No of lesions	Manual lesion		Automatic lesion	
		TP	FP	TP	FP
1	2	2	0	1	0
2	2	2	0	2	0
3	1	1	0	0	1
4	1	1	0	1	0
5	0	0	0	0	0
6	1	1	0	1	0
7	0	0	0	0	1
8	1	1	0	1	0
9	1	1	0	1	0
10	0	0	0	1	0
9	1	1	0	1	0
10	2	2	0	1	0
11	2	2	0	1	0
12	2	2	0	1	0
13	0	0	0	1	0
14	2	2	0	2	0
15	1	1	0	1	1
16	2	1	0	1	0
17	2	2	0	2	0
18	1	1	0	1	0
19	2	2	0	2	0
20	2	2	0	2	0
21	1	1	0	1	0
22	2	2	0	1	0
23	1	1	0	1	0
24	2	2	0	2	0
25	2	2	0	1	0
26	1	1	0	1	0
27	0	1	0	1	0
28	2	1	1	1	0
29	1	1	0	1	0
30	1	1	0	1	1
31	1	1	0	1	0
Total	42	41	1	38	4

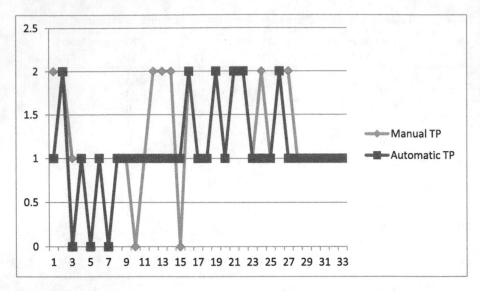

Fig. 5. Manual   segmentation   True   Positive   (TP)   V/S   Automatic   Segmentation
(TP) comparisons

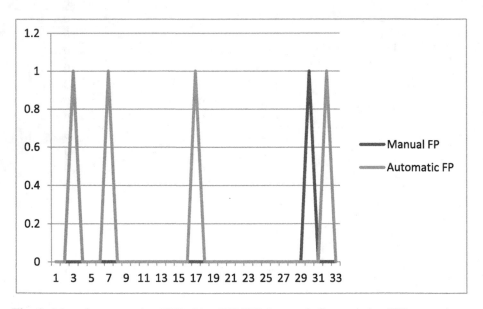

Fig. 6. Manual segmentation FP Positive (FP) V/S Automatic Segmentation (FP) comparisons

6 Conclusion

The proposed research presents a fully automated liver and lesion segmentation system, using morphological operations, for abdominal CT scans. The obtained results suggest that fully automated HCC detection can be efficiently used to aid medical professionals in diagnosing HCC. It has been shown that morphological operations require less computational power when compared to other conventional image segmentation algorithms. A limitation of this research is that the performance was evaluated on a small dataset, which does not allow us to evaluate robustness. For future work, we will collect additional clinical and CT image data to ensure comprehensive evaluation and clinical validation.

We also intend to apply this automated HCC detection and diagnosis system to Positron Emission Tomography (PET) and Magnetic Resonance Imaging (MRI) datasets, as well as adapting it for diagnosing different liver diseases using state-of-the-art feature extraction and se lection, and machine learning classification techniques.

Acknowledgments. This research is funded by the University of Stirling (Scotland, UK), and Ucare Foundation, as part of a collaborative PhD IMPACT project. Professor A. Hussain is also supported by the UK Engineering and Physical Sciences Research Council (EPSRC) grant no. EP/M026981/1, and the Digital Health & Care Institute (DHI) funded Exploratory project: PD2A. The authors are grateful to the anonymous reviewers for their insightful comments and suggestions, which helped improve the quality of this paper.

References

1. Bongartz, G., Merkle, E.M., Zech, C.J., Kircher, A.: Rational imaging of hepatocellular carcinoma. Chall. Multim. Diagn. Criteria **54**, 664–672 (2014). Springer
2. Hussain, A., Wajid, S.K.: Local energy-based shape histogram feature extraction technique for breast cancer diagnosis. In: Expert Systems with Applications, pp. 6990–6999 (2015)
3. Bischof, L., Adams, R.: Seeded region growing. In: IEEE Transactions on Pattern Analysis and Machine Intelligence, Division of Mathematics & Statistics CSIRO, North Ryde (2002)
4. Moni, R.S., Rajeesh, J., Kumar, S.S.: An automatic computer-aided diagnosis system for liver tumours on computed tomography images. Comput. Electr. Eng. **39**, 1516–1526 (2013)
5. Chen, Y.-W., Tsubokawa, K., Foruzan, Amir, H.: Liver segmentation from low contrast open MR scans using K-means clustering and graph-cuts. In: Zhang, L., Lu, B.-L., Kwok, J. (eds.) ISNN 2010. LNCS, vol. 6064, pp. 162–169. Springer, Heidelberg (2010). doi:10.1007/978-3-642-13318-3_21
6. Ali, A.-R., Couceiro, M., Anter, A., Hassanien, A.-E.: Particle swarm optimization based fast fuzzy C-means clustering for liver CT segmentation. In: Hassanien, A.-E., Grosan, C., Tolba, M.F. (eds.) Applications of Intelligent Optimization in Biology and Medicine, vol. 96, pp. 233–250. Springer International Publishing, Switzerland (2016)
7. Li, N., Huang, W., et al.: Liver tumor detection and segmentation using kernel-based extreme learning machine, Osaka (2013)
8. Richbourg, W.J., Liu, J., Watt, J.M., Pamulapati, V., Wang, S., Summers, R.M., Linguraru, M.G.: Tumor burden analysis on computed tomography by automated liver and tumor segmentation. IEEE Trans. Med. Imaging **31**, 1965–1976 (2012)

9. Raj, K., Kiruthika, S.: Liver extraction using histogram and morphology. IJRET: Int. J. Res Eng. Technol. **5**(01), 245–249 (2016)

10. Zayane, O., Jouini, B., Mahjoub, M.A.: Automatic liver segmentation method in CT images. Can. J. Image Process. Comput. Vis. **2**(8) (2011)

11. Hussain, A. Ali, L., et al.: Intelligent image processing techniques for cancer progression detection, recognition and prediction in the human liver. In: 2014 IEEE Symposium on Computational Intelligence in Healthcare and e-health (CICARE) (2014)

12. Hussain, A., Wajid, S.K.: Local energy-based shape histogram feature extraction technique for breast cancer diagnosis. Expert Syst. Appl. **42**, 6990–6999 (2015)

13. Bekes, G., Ruskó, M.F.L.: Automatic segmentation of the liver from multi- and single-phase contrast-enhanced CT images. Med. Image Anal. **13**, 871–882 (2009). Elsevier

14. Ruskó, L., Perényi, Á.: Automated liver lesion detection in CT images based on multi-level geometric features. Int. J. Comput. Assist. Radiol. Surg. **9**(4), 577–593 (2013). Springer

15. Scharcanski, J., Cavalcanti, P.G.: Segmentation of pigmented skin lesions using non-negative matrix factorization. IEEE (2014)

A New Biologically-Inspired Analytical Worm Propagation Model for Mobile Unstructured Peer-to-Peer Networks

Hani Alharbi[1(✉)], Khalid Aloufi[2], and Amir Hussain[1]

[1] Department of Computing Science and Mathematics, University of Stirling, Stirling, UK
{hsa,ahu}@cs.stir.ac.uk
[2] College of Computer Engineering, Taibah University, Medina, Saudi Arabia
koufi@taibahu.edu.sa

Abstract. Millions of users world-wide are sharing content using the Peer-to-Peer (P2P) client network. While new innovations bring benefits, there are nevertheless some dangers associated with them. One of the main threats is P2P worms that can penetrate the network even from a single node and can then spread very quickly. Many attempts have been made in this domain to model the worm propagation behaviour, and yet no single model exists that can realistically model the process. Most researchers have considered disease epidemic models for modelling the worm propagation process. Such models are, however, based on strong assumptions which may not necessarily be valid in real-world scenarios. In this paper, a new biologically-inspired analytical model is proposed, one that considers configuration diversity, infection time lag, user-behaviour and node mobility as the important parameters that affect the worm propagation process. The model is flexible and can represent a network where all nodes are mobile or a heterogeneous network, where some nodes are static and others are mobile. A complete derivation of each of the factors is provided in the analytical model, and the results are benchmarked against recently reported analytical models. A comparative analysis of simulation results indeed shows that our proposed biologically-inspired model represents a more realistic picture of the worm propagation process, compared to the existing state-of-the-art analytical models.

1 Introduction

The invention of the internet has changed social, financial and academic aspects of human life. While the internet undoubtedly provides irreplaceable benefits to society, it nevertheless poses certain serious threats that can even result in social and economic losses. Considerable and wide-ranging research is needed to understand and cope with all the various emerging issues and challenges, the most important of which being to understand the large-scale P2P network dynamics when confronted by a continuously changing peer population, peer mobility and peer heterogeneity. Heterogeneity is the hallmark of the network due to the presence of peers with different operating systems, packages, frameworks and software. Designing a heterogeneous peer population with a

© Springer International Publishing AG 2016
C.-L. Liu et al. (Eds.): BICS 2016, LNAI 10023, pp. 251–263, 2016.
DOI: 10.1007/978-3-319-49685-6_23

perfectly diverse capacity and network bandwidth is indeed challenging. Another question concerns modelling the propagation behaviour of worms for large P2P networks in which a large portion of the peers consists of mobile devices [10]. Another research dimension is the presence of worms, viruses, Trojans and other variants that have been persistent threats to the internet from the early 1980's and have caused a large part of the internet to become inaccessible to the user. Although the users of P2P overlay enjoy sharing benefits, they still remain vulnerable to active, passive and reactive worms.

The objective of this paper is to develop an analytical model for worm propagation that accommodates factors such as configuration diversity, user behaviour, mobility of nodes and infection time lag. The paper is organized as follows: Sect. 2 presents related work, Sect. 3 provides the analytical model, Sect. 4 provides the results and a discussion of them, Sect. 5 discusses the impact of different factors based on the results achieved using the analytical model, and Sect. 6 concludes the paper by identifying future directions.

2   Related Work

Worms in P2P networks pose serious threats to all peers in the network [1]. A worm attack can make a large portion of the internet unavailable. To take the appropriate safety measures, carry out the efficient patching of nodes and apply proper immunization to the influential nodes, it is essential to understand the propagation behaviour of worms. The approaches followed in the research are concerned with creating an analytical mathematical model and a generation of simulation of worm propagation in order to understand the behaviour of the worm. This helps in applying security updates, immunization strategies and recovery options. However, with this approach, it is impossible to analyse a large-scale network consisting of millions of nodes [1]. These models and simulations help in developing detection, containment and counterfeiting strategies against propagating worms. The analytical and simulation models are inspired by the epidemiological disease spread models such as Sin SIS and SIR.

Different models exist in the literature that addresses different areas. A stochastic, discrete time model for active-worm propagation is based on the SIR epidemiological model, proposed in [2] and called the STAWP model. The model considers the flooding behaviour (Gnutella) of message propagation. A major contribution of this work is to consider the dynamicity of network topology during active-worm propagation. It assumes the infection time lag as unit time, which is an important parameter in the infection process [3]. However, the impact of important factors such as node mobility, configuration diversity and user-behaviour are not considered in this model.

The surveys conducted in [4, 5] identified that node mobility, the configuration diversity of a network, and the impact of user-behaviour on worm propagation are all open issues. They also emphasized the need for a general analytical model covering the major factors that affect worm propagation.

2.1 Biologically-Inspired Worms

While there exist numerous biological worms in the literature, it is nevertheless vital to study their propagation behaviour and to derive the factors that affect the worm propagation process. For instance, hookworms have affected humans all over the world. This parasite draws blood from the small intestine and requires human faeces and soil to propagate before the hookworm larvae can reinvest in their hosts. This makes such creatures particularly suitable for observation [6]. It has been observed that different people have different immunity and the infection probability from hookworms is, therefore, directly proportional to a person's immunity to such worms. This is related to the configuration diversity factor that exists in many analytical models. It has also been noted that mobile working populations are less likely to be exposed to the risk of infection from hookworm larvae than sedentary working populations for the reasons set out in [7]. Their surveys demonstrated that repeatedly visiting the same defecation site increases the likelihood of exposure to hookworm infection, as it is in such areas that one is more likely to find a greater degree of soil pollution and soil infestation. The mobility factor is in fact the one least addressed in the worm propagation process. The impact of the frequency of visits to the infectious location in hookworm transmission can be added to the current analytical models.

The Ebola epidemic began in Guinea during December 2013 and affected at least five countries. The Ebola virus is spread mainly through contact with the body fluids of symptomatic patients, and transmission can be stopped by a combination of early diagnosis, contact tracing, patient isolation and care, infection control, and safe burial [8]. The incubation period, which is the time between infection and the onset of symptoms, is referred to as the infection time-lag.

Moreover, a further epidemic is known as an "oriental Eyeworm" because of its occurrence in Far Eastern countries such as Indonesia, Thailand, China, Korea, Myanmar, India and Japan. This nematode infection provokes mild-to-severe ocular manifestations in animals, as well as in humans [9]. The spread of this worm is affected by the immunity of each individual, the time required to get infected and the location of the individual. The aforementioned discussion shows how a new model can be proposed, inspired by these biological worms and yet also addressing multiple factors.

3 A Discrete-Time Active Worm Propagation Model

The proposed analytical model is an extension of the SIR (Suspected-Infectious-Recovered) epidemiological model. The proposed model introduces an additional "exposed" state to handle the infection time-lag problem. In the derivation of this analytical model, only unstructured peer-to-peer networks (Gnutella) are considered.

The major focus of this model is to study factors such as the configuration diversity [10, 11] of nodes in a network, the impact of variation in user behaviour and of the infection time-lag on worm propagation. All these factors are assumed to be independent variables that affect the process of worm propagation. A graphical representation is provided in Fig. 1.

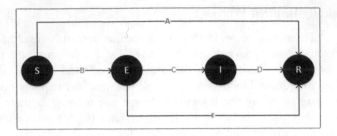

Fig. 1. States and transitions

"R" is an acronym for the Recovered state and this state is an absorbing state. For a steady state, all the nodes are in a susceptible state. There are four states and five state-transitions. These transitions are explained below:

a. A node can transit from a suspected to a recovered state. The rate "a" depends on configuration diversity, user-behaviour and the degree of the node.
b. A node can transit from a suspected to an exposed state at rate "b". The rate is dependent on configuration diversity, user-behaviour and the degree of the node.
c. The exposure to infectious state transition is only dependent on the birth and death rates of nodes in the network.
d. The infectious-to-recover transition is done at rate "γ" and the number of nodes from the infectious-to-recovered state at time t is $\gamma I (t)$.
e. The node can go from an exposed to a recovered state at rate "e". The factors that can affect this state transition are configuration diversity and node mobility. It is important to note that once a node is exposed, it will eventually be infectious, even if disconnected from the network due to mobility. However, a disconnected infectious node does not have an impact on worm propagation in the network.

The state transition takes fractions of seconds to be executed. A human response is impossible within this short period of time. The state transition varies from node to node due to the variation of configuration on the node.

3.1   Model Assumptions

The assumptions taken to develop the analytical model are as follows:

1. The configuration diversity (δ) and user behaviour (β) are taken as random variables that are generated from Gaussian distribution with Mean = 0 and Standard deviation = 1. The values of the random variables range from $0 \leq \delta \leq 1$ and $0 \leq \beta \leq 1$.
2. The factors (δ, β and η) are independent of each other.
3. The total number of nodes in the network, N = 500.
4. At any given time, a node can be in any of the four states that are susceptible S(t), Exposed E(t), Infected I(t) and Recovered R(t) where S(t) + E(t) + I(t) + R(t) = N.
5. Initially, all the nodes are in a suspected state.

Table 1. Notations and Descriptions

Notation	Description
N	Total number of nodes in the network
S(t)	Number of suspected nodes at time (t)
E(t)	Number of exposed nodes at time (t)
I(t)	Number of infectious nodes at time (t)
R(t)	Number of recovered nodes at time (t)
δ	Configuration diversity. $0 \leq \delta \leq 1$
β	User behaviour. $0 \leq \beta \leq 1$
K_i	Degree of node i
ε	Infection time-lag
γ	Infectious-to-removal rate
λ	Rate of transition from exposed to infected state
$\wedge$	Birth-rate of nodes in the network
$\vee$	Death-rate of nodes in the network
η	Node mobility
ϕ	Super spreading parameter

6. Initially, infection-starting nodes are chosen randomly.
7. Mean-direction: a seed value for random computation of the mean speed.
8. Mean-angle: a seed value for the random computation of the mean angle.
9. Gaussian Factor: a factor used in the Gauss-Markov mobility model to compute the coordinates of the nodes.
10. Mobile-node: the number of mobile nodes in the network. Each mobile node is rounded by a circle to represent the effective radius of the base station.

3.2   Complete System

Consider a network of N peers, then the probability of a peer being attacked by at least one attacker is 1/N. If (β) is the user behaviour, then the probability of a peer being attacked by one attacker is (1-β)/N and the probability of not being attacked is $(1 - ((1-\beta)/N))$. If K_i is the degree of the node, then the probability of not being attacked by K_i neighbours is $(1 - ((1-\beta) K_i/N))$.

Most empirical networks share common properties in terms of their local features. For example, some networks have considerable skew degree distribution so that most individuals have few neighbours but there are a few exceptional individuals that have high degree distribution. The latter type of nodes is often called a 'hub' or a 'super-spreader'. In the context of P2P networks, it is called a 'super-peer'. The skewed distribution is often modelled using a power-law where it is assumed that for some $\phi \geq 1$, $P(k) \sim k^{-\varphi}$ for large degrees, where k is the degree of a node [12]. The case where $2 < \phi < 3$ gained significant attention is called scale-free distribution [12]. To calculate the value of ϕ using networks structure, let $\{K_1, K_2, K_3, \ldots, K_N\}$ be the degree of each node in the network and Mean, $M = \frac{\sum_{i=1}^{N} Ki}{N}$. The super-spreading parameters, ϕ, can be computed as:

$$\phi = \sqrt{\sum_{i=1}^{N} |K_i - M| + 1} \tag{1}$$

Where $\phi \geq 1$. It is to be noted that the mass action law applies with the homogeneous mixing assumption that each individual has the same chance of coming into contact with an infected individual. This hypothesis eliminates the need to know the precise contact network by means of which the disease spreads. However true populations violate some mass-action assumptions in a manner affecting the epidemic dynamics. The true population is based on a random mixing assumption.

If a suspected node is attacked, it has the probability $(1 - \delta)$ to be exposed. So the number of exposed hosts from time (t) to (t + 1).

$$E(t+1) = S(t)(I(t))^{\phi}(1-\delta) \times (1 - (1 - (1 - \beta))) - \lambda E(t) \tag{2}$$

So the number of peers in recovered state are:

$$R(t+1) = \gamma I(t) + S(t)(I(t))^{\phi}(\delta) \times (1 - (1 - (\beta))) - vR(t) \tag{3}$$

The number of nodes in an infectious state are:

$$I(t+1) = \lambda E(t) - v I(t) - \gamma I(t) \tag{4}$$

The number of nodes in a susceptible state are:

$$S(t + 1) = -S(t)(I(t))^{\phi}[((1 - \delta) \times (1 - (1 - ((1 - \beta)))) \\ + \delta \times (1 - (1 - (\beta))] + \hat{N} - v S(t) \tag{5}$$

3.2.1   Integrating the Gauss-Markov Mobility Model

The mobility of a node is an important factor, which could be constrained and limited by the physical laws of acceleration, velocity and rate of change of direction. Hence, the current velocity of a mobile node may depend on its previous velocity. Thus the velocities of a single node at different time slots are 'correlated'. We call this mobility characteristic the Temporal Dependency of velocity. The Gauss-Markov (GM) mobility model [13] works with temporal dependence. In this model we have integrated the Gauss-Markov (GM) mobility model with the SEIR model so that the impact of the mobility of the nodes on the worm propagation process can be observed. The position of a node related to the base station can be computed using Eqs. (6) and (7).

$$X_t = X_{t-1} + S_t \times \text{Cos}(\theta_t) \tag{6}$$

$$Y_t = Y_{t-1} + S_t \times \text{Sin}(\theta_t) \tag{7}$$

Where S_t and θ_t are the speed and angle of mobile node at time 't' from the base station. The distance, d, of mobile node from the base station can be calculated using Eq. (8).

$$d = \sqrt{(X_t - X_0)^2 + (Y_t - Y_0)^2} \tag{8}$$

Thus the mobility factor can be computed as $\eta = d/r$, for all $d \leq r$. It is assumed that the mobile node is connected to the P2P network via the hotspot/base station, which has the predefined effective radius 'r'. The P2P network is considered to be heterogeneous where some nodes are mobile and some nodes are static. The ratio of both types of node varies at different instants of time. All of the nodes could be mobile or all of the nodes could be static. If the mobile node is at the centre of its base station, the distance 'd' of the mobile node from the base station/hotspot is zero; hence the mobility factor is also zero and the node is considered to be a static node. The GM model operates in a discrete time fashion and with each time tick 't', the mobility factor of the mobile nodes is updated. The value of the mobility factor is updated with each unit of time for a mobile node and affects the worm propagation process.

If (η) is the mobility factor, then the SEIR model can be extended as follows:

$$\begin{cases} E\,(t + 1) = S\,(t)(I(t))^{\phi}(1-\delta) \times (1 - (1 - (1 - \beta)(1 - \eta))) - \lambda\,E\,(t) \\ R\,(t + 1) = \gamma\,I\,(t) + S\,(t)(I(t))^{\phi}\,(\delta) \times (1 - (1 - (\beta)(\eta))) - v\,R\,(t) \\ \qquad I\,(t + 1) = \lambda\,E\,(t) - v\,I\,(t) - \gamma\,I\,(t) \\ S\,(t + 1) = -S\,(t)(I(t))^{\phi}[((1-\delta) \times (1 - (1 - (1 - \beta)(1 - \eta))) + \\ \qquad \delta \times (1 - (1 - (\beta)(\eta))] + {}^{\wedge}N - vS\,(t) \end{cases} \tag{9}$$

Where $S(t) + E(t) + I(t) + R(t) = N(t)$ if, and only if, the birth-rate of nodes in the network is equal to the death-rate in the network i.e. $v = {}^{\wedge}$. The enhanced model is called an M-SEIR model.

4 Results and Discussion

In this section, three benchmark studies with their worm propagation analytical models have been selected to compare the results of the proposed analytical model (M-SEIR). These studies are the STAWP Model [2], the AMM framework [14], and the Time Four-Factor Model [10]. To measure the worm infection with time, a scale-free network (SFN) of 500 nodes is generated using the Barabasi-Albert (BA) algorithm [15]. The implementation of all these models is done in Matlab for Gnutella protocol.

Configuration Diversity: The configuration diversity is addressed by the Four-Factor and SEIR models. The results of different values of configuration diversity and the impact on worm propagation are shown in Figs. 2(a) and (b). The STAWP model shows rapid increase in the worm propagation process, quickly reaching the range from 400–450 and then dropping linearly. This is because of the absence of handling of any factors of interest. In the meantime, the Four-Factor and M-SEIR models show an exponential increase in node infection, reaching a maximum value of between 100–200 for a configuration diversity of 0.3 and 0.5 for Four-Factor and M-SEIR models. There are two major differences in the graphs of the Four-Factor and M-SEIR models. It can be seen in Fig. 2(a) that the infected nodes in Four-Factor models are almost 10% more than in the M-SEIR model (Table 2). The reason for this is that our model involves an additional exposed state, from which some nodes directly transit to the recovery state instead of going to the infectious state. So this difference in the number of infectious nodes depends on the rate of transition to the recovery state in the exposed state. The second observation is the delay in the M-SEIR graph when compared to the Four-Factor model. The reason is again the infection time-lag in the exposed state due to the presence of different installed packages on the node.

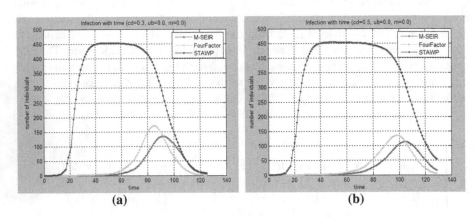

Fig. 2. (a): Configuration diversity = 0.3, (b): Configuration diversity = 0.5

Table 2. Impact of configuration diversity on different models

Configuration diversity								
Protocols	M-SEIR				Four-Factor				STAWP
	0.3		0.5		0.3		0.5		n/a
	M[a]	SD[b]	M	SD	M	SD	M	SD	M
Gnutella	27%	1.22	22.5%	1.09	35.8%	1.32	27.3%	1.22	90%

[a] Mean
[b] Standard Deviation

User behaviour: The user behaviour parameter accounts for the user actions in front of P2P clients. These actions affect the worm propagation process. A typical example of un-fair user behaviour is the free-rider problem that exists in many P2P networks. User-behaviour includes, but is not limited to, the setting up of an upload/download limit of the P2P client, a start/stop/pause in the file transfer, and P2P application/client on/off behaviour. All of these factors combine to form the single factor known as 'user-behaviour'. The results of different values of user-behaviour are shown in Figs. 3 (a) and (b). Since this parameter does not have any impact on the Four-Factor and

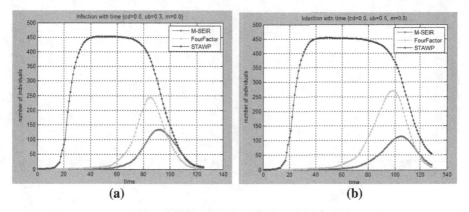

Fig. 3. (a): User behaviour = 0.3, (b): User behaviour = 0.5

STAWP models, the observed node infection value for these models is much higher than that of the M-SEIR model. The results are generated by considering the homogeneous network of the nodes i.e. their configuration diversity is equal to zero. The intent is to highlight the impact of a factor on the worm propagation process, when compared with other analytical models. It can be seen that the infection density is 20% less than that from the Four-Factor model with a value of 0.3 for user behaviour while it is more than 30% less than that from the Four-Factor model with a value of 0.5 for user behaviour (Table 3). The reason for this is that the M-SEIR model incorporates user behaviour while the Four-Factor model does not consider it.

Table 3. Impact of user behaviour on different models

User behaviour									
Protocols	M-SEIR				Four-Factor				STAWP
	0.3		0.5		0.3		0.5		n/a
	M	SD	M	SD	M	SD	M	SD	M
Gnutella	27.2%	1.39	22.2%	1.20	49	1.06	57.7%	2.1	90%

Mobility: While the computing is shifting to mobile peers, it becomes important to consider the impact of mobility on the peer-to-peer worm propagation process. The previous benchmark models do not address this factor. Even the newly proposed framework (AMM) provides only limited information about the mobility models and the details of implementation to achieve the demonstrated results. The results of mobility as a factor in the M-SEIR model under the Gnutella protocol are shown in Figs. 4(a) and (b). The mobility of a node at any instant of time is computed using the GM mobility model. The input parameters, such as direction, speed, and number of mobile nodes in the network are provided. The M-SEIR model assumes that mobile nodes are moving at the same speed and in the same direction. Other factors such as configuration diversity and user-behaviour are kept constant and assigned a zero value. A decrease in the number of infected nodes is observed as soon as the mobile node moves away from the base station and, as a result, the mobility factor increases. The

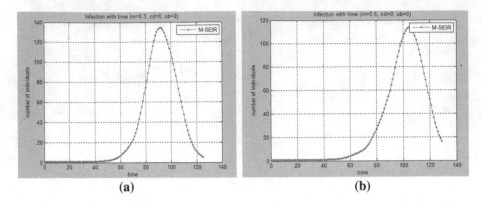

Fig. 4. (a) Mobility = 0.3, (b) Mobility = 0.5

reason for the decrease in node infection is due to the fact that as soon as a node moves away from the base station, different factors, such as the loss in signal strength, the channel path fading and interference, reduce the throughput achieved by the node.

Impact of Random Values on Infection Propagation: The M-SEIR model considers mobility, user behaviour and configuration diversity as factors that impact on the worm propagation process in P2P networks. Let us consider a more realistic network in which all the nodes are affected by all of the factors under consideration. The infection density with time is computed in such a network and shown in Fig. 5. The results demonstrate that for a heterogeneous scale-free network, in which users are continuously affecting the P2P clients, the infection density is very low, being around 20–30% of the total susceptible population. A 30–40% drop in the infection ratio can also be observed in the Four-Factor model because it considers the impact of configuration diversity on the worm propagation process (Table 4). However, there is no impact of any of the factors on the worm propagation process in the STAWP model and this shows a high infection density of more than 90%.

Impact of Node Mobility in a Heterogeneous Network: Mobility is an important aspect related to mobile nodes in P2P networks. The closest to the proposed M-SEIR

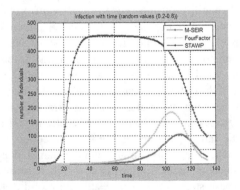

Fig. 5. Impact of random values

Table 4. Impact of random values of parameters on different models

Random parameter values (0.2–0.8)				
Protocols	M-SEIR		Four-Factor		STAWP
	M	SD	M	SD	M
Gnutella	20.5%	1.43	37.87%	2.10	90%

model is the AMM framework [14], which considers mobility models. The results provided by the AMM framework are limited only to ABM and no implementation details are provided.

To achieve the mobility of node, use is made of a GM mobility model [13] which keeps track of the previous values of the coordinates of the mobile nodes. The Random Way Point (RWP) model is not used because of its memory-less nature regarding the velocity and position of a node. The GM model introduces parameters to handle the random movement of nodes. The value of zero indicates completely random movement just like the RWP mode when value $0 < alpha < 1$ defines the degree of randomness. The implementation of the mobility model and the impact of node mobility on worm propagation is given in subsequent sections. The density of infected nodes decreases with the increased values of the mobility factor (Fig. 6).

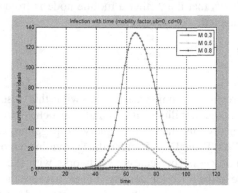

Fig. 6. Impact of mobility

5   Impact of Different Factors

Concerning the impact of configuration diversity under the Gnutella protocol for all benchmark models in Fig. 2(a) and (b), all the results verify that (1) the infection density is lowest, compared with the Four-Factor or STAWP models, due to the handling of additional parameters and (2) the higher the configuration diversity, the lower will be the infection density with time. This rule applies to both the M-SEIR and the Four-Factor models. The STAWP model is not affected by the configuration diversity value. The impact of user-behaviour under the Gnutella protocol for all benchmark models using conventional tools is shown in Fig. 3(a) and (b). (3) The user-behaviour combined with the configuration diversity of the network results in the lowest infection density value, compared to the Four-Factor and STAWP models and (4) the Four-Factor and STAWP models, do not have any impact on the worm propagation process. The mobility of the nodes in P2P networks has not been covered by the STAWP and Four-Factor models. The aspect of mobility is introduced in the M-SEIR model by computing the mobility factor from the Gauss-Markov mobility model. The impact on the infection density due to the mobility of nodes was discussed in the previous section. The results show that the infection density decreases with an increase in the number of mobile nodes. This is due to the weak signal strength of the wireless link, path fading and other related wireless network issues that exist in all wireless networks. Another reason for this decrease in the infection ratio is that the moving nodes go out of range from the base station in a suspected state and thus cannot be infected. The value of the speed of mobile nodes plays an important role in infection propagation.

To achieve more realistic results, random values of configuration diversity and user-behaviour are taken in the range of 0 to 1. The results are shown in Fig. 5 with the additional finding of the concept of a super-peer. For a network which has skew-degree distribution, a sudden increase in infection density is observed over time. The reason for this is that the worm or query reaches a node which is highly connected and spreads the query or worm very quickly. Moreover, the worm propagation process slows down in the presence of random values of configuration diversity and user-behaviour. In Fig. 6 different values of mobility have been taken as representing different positions for mobile nodes. It shows that the farther a mobile node is from the base station, the less likely will it be infected.

6 Conclusion

There are many interesting findings associated with this research. Configuration diversity, infection time-lag, mobility of nodes and user-behaviour combine together to show less infection density, and hence less query propagation, compared with other benchmark models (STAWP and Four-Factor), thus providing a more realistic picture of the worm propagation process. The scale-free networks with skew-degree distribution show a sudden increase in the infection density. This is because the degree is not evenly distributed and a worm on a high-capacity node causes a sudden increase in infection density. The aspect of mobility is introduced into the M-SEIR model by computing the mobility factor from the Gauss-Markov mobility model. It was observed that the M-SEIR model could easily be mapped to incorporate the biological worm. A detailed study of this and its results, however, will have to remain the subject of future work.

References

1. Zhou, L., Zhang, L., McSherry, F., Immorlica, N., Costa, M., Chien, S.: A first look at peer-to-peer worms: threats and defenses. In: Castro, M., Renesse, R. (eds.) IPTPS 2005. LNCS, vol. 3640, pp. 24–35. Springer, Heidelberg (2005). doi:10.1007/11558989_3
2. Jafarabadi, A., Azgomi, M.A.: A stochastic epidemiological model for the propagation of active worms considering the dynamicity of network topology. Peer Peer Netw. Appl. 8(6), 1008–1022 (2015)

3. Mojahedi, E., Azgomi, M.A.: Modeling the propagation of topology-aware P2P worms considering temporal parameters. Peer Peer Netw. Appl. **8**(1), 171–180 (2013)
4. Peng, S., Yu, S., Yang, A.: Smartphone malware and its propagation modeling: a survey. IEEE Commun. Surv. Tutorials **16**(2), 925–941 (2014)
5. Wang, Y., Wen, S., Xiang, Y., Zhou, W.: Modeling the propagation of worms in networks: a Survey. IEEE Commun. Surv. Tutorials **16**(2), 942–960 (2014)
6. Couacaud, L.: Hookworm disease and its relationship to capitalism and urban development. Singap. Med. J. **2**(3), 350 (2014)
7. Hotez, S., Brooker, P.J., Bethony, S., Bottazzi, J.M., Loukas, M.E., Xiao, A.: Hookworm infection. N. Engl. J. Med. **351**(8), 799–807 (2004)
8. WHO Ebola Response Team: Ebola virus disease in West Africa — the first 9 months of the epidemic and forward projections. N. Engl. J. Med. **371**, 1481–1495 (2014)
9. Hodžić, A., Latrofa, M.S., Annoscia, G., Alić, A., Beck, R., Lia, R.P., Dantas-Torres, F., Otranto, D.: The spread of zoonotic Thelazia callipaeda in the Balkan area. Parasit. Vectors **7**, 352 (2014)
10. Zhang, X., Chen, T., Zheng, J., Li, H.: Proactive worm propagation modeling and analysis in unstructured peer-to-peer networks. J. Zhejiang Univ. Sci. C **11**(2), 119–129 (2010)
11. Hosseini, S., Azgomi, M.A., Rahmani, A.T.: Malware propagation modeling considering software diversity and immunization. J. Comput. Sci. **13**, 49–67 (2016)
12. Diekmann, O., Heesterbeek, H., Britton, T.: Mathematical Tools for Understanding Infectious Disease Dynamics, p. 502. Princeton University Press, Princeton (2013)
13. Liang, B., Haas, Z.J.: Predictive distance-based mobility management for multidimensional PCS networks. IEEE/ACM Trans. Netw. **11**(5), 718–732 (2003)
14. Kamesh, Sakthi Priya, N.: Security enhancement of authenticated RFID generation. Int. J. Appl. Eng. Res. **9**(22), 5968–5974 (2014)
15. Barabási, A.-L., Albert, R.: Emergence of scaling in random networks. Science **286**(5439), 11 (1999). (80)

EEG Brain Functional Connectivity Dynamic Evolution Model: A Study via Wavelet Coherence

Chunying Fang[1,2], Haifeng Li[1(✉)], and Lin Ma[1]

[1] School of Computer Science and Technology, Harbin Institute of Technology, Harbin, China
{Lihaifeng,malin_li}@hit.edu.cn
[2] School of Computer and Information Engineering,
Heilongjiang University of Science and Technology, Harbin, China
fcy3333@163.com

Abstract. Estimating the functional interactions and connections between brain regions to corresponding process in cognitive, behavioral and psychiatric domains are central pursuits for understanding the human connectome. Few studies have examined the effects of dynamic evolution on cognitive processing and brain activation using wavelet coherence in scalp electroencephalography (EEG) data. Aim of this study was to investigate the brain functional connectivity and dynamic programming model based on the wavelet coherence from EEG data and to evaluate a possible correlation between the brain connectivity architecture and cognitive evolution processing. Here, We present an accelerated dynamic programing algorithm that we found that spatially distributed regions coherence connection difference, for variation audio stimulation, dynamic programing model give the dynamic evolution processing in difference time and frequency. Such methodologies will be suitable for capturing the dynamic evolution of the time varying connectivity patterns that reflect certain cognitive tasks or brain pathologies.

Keywords: Wavelet coherence · Brain functional connectivity · Dynamic evolution model

1 Introduction

Brain functional connectivity has played a variety of roles in the study of human cognition and behavior over the past four decades. Functional connectivity has revealed the reorganization of brain networks during cognitive tasks [1]. Initially, computed tomography (CT) and then magnetic resonance imaging (MRI) were used to probe the large-scale organization of the brain which is estimated by correlation of BOLD activity, identifies coherent brain activity in distributed and reproducible networks [2]. More recently, a variety of imaging modalities—including structural and functional MRI and positron emission tomography (PET) studies have shown characteristic changes in the brains, but thus far has been limited in its capacity to study their temporal evolution. Therefore, the purpose of this paper is to present a data-driven dynamic construction of

© Springer International Publishing AG 2016
C.-L. Liu et al. (Eds.): BICS 2016, LNAI 10023, pp. 264–273, 2016.
DOI: 10.1007/978-3-319-49685-6_24

the state space for the one-pass algorithm so that only the actually active hypotheses are explicitly generated during the process of recognition.

A fair amount of investigation has been directed at linking spiking activity to the fMRI blood oxygenation level–dependent (BOLD) response [3], but far less research has sought to relate spiking activity and EEG. The EEG is thought to reflect the post-synaptic potentials in the apical dendrites of pyramidal cells resulting from their mutual alignment, which allows summation of electric fields [4]. The strength of the signal is related to both the magnitude of the postsynaptic activity and its coherence: postsynaptic currents with low spatiotemporal coherence tend to destructively interfere at the level of the scalp [5, 6]. The common synaptic activity that drives variability in the EEG signal likely also generates spike count correlation across neurons. Their cortical generator was calculated using wavelet coherence for each group. Coherence analysis has been extensively applied to the study of neural activity. To overcome the problems due to non-stationarity raised in the previous section, it has recently been proposed to apply wavelet analysis for the estimation of coherence among non-stationary signals [7, 8]. In contrast to Fourier analysis, wavelet analysis has been devised to analyze signals with rapidly changing spectra [9]. It performs what is called a time-frequency analysis of the signal, which means the estimation of the spectral characteristics of the signal as a function of time. In some sense, wavelet analysis is close to the windowed short-term Fourier transform, especially when using the Morlet wavelet [10], but the major difference is that the size of the window is fixed for the short-term Fourier, and it is adapted to the frequency of the signal in wavelet analysis. Because of this difference, wavelet analysis has a more accurate time-frequency resolution [11, 12]. However, the utility of wavelet analysis is that it provides not only the time-varying power-spectrum, but also the phase spectrum, which is needed to compute the coherence. This makes wavelet analysis a natural choice for the estimation of coherence between non-stationary signals [13]. The aim of the present study was to evaluate a possible correlation between the brain connectivity architecture and dynamic evolution processing as extracted from EEG recordings. EEG recording in the brain functional connectivity via wavelet coherence can be technically challenging. We aimed to assess the feasibility and the efficacy of auditory stimuli EEG [14].

2 The Wavelet Coherence Analysis

We discuss the cross wavelet transform and wavelet coherence for examining relationships in time frequency space between two time series, the advantage of wavelet analysis over Fourier transformation and time series techniques is that wavelet analyses consider time domain as well as frequency domain [5].

2.1 Wavelet Transform

The related wavelet analyses can be classified into two main groups; (a) discrete wavelet transform (DWT) and (b) continuous wavelet transform (CWT). The CWT can be launched with efficient frequency and time parameters. A wavelet theory, then, can be defined by Eqs. (1) and (2). Equation (3) yields, then, CWT. Given a time series $f(t)$:

$$W_\psi f(a,b) = \frac{1}{\sqrt{|a|}} \int_{-\infty}^{+\infty} f(t)\psi * (\frac{t-b}{a})dt. \tag{1}$$

$$\begin{aligned} W_f(a,b) &= \langle f(t), \psi_{a,b}(t) \rangle = \int_{-\infty}^{\infty} f(t)\psi_{a,b}^*(t) \\ &= \int_{-\infty}^{\infty} f(t)\frac{1}{\sqrt{a}}\psi^*(\frac{t-b}{a})dt \quad (a > 0, f \in L^2(R)) \end{aligned} \tag{2}$$

Where $\psi_{a,b}(t) = \frac{1}{\sqrt{a}}\psi\left(\frac{t-b}{a}\right)$,

if $f(t) = f(k\Delta t), \quad t \in (k, k+1)$ then

$$\begin{aligned} W_f(a,b) &= \sum_k \int_k^{k+1} f(t)|a|^{-1/2}\psi^*\left(\frac{t-b}{a}\right)dt \\ &= \sum_k \int_k^{k+1} f(k)|a|^{-1/2}\psi^*\left(\frac{t-b}{a}\right)dt \\ &= |a|^{-1/2} \sum_k f(k)\left(\int_{-\infty}^{k+1} \psi^*\left(\frac{t-b}{a}\right)dt - \int_{-\infty}^{k} \psi^*\left(\frac{t-b}{a}\right)dt\right) \end{aligned} \tag{3}$$

Where $a \in R, a \neq 0$. * represents complex conjugate. The parameter a controls the width of the wavelet and indicates the position of wavelet in frequency domain, and b controls the location of the wavelet and represents the position of wavelet in time domain.

2.2 Wavelet Coherence

The CWT, therefore, decomposes times series into function of time and frequency variables [15, 16]. In order to study the relationship between two nonstationary processes, definitions of cross spectrum and coherence are required. Given two processes x and y with their time–frequency representations wavelet power spectrum $W_x(a,b)$ and $W_y(a,b)$, the time–frequency cross spectrum between them is defined as Wavelet power spectrum for WCS (Wavelet Cross Spectrum), and cross wavelet power spectrum are denoted by Eq. (4).

$$WCS_{x,y}(a,b) = W_x(a,b) \cdot W_y^*(a,b). \tag{4}$$

It can be seen that the $WCS_{xy}(a,b)$ represent the time frequency similarity of two signal x and y. Schwartz inequality guaranteed $WC_{xy}(a,b)$ between 0 and 1. 0 indicates that the corresponding time position of the two signal is independent, and the 1 represents the complete correlation. The wavelet power, then, yields the squared absolute value of wavelet coefficients of x and y. The wavelet power spectrum and cross wavelet power spectrum, thus, represent the local variance of x (or y) and local covariance between x and y, respectively, through time and frequency. Therefore, one may depict complex wavelet coherence by Eq. (5).

$$WC_{xy}(a, b) = \frac{S(WCS_{xy}(a, b))}{\sqrt{S(|W_x(a, b)|^2)}\sqrt{S(|W_y(a, b)|^2)}}. \tag{5}$$

Where scale denotes smoothing along the wavelet scale axis and S time smoothing in time. It is natural to design the smoothing operator so that it has a similar footprint as the wavelet used. Smoothing is achieved by removing high frequencies and retains low frequencies. Notice that this definition closely resembles that of a traditional correlation coefficient, and it is useful to think of the wavelet coherence as a localized correlation coefficient in time frequency space. For the Morlet wavelet a suitable smoothing operator is given.

$$S_t(W_x(a, b)) = W_x(a, b) * c_1 e^{-\frac{t^2}{2a^2}}. \tag{6}$$

$$S_a(W_x(a, b)) = W_x(a, b) * c_2 \Pi(0.6a). \tag{7}$$

Where c_1 and c_2 are normalization constants and Π is the rectangle function. The factor of 0.6 is the empirically determined scale decorrelation length for the Morlet wavelet. In practice both convolutions are done discretely and therefore the normalization coefficients are determined numerically.

The smoothing function S by Eqs. (6), (7) and (8).

$$S(W) = S_a[S_t(W)]. \tag{8}$$

3 Experiment and Methods

3.1 Experiment

Auditory Stimuli were recorded by two adult (male and female, for eliminating the gender difference) native Chinese speakers. The congruent stimuli consisted of the word/Da/(means loud voice) spoken loudly and the word/Xiao/(means low voice) spoken lowly. The incongruent stimuli consisted of the word/Da/spoken lowly and the word/Xiao/spoken loudly. Loudness difference between the low stimuli and the loud stimuli were adjusted at 30 dB. These two words have similar vowel and consonant duration (both of them are two-syllable words, and the cues of both words were located in the same character of the words), as well as similar appearance frequency in Chinese daily language. In the task, participants were instructed to identify the volume of the words and press the upper button (↑) for a loud volume or the lower button (↓) for a low volume, regardless of the meaning of the words. The task consisted of 320 trials. The four kinds of stimuli were randomly presented with equal probability (0.25) by the audio amplifier, which is limited to less than 60 dB. The duration of every auditory stimulus was 400 ms, and the interval between every two stimuli was 2000,2100,2200,2300 or 2400 ms.

3.2   Method

To obtain a topographic view of the whole brain, brain connectivity was computed with wavelet coherence. Brain activity is typically measured using high-density electroencephalography (EEG). Functional connectivity between brain regions is defined as the statistical dependence between neurophysiological signals in different brain areas and is typically determined by calculating the relationship between regional times series using wavelet coherence, The nodes of the network are EEG channels, and the edges of the network are weighed by the wavelet coherence values, a weighted graph is a mathematical representation of a set of elements (vertices) that may be linked through connections of variable weights (edges). In the present study, weighted and undirected networks were built. The vertices of the networks are the estimated cortical sources in the EEG, and the edges are weighted by the wavelet coherence within each pair of vertices.

The following figure is the normalization of the shortest path length and high clustering coefficient in the word/Da/(means loud voice) spoken loudly. EEG recordings is into distinct frequency bands, namely delta (0.5–4 Hz), theta (4–8 Hz), alpha (8–13 Hz), beta (13–30 Hz) and gamma (30–90 Hz). Furthermore, each frequency band is associated with distinct cognitive functions. The undirected networks are constructed by the weighted clustering coefficient Cw and shortest path length Lw. In addition, the function show the small-world effect, which may shed some light on the great efficiency and high speed of brain information processing. There are the smallest path length because of the small-world effect. So wavelet coherence threshold is 0.64 in Fig. 1 (right, The X axis represents the normalization path length and clustering coefficient, the Y axis represents the wavelet coherence threshold, generating binary network. So the thick lines represent alpha band is significantly different in Fig. 1 (left, The Y axis represents the path length and the X axis represents the wavelet coherence threshold), so the alpha frequency analysis is choice firstly.

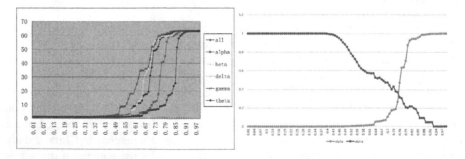

Fig. 1. The shortest path length in difference frequency (left), the normalization of the alpha shortest path length in/Da/spoken loudly (right)

We used functional EEG and dynamic evolution modeling to firstly investigate the cortical dynamics among the region. The brain activation of the intelligibility effect and the effective connectivity among the brain regions were analyzed for both language groups under identical procedures and then put together for comparison. Deciding on the most appropriate connectivity measure can be arduous, as several issues should be considered. This includes the consideration of linear or nonlinear relations, analysis in time or frequency domain, using an amplitude or phase-based measure, obtaining directed or undirected information, wavelet coherence is to investigate connectivity of the brain, which has been used for several decades and are relatively straightforward in terms of computation and interpretation in Fig. 2. Functional networks are based on the strength or consistency of functional interactions between the network nodes. So the degree is chose to represent the dynamic evolution parameter.

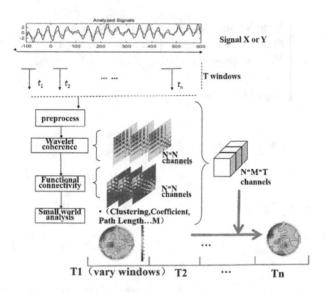

Fig. 2. Functional connectivity dynamics analysis model

The brain network construction based on wavelet coherence analysis, as shown quantitatively in Fig. 2. Sliding-window is 30 ms from −100 ms to 600 ms. In graph theory, the degree of a vertex of a graph is the number of edges incident to the vertex, with loops counted twice.

The time horizon is sampled into T discrete stages that are equally spaced along the length of the driving cycle. The vertical axis is quantized into S different states. The state vector u is composed of degree levels that range in equal steps. The paper deals with degree of node and battery to maximize the cost function. For this reason, the node and the degree can be considered as the state vector. By fixing one, the other can be derived from the degree balance equation, hence the degree is natural to program. In this case, Fig. 3, reveals a model of the network along with all interconnected nodes. The total number of nodes is S_T which depends on the number of selected states and time samples. Each of these nodes (N) is indexed according to its current stage location and corresponding state. For example node N_{iu_j} corresponds to the node at stage i and state u_j. At the first stage each node is characterized with a cost function D_{iu_j} symboled as nodal cost. This is a discrete closed form function that defines a certain objective. The nodal cost represents the cost of being in the associated state. Starting the second stage until t ¼ T, each node has two associated costs which are the nodal cost and the transition cost. The transition cost R_{u_k,iu_j} is the cost of moving from the previous states u_k at i 1 to the current state i at i. The total cost F_iu_j associated with each node at a certain stage is the sum of its nodal cost and the maximum value of all transition costs to the node from previous stage as shown in Eq. (9) and this processing is in Algorithm 1 [17].

$$\text{Index} \begin{cases} \text{State Vector}: u = \left[u_1\ u_2\ ...\ u_j\ ...\ u_s\right] j = 1{:}S \\ \text{Stage Vector: Stage} = [1\ 2\ ...\ i\ ...\ T]\ i = 1{:}T \\ \text{Node Representation: } N_{iu_j} \\ \text{Node Cost}: D_{iu_j} \\ \text{Transition Cost}: R_{u_k,iu_j}\ \ k = 1{:}S \end{cases} \tag{9}$$

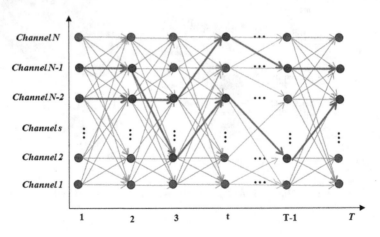

Fig. 3. Dynamic evolution sketch

Algorithm 1 dynamic evolution Algorithm
1:     **for** i such that i=1:T **do**
2:     **for** j such that j=1:S **do**
3:     **for** k such that k=1:S **do**
4:     Compute D_{iu_j}
5:     Compute R_{u_k,iu_j} $\forall k$
6:     Locate maximum of R_{u_k,iu_j}
7:     Save index of max $Max = [i,k_{max}]$ for max of R_{u_k,iu_j}
8:     Compute $F_{iu_j} = D_{iu_j} + R_{u_k,iu_j} + D_{(i-1)u_k}$
9:     **end for**
10:     **end for**
11:     **end for**

3.3 Result

The dynamic evolution processing mapping is presented in Fig. 4 based on node degrees in binary network in incongruent minus congruent. Moreover, our further research is studying brain oscillations mechanisms of auditory cognitive control processing based the dynamic evolution model. We found that the different auditory stimuli arouse different brain areas. This finding provides evidence for an auditory conflict processing signal. More specifically, we proposed a new model to investigate the different cognition processing in Fig. 4 that corresponds to Fig. 5 in 30 ms time windows. High wavelet coherence represents high synchronization of neurons, The dynamic evolution processing mapping (incongruent minus congruent) is that the bigger node degree the greater the color is depth, It can be seen that the degree of synchronization in the former stage, the front right brain area synchronization is higher than other areas, At the later stage, the middle frontal brain area in incongruent is higher than other areas. The results are consistent with auditory cognitive control.

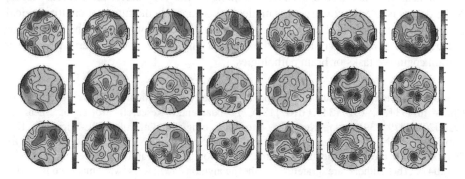

Fig. 4. The dynamic evolution processing mapping (incongruent minus congruent)

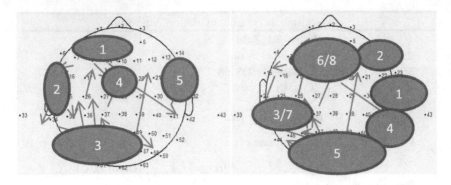

Fig. 5. The dynamic evolution processing in different auditory input

Moreover, the stronger forward connections between the anterior temporal poles and Broca's area may be due to further semantic processing that is included in word identification through phonological information in Chinese in Fig. 5 (left: word/da/spoken loudly and right:word/Xiao/spoken loudly). It can be seen in the process of auditory cognitive control, the high synchronization brain areas change in time and area. This preliminary result for auditory stroop suggests an integrated forward processing of mapping the phonological information to the semantic-related representation from both hemispheres in this tonal language.

4   Conclusion

The model indicate that a complete cognitive control process are perceptual detection, identification detection, and conflict resolution during the auditory stroop task. Understanding the role EEG oscillations is important for comprehending mechanisms of cognitive decline in the network dynamics of auditory stimuli and could serve as a model for understanding large-scale brain network dynamics and their relation to other cognitive phenomena or structural modulations. This study opens interesting avenues into future researches investigating eventual modifications of brain connectivity in the evolution of neurodegenerative processes beginning at the very early, pre-clinical stages. Node degree is used to construct the model in this paper, in the future, more topological parameters are considered to build the model. Such methodologies will be suitable for capturing the dynamic evolution of the time varying connectivity patterns that reflect certain cognitive tasks or brain pathologies.

Acknowledgement.   Our thanks to supports from the National Natural Science Foundation of China (61171186, 61271345, 61671187), Foundamental Research Project of Shenzhen (JCYJ20150929143955341), Key Laboratory Opening Funding of MOE-Microsoft Key Laboratory of Natural Language Processing and Speech (HIT.KLOF.20150xx, HIT.KLOF. 20160xx), and the Fundamental Research Funds for the Central Universities (HIT.NSRIF. 2012047). The authors are grateful for the anonymous reviewers who made constructive comments.

References

1. Sporns, O.: Networks of the Brain. MIT Press, Cambridge (2010)
2. Vincent, J.L., Snyder, A.Z., Fox, M.D., et al.: Coherent spontaneous activity identifies a hippocampal-parietal memory network. J. Neurophysiol. **96**(6), 3517–3531 (2006)
3. Nagai, Y., Critchley, H.D., Featherstone, E., et al.: Brain activity relating to the contingent negative variation: an fMRI investigation. Neuroimage **21**(4), 1232–1241 (2004)
4. Kopal, J., Vyšata, O., Burian, J., et al.: Complex continuous wavelet coherence for EEG microstates detection in insight and calm meditation. Conscious. Cogn. **30**, 13–23 (2014)
5. Lachaux, J.P., Lutz, A., Rudrauf, D., et al.: Estimating the time-course of coherence between single-trial brain signals: an introduction to wavelet coherence. Neurophysiol. Clin./Clin. Neurophysiol. **32**(3), 157–174 (2002)
6. Onnela, J.P., Saramäki, J., Kertész, J., et al.: Intensity and coherence of motifs in weighted complex networks. Phys. Rev. E **71**(6), 065103 (2005)
7. Van Milligen, B., Sanchez, E., Estrada, T., Hidalgo, C., Branas, B., Carreras, B.: Wavelet bicoherence: a new turbulence analysis tool. Phys. Plasmas **2**, 3017–3032 (1995)
8. Santoso, S., Powers, E., Bengtson, R., Ouroua, A.: Time-series analysis of nonstationary plasma fluctuations using wavelet transforms. Rev. Sci. Instrum. **68**, 898–901 (1997)
9. Torrence, C., Compo, G.P.: A practical guide to wavelet analysis. Bull. Am. Meteorol. Soc. **79**(1), 61–78 (1998)
10. Osofsky, S.S.: Calculation of transient sinusoidal signal amplitudes using the Morlet wavelet. IEEE Trans. Sig. Process. **47**(12), 3426–3428 (1999)
11. Lachaux, J.P., Rodriguez, E., Martinerie, J., Adam, C., Hasboun, D., Varela, F.J.: A quantitative study of gamma-band activity in human intracranial recordings triggered by visual stimuli. Eur. J. Neurosci. **12**, 2608–2622 (2000)
12. Bonato, P., Gagliati, G., Knaflitz, M.: Analysis of myoelectric signals recorded during dynamic contractions. IEEE Eng. Med. Biol. Mag. **15**, 102–111 (1996)
13. Lachaux, J.P., Rodriguez, E., Martinerie, J., Varela, F.J.: Measuring phase synchrony in brain signals. Hum. Brain Mapp. **8**, 194–208 (1999)
14. Kronland-Martinet, R., Morlet, J., Grossmann, A.: Analysis of sound patterns through wavelet transforms. Int. J. Pattern Recogn. Artif. Intell. **1**(2), 97–126 (1987)
15. Faust, U.O., Acharya, R., Adeli, H., Adeli, A.: Wavelet-based EEG processing for computer-aided seizure detection and epilepsy diagnosis. Seizure **26**, 56–64 (2015)
16. Ghorbanian, P., Devilbiss, D.M., Hess, T., et al.: Exploration of EEG features of Alzheimer's disease using continuous wavelet transform. Med. Biol. Eng. Comput. **53**(9), 1–13 (2015)
17. Farcs, D., Chedid, R., Panik, F., et al.: Dynamic programming technique for optimizing fuel cell hybrid vehicles. Int. J. Hydrogen Energy **40**(24), 7777–7790 (2015)

Predicting Insulin Resistance in Children Using a Machine-Learning-Based Clinical Decision Support System

Adam James Hall[1(✉)], Amir Hussain[1], and M. Guftar Shaikh[1,2]

[1] Department of Computer Science and Mathematics, School of Natural Sciences,
University of Stirling, Stirling, Scotland
adam@adamshall.co.uk, ahu@cs.stir.ac.uk,
guftar.shaikh@nhs.net
[2] Department of Endocrinology, Glasgow Royal Hospital for Children, Glasgow, Scotland

Abstract. This study proposes a new diagnostic approach based on application of machine learning techniques to anthropometric patient features in order to create a predictive model capable of diagnosing insulin resistance (HOMA-IR).

As part of the study, a dataset was built using existing paediatric patient data containing subjects with and without insulin resistance. A novel machine learning model was then developed to predict the presence of insulin resistance based on dependent biometric variables with an optimal level of accuracy. This model is made publicly available through the implementation of a clinical decision support system (CDSS) prototype. The model classifies insulin resistant individuals with 81% accuracy and 75% of individuals without insulin resistance. This gives an overall accuracy of 78%. The user testing feedback for the CDSS is largely positive.

Best practices were followed for building the model in accordance to those set out in previous studies. The biometric profile of insulin resistance represented in the model is likely to become better fitted to that of insulin resistance in the general population as more data are aggregated from sources. The infrastructure of the CDSS has also been built so that cross platform integration will be possible in future work.

The current methods used by clinicians to identify insulin resistance in children are limited by invasive and clinically expensive blood testing. The benefits of this model would be to reduce the cost of clinical diagnosis and as a result, could also be used as a screening tool in the general childhood population.

Keywords: Machine learning · Ensemble learning · Clinical Decision Support System · Insulin resistance · Diabetes · Paediatrics

1 Introduction

1.1 Clinical Decision Support Systems (CDSSs)

One of the earliest and most definitive examples of using automated tools to help with the processing of clinical data appeared in 1969. This was an essay published by Gerald Goertzel called "Clinical Decision Support System" [2]. In this essay, Goertzel reports upon work he has been involved with concerning the development of a computer system

© Springer International Publishing AG 2016
C.-L. Liu et al. (Eds.): BICS 2016, LNAI 10023, pp. 274–283, 2016.
DOI: 10.1007/978-3-319-49685-6_25

that will assist in patient care. Goertzel outlines that a system of this description would help to alleviate the pressures placed on large public hospitals by the lack of physicians. Goetzels specified that the system should have the following features:

- The system will assist in acquiring patient data.
- The system will present data in the form of a summary.
- The system will suggest appropriate decisions.

Forty years have passed and the fundamental concept of the CDSS remains the same. However, the implementations of this concept vary with their application. Modern CDSS's have been categorised into two groups: knowledge based and non-knowledge based [3]. The non-knowledge based support systems will be the focus of the present study. Non-knowledge based support systems rely on machine learning (ML) techniques that find patterns in clinical data.

One of these studies was called "A predictive model to aid the diagnosis of dementia" [4]. This was developed in the attempt to augment the diagnosis of early dementia. Typically, clinicians find difficulty in diagnosing this due to the inherent complexity of the process of dementia and the lack of comprehensive, exacting diagnostic tools.

A noteworthy aspect of the Mazzocco study is that the knowledge-based CDSS that previously existed for this task was outperformed. In this case, the knowledge recorded by domain experts was noticeably improved upon by the model identified in the logistic regression algorithm. This may indicate the potential for ML in non-knowledge-based CDSS's to supersede current knowledge-based approaches.

1.2   The Problem of Insulin Resistance Diagnosis

Diabetes mellitus in the UK is a growing problem. Around 6% of the population experience the effects of this disease involving disordered glycaemic control [5]. Approximately 90% of this group has type II diabetes (T2DM) and most of the remaining 10% have type I (T1DM) [6]. The two disease processes affect different age groups in their onset. The highest incidence rate of T1DM is in children and adolescents, while the rate of T2DM diagnosis increases from middle age onwards. However, with the increasing worldwide obesity epidemic, T2DM is increasingly seen in children and adolescents [6].

Insulin is the pancreatic hormone that regulates glucose in the blood by signalling for its uptake into adipose tissue and skeletal muscle. It is specifically the beta-cells of the Islets of Langerhans that release insulin in response to a rise in blood glucose. The pathophysiology of diabetes is the result of this system becoming ineffective. T2DM describes the acquired condition of an inability to produce enough insulin when combined with an insensitivity of the target cells to the insulin produced [7]. The dysfunctional point in the pathway is not fully understood with regard to insulin resistance and T2DM. However, low physical activity and excessive weight are strongly associated with the pathophysiology of the disease.

Insulin resistance currently cannot be easily identified by means of any one method of examination. Diagnosis is based on biochemical findings through a multitude of laboratory tests. Individual patients are screened for these based on the presence of simultaneously occurring conditions. Clinical findings can be placed into the following categories:

- Anthropometric factors
- Cardiovascular disease
- Other insulin-resistant states

The present study will look at using anthropometric factors to screen for the presence of insulin resistance. Anthropometric indicators are extremely suitable for use in our model. These factors, such as body mass index (BMI), age and ethnicity are commonly recorded and require little pre-processing before they can be included in our training dataset.

1.3 Machine Learning for Predicting Insulin Resistance

There have been some historical attempts at using forms of machine learning for predicting diabetic symptoms in general populations.

A paper was released in 2010 regarding the successful utilization of Support Vector Machines (SVM) for the diagnosis of Diabetes Mellitus [7]. This study used an additional explanation module to allow for an intelligible summary of the SVMs decision. The model was able to achieve an overall prediction accuracy of 94%. This accuracy is considerably higher than that given by the classifier proposed by the current study. This author would attribute the greater performance of this classifier to the fact that it applies to an adult population and not children. Diabetes Mellitus is generally the result of poor glycemic control sustained over a long period of time. Thus, as the patient gets older, the probability of Diabetes occurring is higher.

Another paper was released in 2010 which attempts to classify T2DM through the analysis of associated gene-gene interactions [8]. The classification technique used was, again, SVM. This paper yielded a prediction rate of 65.3%. While this is not as high a prediction rate as in the previously mentioned study, it was concluded that the SVM machine based feature selection method found novel association between single nucleotide polymorphism and T2DM in a Korean population.

For the purposes of the present study, a heterogeneous ensemble learning approach has been used. Heterogeneous ensemble learning classifiers are amalgamations of separate ML classifiers. The aspects of this methodology have been implemented are stacking and randomisation.

2 Proposed CDSS

2.1 Architecture

Dataset. The dataset used in this study was taken from the Paediatrics Department of the Southern General Hospital in Glasgow. The following data points were used to train the model:

- Height
- Weight
- BMI
- Age

- Sex
- Ethnicity
- Postcode
- Family History of Diabetes
- HOMA-IR [7] score

These are all easily accessible to users at the time of diagnosis.

Height, weight and BMI are further pre-processed on the server side with LMSGrowth data [11]. The LMS method summarises changing distribution using three curves representing the median (M), coefficient of variation (S) and skewness (L), the skewness being expressed as a Box-Cox power. The three curves are fitted as cubic splines by non-linear regression using penalised likelihood. The extent of smoothing required can be expressed in terms of smoothing parameters or equivalent degrees of freedom.

This allows the variables to be placed on a population distribution graph for the average values of the age group of that sex. The model is then able to take in to account how many standard deviations patients are above or below the population average.

This is necessary when examining anthropometric indicators in children such as BMI, as children tend to be in different physical proportions to adults. The LMS method allows us to define patients in relation to others their age [12].

The LMS method also allows us to generalize data across age groups. Where a 15-year-old and an 8-year-old would have been incomparable, we can use the LMS method to distill the patient measurements into their relationship with others their age. This gives us a standardised z-score.

The formula for the LMS method can be found in formula one.

$$z = \frac{\left[(Measurement/M\ )^L - 1\right]}{L \times S} \tag{1}$$

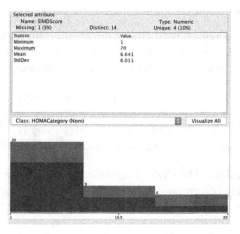

Fig. 1. Diabetic and non-diabetic patient scottish index of multiple depravation scores

Postcode strings are processed using the Scottish index for multiple deprivation. A list of all postcodes in Scotland are held on the server side of the clinical decision support system next to their quintile rank in terms of deprivation. The quintile rank is returned for use by the model. While postcode may seem irrelevant to T2DM on the outset, it is an effective indicator of social condition. Social condition plays a dramatic effect on the development of T2DM. A far higher proportion of T2DM sufferers can be found in those existing in areas of higher deprivation. This can be observed in the histogram shown in Fig. 1. IR sufferers are shown in blue with lower SIMD scores shown on the left.

The dependent variable to be predicted here is whether the HOMA-IR score of the individual was over three. HOMA-IR score is arrived at through interpreting blood test results using homeostatic model assessment. This is achieved through formula 2.

$$HOMA - IR = \frac{Glucose(mmol/L) * Insulin(mmol/L)}{22.5} \tag{2}$$

Classifier Used for Prediction. The model was developed using best practices as described in previous papers [4]. This was an iterative process and an ensemble classifier provided the best level of accuracy with the training set. A similar approach was used in a recent paper for breast cancer diagnosis [9]. The ensemble classifier consists of a heterogeneous stack of the following methodologies:

- Multilayer Perceptron
- Decision Tree
- Naïve Bayesian Network
- SVM
- Logistic Regression
- Decision Forest

These were stacked using probability vote and preprocessed using the following algorithms:

- Synthetic Minority Over-sampling Technique
- Spread Subsample

This preprocessing approach is advocated for dealing with imbalanced datasets [10]. The model is trained independently of the CDSS. It is then dropped into the server side of the application, so that predictions can be made without generating the model each time.

CDSS. The CDSS backend is implemented on an Apache Tomcat Servlet. This allows for ML repositories to be imported from Weka ML tool on the server side for predictions based on input data [11]. The front end is implemented using HTML and CSS. A demo is available for download free of charge on the Stirling University CogBID Lab.[1]

CDSS Front End Design. The CDSS is designed to summarise medical information for non-technical users. The purpose of this is to allow for the system to be used by the public without the presence of a medical professional. As such, the user interface of the

---

[1] http://cosipra.cs.stir.ac.uk/.

system has taken a toy-like appearance. The data summary page has been animated using CSS with icons aimed at children. The data entry page can be observed in Fig. 2.

Fig. 2. CDSS data entry page

When the data are entered the page then folds out into a results section. The patient's height, weight and BMI are plotted on a population distribution curve and the decision arrived at by the classifier is displayed in the bottom right. A text box with advice for the patient is displayed at the lower left of the page. This can be observed in Fig. 3.

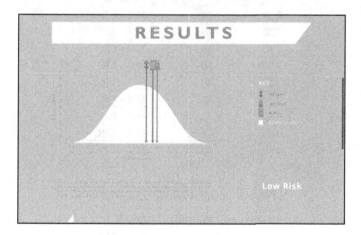

Fig. 3. CDSS data output page

3   Simulation Results and Discussion

The prediction output takes the form of a 'Low Risk' (LR), 'Medium Risk' (MR) and 'High Risk' (HR) categorical variable. Low risk when the probability vote result is less than 0.5, Medium Risk when output is between 0.5 and 0.7 and High Risk when output is above 0.7.

The CDSS behaves as expected giving HR results when individuals with data fitting the biometric profile of insulin resistance are submitted; high BMI, older, positive family history of diabetes, and low postcode deprivation score. LR results are typical when these values are not present or negated. Simulation results for a 12-year-old, male population are shown in Tables 1, 2 and 3.

Table 1. White simulation table

Height(cm)	Weight(kg)	Result
120	32	36% - LR
120	40	55% - MR
120	48	59% - MR
150	32	35% - LR
150	40	35% - LR
150	48	35% - LR
180	32	55% - MR
180	40	56% - MR
180	48	35% - LR

Table 2. African simulation table

Height(cm)	Weight(kg)	Result
120	32	41% - LR
120	40	68% - MR
120	48	73% - HR
150	32	35% - LR
150	40	36% - LR
150	48	45% - LR
180	32	48% - LR
180	40	51% - MR
180	48	35% - LR

Table 3. South Asian simulation table

Height(cm)	Weight(kg)	Result
120	32	51% - MR
120	40	72% - HR
120	48	75% - HR
150	32	35% - LR
150	40	45% - LR
150	48	51% - MR
180	32	72% - HR
180	40	73% - HR
180	48	36% - LR

Sample measurements have been chosen based on the average measurements for 12 year old males with a family history of diabetes. The average height of a 12-year-old male is 150 cm. The average weight is 40 kg. Simulation variables include the average, 20% above and below the average. SIMD quintiles have been simulated with the median score; 10. White, African and South Asian results can be observed in Tables 1, 2 and 3.

Noticeably, African and South Asian populations are prone to higher probabilities whereas white populations yield lower probabilities. Higher weight and lower height generally dictate insulin resistance although high BMI can dictate the prediction. Decisions are arrived at through interpreting percentage probability from the ensemble classifiers probability vote. This three value estimation of risk is acceptable although ideally this would be able to indicate the presence or absence of insulin resistance absolutely and not just a risk assessment.

The model was evaluated on the training set using 10-fold cross validation. These results are shown in Fig. 4.

```
=== Confusion Matrix ===

  a  b   <-- classified as
 17  4 |  a = true
  4 12 |  b = false
```

Fig. 4. Model validation results

These are further summarized by the ROC curve in Fig. 5.

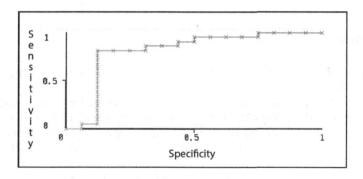

Fig. 5. ROC curve showing classifier errors

4   Conclusions and Future Work

The original aims of the CDSS were to create a system capable of diagnosing insulin resistance based on biometric factors. This has been achieved with 78% overall accuracy-when results are interpreted as >0.5 being positive and <0.5 being negative. The model has a specificity of 75% and a sensitivity of 81%. To this end the study has been successful.

However, the objectives of the study can be better fulfilled through further development. Crucially, the model needs to be trained on a larger data set. This should allow for a model that better fits the biometric profile of insulin resistance. This will not require any changes to the system in place, as the model is trained externally and the format of the set has already been defined. With enough data, the system should be able to make a definitive prediction as to the presence of insulin resistance.

Another avenue for improvement which could be explored is to add more data items targeted at capturing individual genetic and environmental factors. These are both complex issues and difficult to address with just SIMD scores and family history values.

A final aspect of the study to be fulfilled is integration into mobile devices. This will be achieved through writing front ends for both IOS and Android. Again, this will not require much change to the working system as it will be a case of writing an external app interface to be downloaded by the client machine, which receives processed data from the server side. The server side will require an extra interface for passing data to the app client.

The current methods used by clinicians to identify insulin resistance in children are limited by invasive and clinically expensive blood testing. The benefits of this model would be to reduce the cost of clinical diagnosis and as a result, could also be used as a screening tool in the general childhood population.

Acknowledgments. Professor A. Hussain was supported by the UK Engineering and Physical Sciences Research Council (EPSRC) grant no. EP/M026981/1, and the Digital Health & Care Institute (DHI) funded Exploratory project: PD2A. The authors are grateful to the anonymous reviewers for their insightful comments and suggestions, which helped improve the quality of this paper.

References

1. Goertzel, G.: Clinical decision support system. Ann. New York Acad. Sci. **161**(2), 689–693 (1969)
2. Anooj, P.: Clinical decision support system: risk level prediction of heart disease using weighted fuzzy rules. J. King Saud Univ. Comput. Inform. Sci. **24**(1), 27–40 (2012)
3. Mazzocco, T.: Toward a novel predictive analysis framework for new-generation clinical decision support systems. University of Stirling (2014). http://hdl.handle.net/1893/21684. Accessed 12 Jul 2016
4. Diabetes UK: Diabetes Prevalence 2013, February 2014. https://www.diabetes.org.uk/About_us/What-we-say/Statistics/Diabetes-prevalence-2013/. Accessed 12 Jul 2016
5. Scottish Diabetes Survey Monitoring Group: Scottish Diabetes Survey 2012, NHS Scotland (2012). http://www.diabetesinscotland.org.uk/publications/sds%202012.pdf. Accessed 12 Jul 2016
6. Sabin, M.A., Kao, K.-T.: Type 2 diabetes mellitus in children and adolescents. Aust. Fam. Phys. **45**(6), 401–406 (2016)
7. Leahy, J.: Pathogenesis of type 2 diabetes mellitus. Arch. Med. Res. **36**(3), 197–209 (2005)
8. Bradley, A.P., Barakat, M.N.H., Barakat, N.: Intelligible support vector machines for diagnosis of diabetes mellitus. IEEE Trans. Inform. Technol. Biomed. **14**(4), 1114–1120 (2010)

9. Heo, J.Y., Oh, K.-S., Park, K.-J., Ban, H.-J.: Identification of type 2 diabetes-associated combination of SNPs using support vector machine. BMC Genet. **11**, 26 (2010)
10. Levy, J.C., Matthews, D.R., Wallace, T.M.: **27**(6), 1487–1495 (2004). http://care. diabetesjournals.org/content/27/6/1487
11. Cole, T., Pan, H.: (2012). http://www.healthforallchildren.com/shop-base/shop/software/ lmsgrowth/. Accessed Jul 2016
12. Cole, T.J.: The LMS method for constructing normalized growth standards. Eur. J. Clin. Nutr. **44**(1), 45–60 (1990)
13. Qamar, U., Khan, F.H., Bashir, S.: Heterogeneous classifiers fusion for dynamic breast cancer diagnosis using weighted vote based ensemble. Qual. Quant. **49**(5), 2061–2076 (2015)
14. Bowyer, K.W., Hall, L.O., Kegelmeyer, W.P., Chawla, N.V.: SMOTE: synthetic minority over-sampling technique. J. Artif. Intell., June 2002. https://www.jair.org/media/953/ live-953-2037-jair.pdf. Accessed Jul 2016
15. Frank, E., Holmes, G., Pfahringer, B., Reutemann, P., Witten, I.H., Hall, M.: The WEKA data mining software: an update. SIGKDD Explor. **11**(1), 10–18 (2009)

An Ontological Framework of Semantic Learner Profile in an E-Learning System

T. Sheeba[1(✉)] and Reshmy Krishnan[2]

[1] Department of Computer Science and Engineering, Karpagam University,
Coimbatore, Tamil Nadu, India
tsheebat2002@yahoo.co.in
[2] Department of Computing, Muscat College, P.O.Box: 2910, 112 Ruwi,
Sultanate of Oman
reshmy_krishnan@yahoo.co.in

Abstract. The success of E-Learning system depends on the retrieval of relevant learning contents of learner. The best method to acquire learner needs is to construct an efficient learner profile which has to comply with the Semantic Web. Semantic Web relies heavily on formal ontologies to structure data.

The proposed work suggests an approach to construct an efficient ontology based semantic learner profile by achieving the following objectives: First step is to collect static data using questionnaire and dynamic data using web log files. Second step is to preprocess weblog files to retrieve learner interest using semantic representation of WordNet and to retrieve learning style using decision tree classifier with significant rules. Third step is to construct an ontology using the retrieved data and to update ontology automatically using semantic similarity with WordNet. Finally an efficient fuzzy semantic retrieval is obtained using fuzzy linguistic variable which improves information retrieval and filtering.

Keywords: E-Learning · Semantic Web · Learner profile · Ontology · Fuzzy semantic retrieval

1 Introduction

E-Learning is the use of technology to enable people to learn anytime and anywhere. Due to the rapid increase of learning content in the E-Learning systems, it is time consuming for the learners to find content what they really want to and need to study. The E-Learning systems would also perform exactly the same way for all learners as it has no background details of the learner using the system. The success of any E-Learning system depends on the retrieval of relevant learning contents based on the requirements of the learner. In order to satisfy the requirements of the learner and to design an adaptive learning system, there is a necessity to enable the delivery of learning content according to particular learner's needs. The best method used to acquire the needs of the learner is to construct an efficient learner profile which would reflect the true learner needs. A learner profile is basically information relating to individual learners who are engaged in the learning environment. It includes information on learner's knowledge, interest, learning preferences and styles, goals, background etc. The main

© Springer International Publishing AG 2016
C.-L. Liu et al. (Eds.): BICS 2016, LNAI 10023, pp. 284–297, 2016.
DOI: 10.1007/978-3-319-49685-6_26

challenges in the construction of learner profiles is to accurately identify the learner information and organizing the information in such a way that facilities semantic retrieval. In order to develop the learner profile in a conceptual manner, E-Learning system has to comply with the Semantic Web. Semantic Web act as a very suitable platform for implementing an E-Learning system, because it provides all means for E-Learning system such as ontology development, ontology-based annotation of learning materials etc. through E-Learning portals. Ontology is used as a standard knowledge representation for the semantic web. Ontology-based semantic information retrieval is one of the motivations of the Semantic Web.

Various research studies were encountered in the process of creation of user profile. User profile can be created from both static and dynamic characteristics of the user. A user profile model [1] is created using static characteristics in which profile properties of individual user is collected using questionnaire. The dynamic and temporal characteristics are not incorporated. Dynamic characteristics learner interest is considered in the following user profile construction: A user profile [3] is created in "music" domain using user's current interests and new interests by analyzing user web logs. Then the user profile is updated with the new interest using a newly introduced concept of ontology based semantic similarity. Interested terms [6] of the learner are extracted by analyzing the web log. Vector Space Model (VSM) is used to extract feature from document and a fuzzy clustering method is used to classify the learners on their interests. This paper recommends to use ontology based user profiles to maintain sophisticated representations of personal interest profiles. Each user profile [5, 21] is built from learning objects published by the user himself. Automatically generated fuzzy ontology is used to represent the user profile based on the user's interests and preferences which enhances the user's activities into e-learning environments. An ontology based user profile [4, 11] is constructed using fuzzy clustering technique. The method allows some information to belong to several user profiles simultaneously with different degrees of accuracy. User profile [24] is created by collecting information using meta search in user's blog, personal/organization, web page, and any other sites. WordNet and Lexico-Syntactic pattern for hyponyms were used to extract feature from document. This profile is further improved by applying an ontology matching approach to learn the profile with other similar user. For learning style, [12, 13] compares the existing algorithms used for the learning style classification in the learning environments. [14–19] shows the implementation of algorithms such as Bayesian network, Decision Tree, Genetic Algorithms, Neural Network, Genetic algorithms with K-NN etc. with the accuracy obtained using FSLM learning style model. Fuzzy semantic retrieval is proposed in Electronic Commerce [25] and Traffic Information Service domain [26] using the concept of fuzzy linguistic variable. Query expansion done in SPARQL query language by semantic relations between fuzzy concepts and achieved semantic retrieval of e-commerce and traffic information through fuzzy concepts on the Semantic Web.

The proposed work suggests an approach to construct a ontology based semantic learner profile which would provide an intelligent portal for an adaptive learning in E-Learning system by achieving the following objectives: First step is data collection in which static data is collected using questionnaire and dynamic information such as interest and learning style are obtained from web log files. Second step is data preprocessing in which learner interest and learning style are retrieved from the web log files. The learner interest is retrieved using Vector Space Model (VSM) algorithm with WordNet to achieve semantic representation of documents selected by the learner. Learning style is retrieved using decision tree classifier algorithm with significant rules for reasoning to generate learning style based on Felder-Silverman learning style model. Third step is to construct an ontology using the retrieved static and dynamic data and to update this created ontology automatically using semantic similarity algorithm with WordNet to incorporate dynamic characteristics of the learner. Finally an efficient fuzzy semantic retrieval of learner information is obtained from learner profile by taking advantage of the concept of fuzzy linguistic variable which improves the efficiency of information retrieval and filtering. The proposed ontology based semantic representation of learner profile would provide personalized learning process to the learner based on their individual characteristic such as age, education, interest, learning style etc. It would help staff to understand the learning process of learners, and adjust the pedagogical activities, and support the course development. It would also supports self directed learning and collaborative learning. It would enhance the performance of tasks such as filtering, information retrieval, classification, information management etc. from learner profile.

2   System Model

The proposed approach can provide learner profile according to the learner's individual differences which enhance the process of locating precise learning resources. The system intervenes at four stages during the process of learner profile construction as shown in Fig. 1. First stage is data collection which controls the process of collecting static and dynamic data of the learner. Second stage is data preprocessing in which weblog analysis is done to retrieve learner interest and learning style. Third stage is learner profile construction which uses ontology to construct learner profile based on the collected information and learner profile updating which updates the learner profile automatically during the adaptation process. Final stage is the fuzzy semantic retrieval which performs retrieval of semantic information from learner profile with the help of fuzzy linguistic variable.

3   Methods

3.1   Data Collection

Two types of data are available about the learner: knowledge based and behavior based data. Knowledge based information are otherwise called as static information. It includes personal information of learner such as gender, age, place (city, state, and country), education etc. It is obtained using the questiontionnaire when the learner fills while visiting the site and this profile is stored in the database. Behavior based information are otherwise called as dynamic information. It includes information such as learner interest, learning style, learner preferences etc. It is obtained by analyzing the

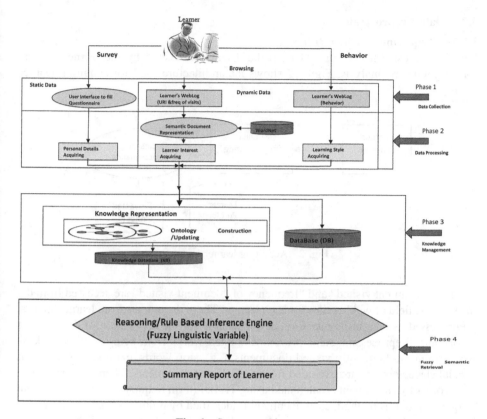

Fig. 1. System architecture

web pages that the learner visits (i.e., web access patterns) in web server logs. Learner Interest and Learning style are considered in the proposed system as it of particular importance for most learner profiles.

WebLog files: Web log files are files that collect the actions of the learners when the learner access the web server. The log files are maintained in the web server automatically when the learner browses the system. These web log files are stored in the web server. The basic information present in the log files are.

Time: The time and date on which the learner access the page while using the learning management system.

IP address: This is the temporary address that is assigned to the computer by the Internet Service provider (ISP) which is used to identify the learner. This address is also used to identify the revisit of the learner.

User full name: This identifies the learner who had visited the learning management system.

Action: This includes the actions and behavior of the learner who access the learning management system.

Information: The resources accessed by the learner.

Course: The course accessed by the learner.

3.2   Data Preprocessing

3.2.1   Acquiring Learner Interest

Learner Interest can be obtained from the documents visited by the learner by performing web log analysis. Figure 2 shows the architecture used for acquiring learner interest.

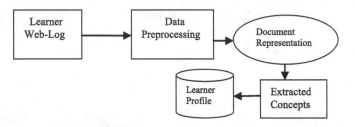

Fig. 2.   Acquiring learner interest

The "document visited" and "frequency of document visited" are accessed from the information field of weblog files for each learner. These documents from learner are first preprocessed as data in its raw form is not suitable for the application of data mining algorithms. Preprocessing steps prevent unwanted words from being selected as keywords from the frequently visited documents. E.g., stop words, extra spaces, number, special characters etc. are excluded from the selected documents. Then the importance of a word is to a document is calculated using TF-IDF(term frequency-inverse document frequency). In this method, each document is identified by n-dimensional feature vector in which each dimension corresponds to a distinct term. Then normalized term frequency (NTF) is calculated which is used to calculate how frequently a word occurs in a document using the formula TF(w) = (No of times word w appears in a document)/ (Total no of words in the document). Then Inverse Document Frequency (IDF) is calculated which is a measure on how important a term is to a document using the formula IDF(w) = log_e(Total no of documents/No of documents with word w in it). Finally the weight of words in the selected document W is calculated using the formula W(w) = TF(w) * IDF(w) as shown in Table 1.

Table 1.   Sample of weighted words in the documents

	network	topology	wireless	interface	cable	devices	logical	installed	perform	physical	equipment	access	security	standards	lans
Document 1	0.04	0.06	0	0.01	0.01	0.01	0.03	0	0.01	0.03	0.01	0.01	0	0	0
Document 2	0.01	0	0.03	0	0.01	0	0	0	0	0	0.01	0.01	0.01	0.01	0.01

The main drawback in method is that it does not represent the semantics to the terms. To improve the performance of this traditional method, semantic representation of keywords using WordNet is used to identify Word Net concepts related to document terms. WordNet is a lexical database developed by George Miller at the Cognitive Science Laboratory at Princeton University. The basic building block of WordNet is synsets. In this WordNet, dictionary is used to find the concept similarity between words. The noun part of the WordNet is considered along with the *hypernymy* and *holonymy* relations. Hypernymy is used to generalize noun and verb meanings to a higher level of abstraction and hyperonymy is the semantic relation between more general words to more specific word. The WordNet concepts selected are finally stored in the database. Table 2 shows the synonyms, hypernyms and its hyponyms obtained from the WordNet 3.1 database.

Table 2. Result from WordNet 3.1 database

Words	Synonyms	Description	Hypernyms	Hyponyms
Topology	Network topology	the configuration of a communication network	Configuration, constellation	Bus topology, loop topology, star topology, mesh topology, physical topology and logical topology
Network	Broadcasting	a communication system consisting of a group of broadcasting stations that all transmit the same programs	Communication system, Communication equipment	–
Wireless	Radio Communication	transmission by radio waves	Telecommunication, telecom	Radio telegraph, radio telegraphy, wireless telegraphy

3.2.2   Acquiring Learning Style

Learning style is typically defined as the way the learner prefers to learn. Everyone has his/her own style on learning which can also vary from one situation to another. This learning style can be identified by the learner action on the site. More profound models are used for learning style. One of the most widely used learning style model in educational systems is Felder-Silverman because it provides an instrument that allows educational practitioners to quantify students' learning style preferences. It has proven to be suitable for use in educational systems and exhibit a good degree of validity and internal consistency. It is suitable for use with an educational system, that it has been widely tested in engineering education, and that it considers learning styles not as fixed traits but as differential preferences for learning.

This model defines four dimensions on learning style such as active/reflective, sensing/intuitive, verbal/visual, sequential/global. The algorithm used to detect learning style is given below: First step is data collection in which web log files are analyzed to retrieve action of students like "forum, chats, assignments, exams, text, ppt and hyperlinks. Second step is to create learning style model using decision tree classifier based on FSLSM Model (Fig. 3) in which leaves represent the learning style to be inferred and the nodes represent the features tracked that lead to learning styles.

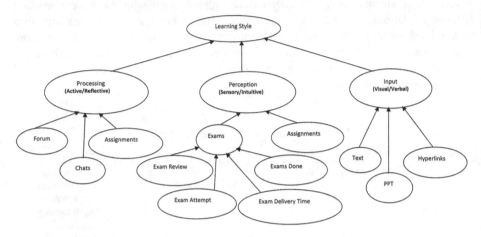

Fig. 3. Learning style model using decision tree classifier

Final step is to predict learning style based on input behavior of learner in which the chosen input behavior are processed to a decision rules (Table 3.) to predict the learning style.

The accuracy and error rate for the learning style system is calculated using the formula in Eq. (1).

$$\text{Accuracy} = \text{Correct Predictions} / \text{Total Number of Predictions}$$
$$\text{Error Rate} = \text{Wrong Predictions} / \text{Total Number of Predictions} \tag{1}$$

We obtained an accuracy of 75% in the processing dimension, 95% in the perception dimension, and 90% in the input dimension. The error rate is 25% in the processing dimension, 5% in the perception dimension and 10% in input dimension. This percentage is calculated by considering the learning styles that could be obtained by the decision tree classifier. By analyzing student's logs and the results obtained from decision tree, we found that most students did most of the exams and exercises provided for the course in the perception dimension and hence did not find most variance in this dimension. In the input dimension, most of the students are interested in using the power point slides and hyperlinks instead of using the theoretical notes for their study and hence shown less variance in the predicted class. In the processing dimension, the students found to use less use of forums and chats facilities and hence found variance in this dimensions.

Table 3. Decision tree rules

Dimensions		Category	Rules	Values (S)
Processing (Active/Reflective)	Forum	Add post to start discussions	No of post	3
		View & Add Post messages	No of view and post	2
		Only View forums & discussions	No of views	1
		No Participation	No participation	0
	Chats	View & Report	No of view and report	2
		Only view	No of view	1
		No Participation	No participation	0
	Assign ments Done	Submit, View-Submit assign form	Makes <10% of assignments	0
			Makes 10% - 30% of assign	1
			Makes 30% - 50% of assign	2
			Makes 50% - 70% of assign	3
			Makes > 70% of assign	4
Perception (Sensory/Intuitive)	Exams	Exam Review	Uses <5% of revision	0
			Uses 5% - 10% of revision	1
			Uses 10% - 15% of revision	2
			Uses 15% - 20% of revision	3
			Uses > 20% of revision	4
		Attempt & Continue Attempt	Uses <10% attempt	0
			Uses 10% - 30% attempt	1
			Uses 30% -50% attempt	2
			Uses 50% - 70% attempt	3
			Uses > 70% attempt	4
		Exam Delivery Time	Uses <40% of time given	0
			Uses 40% - 50% of time given	1
			Uses 50% - 60% of time given	2
			Uses 60% - 70% of time given	3
			Uses > 70% time given	4
		Exams done	Makes <10% of exams	0
			Makes 10% - 30% of exams	1
			Makes 30% - 50% of exams	2
			Makes 50% - 70% of exams	3
			Makes > 70% of exams	4
	Assign ments Done	Submit, View-Submit assign form	Makes <10% of assignments	0
			Makes 10% - 30% of assign	1
			Makes 30% - 50% of assign	2
			Makes 50% - 70% of assign	3
			Makes > 70% of assign	4
Input (Visual/Verbal)	Text	View Course (Word)	No of view (Word)	1
		No view	No of no view (Word)	0
	PPT	View Course (PPT)	No of view (ppt)	1
		No view	No of no view(ppt)	0
	Hyperli nks	View Course (HyperLink)	No of view (HyperLink)	1
		No view	No of no view (HyperLink)	0

S	Value of Processing Dimension
0-1	Extremely Reflective
2-3	Medium Reflective
4-5	Neutral
6-7	Medium Active
8-9	Extremely Active

S	Value of Perception Dimension
0<=S<=4	Extremely Intuitive
4<S<=8	Medium Intuitive
8<S<=12	Neutral
12<S<=16	Medium Sensitive
16<S<=20	Extremely Sensitive

S	Value of Input Dimension
0	-
1	Extremely Verbal
2	Neutral
3	Extremely Visual

3.3   Knowledge Management

3.3.1   Learner Profile Construction

Ontology is used for the learner profile construction. Ontology represents the knowledge in a domain in a structured way. It is a conceptualization of a domain into a human understandable, machine-readable format consisting of entities, attributes, relationships, and axioms. It is used as a standard knowledge representation for the semantic web. The main steps used in the ontology construction are: Enumerate important concepts and terms which collect terms related to learner; Define concepts, slots and relation of concepts which create preliminary concepts and sub concepts and create relationships between the concept; Implementation which is performed with the help of software and Evaluation which check whether the created ontology is accurate or not.

This ontology includes four main components (Fig. 4) to represent the domain such as classes, subclasses, object property, data property and named individuals.

- **Classes:** represent a set of objects within a domain. The classes created are name, id, date of birth, email, phone no, education, profession, address, place of birth, nationality, interest etc.

- **Properties:** express attributes and relations between classes and objects
  - **Object Property:** relation between two classes. Example: <has studid> MCM12207CH; <has dob> 20-May-93; <has nationality> Omani; <has address> alseeb;
  - **Data Property:** relation between classes and a primitive data type. Example <has email> 12207@email.muscatcollege.in
- **Named Individuals:** atoms (objects) which are members of a class. For example, the individuals takes the corresponding values of the created classes for name, id, date of birth, email, phone no, education, profession, address, place of birth, nationality from the excel file. Example: <studid>; <dob>; <nationality>; <address>.

If any new input field is added to the input file, then new relationship is created with all the other existing fields in the input file. The created ontology is finally written automatically to a OWL file. The ontology created in the OWL file is opened using an ontology editor protégé 4.2 beta editor for viewing the created ontology. The below Figs. 4 and 5 shows the view of ontology created in the protégé editor.

Fig. 4. Four components of Ontology

3.3.2   Learner Profile Updating

Learner profile updating allows the inclusion of new concepts into the learner profile when new concepts are selected by learners. Semantic Similarity is the general method used for the learner profile updating. It is used to quantify concept similarities in a given ontology. There are multiple ways of calculating similarity of concepts/ individuals in an ontology. The most efficient method that matches with the human

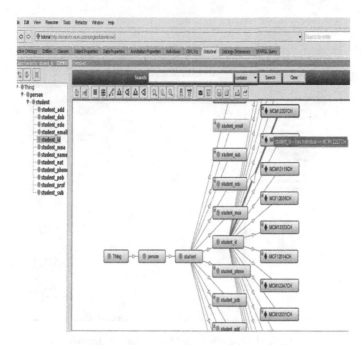

Fig. 5. OntoGraf view of Ontology

intuition is based on ontology nodes (classes). Ontology-based semantic similarity is used to compare items browsed by a user on the web with the items from a learner's profile. In this method, a list of WordNet synets are obtained for each concept to be updated in learner profile. Then, information content similarity between two concepts c1, c2 is calculated using the formula: sim (a1, a2) = 2 log(p(c)) / log(p(c1) + log(p (c2)), c is maximum information content shared by c1 and c2. The concepts having similarity score of threshold (0.5) is added to the learner profile.

Below Figs. 6 and 7 shows an example of updating "Education" of Learner "AnasHashim Abdullah Al Hashmi" from "Diploma" to "BachelorinComputing Science".

3.4 Fuzzy Semantic Information Retrieval

Fuzzy ontology contains fuzzy concepts and fuzzy memberships which allow easy determination of the precise meaning of a word as it relates to a document collection. It can be used in information retrieval to locate precise information, which may be contained in a document content collection. Fuzzy ontology based retrieval system is a system that typically measures the relevance of documents to learner's query based on meaning of dominant words in each document. It determines semantic equivalence between terms in a query and terms in a document by relating the synonyms of query terms with those of document terms.

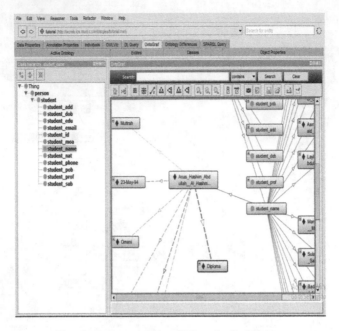

Fig. 6. Before updating "Education" of learner

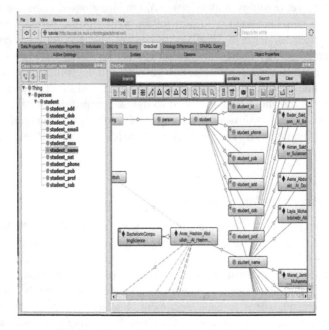

Fig. 7. After updating "Education" of learner

In the proposed system, fuzzy semantic retrieval is performed with the help of fuzzy linguistic variable. This variable is used for the classification and retrieval of learner profile. It uses the following main steps: Define linguistic variable in which linguistic variable values are defined whose values are words or sentences from a natural language, instead of numerical values. A linguistic variable is then generally decomposed into a set of linguistic terms. Example: Age (a) is the linguistic variable. Linguistic terms A(a) = {old, middle-aged, midlife, youth, youngster, adult, ...} covers overall values of the age. Next step is to define membership functions which is used to quantify a linguistic term. Different forms of membership functions used are triangular, trapezoidal, piecewise linear, Gaussian, or singleton. Membership function can be context dependent and generally chosen arbitrarily according to the user experience. Example: Linguistic terms "youngster" ≤ "midlife" ≤ "old" (Fig. 8).

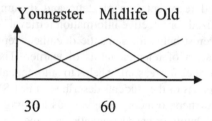

Fig. 8. Triangular membership function

Some of the main fuzzy linguistic variable ontologies used in the system are as following:

O1 = (age, {adult, middle-aged, old, ...});
O2 = (profession, {student, manager, engineer, administrator, ...});
O3 = (education, {highschool, diploma, bachelor, masters......});

The fuzzy logic process is done by applying four conditions to each class. For example, to the class education the fuzzy logic is applied by applying the conditions: low for highschool, medium for diploma, high for bachelor and extreme for masters. After assigning the conditions to the values, score values are calculated for each value. Based on the score values, the whole details are displayed for the selected values. The result would also used to group the students based on the conditions applied in the fuzzy logic process (Tables 4 and 5).

Table 4. Sample data set

Subject	Predicate(property)	Object(value)
Student	Name	Aiman Said Nasser Sulaiman Al Rqadi
Student	DateofBirth	9/28/1988
Student	Email	12347@email.mctcollege.in
Student	Education	Diploma
Student	Profession	Commander in Defence
Student	Nationality	Omani

Table 5. Sample results for individual student

Name	Date of Birth	Nationality	AgeGroup	Profession	Education
Aiman Said Nasser Sulaiman Al Rqadi	9/28/1988	Omani	MiddleAged	Medium Cader	Medium
Manal Jamil Ali Muhammad	6/6/1994	Omani	Youth	Low	Medium
Ziyad Ali Ahmed Al Farsi	8/22/1987	Omani	MiddleAged	Medium Cader	Medium

4 Conclusion

The proposed system is an attempt to implement an ontology based learner profiles that incorporates sophisticated representation of static and dynamic characteristics of a learner which can be utilized for effective information retrieval. The use of WordNet in retrieving the learner interest helps for semantic document representation to obtain a more powerful identification of relevant terms of learner. The use of decision tree classifier with significant rules for reasoning helps to automatically classify the learning style based on the preferences of the students described in FSLSM which would benefit both the educators and learners to incorporate various learning materials based on the student's learning style. Ontology-based semantic information retrieval is one of the motivations of the Semantic Web. The proposed system implements an efficient fuzzy semantic retrieval by using the concept of fuzzy linguistic variable which enhances the performance of tasks such as filtering and information retrieval. The proposed ontology based learner profile would make the E-learning System as an intelligent portal which would help staffs to understand the background details of learners, and adjust the pedagogical activities, and support the course development.

References

1. Maria, G., Akrivi, K., Costas, V., George, L., Constantin, H.: Creating an Ontology for the User Profile: Method and Applications (2006)
2. Fouad, K.M.: Proposed approach to build semantic learner model in adaptive e-learning. Int. J. Comput. Appl. (0975 – 8887) **58**(17), November 2012
3. Reformat, M.: Updating user profile using ontology-based semantic similarity. In: FUZZ-IEEE, 20–24 August 2009
4. Han, L., Chen, G.: A fuzzy clustering method of construction of ontology-based user profiles. Adv. Eng. Softw. **40**, 535–540 (2008)
5. Ferreira-Satler, M., Romero, F., Menendez, V., Zapata, A., Prieto, M.: A fuzzy ontology approach to represent user profiles in e-learning environments. IEEE (2010)
6. Fouad, K.M.: Adaptive e-learning system based on semantic web and fuzzy clustering. Int. J. Comput. Sci. Inform. Secur. **8**(9) (2010)
7. Fouad Ibrahim, K.M.: Semantic retrieval and recommendation in adaptive e-learning system. In: ICCIT (2012)
8. Leiba, M.: Web usage patterns and learning styles in an academic course in engineering

9. Qiu, B.: Student model in adaptive learning system based on semantic web. In: First International Workshop on Education Technology and Computer Science (2009)

10. Wei, C., Huang, C., Tan, H.: A personalized model for ontology-driven user profiles mining. In: International Symposium on Intelligent Ubiquitous Computing and Education. IEEE (2009)

11. Han, L., Chen, G.: A fuzzy clustering method of construction of ontology-based user profiles. Adv. Eng. Softw. **40**(7), 535–540 (2009)

12. Feldman, J., Monteserin, A., Amandi, A.: Automatic detection of learning styles: state of the art. Artif. Intell. Rev., May 2014. doi:10.1007/s10462-014-9422-6. (Print ISSN:0269-2821, Online ISSN:1573-7462, Springer)

13. Al-Azawei, A., Badii, A.: State of the art of learning styles-based adaptive educational hypermedia systems (Ls-Baehss). Int. J. Comput. Sci. Inform. Technol. (IJCSIT) **6**(3), 1–19 (2014)

14. García, P., Amandi, A., Schiaffino, S., Campo, M.: Evaluating Bayesian networks precision for detecting students learning styles. ScienceDirect. doi:10.1016/j.compedu.2005.11.017

15. Abdullah, M., Alqahtani, A., Aljabri, J., Altowirgi, R., Fallatah, R.: Learning style classification based on student's behavior in moodle learning management system. TAMLAI Trans. Mach. Learn. Artif. Intell. **3**(1), 18 February 2015. doi:10.14738/tmlai.31.868. ISSN 2054-7390

16. Yannibelli, V., Godoy, D., Amandi, A.: A genetic algorithm approach to recognise students' learning styles. Interact. Learn. Environ. **14**(1), 55–78 (2006)

17. Chang, Y.C., Kao, W.Y., Chu, C.P., Chiu, C.H.: A learning style classification mechanism for e-learning. Comput. Educ. **53**(2), 273–285 (2009)

18. Kolekar, S.V., Sanjeevi, S.G., Bormane, D.S.: Learning style recognition using artificial neural network for adaptive user interface in e-learning. In: IEEE International Conference on Computational Intelligence and Computing Research (ICCIC), pp. 1–5 (2010). doi:10.1109/ICCIC.2010.5705768

19. Villaverde, J.E., Godoy, D., Amandi, A.: Learning styles' recognition in e-learning environments with feed-forward neural networks. J. Comput. Assist. Learn. **22**(3), 197–206 (2006)

20. Nada, Y.A.: An approach to improve the representation of the user model in the web-based systems. Int. J. Adv. Comput. Sci. Appl. (IJACSA) **2**(12), 152–160 (2011)

21. Ferreirs-Satler, M.: Fuzzy Ontologies-Based User Profiles Applied to Enhance E-Learning Activities. Springer, New York (2011)

22. Li, X., Chang, S.-K.: A Personalized E-Learning System Based on User Profile Constructed Using Information Fusion (2004)

23. Yu, Z., Nakamura, Y., Jang, S., Kajita, S., Mase, K.: Ontology-based semantic recommendation for context-aware e-learning. In: Indulska, J., Ma, J., Yang, L.T., Ungerer, T., Cao, J. (eds.) UIC 2007. LNCS, vol. 4611, pp. 898–907. Springer, Heidelberg (2007). doi:10.1007/978-3-540-73549-6_88

24. Duong, T.H., Uddin, M.N., Li, D., Jo, G.S.: A collaborative ontology-based user profiles system. In: Nguyen, N.T., Kowalczyk, R., Chen, S.-M. (eds.) ICCCI 2009. LNCS (LNAI), vol. 5796, pp. 540–552. Springer, Heidelberg (2009). doi:10.1007/978-3-642-04441-0_47

25. Zhai, J., Li, J., Lin, Y.: Semantic retrieval based on SPARQL and fuzzy ontology for electronic commerce. J. Comput. **6**(10), 2127–2134 (2011)

26. Zhai, J., Chen, Y., Yu, Y., Liang, Y., Jiang, J.: Fuzzy semantic retrieval for traffic information based on fuzzy ontology and RDF on the semantic web. J. Softw. **4**(7), 758–765 (2009)

27. Kaur, T., Kaur, A.: Extension of a crisp ontology to fuzzy ontology. Int. J. Comput. Eng. Res. **2**(6), 201–207 (2012)

Incremental PCANet: A Lifelong Learning Framework to Achieve the Plasticity of both Feature and Classifier Constructions

Wang-Li Hao and Zhaoxiang Zhang$^{(\boxtimes)}$

CAS Center for Excellence in Brain Science and Intelligence Technology, CASIA,
Beijing, China
zhaoxiang.Zhang@ia.ac.cn

Abstract. The plasticity in our brain gives us promising ability to learn and know the world. Although great successes have been achieved in many fields, few bio-inspired methods have mimiced this ability. They are infeasible when the data is time-varying and the scale is large because they need all training data loaded into memory. Furthermore, even the popular deep convolutional neural network (CNN) models have relatively fixed structures. Through incremental PCANet, this paper aims at exploring a lifelong learning framework to achieve the plasticity of both feature and classifier constructions. The proposed model mainly comprises of three parts: Gabor filters followed by maxpooling layer offering shift and scale tolerance to input samples, cascade incremental PCA to achieve the plasticity of feature extraction and incremental SVM to pursue plasticity of classifier construction. Different from CNN, the plasticity in our model has no back propogation (BP) process and don't need huge parameters. Experiments have been done and their results validate the plasticity of our models in both feature and classifier constructions and further verify the hypothesis of physiology that the plasticity of high layer is better than the low layer.

Keywords: Plasticity · Lifelong learning · Incremental PCANet · Incremental SVM

1 Introduction

Recently, bio-inspired visual processing methods have drawn much more attention as they are favorable in guiding people to design effective models in surveillance, automotive safety and robotics application fields. However, few of them have investigated the plasticity like in primates' visual cortex.

HMAX [1], a popular bio-inspired shallow model, has two S layers, two C layers and a view-tuned units layer. Via convoluting with filters, the S layers can extract more and more abstract features. Through max pooling, the C layers can guarantee the scale and position invariant of the images. VisNet [2] has a similar architecture with HMAX. It comprises of Differential of Gaussian (DoG)

© Springer International Publishing AG 2016
C.-L. Liu et al. (Eds.): BICS 2016, LNAI 10023, pp. 298–309, 2016.
DOI: 10.1007/978-3-319-49685-6_27

filters layer and 4 hierarchical layers that correspond to V2, V4, PIT and AIT respectively. Although they are capable of generating some physiological results, they need all data loaded into memory, which makes them insufficient when dealing with the large scale or flow data. Furthermore, they are lack of plasticity.

Drawn inspiration from the hierarchical structures of the visual cortex [6], combining the deep learning [7] and convolutional neural networks [8], the deep models [3–5] emerged. They generally consist of some continuous convolutional layers, pooling layers and full connection layers. From low to high, convolution layers tend to extract more and more complex and abstract features. Recently, deep convolutional neural networks (DCNNs) have been able to achieve impressive performances on very large and difficult object databases such as ImageNet [9]. Inspite the BP process of DCNNs can finetune the deep networks, their training are very expensive and need a lot of parameters.

Refering to convolution neural network, a simple unsupervised deep learning baseline, PCANet, is first proposed by Chan et al. [10]. It consists of cascade PCA and the binarization hashing followed by block-wise histograms. Despite simple architecture, PCANet obtains very well performance in many image classification tasks. Nevertheless, its training process also need all data available and it has no plasticity.

Above all, no matter shallow and deep bio-inspired models, they are not investigate the plasticity or have expensive finetuning cost. In this paper, we first propose the incremental PCANet, a lifelong learning framework to explore the plasticity of both feature and classifier constructions. Our model basically consists of three parts, Gabor convolutional filters with different scales and orientations followed by maxpooling layer, incremental PCANet and incremental SVM. In the view of machine learning, our model has well self-adaption and robustness which should be attributed to its lifelong learning framework. From the respect of brain-inspired fields, our model explores the plasticity of visual pathway from low to high levels.

The contributions of this paper are listed as follows: (1) Since PCANet suffers a performance degeneration when the input images exhibit diverse in scales or poses, the Gabor filters with several scales and orientations followed by max pooling layer are utilized to process the images. (2) The incremental PCANet is first proposed to investigate the plasticity of feature extraction like in the visual cortex. (3) To explore the plasticity of classifier construction, offline linear classifier utilized in the traditional PCANet is alternated with incremental SVM. (4) We first combine the plasticity of both feature extraction and classifier construction together, thus leading to an end to end lifelong learning framework. (5) Through our model, we do some experiments to validate the plasticity of which layer is crucial.

The remainder of this paper is organized as follows. Related works are described in Sect. 2, our method is shown in Sect. 3, experiments are listed in Sect. 4 and we conclude this paper in Sect. 5.

2   Related Works

Inspired by the hierarchical structure of visual cortex, hierarchical neural networks for object categorization have achieved a widespread success in a variety of domains. Neocognitron, one of the earliest hierarchical neural networks was proposed by Fukushima [11]. Other impressive hierarchical neural networks for object recognition contain LeNet [12] and HMAX [1].

In recent years, the deep hierarchical convolutional neural networks showed us a gradual deeper model. Starting from AlexNet [3], VGG [4], Inception [5] to Residual [13] networks. Furthermore, the performance become much better in many image recognition tasks. AlexNet [3], comprises of five convolutional and three fully connected layers, which wins the ILSVRC2012 competition. To investigate the function of the number of internal layers of DCNNs, Simonyan and Zisserman [4] develop deep convolutional networks with 11, 13, 16, and 19 layers. Their results have shown that the more the layer number is, the better the results will be. GoogLeNet, consists of several inception modules, which wins ILSVRC 2014 [5]. The latest residual networks (ResNet) [13] makes further breakthrough in many tasks, it has won ImageNet and COCO 2015 competition.

On the basis of scattering theory, scattering convolution network (ScatNet) [14] is proposed. Its filters are prefixed as they are derived from mathematical functions. Benefit from these filters, ScatNet shows the state-of-the-art performance in many fields, such as texture discrimination and handwritten recognition.

With the explosion of data, incremental techniques that don't need all data loaded into memory emerged to perform many tasks like principal component analysis (PCA), support vector machine (SVM) and so on. The basic principle of incremental PCA is to update the current PCA without recalculating it when the new data arrive. Many techniques have been proposed to realize it, such as perturbation techniques [15], incremental methods [16], and stochastic optimization [17]. The key principle of incremental SVM is to make use of the current SVM solution to simply figure out the quadratic program of the next search. Specifically, when the new data arrive, they are integrated into the quadratic program and the kernel and regularization parameters (C, σ) are then modified correspondingly [18].

Lifelong learning, is very important to the flexible machines. Early studies on lifelong learning was mainly about sharing distance metrics through transferring invariances in neural networks [19] and task clustering [20]. It has also been extended for learning by reading [21].

3   Methods

Among bio-inspired methods, few of them have mimiced the plasticity in primates' visual cortex. To explore the plasticity of both feature extraction and classifier construction, a lifelong learning framework based on incremental PCANet proposed here.

3.1   MulOri_PCANet

Although PCANet has promising performance in some face, hand-written digital, texture and object recognition tasks, when the input data bear diverse scales or poses, the performance of PCANet may decrease. Inspired by the phenomenon that the primate vision cortex (V1) has some shift and scale invariance [1], its similar realization in machine learning, the Gabor filters with several scales and orientations followed by maxpooling layer are employed to process the images before they are sent to PCANet. They can be described as:

$$G(X,Y) = exp(-\frac{X^2 + \gamma^2 Y^2}{2\sigma^2}) \times \cos(\frac{2\pi}{\lambda}X) \tag{1}$$

Where $X = x\cos\theta + y\sin\theta$ and $Y = -x\sin\theta + y\cos\theta$, θ denotes the orientation, σ represents effective width and λ indicates the wavelength.

Assume N input images are $\{I_i\}_{i=1}^N$. Each of them is first convoluted with the above Gabor filters and several feature maps are obtained subsequently. To mimic the shift and position invariances and orientation sensitivity of V1 in visual cortex, these feature maps are first maxpooled among different scales, then maxpooled in certain grid size Q but not pooled in orientations. As a result, the samples flowed into the subsequent PCANet have multiple orientations, specifically, there are four orientations here. The PCANet with Gabor filters followed maxpooling layer is dubbed as MulOri_PCANet and illustrated in Fig. 1.

3.2   Incremental PCANet

Since the training process of traditional PCANet need all data, it's inefficient when dealing with the large scale or time-varying data. Furthermore, it has no

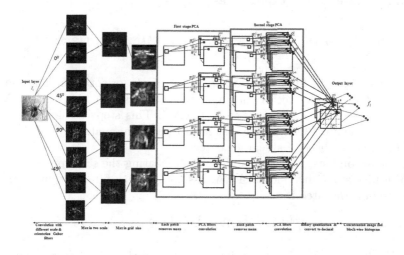

Fig. 1. Detailed structure of MulOri_PCANet.

plasticity. To this end, the incremental PCANet is introduced to explore the plasticity of feature extraction. For simplify, the incremental PCANet is dubbed as IncPCANet.

A. The first stage Incremental PCA: Assume the samples from the Gabor filters flow into the network batch after batch. Let lth batch samples are $\{I_i^{o,l}\}_{i=1}^{N_l}\{o = 1, 2, 3, 4\}$ with size $m \times n$, N_l is the number of input samples of lth batch, o indicts the oth orientation. For each sample, around each pixel, patches with size $k_1 \times k_2$ pixels are extracted, converted into column vectors and concatenated together as $y_{i,1}^{o,l}, y_{i,2}^{o,l}, \cdots, y_{i,\tilde{m}\tilde{n}}^{o,l} \in \mathbb{R}^{k_1 k_2}$, each $y_{i,j}^{o,l}$ indicates the jth patch in $I_i^{o,l}$, here, $\tilde{m} = m - \lceil k_1/2 \rceil$ and $\tilde{n} = n - \lceil k_1/2 \rceil$. Then the mean of patches are subtracted from themselves

$$\bar{Y}_i^{o,l} = [\bar{y}_{i,1}^{o,l}, \bar{y}_{i,2}^{o,l}, \cdots, \bar{y}_{i,\tilde{m}\tilde{n}}^{o,l}] \tag{2}$$

where $\bar{y}_{i,j}^{o,l}$ indicates a patch with its mean removed.

For each orientation samples, by applying the same operators for all input samples and concatenating them together, we obtain

$$Y^{o,l} = [\bar{Y}_1^{o,l}, \bar{Y}_2^{o,l}, \cdots, \bar{Y}_{N_l}^{o,l}] \in \mathbb{R}^{k_1 k_2 \times N_l \tilde{m}\tilde{n}} \tag{3}$$

Since the filter banks of PCANet in every layer are obtained via figuring out several eigenvalues of the convariance matrix Σ correspond to the first largest eigenvalues. Here, Σ is the convariance matrix of the mean-removed pathes of all training samples. To realize the incremental PCANet, instead of storing the mean-removed patches of all training samples of earlier batches, their convariance matrices are just stored and added into that of the current batch. This can significantly save the space and time.

Assume that the pth layer has L_p filters, the filters of the first stage incremental PCA layer can be expressed as

$$W_j^{o,l,1} = mat_{k_1 k_2}(q_p(\sum_{t=1}^{l} Y^{o,t} Y^{o,tT})) \in \mathbb{R}^{k_1 \times k_2}, j = 1, 2, \cdots, L_1 \tag{4}$$

which means the jth filter bank of lth batch of oth orientation. The function $mat_{k_1 k_2}$ is to map the vector into a matrix with size $k_1 \times k_2$ and $q_p(XX^T)$ denotes the pth principle eigenvector of XX^T. This step is crucial for realizing the incremental PCANet, we just need to add the matrix $Y^{o,t} Y^{o,tT}$ of the arriving batch to those of all earlier batches.

B. The second stage Incremental PCA: Repeating the same process of what we do in first stage incremental PCA, assume the jth filter output of the oth orientation of lth batch is

$$I_i^{o,l,j} = I_i^{o,l} * W_j^{o,l,1}, i = 1, 2, \cdots, N_l \tag{5}$$

where $*$ indicates 2D convolution. In order to keep the size of each output $I_i^{o,l,j}$ the same as $I_i^{o,l}$, the boundary of $I_i^{o,l}$ is zero-padded before it convolves with

$W_j^{o,l,1}$. Like in the first stage, all of the overlapping patches of $I_i^{o,l,j}$ are collected and mean-removed to form

$$\bar{Z}_i^{o,l,j} = [\bar{z}_{i,j,1}^{o,l}, \bar{z}_{i,j,2}^{o,l}, \cdots, \bar{z}_{i,j,\tilde{m}\tilde{n}}^{o,l}] \in \mathbb{R}^{k_1 k_2 \times \tilde{m}\tilde{n}} \tag{6}$$

$\bar{z}_{i,j,k}^{o,l}$ means the kth mean-removed patch in $I_i^{o,l,j}$.

Furthermore, let

$$Z^{o,l,j} = [\bar{Z}_1^{o,l,j}, \bar{Z}_2^{o,l,j}, \cdots, \bar{Z}_{N_l}^{o,l,j}] \in \mathbb{R}^{k_1 k_2 \times N_l \tilde{m}\tilde{n}} \tag{7}$$

represents all mean-removed patches of the jth filter output of oth orientation in lth batch.

Concatenate $Z^{o,l,j}$ for all of the filter outputs as

$$Z^{o,l} = [Z^{o,l,1}, Z^{o,l,2}, \cdots, Z^{o,l,L_1}] \in \mathbb{R}^{k_1 k_2 \times L_1 N_l \tilde{m}\tilde{n}} \tag{8}$$

Further, gather $Z^{o,l}$ for all of the orientation outputs as

$$Z^l = [Z^{l,1}, Z^{l,2}, \cdots, Z^{l,4}] \in \mathbb{R}^{k_1 k_2 \times 4L_1 N_l \tilde{m}\tilde{n}} \tag{9}$$

As in the first stage, the incremental PCA filters of lth batch for second stage can be represented as

$$W_j^{l,2} = mat_{k_1 k_2}(q_l(\sum_{t=1}^{l} Z^t Z^{tT})) \in \mathbb{R}^{k_1 \times k_2}, j = 1, 2, \cdots, L_2 \tag{10}$$

For each input $I_i^{o,l,j}$ of the second stage, we can get L_2 output maps of size $m \times n$ via convoluting with $\{W_j^{l,2}\}_{j=1}^{L_2}$

$$O_i^{o,l,j} = \{I_i^{l,j} \times W_j^{l,2}\}_{j=1}^{L_2} \tag{11}$$

The number of output images at the second increment PCA stage is $4L1L2$. The subsequent binarization and histogram pooling can refer to the literature [10], and we don't describe it here.

3.3 Incremental PCANet with Incremental SVM

To analog the plasticity of classifier construction in primates' brain, instead of offline linear SVM classifier [22] used in PCANet [10], incremental SVM in literature [18] is adopted into our model. Since the original incremental SVM algorithm is utilized to deal with two classification problem, we extend it to solve multi classification via one vs one technique here. The IncPCANet with incremental SVM formed a lifelong learning framework that has the plasticity of both feature and classifier constructions.

4 Experiments

To validate the effectiveness of our model, several experiments have been done. They are detailedly depicted as follows.

4.1 Mulori_PCANet: Robust to Input Samples with Diverse Scales or Shifts

For purpose of enforcing the scale and shift invariance of input images flowed into PCANet, Gabor filters with 2 scales $s = \{3,5\}$ and four orientations $\theta = \{-45, 0, 45, 90\}$ are utilized to convolute with them and their responses are maxpooled among different scales and certain gride size $Q = 4$.

To varify the performance of MulOri_PCANet, original PCANet [10], AlexNet [3] and ScatNet [14] are utilized as comparisons. For fair comparison, except the parameters of Gabor filters, the other parameters utilized in PCANet and MulOri_PCANet are set with the same values, the filter size $k_1 = k_2 = 7$, the number filter $L_1 = L_2 = 8$, the block size and the block overlap ration used in block-wise histogram pooling are set as 7×7, 0.5 respectively. In ScatNet, the number of scales and orientations are set as 3 and 8. The parameters of AlexNet are listed in Table 1 and the mean file of imagenet is utilized here.

Table 1. The parameters of AlexNet used on different databases.

Parameters	Test_iter	Test_interval	Lr	Lr_policy	γ	Stepsize	Max_iter	Momentum	Weight_decay
Mnist variations	100	500	0.01	INV	0.1	10000	10000	0.9	0.0005
Caltech101	100	1000	0.01	STEP	0.1	10000	45000	0.9	0.0005

Databases: MNIST variations [23], including background noise, rotations, and background images, to MNIST. The Caltech101 dataset consists of 101 objects and a background category, it can be downloaded from http://www.vision.caltech.edu. In each MNIST databases, there are 10000 train samples and 50000 test samples. For Caltech101, 30 images per category form the training samples and the rest images are used as test samples.

For fair comparison, the linear SVM classifier [22] is utilized for both MulOri_PCANet and PCANet [10].

The results can be found in Table 2. From it, we can see that the performance of our model uniformly better than PCANet and ScatNet-2 most cases, which shows the robustness of MulOri_PCANet. Although MulOri_PCANet performs not better than AlexNet sometimes, it has no data augmentation and the filter learning in MulOri_PCANet don't include adjustments of parameters, meanwhile, its unsupervised learning process with very simple structure is also attractive.

Table 2. The error rate of different algorithms based on several databases.

Databases	bg-img-rot	bg-img	rot	Caltech101
MulOri_PCANet	32.48	9.88	5.89	29.52
PCANet	35.48	10.95	7.37	31.54
ScatNet-2 [14]	50.48	18.40	7.48	46.04
AlexNet [3]	19.26	4.40	7.06	39.30

4.2   IncPCANet: Achieve the Plasticity of Feature Extraction

Inspite great success achieved in many image processing fields, most bio-inspired methods are infeasible when handling the large scale or flow data. This is due to they need all samples available and lack of plasticity. To this end, IncPCANet is proposed, aims at exploring the plasticity of feature extraction.

To validate the effectiveness of IncPCANet, we compare the performance of IncPCANet and traditional PCANet on database with identical distribution, specifically, it is Caltech101. The number of training and testing samples are set the same as in Sect. 4.1. For each database, the whole training samples are divided into 10 batches, these batches are sent to the IncPCANet continuously, after each batch pass, the test samples are utilized to test the model.

To evaluate the effects of filter banks learned by IncPCANet and traditional PCANet, the same number training samples are utilized to train their filter banks. Specifically, the filter banks in PCANet are learned from all arriving batch samples, while those in incremental PCANet are updated just utilize the new arriving data based on earlier batches. For fair comparison, the features are used to train SVM classifier in IncPCANet are the features of all training samples extracted by the current filter banks every time.

The results can be found in Tables 3 and 4. With much less training time, IncPCANet can obtain the comparable results with traditional PCANet, specifically, the Training_Time here means the PCA filter banks' learning time. When dealing with large scale data, IncPCANet is a better choice.

To verify the plasticity of feature extraction of IncPCANet, we compare the performance of IncPCANet and PCANet on databases with different distributions. Here, the Mnist variations are utilized as a database with different distributions. The database is organized with the order of Mnist_basic, Mnist_bg_img, Mnist_bg_rand, Mnist_rot, each of them have 4000 training samples and 5000 test samples, further, the same distribution samples are arriving together and 1000 training samples are seen as a batch.

When the new batch samples arrive, the filter banks of PCANet are updated by utilizing all arriving batch samples no matter the distribution of data has changed or not. Nevertheless, the filter banks of IncPCANet are trained just using the

Table 3. The performance of Incremental PCANet based on Caltech101.

Training numbers	306	612	918	1224	1530	1836	2142	2448	2754	3060
Accuracy	66.64	60.43	51.26	39.77	38.18	34.56	31.55	30.78	30.45	29.81
Training_Time	26.09	26.03	26.82	26.72	26.74	27.48	29.13	26.95	27.09	26.95

Table 4. The performance of PCANet based on Caltech101.

Training numbers	306	612	918	1224	1530	1836	2142	2448	2754	3060
Accuracy	66.96	54.73	46.38	37.68	36.37	33.89	31.72	30.735	29.76	29.40
Training_Time	21.17	39.87	59.77	79.74	101.51	123.41	146.42	169.02	192.53	202.68

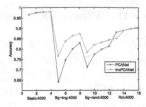

Fig. 2. The comparison of PCANet and IncPCANet based on Mnist database with different distributions.

current arriving batch samples based on the earlier filter banks. The samples are used to train SVM classifier in PCANet are features of all training samples extracted by the current filter banks, while in IncPCANet are just features of all new distribution training samples extracted by the current filter banks.

The results are shown in Fig. 2. In Fig. 2, the name of arriving databases with different distributions and their training numbers are listed in X-axis. From it, we can see that when the distribution of data is changed, the accuracies of PCANet and IncPCANet first decrease and then increase gradually most times, and IncPCANet can obtain better performance than PCANet. This is because when the new data arrive, the filter banks obtained earlier are not suitable for the new situation, so the accuracy decreases. Further, with the number of new samples becomes more and more, the filter banks obtained can better represent the new data, lead to an increase accuracy. However, when Mnist_rot arrive, the performance of two models are not degenerate and IncPCANet first performs worse than PCANet while better than it at last. This is due to Mnist_rot samples have some similarities with the earlier databases, the filter banks of earlier samples can represent Mnist_rot at some extent, so the accuracy of Mnist_rot is not decrease. Furthermore, IncPCANet has less training samples than PCANet at first, which leads to a worse result compared to PCANet. Nevertheless, with the number of Mnist_rot samples becomes more, IncPCANet can quickly adjust the filter banks to better approximate the new data and obtain a better results. Above all, the experimental results in this section reveal IncPCANet has plasticity in feature extraction and owns better self-adaption and robustness compared to PCANet.

4.3   Validate the Effectiveness of the End to End Lifelong Learning Model Based on IncPCANet with Incremental SVM

The plasticity in primates' brain not only include the feature extraction but also classifier construction. Incremental PCANet with incremental SVM (dubbed as IncPCANetIncSVM) is expected here to analog this end to end plasticity. In this section, we first validate the effectiveness of IncPCANetIncSVM and in the next section further verify the plasticity in visual cortex.

To varify the performance of IncPCANetIncSVM, the incremental PCANet with offline SVM (IncPCANetSVM) and PCANet with incremental SVM (PCANetIncSVM) are employed as comparisons. Mnist_rot is utilized as their

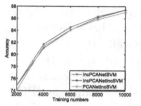 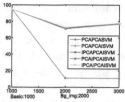

(a) The comparison of different models based on M-nist_rot.

(b) The comparison of different models based on M-nist database with different distributions.

Fig. 3. The validations of the model's plasticities based on different levels.

databases and the numbers of training and testing samples are 10000 and 50000 respectively. For fair comparison, the offline SVM we also use the batch SVM offered in [18] other than linear SVM [22].

The result is shown in (a) subfigure of Fig. 3. Along with the number of training samples increased, the results of three models become better. Furthermore, with much less time and space cost, the IncPCANetIncSVM can obtain comparable or even better performance compared to other two models, which reveal the efficient and effectiveness of IncPCANetIncSVM.

4.4 Analog and Validate the Functions of Plasticity of Different Layers in Visual Cortex

Assume the databases with different distributions flow into the incremental PCANet, when the data distribution is changed, to validate the plasticity of which layer is crucial, we freeze some layer and adjust the rest layers. Here, the adjustment operations via incremental technique to realize.

- Feature layers and classifier layer with no adjustments (dubbed as PCAP-CASVM)
- Feature layers with no adjustments and classifier layer with adjustment (dubbed as PCAPCAISVM)
- Low level feature layer and classifier layer with adjustments and high level feature layer with no adjustment (dubbed as IPCAPCAISVM)
- High level feature layer and classifier layer with adjustments and low level feature layer with no adjustment (dubbed as PCAIPCAISVM)
- Feature and classifier layers with adjustments (dubbed as IPCAIPCAISVM).

Mnist variations which include Mnist_basic and Mnist_bg_img are utilized as database with different distributions to validate the performance of above different models. Here the Mnist_basic has 1000 training samples and 5000 test samples, Mnist_bg_img has 2000 training samples and 5000 test samples.

The results are show in (b) subfigure in Fig. 3. From it, we can see that when the data distribution is changed, with no feature and classifier layers adjustments, the performance decreased heavily. As long as the classifier layer has adjusted, the accuracy increase dramatically and becomes better along with the number of training samples increase. This is because the high level classifier layer similar like the neural center, it's very effective by utilizing the supervised information to adjust the model. Furthermore, the feature layers adjustments also have effect in updating the model even the function of it is very smaller when compared to that of the classifier layer. Finally, the IPCAIPCAISVM has best results while the PCAPCAISVM has the worst among all compared models. These results validate the hypothesis of physiology that the plasticities exist in every layer of brain cortex and the plasticity in high level is more efficient and effective than the low level. However, it seems because the effect of the error accumulation, PCAIPCAISVM has no better results than IPCAPCAISVM. This is just the preliminary experiments and the further experiments are ongoing.

5   Conclusion

Inspired by the plasticity in primates' visual cortex, a lifelong learning framework based on incremental PCANet is proposed here to explore the plasticity of both feature extractor and classifier construction. Gabor filters with maxpooling layer are used to enforce the scale and shift tolerance to input samples. Incremental PCANet dedicated to investigate the plasticity of feature extraction and the incremental SVM devoted to validate the plasticity in classifier construction. Experiment results show that our model have better self-adaption and robustness compared to PCANet. Further, in the view of physiology, the incremental PCANet with incremental SVM has achieved the plasticity of both feature and classifier constructions. Finally, via our model, we validate the plasticity of high level classifier layer is much better than that of the low feature extraction layers, which is consist with the hypothesis of physiology.

References

1. Jim, M., David, L.G.: Multiclass object recognition with sparse, localized features. In: IEEE Computer Society Conference on Computer Vision and Pattern Recognition (CVPR 2006), vol. 1, pp. 11–18 (2006)
2. Rolls, E.T., Milward, T.: A model of invariant object recognition in the visual system: learning rules, activation functions, lateral inhibition, and information-based performance measures. Neural Comput. **12**(11), 2547–2572 (2000)
3. Krizhevsky, A., Sutskever, I., Hinton, G.E.: Imagenet classification with deep convolutional neural networks. In: Advances in Neural Information Processing Systems, pp. 1097–1105 (2012)
4. Simonyan, K., Zisserman, A.: Very deep convolutional networks for large-scale image recognition. arXiv preprint arXiv:1409.1556 (2014)
5. Szegedy, C., Liu, W., Jia, Y., Sermanet, P., Reed, S., Anguelov, D., Erhan, D., Vanhoucke, V., Rabinovich, A.: Going deeper with convolutions. In: Proceedings of the IEEE Conference on Computer Vision and Pattern Recognition, pp. 1–9 (2015)

6. Thorpe, S., Fize, D., Marlot, C.: Speed of processing in the human visual system. Nature **381**(6582), 520–522 (1996)
7. Schmidhuber, J.: Deep learning in neural networks: an overview. Neural Netw. **61**, 85–117 (2015)
8. LeCun, Y., Bengio, Y.: Convolutional networks for images, speech, and time series. In: The Handbook of Brain Theory and Neural Networks, vol. 3361, MIT Press, Cambridge (1995). (10)
9. LeCun, Y., Bengio, Y., Hinton, G.: Deep learning. Nature **521**(7553), 436–444 (2015)
10. Chan, T.H., Jia, K., Gao, S., Lu, J., Zeng, Z., Ma, Y.: PCANet: a simple deep learning baseline for image classification? IEEE Trans. Image Process. **24**(12), 5017–5032 (2015)
11. Fukushima, K.: Neocognitron: a self-organizing neural network model for a mechanism of pattern recognition unaffected by shift in position. Biol. Cybern. **36**(4), 193–202 (1980)
12. LeCun, Y., Boser, B., Denker, J.S., Henderson, D., Howard, R.E., Hubbard, W., Jackel, L.D.: Backpropagation applied to handwritten zip code recognition. Neural Comput. **1**(4), 541–551 (1989)
13. He, K., Zhang, X., Ren, S., Sun, J.: Deep residual learning for image recognition. arXiv preprint arXiv:1512.03385 (2015).
14. Nguyen, V.L., Vu, N.S., Gosselin, P.H.: A scattering transform combination with local binary pattern for texture classification. In 2016 14th International Workshop on Content-Based Multimedia Indexing (CBMI), pp. 1–4, IEEE (2016)
15. Hegde, A., Principe, J.C., Erdogmus, D., Ozertem, U., Rao, Y.N., Peddaneni, H.: Perturbation-based eigenvector updates for on-line principal components analysis and canonical correlation analysis. J. VLSI Signal Process. Syst. Signal Image Video Technol. **45**(1–2), 85–95 (2006)
16. Weng, J., Zhang, Y., Hwang, W.S.: Candid: covariance-free incremental principal component analysis. IEEE Trans. Pattern Anal. Mach. Intell. **25**, 1034–1040 (2003)
17. Krasulina, T.: Method of stochastic approximation in the determination of the largest eigenvalue of the mathematical expectation of random matrices. Autom. Remote Control., 50–56 (1970)
18. Diehl, C.P., Cauwenberghs, G.: SVM incremental learning, adaptation and optimization. In: Proceedings of the International Joint Conference on Neural Networks, 2003, vol. 4, pp. 2685–2690. IEEE (2003)
19. Thrun, S.: Explanation-Based Neural Network Learning: A Lifelong Learning Approach. Kluwer Academic Publishers, Boston (1996)
20. Thrun, S., O'Sullivan, J.: Discovering structure in multiple learning tasks: the TC algorithm. ICML **96**, 489–497 (1996)
21. Carlson, A., Betteridge, J., Kisiel, B., Settles, B., Hruschka, E.R., Mitchell, T.M.: Toward an architecture for never-ending language learning. In: AAAI, vol. 5, p. 3 (2010)
22. Fan, R.E., Chang, K.W., Hsieh, C.J., Wang, X.R., Lin, C.J.: LIBLINEAR: a library for large linear classification. J. Mach. Learn. Res. 1871–1874 (2008)
23. Larochelle, H., Erhan, D., Courville, A., Bergstra, J., Bengio, Y.: An empirical evaluation of deep architectures on problems with many factors of variation. In: Proceedings of the 24th International Conference on Machine learning, pp. 473–480. ACM, June 2007

PerSent: A Freely Available Persian Sentiment Lexicon

Kia Dashtipour[1(⊠)], Amir Hussain[1], Qiang Zhou[2],
Alexander Gelbukh[3], Ahmad Y.A. Hawalah[4], and Erik Cambria[5]

[1] Department of Computing Science and Mathematics,
University of Stirling, Stirling FK9 4LA, Scotland
kd28@cs.stir.ac.uk
[2] Tsinghua University, Beijing, China
[3] CIC, Instituto Politécnico Nacional, 07738 Mexico City, Mexico
[4] Taibah University, Madina, Saudi Arabia
[5] School of Computer Engineering, Nanyang Technological University,
Singapore, Singapore

Abstract. People need to know other people's opinions to make well-informed decisions to buy products or services. Companies and organizations need to understand people's attitude towards their products and services and use feedback from the customers to improve their products. Sentiment analysis techniques address these needs. While the majority of Internet users are not English speakers, most research papers in the sentiment-analysis field focus on English; resources for other languages are scarce. In this paper, we introduce a Persian sentiment lexicon, which consists of 1500 words along with their part-of-speech tags and polarity scores. We have used two machine-learning algorithms to evaluate the performance of this resource on a sentiment analysis task. The lexicon is freely available and can be downloaded from our website.

1 Introduction

In recent years, with fast growing of Internet people all around the world share their opinions on different topics. This huge amount of unstructured data available online in different languages is very useful for companies and organisations to improve their products and services (Poria et al. 2014).

The corresponding field of science and technology is called sentiment analysis (SA). SA techniques involve a number of tasks, among them identification of the polarity (positive/negative) or emotion (happy, sad, angry, etc.) expressed the text or in a sentence (Turney 2002). Sentiment polarity can be binary or can involve multiclass classification, such as strongly positive, positive, neutral, negative, and strongly negative. Most of research is focused on the binary polarity classification, though identifying at least the neutral opinion in the sentence is more helpful (Tang et al. 2009).

In the recent years, sentiment analysis has been a very active area of research. There have been compiled numerous lexical resources and datasets for English language. However, much less effort has been devoted to the development of lexical resources in other languages, which makes is difficult for researchers to analyze the text in

© Springer International Publishing AG 2016
C.-L. Liu et al. (Eds.): BICS 2016, LNAI 10023, pp. 310–320, 2016.
DOI: 10.1007/978-3-319-49685-6_28

languages other than English because of lack of available lexical resources (Dashtipour et al. 2016).

In particular, there is no well-known dataset or lexicon available for Persian language (Neviarouskaya et al. 2011). In this paper, we present PerSent, a Persian polarity lexicon for sentiment analysis, which contains words and phrases along with their polarity and part-of-speech tag. We evaluate its quality and performance via applications to a sentiment analysis task using different features such as POS-based features, the presence and frequency of sentiment words, average polarity of words, etc., and two machine-learning algorithms: SVM and Naïve Bayes.

The lexicon is freely available for the research community and can be downloaded from the URL http://www.gelbukh.com/resources/persent.

This paper is organized as follows. Section 2 discusses related work on lexicons in languages other than English; Sect. 3 presents PerSent, our Persian sentiment lexicon; Sect. 4 describes our evaluation methodology, and Sect. 5 gives the evaluation results. Section 6 concludes the paper.

2 Related Work

Data analysis is important for small and large companies. They gather opinions from texts available in Internet. Analysis of such opinions has great impact on customer relationships. Companies use customer comments about negative features of products to improve their products (Cambria et al. 2016). Moreover, sentiment analysis is not only restricted to product reviews but is also used in other fields such as politics, sport, etc.

In this section, we give some background on sentiment classification and discuss related work.

2.1 Types of Sentiment Analysis

Approaches to sentiment classification can be divided into three groups: statistical approaches, knowledge-based approaches, and hybrid approaches.

Statistical approaches use machine-learning algorithms such as SVM or Naïve Bayes to classify text. They can use supervised or unsupervised learning methods. Supervised methods use labelled data to classify the text, while unsupervised ones use only raw data (Maynard and Funk 2012). Statistical approaches are usually used, for example, to detect sentiments holders and target (Cambria et al. 2013).

Knowledge-based approaches classify the text by affect categories based on the presence of unambiguous affect words such as *sad*, *happy*, *afraid*, or *bored* (Cambria 2016). They use lexicons to calculate the statistics of positive and negative words in the given text: for example, the word *good* is known to be positive and the word *bad* negative. The lexicon can contain single words or phrases. The advantage of knowledge-based approaches is that they do not require trained data; the main disadvantage is lack of scalability.

Hybrid approaches combine statistical and knowledge-based methods to improve performance and accuracy (Maynard and Funk 2012; Cambria 2016). Pak and Paroubek

(2010) developed a dataset that contains positive and negative documents; for classi-fication, they calculate the cosine similarity between the given document and the doc-uments with known polarity. They evaluated their method using the Naïve Bayes algorithm.

2.2 Knowledge-Based Approaches

Various lexicon-based approaches have been used for sentiment classification of doc-uments in different languages; see Table 1. Most of the lexicon-based approaches used adjectives to identify the polarity of the text. There have been suggested different methods to develop sentiment lexicons, such as manual, corpus-based, and dictionary-based compilation. Manual construction is time consuming; it is usually combined with other methods to improve performance.

Corpus-based methods use lists of sentiment words along with their polarity and syntactic patterns to find more sentiment words and their polarity. For example, Hatzivassiloglou and McKeown (1997) developed graph-based technique for learning lexicons; they identified polarity of adjectives using conjunctions. They used a clus-tering algorithm to divide words into positive and negative. They achieved 82% of accuracy.

Table 1. Existing sentiment lexicons for various languages

Reference	Lexicon name	Language	Comments
(Elarnaoty et al. 2012)	MPQA Subjectivity Lexicon	Arabic	Arabic news. POS tags
(Elhawary and Elfeky 2010)	Arabic Lexicon for business reviews	Arabic	Word polarity. 200 positive, 250 negative
(Abdul-Mageed and Diab 2014)	SANA	Arabic and dialects	3,325 adjectives, 617 positive, 550 negative, 2158 objective
(Dehkharghani et al. 2015)	SentiTurkNet	Turkish	15,000 synsets positive, negative and neutral. POS tags
(Sidorov et al. 2013)	SEL	Spanish	Emotion lexicon. 2036 words on different emotions such as joy, sadness, surprise, disgust
(Remus et al. 2010)	SentiWortSchatz	German	1818 positive, 1650 negative. Adjectives, adverbs, nouns, verbs. POS tags
(Waltinger 2010)	German Polarity Clues	German	10,141 features associated with positive, negative and neutral
(de Albornoz et al. 2012)	SentiSense	English	5,496 words and 2,190 synsets labelled with an emotion
(Mahyoub 2014)	ArabicWordNet	Arabic	23481 words: 15,890 nouns, 6,048 verbs, 1,234 adjectives, 264 adverbs

Dictionary-based approaches do not require pre-compiled lists of sentiment words. They are used to collect sentiment words and their orientation manually and look up synonyms and antonyms in a dictionary. The main disadvantage of this method is that it unable to find sentiment words with domain-specific orientation: sentiment words can be positive in one domain and negative in another. For example, the word *large* is positive when it refers to a computer screen, but negative when it refers to a mobile phone (Hu and Liu 2004).

2.3   Persian Language

Persian uses 32 letters, which cover 28 Arabic letters. Its writing system includes special signs and diacritic marks that can be used in different forms or omitted from the word. Short vowels are not indicated in writing. There are letters with more than one Unicode encoding. Some words have more than one spelling variants. Spelling of some words changes with time. All this increases the number of both homographs and synonyms, which presents problems in computational treatment of Persian (Karimi 1989; Seraji et al. 2012).

Saraee and Bagheri (2013) proposed a method for feature selection in Persian sentiment analysis able to calculate the co-occurrence of Persian words in different classes. They used customer reviews to evaluate the performance of the approach. Naïve Bayes algorithm has been used in evaluation. The overall accuracy of their approach was 75%. The advantage of this approach is its simplicity; a disadvantage is the need of a great amount of training data.

Chen and Skiena (2014) proposed a lexicon for major languages such as English, Arabic, Japanese, and Persian. The English data has been collected online. They used Google translator to translate data into different languages and WordNet to gather synonyms and antonyms for English; these words and phrases were translated into different languages. They used Wikipedia pages to evaluate the performance of their lexicon, and obtained the overall performance of 45.2%. An advantage of this approach is its ability to develop lexicons for 136 languages; a disadvantage is that the lexicons for most of these languages were only of less than one hundred words and phrases.

3   PerSent Persian Sentiment Lexicon

Many researchers note that the main problem of the multilingual sentiment analysis is the lack of resources. To overcome this issue, we developed a Persian lexicon of 1500 Persian words along with their polarity and part of speech tag, which we called PerSent. Table 2 shows some examples.

Most of the previous research on sentiment used adjectives to identify the polarity of sentences (Hu and Liu 2004). Some researchers used adverbs and adjectives together to build a lexicon (Benamara et al. 2007); some used adjectives, adverbs, and verbs (Taboada et al. 2011). For our Persian sentiment lexicon, we used adjectives, adverbs, verbs, and nouns, because all these words and phrases are useful to determine the polarity of the sentence.

Table 2. Examples from our Persian sentiment lexicon

Word	Translation	POS	Polarity	Score
خوب	good	adjective	positive	+0.7
بد	bad	adjective	negative	−0.69
زشت	ugly	adjective	negative	−0.7
آزردن	annoying	verb	negative	−0.1689

Table 3. Statistics by POS

Part of speech	Words
Adjective	556
Adverbs	51
Nouns	371
Verbs	522

A lexicon can be developed in different ways, such as manually or using existing lexicons such as SentiWordNet (Esuli and Sebastiani 2006) or General Inquirer (Stone et al. 1966). The words and phrases used in our lexicon were taken from different resources such as movie review website, weblogs, and Facebook. There were four different categories of sources, namely, websites related to movies, news, mobile phones, and computers.

We manually assigned polarity between −1 and +1 to each word and phrase. The degree of intensity was indicated: e.g., "خوشحال" (*happy*), "بشاش" (*cheerful*), and "شاد" (*delighted*) have different positive values. In order to assign polarity manually to some words and phrases, we used the TextBlob Python package, used to assign polarity to words, phrases, and sentences in English (Yang 2015. For this, we translated Persian words into English. We also manually assigned a part of speech (POS) tag to each word or phrase. Table 3 shows the distribution of the POS tags in the lexicon.

4 Evaluation Methodology

In order to evaluate the performance of our lexicon, we used two classification algorithms; we used our lexicon to assign polarity to the features extracted from the dataset. Figure 1 shows the general framework we used to evaluate the performance of our lexicon. Below we describe each processing steps.

Pre-processing. The pre-processing step consisted of four parts, tokenisation, normalisation, stop-word removal, and stemming. Normalization was used to remove noise from the text. Stemming was used to remove inflection of infected forms: the lexicon only provides the base form of the words.

Feature selection. The purpose of the feature selection was to remove unnecessarily features, which improved the performance and efficiency of the classification.

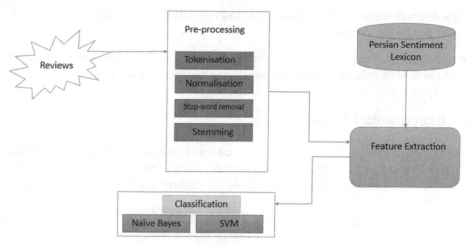

Fig. 1. The Persian framework

Table 4. Features used

Category	Features
Presence and frequency of sentiment words	Frequency of positive words
	Frequency of negative words
	Presence of positive words
	Presence of negative words
POS-based features	Frequency of positive and negative adjectives
	Frequency of positive and negative adverbs
	Frequency of positive and negative verbs
	Frequency of positive and negative nouns
Word polarity	Overall polarity of negative words
	Overall polarity of positive words

The features we used were based on word polarity, POS tag, and presence and frequency of sentiment words; see Table 4.

Presence and frequency of sentiment words. The sentiment words identify the overall polarity for sentiment classification. Example of positive words in Persian are "زیبا" (*beautiful*) and "عالی" (*excellent*), and of negative words are "زشت" (*ugly*) and "بد" (*bad*). The features of presence of positive and of negative words (two different features) are binary, without considering the number of occurrences of a given word, while the other two features are integer and indicate the number of occurrences of positive and of negative works, correspondingly.

POS-based features. Our lexicon contains words along with their POS tag, such as adverb, verb, noun, or adjective. Most of the previous research used only adjectives and nouns to identify the polarity of sentences (Kouloumpis et al. 2011), but we consider eight different features: the frequencies of positive and of negative adjectives, adverbs, verbs, and nouns, correspondingly.

Word Polarity. Our lexicon gives polarity for words. As two different features, we used the overall polarity of negative and of positive words, correspondingly.

5 Experimental Results

We applied simple baseline approaches to sentiment analysis using our lexicon to the Persian VOA (Voice of America) news corpus, which contains 500 positive and 500 negative news headlines. We then measured the performance in terms of accuracy:

$$\text{Accuracy} = \frac{number\ of\ data\ classified\ correctly}{total\ number\ of\ data}$$

5.1 Results

We used support vector machine (SVM) and Naïve Bayes classifier for evaluation. The support vector machine gave better results than Naïve Bayes; see Table 5. In this experiment all the features were used.

Table 5. Performance of different classifiers with all features

Classifier	Accuracy
SVM	**69.54%**
Naïve Bayes	65.02%

We also compared the effectiveness of different features in order to determine their importance; see Table 6. The accuracy varied from 46% to 63%. SVM gave uniformly better results than Naïve Bayes did. The experiment showed that the mere presence of opinion words gives better performance than their frequency.

Table 6. Performance of the frequency features

	SVM	Naïve Bayes
Frequency of positive words	54.28%	53.74%
Frequency of negative words	52.01%	46.02%
Presence of positive words	61.12%	52.39%
Presence of negative words	59.98%	46.17%
All frequency features	**63.00%**	59.23%

We also compared the POS features, such as the frequency of positive and negative adjectives, adverbs, verbs, and nouns, correspondingly; see Table 7. SVM again almost uniformly outperformed Naïve Bayes.

Table 7. Performance of the POS features

	SVM	Naïve Bayes
Frequency of positive and negative adjectives	65.01%	61.23%
Frequency of positive and negative adverbs	63.83%	59.07%
Frequency of positive and negative verbs	64.25%	61.04%
Frequency of positive and negative nouns	61.49%	63.34%
All POS features	**69.29%**	63.19%

Table 8 shows the results for overall polarity of negative and of positive words. Positive words outperformed negative words, and SVM outperformed Naïve Bayes.

Table 8. Performance of the overall polarity feature

	SVM	Naïve Bayes
Overall polarity of negative words	57.23%	56.49%
Overall polarity of positive words	66.02%	64.97%

5.2 Discussion

Based on related work on lexicon-based methods, we expected that PerSent lexicon would perform better. Classification of news into positive and negative is, however, a difficult task, because most of the bad news do not contain any subjective terms that would help to classify them as negative.

The main problem of our lexicon is its relatively small size: 1500 words are not enough for Persian because it has many dialects and actively us idiomatic expressions, and thus requires a larger lexicon, development of which would take time and effort (He and Zhou 2011).

Another problem is that our simple application did not properly handle sarcasm. A much more sophisticated system should be developed to be able to identify sarcasm in the texts. Further study is required to detect ironic and sarcastic sentences. Sarcasm should be studied independently and another tool needs to be developed to handle sarcasm in order to improve our classification performance.

Similarly, our simple testing application did not properly handle code switching between Persian and English: some sentences used a mixture of Persian and English words.

Adjectives gave better results in comparison with other parts of speech, because the examination of adjectives in a sentence is easier as compared with other words. For example, in "عکس زیبایی است", which means "It is beautiful picture", the adjective clearly indicates the sentiment.

Rather not surprisingly, all features together gave better results than individual features separately, because in this way the algorithm had access to more information.

6 Conclusions

We have developed a new lexicon for Persian language, which can be used for Persian sentiment analysis. The lexicon contains 1500 Persian words along with their polarity on a numeric scale from −1 to +1 and the part of speech of tag. The majority of the values were assigned manually. The new lexicon is freely available for download from the URL http://www.gelbukh.com/resources/persent.

Our experiment results show that our lexicon is a useful tool to determine the polarity of sentences in Persian. In the experiments, we used two classifiers: SVM and Naïve Bayes, of which SVM gave better results.

As future work, we plan to extend our lexicon, try computer-assisted methods of its compilation, as well as to apply our lexicon to a wider variety of tasks and corpora. In addition, we will combine knowledge-based methods with deep textual features for sentiment classification (Poria et al. 2015a). An end-to-end Persian sentiment analysis framework based on the linguistic patterns and common-sense knowledge is another important work to be done (Poria et al. 2015b, 2012; Cambria et al. 2015). Aspect-based sentiment analysis (Poria et al. 2016) and disambiguating sentiment words (Pakray et al. 2011a, 2011b, 2010) will play a major role in such a framework.

References

Abbasi, A., Chen, H., Salem, A.: Sentiment analysis in multiple languages: feature selection for opinion classification in Web forums. ACM Trans. Inf. Syst. (TOIS) **26**(3), 12 (2008)

Abdul-Mageed, M., Diab, M.T.: SANA: a large scale multi-genre, multi-dialect lexicon for arabic subjectivity and sentiment analysis. In: LREC, pp. 1162–1169 (2014)

Benamara, F., Cesarano, C., Picariello, A., Recupero, D.R., Subrahmanian, V.S.: Sentiment analysis: adjectives and adverbs are better than adjectives alone. In: ICWSM (2007)

Cambria, E.: Affective computing and sentiment analysis. IEEE Intell. Syst. **31**(2), 102–107 (2016)

Cambria, E., Howard, N., Xia, Y., Chua, T.S.: Computational intelligence for big social data analysis. IEEE Comput. Intell. Mag. **11**(3), 8–9 (2016)

Cambria, E., Poria, S., Bisio, F., Bajpai, R., Chaturvedi, I.: The CLSA model: a novel framework for concept-level sentiment analysis. In: Gelbukh, A. (ed.) CICLing 2015. LNCS, vol. 9042, pp. 3–22. Springer, Heidelberg (2015). doi:10.1007/978-3-319-18117-2_1

Cambria, E., Schuller, B., Xia, Y., Havasi, C.: New avenues in opinion mining and sentiment analysis. IEEE Intell. Syst. **28**(2), 15–21 (2013)

Cambria, E., Speer, R., Havasi, C., Hussain, A.: SenticNet: a publicly available semantic resource for opinion mining. In: Common-sense Knowledge, AAAI Fall Symposium series, vol. 10 (2010)

Chen, Y., Skiena, S.: Building sentiment lexicons for all major languages. In: ACL, vol. 2, pp. 383–389 (2014)

Dashtipour, K., Poria, S., Hussain, A., Cambria, E., Hawalah, A.Y., Gelbukh, A., Zhou, Q.: Multilingual sentiment analysis: state of the art and independent comparison of techniques. Cogn. Comput. **8**, 1–15 (2016)

Dehkharghani, R., Saygin, Y., Yanikoglu, B., Oflazer, K.: SentiTurkNet: a Turkish polarity lexicon for sentiment analysis. Lang. Resour. Eval. **50**, 1–19 (2015) de Albornoz, J.C., Plaza, L., Gervás, P.: SentiSense: an easily scalable concept-based affective lexicon for sentiment analysis. In: LREC, pp. 3562–3567 (2012)

Elhawary, M., Elfeky, M.: Mining Arabic business reviews. In: 2010 IEEE International Conference on Data Mining Workshops (ICDMW), pp. 1108–1113. IEEE (2010)

Elarnaoty, M., AbdelRahman, S., Fahmy, A.: A machine learning approach for opinion holder extraction in Arabic language. arXiv preprint arXiv:1206.1011 (2012)

Esuli, A., Sebastiani, F.: Sentiwordnet: a publicly available lexical resource for opinion mining. In: Proceedings of LREC, Vol. 6, pp. 417–422 (2006)

Hatzivassiloglou, V., McKeown, K.R.: Predicting the semantic orientation of adjectives. In: Proceedings of the 35th Annual Meeting of the Association for Computational Linguistics and Eighth Conference of the European Chapter of the Association for Computational Linguistics, pp. 174–181. Association for Computational Linguistics (1997)

He, Y., Zhou, D.: Self-training from labeled features for sentiment analysis. Inf. Process. Manage. **47**(4), 606–616 (2011)

Hu, M., Liu, B.: Mining and summarizing customer reviews. In: Proceedings of the Tenth ACM SIGKDD International Conference on Knowledge Discovery and Data Mining, pp. 168–177. ACM (2004)

Karimi, S.: Aspects of Persian syntax, specificity, and the theory of grammar. University of Washington (1989)

Kouloumpis, E., Wilson, T., Moore, J.D.: Twitter sentiment analysis: the good the bad and the omg!. In: ICWSM, vol. 11, pp. 538–541 (2011)

Mahyoub, F.H., Siddiqui, M.A., Dahab, M.Y.: Building an Arabic sentiment lexicon using semi-supervised learning. J. King Saud Univ. Comput. Inf. Sci. **26**(4), 417–424 (2014)

Maynard, D., Funk, A.: Automatic detection of political opinions in tweets. In: García-Castro, R., Fensel, D., Antoniou, G. (eds.) ESWC 2011. LNCS, vol. 7117, pp. 88–99. Springer, Heidelberg (2012). doi:10.1007/978-3-642-25953-1_8

Neviarouskaya, A., Prendinger, H., Ishizuka, M.: SentiFul: a lexicon for sentiment analysis. IEEE Trans. Affect. Comput. **2**(1), 22–36 (2011)

Pak, A., Paroubek, P.: Twitter based system: using Twitter for disambiguating sentiment ambiguous adjectives. In: Proceedings of the 5th International Workshop on Semantic Evaluation, pp. 436–439. Association for Computational Linguistics, July 2010

Pakray, P., Neogi, S., Bhaskar, P., Poria, S., Bandyopadhyay, S., Gelbukh, A.: A textual entailment system using anaphora resolution. In: System Report, Text Analysis Conference Recognizing Textual Entailment Track (TAC RTE) Notebook, November 2011a

Pakray, P., Pal, S., Poria, S., Bandyopadhyay, S., Gelbukh, A.: JU_CSE_TAC: textual entailment recognition system at TAC RTE-6. In: System Report, Text Analysis Conference Recognizing Textual Entailment Track (TAC RTE) Notebook (2010)

Pakray, P., Poria, S., Bandyopadhyay, S., Gelbukh, A.: Semantic textual entailment recognition using UNL. Polibits **43**, 23–27 (2011b)

Poria, S., Cambria, E., Gelbukh, A.: Deep convolutional neural network textual features and multiple kernel learning for utterance-level multimodal sentiment analysis. In: Proceedings of EMNLP, pp. 2539–2544 (2015a)

Poria, S., Cambria, E., Gelbukh, A.: Aspect extraction for opinion mining with a deep convolutional neural network. Knowl.-Based Syst. **108**, 42–49 (2016)

Poria, S., Cambria, E., Gelbukh, A., Bisio, F., Hussain, A.: Sentiment data flow analysis by means of dynamic linguistic patterns. IEEE Comput. Intell. Mag. **10**(4), 26–36 (2015b)

Poria, S., Cambria, E., Winterstein, G., Huang, G.B.: Sentic patterns: dependency-based rules for concept-level sentiment analysis. Knowl.-Based Syst. **69**, 45–63 (2014)

Poria, S., Gulbukh, A., Das, D., Bandyopadhyay, S.: Fuzzy clustering for semi-supervised learning–case study: construction of an emotion lexicon. In: Mexican International Conference on Artificial Intelligence, pp. 73–86, October 2012

Remus, R., Quasthoff, U., Heyer, G.: SentiWS – a publicly available german-language resource for sentiment analysis. In: LREC, May 2010

Saraee, M., Bagheri, A.: Feature selection methods in Persian sentiment analysis. In: Métais, E., Meziane, F., Saraee, M., Sugumaran, V., Vadera, S. (eds.) NLDB 2013. LNCS, vol. 7934, pp. 303–308. Springer, Heidelberg (2013). doi:10.1007/978-3-642-38824-8_29

Seraji, M., Megyesi, B., Nivre, J.: A basic language resource kit for Persian, In: LREC, pp. 2245–2252 (2012)

Shi, H.X., Li, X.J.: A sentiment analysis model for hotel reviews based on supervised learning. In: 2011 International Conference on Machine Learning and Cybernetics (ICMLC), vol. 3, pp. 950–954. IEEE (2011)

Sidorov, G., et al.: Empirical Study of Machine Learning Based Approach for Opinion Mining in Tweets. In: Batyrshin, I., González Mendoza, M. (eds.) MICAI 2012. LNCS (LNAI), vol. 7629, pp. 1–14. Springer, Heidelberg (2013). doi:10.1007/978-3-642-37807-2_1

Stone, P., Dunphy, D.C., Smith, M.S., Ogilvie, D.M.: The general inquirer: a computer approach to content analysis. J. Reg. Sci. 8(1), 113–116 (1968)

Subrahmanian, V.S., Reforgiato, D.: AVA: adjective-verb-adverb combinations for sentiment analysis. IEEE Intell. Syst. 23(4), 43–50 (2008)

Tang, H., Tan, S., Cheng, X.: A survey on sentiment detection of reviews. Expert Syst. Appl. 36(7), 10760–10773 (2009)

Taboada, M., Brooke, J., Tofiloski, M., Voll, K., Stede, M.: Lexicon-based methods for sentiment analysis. Comput. Linguist. 37(2), 267–307 (2011)

Taghva, K., Beckley, R., Sadeh, M.: A stemming algorithm for the farsi language. In: ITCC, vol. 1, pp. 158–162, April 2005

Turney, P.D.: Thumbs up or thumbs down?: semantic orientation applied to unsupervised classification of reviews. In: Proceedings of the 40th Annual Meeting on Association for Computational Linguistics, pp. 417–424. Association for Computational Linguistics (2002)

Waltinger, U.: GermanPolarityClues: a lexical resource for german sentiment analysis. In: Proceedings of the Seventh International Conference on Language Resources and Evaluation (LREC) (2010)

Yang, Y.: Application of Latent Dirichlet Allocation in Online Content Generation. Ph.D. thesis, University of California, Los Angeles (2016)

Low-Rank Image Set Representation
and Classification

Youxia Cao, Bo Jiang$^{(\boxtimes)}$, Zhuqiang Chen, Jin Tang, and Bin Luo

School of Computer Science and Technology, Anhui University,
No.111 Jiulong Road, Hefei, China
{ahu_youxia,zoeczq}@foxmail.com, {jiangbo,tj,luobin}@ahu.edu.cn

Abstract. Image set representation and classification is an important problem in computer vision and pattern recognition area. In real application, image set data often come with kinds of noises, corruptions or large errors which usually make the recognition/learning tasks of image set more challengeable. In this paper, we utilize the low-rank representation/component of image set to represent the observed image set which is called Low-rank Image Set Representation (LRISR). Comparing with original observed image set, LRISR is generally noiseless and thus can encourage more robust learning process. Based on LRISR, we then use covariate-relation graph to encode the geometric relationship between covariates/features of LRISR and thus extract description vectors for LRISR classification task. Experimental results on several datasets demonstrate the benefits of the proposed image set representation and classification method.

Keywords: Low-rank representation · Image set classification · Linear discriminant analysis

1 Introduction

Many problems in pattern recognition and computer vision area can be formulated as object recognition based on visual content. Recently, image set based object recognition attracts more and more interest. The aim of image set based object recognition is to conduct object recognition task using multiplier images that belong to one single object. Image set based object description contains more variations of the object appearance, such as pose, lighting, non-rigid deformation etc., and thus involves more visual information for object recognition task [3,14,20,25].

One main issue for image set based object recognition is how to represent an image set effectively [5,9,11,23,27]. Recently, many methods have been proposed for image set representation and classification. Mutual Subspace Method (MSM) [26] and Discriminant-analysis of Canonical Correlations (DCC) [14] aim to represent an image set with a single linear subspace and measure the similarity between two image sets using the principal angles of two linear subspaces.

© Springer International Publishing AG 2016
C.-L. Liu et al. (Eds.): BICS 2016, LNAI 10023, pp. 321–330, 2016.
DOI: 10.1007/978-3-319-49685-6_29

Grassmann Discriminant Analysis (GDA) [9] and Grassmann Embedding Discriminant Analysis (GEDA) [10] formulate the problem as classifying points on the Grassmann manifold and further define a kernel based on principal angles to measure the similarity between image sets. In additional to linear subspace, nonlinear manifold methods have also been used for image set representation [4,7,22,24]. Manifold-Manifold Distance (MMD) [24] represents each image set as a nonlinear manifold and then segment it into several linear subspaces. Manifold Discriminant Analysis (MDA) [22] further extends MMD to a more discriminative feature space. Recently, statistical methods have also been proposed to represent image set [1,18,21,25]. For example, Manifold Density Method (MDM) [1] represents each image set with Gaussian Mixture Model (GMM), and measures the similarity between image sets using Kullback-Leibler Divergence (KLD) of their gaussian components. Wang et al. proposed a method [25] which further learns the discriminative information based on GMM modeling and measure the similarity of image sets with kernel based distances. Covariance Discriminative Learning (CDL) [23] aims to model the image set with covariance matrix and define a similarity measurement based on kernel function.

Overall, previous works generally focus on effective image set representation and classification method. However, little attention has been put into the image set itself. Indeed, in real-world applications, the observed images often come with noises, corruptions or large errors due to different reasons, for example images are corrupted, data components are missing, errors due to human recording or machine malfunction. These noises and corruptions may make the representation of image set and thus the recognition/learning task more challengeable and significantly affect the recognition results. This motivates us to utilize the low-rank recovery/representation method [17,19,28] to recover the clear image samples from original observed image set. We call it as Low-rank Image Set Representation (LRISR). It is known that Low-rank representation has been widely used in many data learning tasks in recent years. However, to the best of our knowledge, this technique has been not or less studied for image set learning problem. Based on the proposed LRISR, we propose to use covariate-relation graph [6] for LRISR description. At last, we implement image set classification task by using Kernel Linear Discriminant Analysis (KLDA) [2] and nearest neighbor classification method. Experimental results on several datasets show the benefits and robustness of the proposed method.

2   Image Set Representation

2.1   Problem Formulation and Motivation

Our aim in this paper is to propose an effective and robust representation for an image set and thus conduct image set classification effectively. Let $X = (x_1, x_2, ..., x_n) \in \mathbb{R}^{p \times n}$ be an observed image set containing n images. Each column $x_i \in \mathbb{R}^p$ is the linearized array of pixels gray levels. In pattern recognition and machine learning area, an image set X generally contains multiplier visual content information that belongs to one single object. The aim of image set representation is to exact a vectorized feature description for image set X. In real applications, images $x_i \in X$ usually contains some noises, corruptions or large errors due to different reasons. Note that these images $x_i \in X$ are generally highly correlated with each other because (1) they belong to one single object and (2) noises or errors often exist randomly. This motivates us to utilize a low-rank representation/recovery model which aims to recover the clear component Z from observed noise images X using the inherent correlation information among them and then use some feature extraction method to generate a robust vectorized feature for Z. In the following, we first propose our low-rank representation of image set and then use covariate-relation graph [6] to exact a feature description for it. At last, we conduct image set classification task based on the proposed image set representation method.

2.2 Low-Rank Representation of Image Set

Formally, the aim of the proposed low-rank representation of image set X is to obtain the optimal low-rank image set $Z = (z_1, z_2, ..., z_n) \in \mathbb{R}^{p \times n}$ that best approximates the observed set X. This can be formulated as the following optimization,

$$\min_{Z} \|X - Z\|_p \qquad s.t. \quad \text{rank}(Z) \leq k \qquad (1)$$

where $k \ll p$ and $\| \cdot \|_p$ denotes some certain norms, such as Frobenius norm, $\ell_{2,1}$ norm, ℓ_1 norm and so on.

It is known that the explicit rank constraint $\text{rank}(Z)$ is difficult to enforce in numerical computation. Many works have been proposed to use a replacement formulation to enforce the rank constraint. One popular way is to use low-rank matrix factorization formulation.

$$\min_{Z,U,V} \|X - Z\|_p \qquad s.t. \quad Z = UV, \quad U^T U = I \qquad (2)$$

This is equivalent to the following,

$$\min_{U,V} \|X - UV\|_p \qquad s.t. \quad U^T U = I \qquad (3)$$

where $U \in \mathbb{R}^{p \times k}, V \in \mathbb{R}^{k \times n}$. The orthogonal constraint $U^T U = I$ is used to avoid scale problem. Let U^*, V^* be the optimal solution of the above problem, then $Z = U^* V^*$ provides a low-rank representation of X. Here, the key point is low-rank of U and V and thus the low-rank of Z. Comparing with original observed set X, the noise of images can be suppressed in Z. When $p = 2$, it is well-known that the solution of this problem is given by the singular value decomposition method. When $p = 1$, this problem becomes to ℓ_1-norm PCA [12] and can be effectively solved using the Augmented Lagrange Multiplier (ALM) [28], as shown in Algorithm 1.

Algorithm 1. ℓ_1-LRISR Algorithm

Require: Image set X, parameter k
Ensure: Low-rank image set representation Z
1: Initialize $\mu = 1/\|X\|_2, \rho = 1.2, E = 0, \Lambda = 0$
2: **while** not convergence **do**
3:    Compute the first k largest singular values and associated singular vectors

$$\{F_k, \Sigma_k, G_k\} = \text{SVD}(X - E + \frac{\Lambda}{\mu})$$

4:    Compute U, V: $U = F_k, V = \Sigma_k G_k^T$
5:    Compute E: $E_{ij} = \text{sign}(P_{ij})(|P_{ij} - \frac{1}{\mu}|)_+, \quad P = X - UV + \frac{\Lambda}{\mu}$
6:    Update Λ, μ: $\Lambda = \Lambda + \mu(X - UV - E), \quad \mu = \min\{\mu\rho, 10^{10}\}$
7: **end while**
8: Compute the optimal low rank representation $Z = UV$

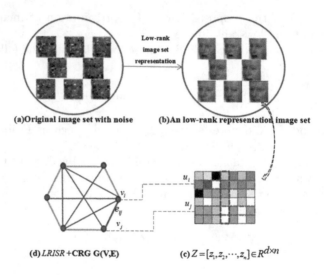

Fig. 1. Illustration of the LRISR and CRG. (a) Original image set X with several kinds of noises. (b) Low-rank representation Z of image set X. (c) Low rank data matrix and its covariates, where covariate u_i is i-th row of data matrix Z. (d) CRG generation on Z. Each node v_i represents the corresponding covariate u_i and edge e_{ij} denotes the relationship r_{ij} between u_i and u_j.

2.3   Covariate-Relation Graph

In this section, we propose to use covariate-relation graph (CRG) model [6] to represent the low-rank image representation $Z = [z_1, z_2, \cdots z_n] \in \mathbb{R}^{p \times n}$ be the low-rank representation of image set X. Let $u_i, i = 1, ..., p$ be the i-th covariate denoting the i-th dimension feature throughout the n data points, i.e., the i-th row of low-rank representation matrix Z.

The aim of CRG is to construct a graph $G = (V, E)$, where each node $v_i, v_i \in V$ in G represents a covariate/feature u_i, and the edge e_{ij} between node v_i and v_j denotes some relationship r_{ij} between covariate u_i and u_j. When this relationship refers to correlation, CRG degenerates to Covariance Discriminative Learning (CDL) representation [23]. In this paper, we use the Heat Kernel function to compute the weight r_{ij} between node v_i and v_j, i.e.,

$$r_{ij} = e^{-\frac{\|u_i - u_j\|^2}{\sigma}}. \tag{4}$$

where σ is scaling parameter. Indeed, the above kernel function can be factorized as

$$r_{ij} = e^{-\sum_{k=1}^{n} \frac{(u_{ik} - u_{jk})^2}{\sigma}} = \prod_{k=1}^{n} e^{-\frac{(u_{ik} - u_{jk})^2}{\sigma}}. \tag{5}$$

where u_{ik} is the i-th feature of the k-th image and $e^{-\frac{(u_{ik} - u_{jk})^2}{\sigma}}$ can be regarded as a kind of relationship/similarity between i-th and j-th feature for the k-th image. This demonstrates that CRG is a kind of graph which encodes the average geometrical relationship between features across n images in Z. CRG is a weighted graph, one can use an adjacency matrix A to represent it, i.e.,

$$A(i, j) = \begin{cases} r_{ij}, & \text{if } i \neq j, \\ 0, & \text{otherwise.} \end{cases} \tag{6}$$

3   Image Set Classification

The classification process contains three main steps.

Step 1: Based on the above LRISR and CRG representation, we define a kind of kernel/similarity between two CRG graphs. Similar to work [6], we define the similarity $s(G_i, G_j)$ between two CRG graph G_i and G_j by computing the inner product of projected adjacency matrices in the Euclidean space, i.e.,

$$s(G_i, G_j) = k(A_i, A_j) = tr(\log(A_i) \cdot \log(A_j))$$
$$= < \log(A_i), \log(A_j) > \tag{7}$$

where $tr(\cdot)$ is the trace operator of a matrix and $< \cdot, \cdot >$ is the inner product of matrices.

Step 2: We use Kernel variant of Linear Discriminant Analysis (KLDA) [2,23] method to learn a kind of discriminative feature representation for image set.

Step 3: We use nearest neighbor classification to classify image set in learned discriminant space using KLDA method [23].

4   Experiments

In this section, we evaluate our experiments on four datasets and compare our LRISR method with other some classical methods, the detail settings are introduced as follows. An intuitive illustration of LRISR and CRG generation is shown in Fig. 1.

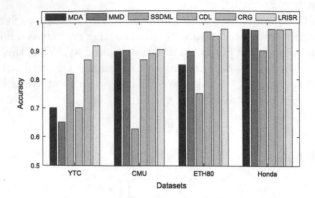

Fig. 2. Average accuracies of different methods on four datasets.

4.1 Datasets and Settings

We test our LRISR method on four datasets including YouTube Celebrities (YTC) [13], ETH-80 [16], Honda/UCSD [15] and CMU MoBo [8]. We resize all the images of the above four datasets into 20×20 intensity images and the four datasets are described as following.

- Honda/UCSD [15] dataset consists of 59 video sequences belonging to 20 different persons. Each sequence contains about 400 frames covering large variations. For this dataset, we randomly select one sequence for training set and the rest for testing.
- YouTube-Celebrities(YTC) [13] dataset contains 1910 video clips of 47 celebrities, most of the videos are low resolution and highly compression, which leads to noisy, low-quality image frames. Each clip contains hundreds of frames. For this dataset, we randomly chose 3 sets for training and 6 sets for testing.
- ETH-80 [16] dataset contains image sets of 8 subjects and each subject contains 10 subcategories. Each subcategory contains 41 images from different views. For each subject of this dataset, we randomly choose 5 sets for training and the rest 5 object for testing.
- CMU MoBo [8] dataset has 96 sequences of 24 persons and the sequences are captured from different walking situations. Each video further divided into four illumination sets, the first set for training and the rest sets for testing.

We have compared our method with some other classical methods: Manifold-Manifold Distance(MMD) [24], Manifold Discriminant Analysis(MDA) [22], Covariance Discriminative Learning (CDL) [23] and Set to Set Distance Metric Learning (SSDML) [29]. According to [24], MMD method does the subspaces learning with 95% data energy based on PCA. For MDA, the subspace dimension is the same as the original reference [22]. For the discriminative learning method of CDL, we choose KLDA to do the learning task.

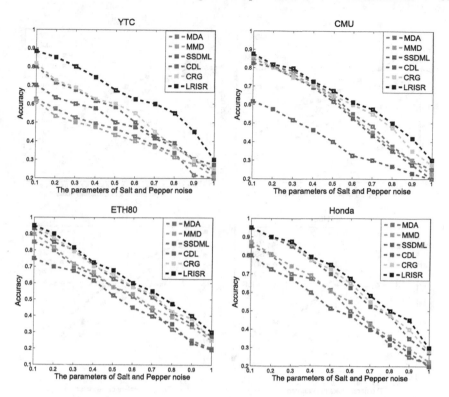

Fig. 3. The classification accuracies of different methods on four datasets with 'Salt and Pepper' noise.

4.2 Results Analysis

The average classification accuracies of different methods on four datasets are summarized in Fig. 2. From Fig. 2, we can know that our LRISR method can generally obtain better performance than other compared methods on the four datasets used in this experiments, especially on YTC dataset. This obviously demonstrates the effectiveness and robustness of the proposed LRISR method.

To further evaluate the robustness of the proposed method, we further conduct the classification experiments on four datasets with different noises including 'salt&pepper' and Gaussian noise. Here, for each kind of noise, we add various levels of the noises and test our method on these noise image set data. Figures 3 and 4 show the accuracies of all the comparison methods on four datasets. From the results, we can note that the classification accuracies of all the methods are decreasing as the level of noise increasing. However, our LRISR method still maintains better performance comparing with some other compared methods. This obviously indicates that our LRISR method performs more robustly than other compared methods.

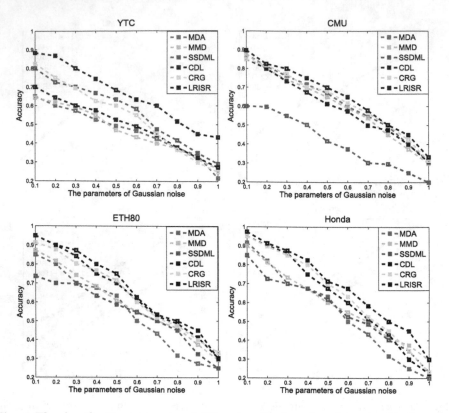

Fig. 4. The classification accuracies of different methods on four datasets with Gaussian noise.

5   Conclusion

In this paper, we propose to utilize the low-rank representation/component of set to represent observed image set which is called Low-rank Image Set Representation (LRISR). LRISR aims to recover clear image set from observed image set with kinds of noises and thus encourages more robust learning and recognition process. Experimental results on several datasets demonstrate the robustness and better performance of the proposed image set representation and classification method.

Acknowledgments. This work was supported by the National Nature Science Foundation of China (61602001,61671018,61472002); Natural Science Foundation of Anhui Higher Education Institutions of China (KJ2016A020), Natural science foundation of Anhui Province (1508085QF127); The Open Projects Program of National Laboratory of Pattern Recognition.

References

1. Arandjelovic, O., Shakhnarovich, G., Fisher, J., Cipolla, R., Darrell, T.: Face recognition with image sets using manifold density divergence. In: IEEE Computer Society Conference on Computer Vision and Pattern Recognition, CVPR 2005, pp. 581–588. IEEE (2005)
2. Baudat, G., Anouar, F.: Generalized discriminant analysis using a kernel approach. Neural Comput. **12**(10), 2385–2404 (2000)
3. Cevikalp, H., Triggs, B., Face recognition based on image sets. In: 2010 IEEE Conference on Computer Vision and Pattern Recognition (CVPR), pp. 2567–2573. IEEE (2010)
4. Chen, S., Sanderson, C., Harandi, M.T., Lovell, B.C.: Improved image set classification via joint sparse approximated nearest subspaces. In: 2013 IEEE Conference on Computer Vision and Pattern Recognition (CVPR), pp. 452–459. IEEE (2013)
5. Chen, S., Wiliem, A., Sanderson, C., Lovell, B.C.: Matching image sets via adaptive multi convex hull. In: 2014 IEEE Winter Conference on Applications of Computer Vision (WACV), pp. 1074–1081. IEEE (2014)
6. Chen, Z., Jiang, B., Tang, J., Luo, B.: Image set representation and classification with covariate-relation graph. In: IEEE Conference on Asian Conference and Pattern Recognition, ACPR 2015, pp. 750–754. IEEE (2015)
7. Cui, Z., Shan, S., Zhang, H., Lao, S., Chen, X.: Image sets alignment for video-based face recognition. In: 2012 IEEE Conference on Computer Vision and Pattern Recognition (CVPR), pp. 2626–2633. IEEE (2012)
8. Gross, R., Shi, J.: The CMU motion of body (MoBo) database. Technical report CMU-RI-TR-01-18, Robotics Institute, Carnegie Mellon University (2001)
9. Hamm, J., Lee, D.D.: Grassmann discriminant analysis: a unifying view on subspace-based learning. In: Proceedings of the 25th International Conference on Machine Learning, pp. 376–383. ACM (2008)
10. Harandi, M.T., Sanderson, C., Shirazi, S., Lovell, B.C.: Graph embedding discriminant analysis on Grassmannian manifolds for improved image set matching. In: 2011 IEEE Conference on Computer Vision and Pattern Recognition (CVPR), pp. 2705–2712. IEEE (2011)
11. Hu, Y., Mian, A.S., Owens, R.: Sparse approximated nearest points for image set classification. In: 2011 IEEE Conference on Computer Vision and Pattern Recognition (CVPR), pp. 121–128. IEEE (2011)
12. Ke, Q., Kanade, T.: Robust L1 norm factorization in the presence of outliers and missing data by alternative convex programming. In: 2005 IEEE Computer Society Conference on Computer Vision and Pattern Recognition (CVPR 2005), pp. 739–746. IEEE (2005)
13. Kim, M., Kumar, S., Pavlovic, V., Rowley, H.: Face tracking and recognition with visual constraints in real-world videos. In: IEEE Conference on Computer Vision and Pattern Recognition, CVPR 2008, pp. 1–8. IEEE (2008)
14. Kim, T.-K., Kittler, J., Cipolla, R.: Discriminative learning and recognition of image set classes using canonical correlations. IEEE Trans. Pattern Anal. Mach. Intell. **29**(6), 1005–1018 (2007)
15. Lee, K.C., Ho, J., Yang, M.H., Kriegman, D.: Video-based face recognition using probabilistic appearance manifolds. In: Proceedings of the 2003 IEEE Computer Society Conference on Computer Vision and Pattern Recognition, pp. 313–320 (2003)

16. Leibe, B., Schiele, B.: Analyzing appearance and contour based methods for object categorization. In: Proceedings of the 2003 IEEE Computer Society Conference on Computer Vision and Pattern Recognition, pp. 409–415. IEEE (2003)

17. Liu, G., Lin, Z., Yu, Y.: Robust subspace segmentation by low-rank representation. In: Proceedings of the 27th International Conference on Machine Learning (ICML 2010), pp. 663–670 (2010)

18. Lu, J., Wang, G., Moulin, P.: Image set classification using holistic multiple order statistics features and localized multi-kernel metric learning. In: 2013 IEEE International Conference on Computer Vision (ICCV), pp. 329–336. IEEE (2013)

19. Nie, F., Huang, H., Cai, X., Ding, C.H.: Efficient and robust feature selection via joint 2, 1-norms minimization. In: Advances in Neural Information Processing Systems, pp. 1813–1821 (2010)

20. Nishiyama, M., Yamaguchi, O., Fukui, K.: Face recognition with the multiple constrained mutual subspace method. In: Kanade, T., Jain, A., Ratha, N.K. (eds.) AVBPA 2005. LNCS, vol. 3546, pp. 71–80. Springer, Heidelberg (2005). doi:10. 1007/11527923_8

21. Shakhnarovich, G., Fisher, J.W., Darrell, T.: Face recognition from long-term observations. In: Heyden, A., Sparr, G., Nielsen, M., Johansen, P. (eds.) ECCV 2002. LNCS, vol. 2352, pp. 851–865. Springer, Heidelberg (2002). doi:10.1007/ 3-540-47977-5_56

22. Wang, R., Chen, X.: Manifold discriminant analysis. In: IEEE Conference on Computer Vision and Pattern Recognition, CVPR 2009, pp. 429–436. IEEE (2009)

23. Wang, R., Guo, H., Davis, L.S., Dai, Q.: Covariance discriminative learning: a natural and efficient approach to image set classification. In:2012 IEEE Conference on Computer Vision and Pattern Recognition (CVPR), pp. 2496–2503. IEEE (2012)

24. Wang, R., Shan, S., Chen, X., Gao, W.: Manifold-manifold distance with application to face recognition based on image set. In: IEEE Conference on Computer Vision and Pattern Recognition, CVPR 2008, pp. 1–8. IEEE (2008)

25. Wang, W., Wang, R., Huang, Z., Shan, S., Chen, X.: Discriminant analysis on Riemannian manifold of Gaussian distributions for face recognition with image sets. In: Proceedings of the IEEE Conference on Computer Vision and Pattern Recognition, pp. 2048–2057 (2015)

26. Yamaguchi, O., Fukui, K., Maeda, K.-I.: Face recognition using temporal image sequence. In: Proceedings of the Third IEEE International Conference on Automatic Face and Gesture Recognition, pp. 318–323. IEEE (1998)

27. Yang, M., Zhu, P., Van Gool, L., Zhang, L.: Face recognition based on regularized nearest points between image sets. In: 2013 10th IEEE International Conference and Workshops on Automatic Face and Gesture Recognition (FG), pp. 1–7. IEEE (2013)

28. Yu, L., Zhang, M., Ding, C.: An efficient algorithm for L1-norm principal component analysis. In: 2012 IEEE International Conference on Acoustics, Speech and Signal Processing (ICASSP), pp. 1377–1380. IEEE (2012)

29. Zhu, P., Zhang, L., Zuo, W., Zhang, D.: From point to set: extend the learning of distance metrics. In: 2013 IEEE International Conference on Computer Vision (ICCV), pp. 2664–2671. IEEE (2013)

A Data Driven Approach to Audiovisual Speech Mapping

Andrew Abel[1], Ricard Marxer[2], Jon Barker[2], Roger Watt[1], Bill Whitmer[3], Peter Derleth[4], and Amir Hussain[1(✉)]

[1] University of Stirling, Stirling FK9 4LA, Scotland
{aka,ahu}@cs.stir.ac.uk, r.j.watt@stir.ac.uk
[2] University of Sheffield, Sheffield S1 4DP, UK
{r.marxer,j.barker}@sheffield.ac.uk
[3] MRC/CSO IHR - Scottish Section, GRI, Glasgow G31 2ER, Scotland
william.whitmer@nottingham.ac.uk
[4] Sonova AG, 8712 Staefa, Switzerland
peter.derleth@sonova.com

Abstract. The concept of using visual information as part of audio speech processing has been of significant recent interest. This paper presents a data driven approach that considers estimating audio speech acoustics using only temporal visual information without considering linguistic features such as phonemes and visemes. Audio (log filterbank) and visual (2D-DCT) features are extracted, and various configurations of MLP and datasets are used to identify optimal results, showing that given a sequence of prior visual frames an equivalent reasonably accurate audio frame estimation can be mapped.

Keywords: Audiovisual · Speech processing · Speech mapping · ANNs

1 Introduction and Background

There has been much recent research investigating the use of visual information as part of speech processing systems. The relationship between audio and visual aspects of speech production and perception has been heavily investigated in the literature, proving the relationship between audio speech and lip movements [12,17]. A detailed summary can be found in Abel and Hussain [1]. A number of multimodal approaches have been proposed for speech filtering, including using visual information for beamforming and noise cancellation [1,3]. There have also been attempts to map audio and visual speech to each other [6,10,14].

Recent work such as [4,11], attempts to use visual data for "lip reading", by mapping lip information to audio phonemes or words, which is a linguistic basis to work from. For this, they generate visemes and compare them to speech units such as words, syllables, or phonemes. By viseme, as discussed by [4], there is no standard definition, with a range of possible definitions such as "a set of phonemes that have identical appearance on the lips" [5]. However, there are

© Springer International Publishing AG 2016
C.-L. Liu et al. (Eds.): BICS 2016, LNAI 10023, pp. 331–342, 2016.
DOI: 10.1007/978-3-319-49685-6_30

some limitations with this approach. There is not a complete one-to-one mapping of phonemes to visemes, as one viseme can be mapped to several phonemes [4], which makes classification challenging. Another issue with using visemes is co-articulation, where a speaker starts to form words before they are spoken, resulting in a phone being pronounced differently due to the effect of adjacent phonemes, which was identified to have a negative effect on lipreading results [4]. Finally, while a linguistic approach (using phonemes and linguistic information) can be particularly useful for speech recognition, in speech filtering technologies, a frame based approach [7] is often used, i.e. processing on a frame-by-frame basis, rather than using discrete linguistic units.

Other research has considered the use of visual information to estimate an audio frame for speech filtering [1,3], by estimating clean audio from visual information as part of a Wiener filter to remove noise from speech. However, the results are extremely limited, due to the narrow range of data used for the audiovisual speech models, and also the limited evaluation of the mapping performance alone. To develop an improved system, it is considered necessary to first evaluate the mapping process alone. Although this approach may not capture the fine time information required to produce a detailed speech estimation (which would be required for synthesis) [15], it has been argued [3] that this could produce a smoothed estimation which could be feasibly used for filtering.

This paper contributes a new initial investigation of visual to audio mapping. Rather than working on a linguistic basis, it purely considers the data on a frame-by-frame basis, and attempts to identify conditions that produce the best audiovisual mapping. A large multi-speaker dataset (the Grid corpus [8]) and different configurations of a non-linear neural network are used to identify optimal parameters and the best use of data for estimating an audio feature vector, given only visual information as input. This could arguably be considered to be a data driven, rather than a language driven, approach.

2   Dataset and Feature Extraction

2.1   Grid Corpus

For the research in this paper, we used the Grid Corpus [8], an audiovisual dataset which contains 34 speakers, each reciting 1000 command sentences (e.g. "bin blue on red seven now"). Clean audio and video recordings are available. We use five speakers, two white males, two white females, and one black male speaker. This means that there are clear differences between speakers. Two different sets of sentences were used. Firstly, the full fixed length Grid sentences, and also an end pointed set, where the sentences were cut to exclude all silences preceding and following the sentence, which will be referred to as the aligned sentences.

2.2   Audio Feature Extraction

This work uses log filterbank (log-fb) audio features, and assumes a filterbank (fb) of 23 filters, based on other work in the literature [1,3]. The fb of the audio signal is logarithmically compressed to produce the log-fb signal. This is very similar to the implementation found in previous work [2]. First, given an audio signal S, this is windowed and overlapped using a hamming window to produce 100 vectors per second, which at the chosen sampling rate of 50 kHz results in N 16 ms frames $s(n)$, where $n = 1...N$, with a 62.5% increment, with each $s(n)$ consisting of 800 samples. This is then Fourier transformed to produce $s_\Phi(n)$, and the final log-fb output is generated, following the approach outlined in [2]. To create the vector pairings, each extracted audio log-fb vector is matched with its equivalent visual frame (which was interpolated to match the audio frame rate).

2.3   Visual Feature Extraction

Visual data is extracted from video files following the process described fully in [2]. There are three stages. Firstly, the video file is process to extract a full sequence of individual image frames. Secondly, an initial rectangular Region-of-Interest (ROI) is identified in the first frame. For this, we use a widely used Viola-Jones lip detector [19]. This identifies the ROI in the form of a bounding box. Thirdly, using the initially identified ROI, an object tracker is used [16]. This is an online model, in that it does not require training in advance, but is a shape model that adds "good" matches to the model, and learns as the tracking progresses. More detail is provided in [16]. This produces a set of corner points for a rectangular ROI for each frame. Finally, these corner points are used to then crop each raw image to extract only the lip region, for further processing.

This was found in [2] to be an accurate approach, however, as this is an automated process (due to the quantity of data processed), each sentence was manually validated to ensure that examples of poor lip tracking (such as cases where only a partial lip region was correctly cropped) or camera glitches are removed. This was done by manually inspecting a small number of frames from each sentence, and then deleting sentences where the lip region was not confirmed to be fully and correctly identified in any of the inspected frames.

Both the full and aligned sentence datasets were extracted. The majority of removed sentences were cut because of a small portion of the ROI was not precisely captured. This resulted in the datasets given in Table 1.

Table 1. Summary of sentences used from the Grid Corpus, and results of validating fully automated lip tracking, with number of sentences used and removed.

Speaker ID	Grid ID	No. of Sents	Full Sents.		Aligned Sents.	
			Rem.	Used	Rem.	Used
Speaker 1	S1	1000	11	989	11	989
Speaker 2	S15	1000	164	836	164	836
Speaker 3	S26	1000	16	984	71	929
Speaker 4	S6	1000	9	991	9	991
Speaker 5	S7	1000	11	989	11	989

The 2D-DCT (discrete cosine transform) vector $F_v = 2D - DCT(v)$ of each cropped lip region in the sequence is then found, a commonly used technique [2,3,5]. For a V_U x V_V matrix V_P of pixel intensities (i.e. the cropped lip region), a 1D-DCT is applied to each row of V_P and then to each column of the result. The first 24 2D-DCT components of each image are vectorised in a zigzag order to produce the final frame vector. The resulting 2D-DCT sequence is then interpolated to match the equivalent audio sequence. As the video was recorded at 25 fps, it is upsampled to match the 100 frames per second rate of the audio features by using each visual feature frame for four consecutive audio frames, utilising the same approach as described in previous research [1,2].

3   Results

3.1   Methodology

A number of Multi-Layer Perceptron (MLP) neural networks are trained. The datasets were divided into training (80%) and test (20%) sets, with the exact content varying due to the dataset being randomly split for each run. The datasets consist of visual frame vectors as inputs, with the equivalent audio log fb vector used as the label. Although there are many network topologies and approaches available that can be used, including deep learning [14], it was decided that the quantity of data available and the preliminary nature of this work justified the use of an MLP. Deep networks are an very interesting approach to non-linear machine learning, and have been shown to be effective for speech processing work [14,18], and so in this research, we wished to make use of a non-linear method. However, we wished to keep the number of parameters relatively limited, and so decided to make use of a single hidden layer MLP rather than a deep network. A number of parameters were varied, namely the datasets, the number of visual frames used to estimate an audio frame, and the hidden layer size. The networks were trained in Matlab. For each individual configuration, 10 different networks were initialised, with the training and test datasets permuted randomly before each run. It was decided for consistency to focus on a single hidden layer, rather than considering deep networks with multiple hidden layers. The overall network is shown in Fig. 1.

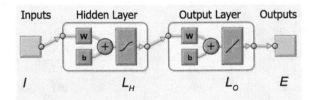

Fig. 1. Structure of MLP network used in this paper, showing number of inputs (I), hidden layer size (L_H), output layer size (L_O), and outputs E.

Figure 1 shows the network, which has a number of parameters that can be varied. The number of inputs, I, depends on how many frames to use as the input. A single frame will use 24 inputs, matching the DCT inputs, whereas using two frames will require 48 inputs, and as the number of chosen frames increases, the number of inputs increases accordingly. The network uses a single hidden layer, and the number of neurons in this is represented by L_H, and this parameter varies depending on the experiment. The outputs (E) and output layer size (L_O) correspond in all experiments to the number of filterbank vectors we wish to estimate, which is 23.

For evaluation, Mean Squared Error (MSE) was used, as this research takes a data driven approach to estimation, and so rather than trying to predict a complete phoneme or word, the aim is to produce the closest match between an estimated audio fb frame generated by the MLP using visual information, and the actual labelled frame. As the resulting MSE performance of each 10 runs of a network was not always symmetrical, it was best to calculate the median rather than the mean, and also use interquartile range (IQR) to signify the deviation.

3.2 Sentence Length Evaluation

Firstly, two possible datasets were considered, using all frames in each chosen sentence, or considering only aligned data. As discussed, five speakers, and 900 (or the maximum number available, see Table 1) sentences from each were used for each configuration. All audio and visual features are extracted, and the resulting vector pairings are shuffled randomly. For full sentences, this resulted in an initial 1,326,364 visual and audio vector pairings to be divided into training and test sets, and for the aligned sentences, 804,160 pairs.

Initially, a comparison was made between full and aligned data for MLP hidden layer sizes ranging between 10 neurons and 150 neurons. Using the structure given in Fig. 1, I is set to 24 (using a single frame) in both cases, L_O and E are set to 23, and the hidden layer size L_H is varied in steps of 10 between 10 and 150. The results of test data evaluation are given in Fig. 2, and results are given in Table 2.

Considering the initial results, it appears that the overall median full sentence results are better than aligned sentences, and that good results can be achieved with a relatively small hidden layer. However, a closer inspection of the individual results within the datasets showed that because the full sentences contained a relatively large number of frames (522,204) that could be classified as silence, the dataset was over-represented for silence, and this resulted in the network being able to very effectively distinguish between silence and non-speech frames, resulting in a potentially good voice activity detector (VAD). However, the main interest in this paper is speech mapping, and so although there is a higher MSE with aligned data, this is of more relevance to this work. As there is an improved balance to the dataset, an inspection of individual results showed an improvement in performance. Rather than learning silence only, it made more attempts to generalise over a greater variety of audio vectors, resulting in a slightly higher MSE. This is reflected in the noticeably smaller IQR, which shows a consistency

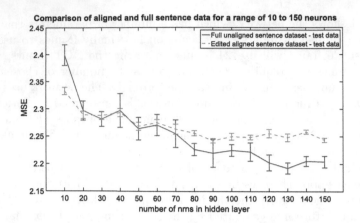

Fig. 2. MSE median test data results of using whole (solid blue line) or aligned (red dashed line) sentences for different MLP hidden layer sizes. (Color figure online)

Table 2. Selected median MSE results of test data for aligned and full sentences for different MLP hidden layer sizes, giving the median and the IQR.

Sentence type	No. nrns	Dataset type			
		Full Sentence		Aligned	
		median	IQR	median	IQR
Full Sentence	10	2.399	0.019	2.333	0.007
	30	2.282	0.014	2.288	0.007
	60	2.271	0.019	2.275	0.006
	90	2.220	0.025	2.242	0.004
	120	2.202	0.014	2.256	0.008
	150	2.204	0.011	2.244	0.004

in results. It can also be seen that a larger hidden layer (i.e. 90+ neurons) does not generate noticeably improved results, with improvement tending to be within the interquartile range, despite the additional time required for training. Given the quantity of data used being quite large, and improved results being found later in this paper, we theorise that the lack of improvement, despite the larger hidden layers, shows the limitations of using a single visual frame for speech estimation, and that this is not an optimal solution. Accordingly, for the remainder of this paper, aligned data is used.

3.3   Use of Multiple Visual Frames for Estimation

The effect of using a different number of visual frames is considered, by concatenating prior frames into one large input visual vector. This would theoretically allow movement information to be captured. Prior experiments (not reported

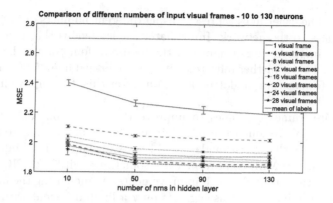

Fig. 3. MSE test data results of using different numbers of visual frames to estimate a single audio frame. (Color figure online)

Table 3. Selected median and IQR of MSE test data results of using different numbers of visual frames to estimate a single audio frame.

No. vis frames	Hidden layer size median results							
	10 nrns		50 nrns		90 nrns		130 nrns	
	MSE	IQR	MSE	IQR	MSE	IQR	MSE	IQR
1	2.399	0.019	2.264	0.021	2.220	0.025	2.192	0.010
4	2.105	0.009	2.044	0.008	2.027	0.010	2.017	0.009
8	2.039	0.011	1.957	0.014	1.941	0.006	1.932	0.009
12	2.007	0.017	1.917	0.007	1.908	0.009	1.9075	0.006
16	1.976	0.007	1.896	0.012	1.899	0.013	1.882	0.011
20	1.977	0.024	1.880	0.017	1.879	0.005	1.869	0.007
24	1.987	0.017	1.879	0.013	1.857	0.005	1.854	0.003
28	1.952	0.038	1.861	0.009	1.848	0.011	1.839	0.008

here for space reasons) showed that using the temporal differences ($\Delta(t)$) was an improvement over only using one frame, but not as good as using multiple visual frames.

A range of visual frames, ranging from one frame to a concatenation of the visual frame with the previous 27 visual frames, are used as I, thus meaning I ranges from 24 to 672. We also experiment with different values of L_H from 10 to 150. The results are shown in Fig. 3, where the x-axis corresponds to changes in L_H, and the different plots correspond to varying I, and in Table 3.

Firstly, the horizontal line at the top of Fig. 3 shows the result of calculating the mean of all the output labels and using this as the prediction for every frame, giving a baseline average value. There is a large improvement when using an ANN, demonstrating that using visual information has a strong relationship to the audio vector. The solid blue line is the MSE for using a single visual frame. The other lines represent using different numbers of visual frames, i.e. more inputs to the network. Immediately, it is obvious that using multiple visual frames improves performance, with the use of four frames showing a big improvement. This is further reflected with 8 (red dashed line), 12 (yellow dotted line), and 16 frames (purple dotted line), but after this, the improvement is less clear.

Using more frames continues to improve the results, but only by a small amount each time. Although the IQR (given as error bars) tends to be smaller for multiple frames than for a single visual frame, for larger visual inputs (20,24, and 28 frames), the MSE improvement is sometimes within the IQR of other results, suggesting extremely small improvements. As increasing the input vector size increases training time, this suggests only a limited benefit with very large input vectors. It can also be seen that network performance continues to improve with a larger hidden layer, but only by a small amount, arguably not justifying the much larger required training time. It is clear that using more visual frames is the biggest improvement that can be identified for audio vector prediction. This the benefit of accounting for lip movement, which makes sense, given that there is more information present in the lips than just static information. Other research has identified co-articulation as an issue present in some speakers, which makes phoneme-viseme mapping more challenging. As we use frame based data rather than a viseme, this should be less of an issue.

3.4   Speaker Dependent Training Comparison

Another optimisation approach is to train and test with individual speakers. This results in a smaller dataset being available, but ensures audio and visual greater consistency between vectors. We consider the results for each individual speaker, considering the use of 14 visual frames as input following Fig. 1, where $I = 336$ ($14 frames X 24 DCT components per frame$), and with hidden layer L_H ranging between 0 and 100 (chosen based on the results in the previous section). Test data results are shown in Fig. 4 and Table 4. These are compared to the results of training models with all five speakers.

It can be seen that using a model trained using the combined five speakers produces a consistently higher MSE at all hidden layer sizes than using any single speaker model. This is not unexpected, as there are differences between how individual speakers articulate and sound, and using five speakers does not appear to fully generalise, suggesting that more speakers or more information are required to train a fully robust multi-speaker model. The individual speaker results show an improvement, varying from speaker to speaker.

Speaker 1 (solid blue line) shows a particularly low MSE, signifying a particularly good performance, with speakers 2 and 4 being noticeably worse. However, it was not simple to identify why. All speakers seem to articulate clearly, the speech contents are similar, and inspecting example spectrograms for the audio files did not identify any obvious differences. One potential issue could be in the tracking approach, with slight differences in results, depending on the speaker. For example, speaker two tends to have a slightly smaller mouth region with

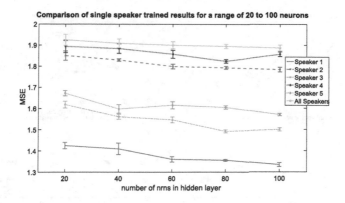

Fig. 4. MSE test data results of using individual speakers. (Color figure online)

Table 4. Selected normalised median MSE results of training and test data for using 14 prior frames, showing the results for individual speaker datasets.

Speaker ID	Hidden Layer Size MSE				
	20 nrns	40 nrns	60 nrns	80 nrns	100 nrns
All	1.925	1.909	1.900	1.895	1.887
S1	1.425	1.410	1.361	1.356	1.335
S2	1.850	1.829	1.799	1.793	1.784
S3	1.618	1.561	1.546	1.492	1.500
S4	1.894	1.884	1.857	1.823	1.857
S5	1.672	1.598	1.615	1.605	1.570

more of the face captured. However, by the same token, speaker 4 tends to have a very close mouth region tracked, with less of the face captured. These could potentially explain the difference, suggesting perhaps some other visual features, such as geometric measurements [13], could be useful.

3.5 Individual Vector Examination

Considering the size of the dataset and the random shuffling involved during the training set, it is challenging to consider individual speech vectors alone, hence the use of MSE as an evaluation metric. For illustrative purposes, six labelled and estimated audio vectors are shown that were generated using the best case model (i.e. a single speaker trained model using 14 prior frames, $I = 14 * 24 = 336$, and 100 neurons in the hidden layer, $L_H = 100$). These are shown in Fig. 5. The frames shown here are selected pseudo-randomly, although care was taken to include at least one good example and one poor example. Each frame in Fig. 5 shows an estimated network output, compared to the actual filterbank output. The x-axis represents each filterbank channel (and accordingly each network

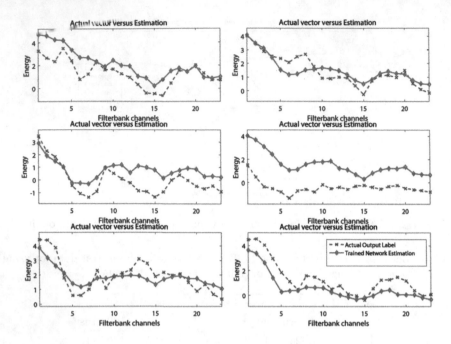

Fig. 5. Examples of individual vector results (Color figure online)

output E), with the y-axis giving the amount of energy in each channel. The network outputs are aiming to generate an estimated filterbank vector.

Figure 5 shows that in general, the estimation is reasonably good. The actual vector (i.e. the ground truth) is shown with a blue dashed line, and the trained estimation from only visual information is shown with a solid red line. The examples show that the fit is not perfect, which is to be expected, represents a reasonably accurate smoothed estimation. However the bottom and middle right examples in Fig. 5 show that where the actual data is for consistent low speech energy, the estimate predicts more noise present, particularly at lower frequencies (i.e. the lower fb channels). Overall, it shows that training using only visual information, without any audio input, and with a fairly basic visual feature vector (i.e. DCT) is successful, and the right combination of visual inputs, speaker selection, and network size, can produce a reasonably good estimation, but that there is also still room for improvement.

As an example of how the training has improved estimation, Fig. 6 shows a similar comparison, but with the addition of an estimation acquired from a network of the same parameters that has not been trained (see the orange line). The weights are therefore in their initial pre-trained randomised state, and it can be clearly seen that the estimation differs radically from both the trained and the actual values, demonstrating that training has improved the initial network outputs significantly. When this is combined with the demonstrated improvement over using an averaged value (as shown in Fig. 3), it demonstrates the value of using a neural network for speech estimation.

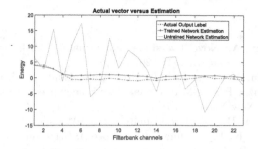

Fig. 6. Examples of individual vector results (Color figure online)

Overall, we can see that the neural network works well, and that reasonably good initial results can be achieved. There are limitations with the potential of achieving perfect speech estimations using only visual information (as discussed previously), but given the fairly constrained corpus and the quantity of data available, the non-linear training discussed here seems to deliver good results, especially when a number of previous frames are also used as input, providing much more information than a single visual frame would. The next step is to consider different visual features, as well as compare these baseline results to using state-of-the-art deep networks [18].

4   Conclusions and Future Work

This paper presented a detailed investigation of audiovisual visual to audio speech mapping. A number of different data and neural network configurations were experimented with, showing that optimal results could be gained with speaker specific data, using a large number of prior visual frames, and that a hidden layer of larger than fifty neurons delivers optimal results. These results verify that visual information can feasibly be used to estimate audio features, and serves as a very useful precursor to the development of a more advanced single channel audiovisual speech enhancement system, as outlined in [2]. However, there is still scope for improvement. Other work in the literature [13] uses a range of features to optimise results, including shape biologically inspired barcode features [9], which should be investigated in more depth. There is also scope for using deep neural networks [14], and finally, although this paper focused on data driven mapping, in future work, it will be of interest to investigate the difference in individual parts of speech, such as phonemes and words, both to compare more closely to other research, and for speaker specific analysis.

Acknowledgements. This work was supported by the UK Engineering and Physical Sciences Research Council (EPSRC) Grant No. EP/M026981/1 (CogAVHearing-http://cogavhearing.cs.stir.ac.uk). In accordance with EPSRC policy, all experimental data used in the project simulations is available at http://hdl.handle.net/11667/81. The authors would also like to gratefully acknowledge Prof. Leslie Smith and Dr Ahsan Adeel at the University of Stirling, Dr Kristína Malinovská at Comenius University in Bratislava, and the anonymous reviewers for their helpful comments and suggestions.

References

1. Abel, A., Hussain, A.: Novel two-stage audiovisual speech filtering in noisy environments. Cogn. Comput. **6**, 1–18 (2013)
2. Abel, A., Hussain, A.: Cognitively Inspired Audiovisual Speech Filtering: Towards an Intelligent, Fuzzy Based, Multimodal, Two-Stage Speech Enhancement System, vol. 5. Springer, New York (2015)
3. Almajai, I., Milner, B.: Effective visually-derived Wiener filtering for audio-visual speech processing. In: Proceedings of Interspeech, Brighton, UK (2009)
4. Bear, H., Harvey, R.: Decoding visemes: improving machine lip-reading. In: International Conference on Acoustics, Speech and Signal Processing (2016)
5. Bear, H.L., Harvey, R.W., Theobald, B.-J., Lan, Y.: Which phoneme-to-viseme maps best improve visual-only computer lip-reading? In: Bebis, G., et al. (eds.) ISVC 2014. LNCS, vol. 8888, pp. 230–239. Springer, Heidelberg (2014). doi:10.1007/978-3-319-14364-4_22
6. Cappelletta, L., Harte, N.: Phoneme-to-viseme mapping for visual speech recognition. In: ICPRAM (2), pp. 322–329 (2012)
7. Chung, K.: Challenges and recent developments in hearing aids part I. speech understanding in noise, microphone technologies and noise reduction algorithms. Trends Amplif. **8**(3), 83–124 (2004)
8. Cooke, M., Barker, J., Cunningham, S., Shao, X.: An audio-visual corpus for speech perception and automatic speech recognition. J. Acoust. Soc. Am. **120**(5 Pt 1), 2421–2424 (2006)
9. Dakin, S.C., Watt, R.J.: Biological bar codes in human faces. J. Vis. **9**(4), 2:1–2:10 (2009)
10. Fu, S., Gutierrez-Osuna, R., Esposito, A., Kakumanu, P.K., Garcia, O.N.: Audio/visual mapping with cross-modal hidden Markov models. IEEE Trans. Multimedia **7**(2), 243–252 (2005)
11. Lan, Y., Theobald, B.J., Harvey, R., Ong, E.J., Bowden, R.: Improving visual features for lip-reading. In: AVSP, pp. 7–3 (2010)
12. McGurk, H., MacDonald, J.: Hearing lips and seeing voices. Nature **264**, 746–748 (1976)
13. Milner, B., Websdale, D.: Analysing the importance of different visual feature coefficients. In: FAAVSP 2015 (2015)
14. Ngiam, J., Khosla, A., Kim, M., Nam, J., Lee, H., Ng, A.Y.: Multimodal deep learning. In: Proceedings of the 28th International Conference on Machine Learning (ICML 2011), pp. 689–696 (2011)
15. Pahar, M.: A novel sound reconstruction technique based on a spike code (event) representation. Ph.D. thesis, Computing Science and Mathematics, University of Stirling, Stirling, Scotland (2016)
16. Ross, D.A., Lim, J., Lin, R.S., Yang, M.H.: Incremental learning for robust visual tracking. Int. J. Comput. Vis. **77**(1–3), 125–141 (2008)
17. Sumby, W., Pollack, I.: Visual contribution to speech intelligibility in noise. J. Acoust. Soc. Am. **26**(2), 212–215 (1954)
18. Tóth, L.: Phone recognition with hierarchical convolutional deep maxout networks. EURASIP J. Audio Speech Music Process. **2015**(1), 1–13 (2015)
19. Viola, P., Jones, M.: Rapid object detection using a boosted cascade of simple features. In: Proceedings of the 2001 IEEE Computer Society Conference on Computer Vision and Pattern Recognition, CVPR 2001, vol. 1, p. I-511. IEEE (2001)

Continuous Time Recurrent Neural Network Model of Recurrent Collaterals in the Hippocampus CA3 Region

Ashraya Samba Shiva and Amir Hussain[(⊠)]

Division of Computing Science and Mathematics, School of Natural Sciences,
University of Stirling, Stirling FK9 4LA, Scotland, UK
{asv,ahu}@cs.stir.ac.uk

Abstract. Recurrent collaterals in the brain represent the recollection and execution of various monotonous activities such as breathing, brushing our teeth, chewing, walking, etc. These recurrent collaterals are found throughout the brain, each pertaining to a specific activity. Any deviation from regular activity falls back to the original cycle of activities, thus exhibiting a limit cycle or attractor dynamics. Upon analysis of some of these recurrent collaterals from different regions of the brain, it is observed that rhythmic theta oscillations play a vital role coordinating the functionalities of different regions of the brain. The neuromodulator acetylcholine, is found to be present in almost all of the regions where recurrent collaterals are present. This notable observation points to an underlying link between the generation and functioning of theta oscillations present in these recurrent collaterals, with the neuromodulator acetylcholine. Further, we show that these recurrent collaterals can be mathematically modeled using continuous time recurrent neural networks to account for the frequency of action potentials which follow the excitatory-inhibitory-excitatory (E-I-E) and inhibitory-excitatory-inhibitory (I-E-I) model. As a first case study, we present a detailed preliminary analysis of the CA3 region of the hippocampus, which is one of the most widely studied recurrent collaterals network in the brain, known to be responsible for storing and recalling episodic memories and also learning tasks. The recurrent collaterals present in this region are shown to follow an E-I-E pattern, which is analyzed using a mathematical model derived from continuous time recurrent neural networks, using inputs from a leaky integrate-and-fire neuronal model.

Keywords: theta oscillations · attractor dynamics · recurrent neural networks · recurrent collaterals · acetylcholine

1 Introduction

Neuronal models of day-to-day activities, some involuntary and some habitual ones such as breathing, locomotory activities, eating, blinking, learning, recollecting from memory, etc. are related to the rhythmic oscillations in the brain. These oscillations require a positive action potential followed by a negative inhibitory feedback action

The authors declare no conflict of interest.

C.-L. Liu et al. (Eds.): BICS 2016, LNAI 10023, pp. 343–354, 2016.
DOI: 10.1007/978-3-319-49685-6_31

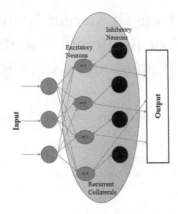

Fig. 1. Recurrent neural network as exhibited by recurrent collaterals

potential [1] and emerge as a result of dynamic interactions between neuronal circuits and the internal cellular mechanisms. While asleep, many neuronal oscillators are active [2]. Many regions of the brain cooperate with each other by the phase-coupling of theta and gamma oscillations to complete an activity [3]. It is also observed that synchronization of several (approximately seven) gamma sub cycles within a single theta cycle representing different spatial information coordinate communication of different regions of the brain [4, 5].

Some of the attributes studied about such networks include the type of neurotransmitter/neuromodulators involved, type of emerging rhythmic oscillations, amplitude of such oscillations, synchronization of oscillations across brain regions, phase-amplitude coupling of oscillations across brain regions, etc. For example, it is observed that stronger gamma frequency oscillations occur while trying to recall well-remembered objects and also while effectively encoding events [6, 7]. Such network of neurons are a feedback system called recurrent collaterals which synapse on their own somata or axons or on neighbouring dendrites as shown in Fig. 1. These recurrent collaterals serve in learning and provide computational capabilities [8].

In this paper, recurrent collaterals in the CA3 region of the hippocampus in the brain is explored in the subsequent sections and a hypothesis based on these observations is presented in the end.

2 Characteristics of CA3 Recurrent Collaterals

The CA3 recurrent collaterals of the hippocampus follow the E-I-E model of execution where the neuromodulator acetylcholine (ACh) is found to be responsible either for excitation or inhibition. The frequency of the resultant oscillations in either the excitatory part of the circuit or the inhibitory part of the circuit is always between 7–12 Hz which falls under the theta oscillations category [9], which is known to be responsible for the effective synchronization and coordination of the whole brain.

Acetylcholine (ACh) is a neuromodulator which alters synaptic connections based on its intrinsic excitatory or inhibitory behaviour enriching the oscillatory behaviour of the recurrent collaterals, where it is found to be present. In hippocampus, it is found to be present as a primary excitatory neurotransmitter in the CA3 recurrent collaterals. Enhancement of memory encoding and learning rate is due to ACh in the CA3 region of the hippocampus which contributes to stronger afferent input given to the feedback loop that adds to the theta oscillations [10].

CA3 recurrent collaterals behave as an associative memory or content-addressable memory, which is due to the attractor dynamics exhibited by this region [11]. As the pattern closes into a particular stored memory, convergence occurs, fulfilling the limit cycle. Thus, any deviation from the attractor pattern ultimately falls back to the same trajectory.

3   CA3 Region of the Hippocampus in the Medial Temporal Lobe

The different regions of the hippocampus is shown in Fig. 2, and a PET scan image of the brain indicating the hippocampus is shown in Figs. 3 and 4. The regions CA1 to CA4 (sandwiched between CA3 and the Dentate Gyrus (DG)) house many pathways such as the Schaffer collaterals, perforant pathways forming the trisynaptic circuit, dealing with remembering and recalling information, learning new tasks, storing spatial map information, etc. In general, the hippocampus is known for episodic memory, learning ability and for storing spatial information. The CA3 region is composed of the recurrent collaterals formed by the excitatory CA3 pyramidal neurons and the inhibitory CA3 interneurons forming a closed feedback circuit giving rise to rhythmic oscillations in the range of 7–12 Hz which is within the theta oscillations. These oscillations synchronize with other rhythmic oscillations of different frequencies such as slow gamma waves (30–60 Hz), fast gamma waves (60–90 Hz), sharp waves (150–200 Hz) [12].

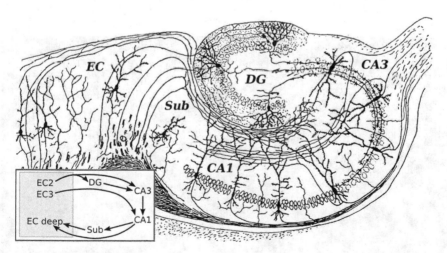

Fig. 2. Hippocampus regions and cells shown by a modified version of drawing of Santiago Ramón y Cajal

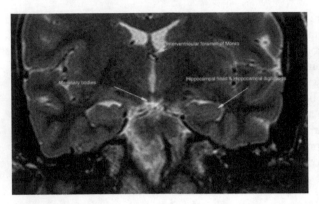

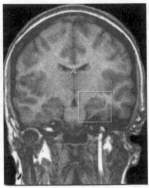

Fig. 3. Location of Hippocampus, closer view, case courtesy of Dr. Azza Elgendy, Radiopaedia.org, rID: 33687

Fig. 4. Location of Hippocampus in the PET scan image of the brain, case courtesy of A. Prof. Frank Gaillard, Radiopaedia.org, rID: 10770

Also, in the CA3 region, the arborization of basket cells is extensive and hence, CA3 pyramidal neurons excite basket cells, wherein, each axon of the pyramidal cell synapses on one basket cell at a single location, thus creating a single release site [13, 14]. The pyramidal cells synapse on the basket cells which in turn synapse on the pyramidal cells forming the E-I-E network. The presence of these inhibitory basket cells regulate the activity of pyramidal cells in CA3 region, thus preventing deviation from the existing pathways resulting in limit cycles or attractors [15].

The different pathways and neuronal circuits found in the hippocampus as explained above, is shown in Fig. 4.

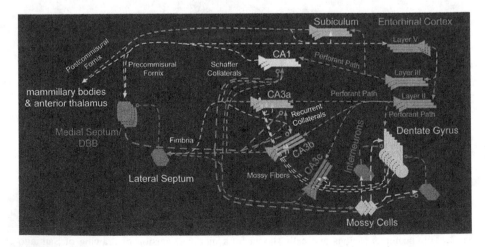

Fig. 5. Neural circuit of hippocampus, taken from R.P. Kesner [24]

As seen from Fig. 5, a major source of input to the CA3 pyramidal neurons are from themselves. This allows for an associative structure which helps in storing information [16]. This is a short term memory which is sustained by the excitatory firing of the recurrent collateral network [17].

CA3 pyramidal neurons receive their inputs from other CA3 axons and also from the dentate gyrus and entorhinal cortex. But they also receive cholinergic inputs from the medial septum which is known to be the origin of theta rhythms [18]. The region of the hippocampus activated during initial learning can be seen at the top of Fig. 6 and the region of the hippocampus activated during initial recall can be seen at the bottom of Fig. 6 [19]. This paper hypothesizes that these recurrent collaterals following an E-I-E model, exhibit attractor dynamics which is responsible for their associativity, also known as content addressable pattern. The fact that *such recurrent collaterals give rise to rhythms in a fixed bandwidth, synchronizing the activity of the whole region, also have neuromodulatory cholinergic connections* [20–23].

4 Proposed Model

The structure and behaviour of the recurrent collaterals is explained in this section.

In 1949, Donald Hebb, proposed the most renowned rule called the Hebb rule, which states that *"When an axon of cell A is near enough to excite cell B or repeatedly or persistently takes part in firing it, some growth process or metabolic change takes place in one or both cells such that A's efficiency, as one of the cells firing B, is increased."* as explained by Sejnowski et al. in [18], for the implementation of synaptic plasticity.

Using the leaky integrate-and-fire model [25], the time dependent current denoted by I is induced by the difference in the membrane potential caused by a stimulus. The ion that opens the gated-ion channels for the release of the neurotransmitter is considered here, since the excitatory or inhibitory effect of the neurotransmitter decides the effect of the action potential in the principal cell. Therefore, accounting for this ion, the current, I output by the system that reduces or increases the action potential of the principal cell is given by,

$$I = C_m \frac{dV_m(t)}{dt} + g_{ion}(V_m(t) - V_{ion}) \tag{1}$$

where, C_m is the membrane capacitance caused by the cell membrane, g_{ion} is the ionic conductances per unit area, V_{ion} is the ionic reverse potential (or Nernst potential of the ion), $V_m(t)$ is the membrane potential which changes due to the flow of ions causing the cell to become depolarized or hyperpolarized. The membrane potential is a time-dependent variable here, as a result of which, the induced current and ionic conductances are time-dependent as well, and the conductances are also dependent on voltage. *The current from the leaky integrate-and-fire model drives the neural network.* In the event of a change in membrane potential, if the current induced exceeds the action potential threshold, then the neuron fires; else if many small currents follow before the induced current dies away, then an action potential is generated by the

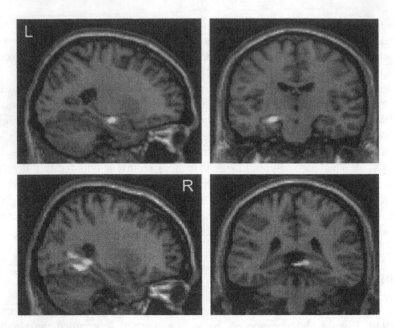

Fig. 6. Initial Learning (top) and initial recall (bottom) MRI scan, taken from G. Grön et al. [19]

cumulative effect of all such currents. From McCulloch & Pitts neuron model, we have the equation of a neuron depicting this general behaviour, with Eq. 1 being the current from each dendrite given as input to the neuron,

$$out_I = \sigma\left(\sum\nolimits_{i=1}^{n} x_i w_{ji} + \theta_i\right) \tag{2}$$

where, out_I is the output vector of the neural network for which the summation of the product of the input vector, x_i and the weight of connection from pre-synaptic node to post-synaptic node, w_{ji} is the input, assuming there are n dendritic inputs and lastly, θ_i is the threshold or the bias of the pre-synaptic neuron. The input in Eq. 2 is the current induced in the neuron. The weight is the strength of synaptic connection between pre- and post-synaptic neuron.

From the observation of the pattern followed in the recurrent collaterals as explained before, this equation can be modified by adding another part to it to include the inhibitory neurons as shown.

$$out_I = \sigma\left(\sum\nolimits_{i=1}^{n} u_i w_{ji}^{(1)} - \sum\nolimits_{j=1}^{m} v_j w_{ij}^{(2)} + \theta\right) \tag{3}$$

where, u_j is the principal neuron and v_j is the inhibitory neuron, assuming there are n principal cells and m interneurons, and a common threshold. The parameters $w_{ji}^{(1)}$ and $w_{ij}^{(2)}$ are the weights from principal cell to inhibitory neuron and vice-versa respectively. The product of the excitatory input and the weight of the principal cell synapse

Table 1. Simulation parameters

Property	Pyramidal cell	Basket cell
Membrane potential (V_m mV)	−62.97	−45
Membrane capacitance (C_m pF)	119.97	151.4
Time constant (τ_m ms)	23.82	13.15
Ionic conductance (g_{ion} mS/cm^2)	17	17
Ionic potential (V_{ion} mV)	140	140

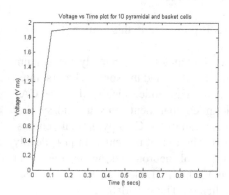 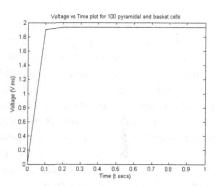

Fig. 7. Action Potential vs. Time

on the inhibitory neuron. Now, the product of the inhibitory neuron input (upon excitation by the principal cell) and the weight of the inhibitory neuron synapse on the principal cell, reducing its strength. This happens to all the dendrites of a neuron which is the end result in out_I.

The activation of the recurrent collaterals changes over time and these collaterals have a time delay due to the feedback loops. A continuous time recurrent neural network model [26–28] can be proposed to account for such recurrent collaterals. For a given neuron, the activation y_i is,

$$\tau_i \frac{dy_i}{dt} = -y_i + out_I \qquad (4)$$

The output from Eq. 2 is the input (out_I) to Eq. 3, to the sigmoidal activation function. τ_i is the time constant of the postsynaptic neuron and y_i is the action potential of the postsynaptic neuron. The differential, $\frac{dy_i}{dt}$ depicts the rate of change of activation of the postsynaptic neuron.

To summarize, the above model inputs the induced current from the leaky integrate-and-fire model from Eq. 1 and adds the inhibitory feedback action on the excitatory potential and inputs it to the sigmoidal activation function to output the rate of change of activation of the postsynaptic neuron.

Using the parameters as shown in Table 1 for CA3 pyramidal cell taken from [14, 29] and for basket cells, taken from [13], considering 100 pyramidal cells and basket cells with each pyramidal cell synapsing on a basket cell creating a single release site, and starting with random weights, it can be seen, as plotted in Fig. 7, that irrespective of the random weights and the number of neurons, the firing of action potentials becomes constant once the weights converge, keeping the voltage across the recurrent collateral network unchanging, which leads us back to the concept of attractor dynamics, or precisely, limit cycles exhibited by the CA3 pyramidal neurons.

5 Discussion, Limitations and Future Work

A discussion of a couple of most relevant models is presented in this section, to make a comparison of them with the model proposed here.

The CA3 pyramidal neuron is composed of 4-compartments namely the stratum lacunosum-moleculare, stratum radiatum, stratum lucidum and the soma. The first three regions constitute the dendritic compartments. We can notice clearly that the CA1 pyramidal neurons do not have the stratum lucidum compartment, since the mossy fiber inputs from the dentate gyrus is received in this region of the CA3 pyramidal neurons, which is absent for CA1 pyramidal neurons [14]. The model presented in [14] deeply analyses each compartment of the CA3 pyramidal neuron, taking in the exact parameters of voltage and conductances, and the Hodgkin-Huxley constants have been evaluated for the CA3 pyramidal neuron specifically. The calculations are also done specifically for the interneuron types present in the CA3 region namely the O-LM cell and the basket cell population.

The biophysical parameters used in the equations as derived from the Hodgkin and Huxley equations, as given in this paper, with definitions of the constants for the ions for CA3 pyramidal cells and interneurons, are as follows:

For the pyramidal cell,

$$
\begin{aligned}
v_0' = I_0 + g_c\left(v_{d,1} - v_s\right) - g_{Na}m_\infty^2(v_s)h_s(v_s - E_{Na}) - g_K n_s(v_s - E_K) \\
- g_A a_s(v_s - E_A) - g_L(v_s - E_L) - g_{ie}s_{ie}(v_s - E_{isyn})
\end{aligned}
\tag{5}
$$

where,

$$
h_s' = \alpha_h(v_s)(1 - h_s) - \beta_h(v_s)h_s
\tag{5a}
$$

$$
n_s' = \alpha_n(v_s)(1 - n_s) - \beta_n(v_s)n_s
\tag{5b}
$$

$$
a_s' = \alpha_a(v_s)(1 - a_s) - \beta_a(v_s)a_s
\tag{5c}
$$

For the O-LM interneuron,

$$
\begin{aligned}
v_0' = I_0 - \left[g_{Na}m_0^3(v_0)h_0 + g_{Nap}m_{po}\right](v_0 - E_{Na}) - g_K n_0^4(v_0 - E_k) \\
- g_H(0.65\lambda_{fo} + 0.35\lambda_{so})(v_0 - E_H) - g_L(v_0 - E_L) + E_{syn} + I_{syn}
\end{aligned}
\tag{6}
$$

where,

$$E_{syn} = -\sum_i g_{eo}S_{eo,i}(v_0 - E_{esyn}) \tag{6a}$$

$$I_{syn} = -g_{io}S_{io}(v_0 - E_{isyn}) \tag{6b}$$

$$m'_0 = \alpha_m(v_0)(1 - m_0) - \beta_m(v_0)m_0 \tag{6c}$$

$$h'_0 = \alpha_h(v_0)(1 - h_0) - \beta_h(v_0)h_0 \tag{6d}$$

$$m'_{po} = \alpha_{mpo}(v_0)(1 - m_{po}) - \beta_{mpo}(v_0)m_{po} \tag{6e}$$

$$n'_0 = \alpha_n(v_0)(1 - n_0) - \beta_n(v_0)n_0 \tag{6f}$$

$$\lambda'_{fo} = \frac{\lambda_{f\infty}(v_0) - \lambda_{fo}}{\tau_{\lambda f}v_0} \tag{6g}$$

$$\lambda'_{so} = \frac{\lambda_{s\infty}(v_0) - \lambda_{so}}{\tau_{\lambda s}v_0} \tag{6h}$$

For the basket cell,

$$B_{pop} = B_{pop} + R(t)[T(t) - \Theta(\tau)] + \sum_{i=1}^{5} \rho_i \tag{7}$$

Next, as proposed by Wilson and Cowan in [30] and adopted by Kali and Dayan in [15], the CA3 recurrent collaterals having excitatory and inhibitory connections is modeled using recurrent neural networks to exhibit the associative property of these collaterals.

$$\tau \dot{u}_i = -u_i + \sum_j J_{ij}g_u(u_j) - hg_v(v)u_i + I_i^{PP} + I_i^{MF} \tag{8}$$

$$\tau' \dot{v} = -v + w \sum_j g_u(u_j) \tag{9}$$

Where u and v are the membrane potentials of the pyramidal and inhibitory cells τ is the membrane time constant, J_{ij} is the weight of neuron j to i. I_i^{PP} and I_i^{MF} are the inputs from perforant path and mossy fibers from the dentate gyrus.

The first model captures the exact biological functionality but does not consider the attractor dynamics involved in the recurrent collaterals. The second model considers a global inhibitory interneuron and also sums up all the neuronal inputs while processing and produces the output.

The model proposed in this paper coalesces both of these models fulfilling the properties exhibited by a neuronal recurrent collateral, adding more to it as explained below.

The convergence of weights in the proposed model implies the network stability on reaching the limit cycle and hence, fulfils the attractor dynamics model. Secondly, biological parameters are used in the model instead of assuming values for each parameter. This emulates a biological neuronal recurrent collateral network. Lastly, in almost all the models, neuron summation on the whole network level is considered, but biologically, there are many dendritic inputs which combine to produce single activity in a neuron. To emulate this property, dendritic summation of inputs in considered on a single neuron level, and such neuronal inputs are given to each inhibitory interneuron which in turn feedback on the pyramidal cell.

Considering the various characteristics explained before, in detail, we hypothesize that the recurrent collaterals found in various regions of the brain all have attractor dynamics, involving acetylcholine neuromodulator for either excitation or inhibition, generating theta rhythms or synchronizing with hippocampal theta rhythms. The limitation of this current paper and future work extending the research involved in this paper is to derive a generic architecture which would consider the various other recurrent collaterals found in the brain, accounting for all the common properties of these recurrent collaterals exhibiting associative network behaviour. With the simulation of these common characteristics in such a generic architecture for the recurrent collaterals in the brain, taking aspiration from the above explained models and extending them to other regions of the brain, it can then be used in many applications which require such content-addressable memory architecture to emulate the monotonicity of activities performed by the brain, both voluntarily and involuntarily.

6   Conclusion

Overall, it can be seen that recurrent collaterals have cholinergic connections that serve as short-term memory, generating or synchronizing with theta oscillations to communicate information to other regions of the brain. The recurrent collaterals present in this region follows an E-I-E pattern which is explained using the mathematical model derived from the continuous time recurrent neural networks using inputs from the leaky integrate-and-fire neuronal model. Also, acetylcholine promotes excitation followed by inhibition based recurrent connections helping in learning and encoding of information. We further intend to extend this model to include many other regions of the brain which has recurrent collaterals, modeling the common characteristics found in these regions.

Acknowledgements. This research is funded by the University of Stirling International Doctoral studentship. Professor A. Hussain is also supported by the UK Engineering and Physical Sciences Research Council (EPSRC) grant no. EP/M026981/1, and the Digital Health & Care Institute (DHI) funded Exploratory project: PD2A. The authors are grateful to Prof B. Graham at the University of Stirling, and the anonymous reviewers for their insightful comments and suggestions, which helped improve the quality of this paper.

References

1. Ermentrout, G.B., Chow, C.C.: Modeling neural oscillations. Physiol. Behav. **77**, 629–633 (2002)
2. Buzsáki, G., Draguhn, A.: Neuronal oscillations in cortical networks. Science **304**, 1926–1929 (2004)
3. Sander, R.: Slow brain waves play key role in coordinating complex activity. UC Berkeley News (2006)
4. Lisman, J.E., Jensen, O.: The theta-gamma neural code. Neuron **77**, 1002–1016 (2013)
5. Bragin, A., Jandó, G., Nádasdy, Z., Hetke, J., Wise, K., Buzsáki, G.: Gamma (40–100 Hz) oscillation in the hippocampus of the behaving rat. J. Neurosci. **15**, 47–60 (1995)
6. Osipova, D., Takashima, A., Oostenveld, R., Fernández, G., Maris, E., Jensen, O.: Theta and gamma oscillations predict encoding and retrieval of declarative memory. J. Neurosci. **26**, 7523–7531 (2006)
7. Colgin, L.L.: Theta–gamma coupling in the entorhinal–hippocampal system. Curr. Opin. Neurobiol. **31**, 45–50 (2015)
8. Taverna, S., Ilijic, E., Surmeier, D.J.: Recurrent collateral connections of striatal medium spiny neurons are disrupted in models of Parkinson's disease. J. Neurosci. **28**, 5504–5512 (2008)
9. Fischer, Y., Gähwiler, B.H., Thompson, S.M.: Activation of intrinsic hippocampal theta oscillations by acetylcholine in rat septo-hippocampal cocultures. J. Physiol. **519**, 405–413 (1999)
10. Hasselmo, M.E.: The role of acetylcholine in learning and memory. Curr. Opin. Neurobiol. **16**, 710–715 (2006)
11. Rennó-Costa, C., Lisman, J.E., Verschure, P.F.: A signature of attractor dynamics in the CA3 region of the hippocampus. PLoS Comput. Biol. **10**, e1003641 (2014)
12. Gray, C.M.: Synchronous oscillations in neuronal systems: mechanisms and functions. J. Comput. Neurosci. **1**, 11–38 (1994)
13. Papp, O.I., Karlócai, M.R., Tóth, I.E., Freund, T.F., Hájos, N.: Different input and output properties characterize parvalbumin-positive basket and Axo-axonic cells in the hippocampal CA3 subfield. Hippocampus **23**, 903–918 (2013)
14. Kunec, S., Hasselmo, M.E., Kopell, N.: Encoding and retrieval in the CA3 region of the hippocampus: a model of theta-phase separation. J. Neurophysiol. **94**, 70–82 (2005)
15. Káli, S., Dayan, P.: The involvement of recurrent connections in area CA3 in establishing the properties of place fields: a model. J. Neurosci. **20**, 7463–7477 (2000)
16. Witter, M.P.: Intrinsic and extrinsic wiring of CA3: indications for connectional heterogeneity. Learn. Memory **14**, 705–713 (2007)
17. Rolls, E.T.: Memory, Attention, and Decision-Making. OUP, Oxford (2008). Chapter 2
18. Sejnowski, T.J., Tesauro, G.: The Hebb rule for synaptic plasticity: algorithms and implementations. In: Neural Models of Plasticity: Experimental and Theoretical Approaches, pp. 94–103 (1989)
19. Grön, G., Bittner, D., Schmitz, B., Wunderlich, A.P., Tomczak, R., Riepe, M.W.: Hippocampal activations during repetitive learning and recall of geometric patterns. Learn. Memory **8**, 336–345 (2001)
20. Vertes, R.P., Hoover, W.B., Di Prisco, G.V.: Theta rhythm of the hippocampus: subcortical control and functional significance. Behav. Cogn. Neurosci. Rev. **3**, 173–200 (2004)
21. Lisman, J.E.: Bursts as a unit of neural information: making unreliable synapses reliable. Trends Neurosci. **20**, 38–43 (1997)

22. Easton, A., Douchamps, V., Eacott, M., Lever, C.: A specific role for septohippocampal acetylcholine in memory? Neuropsychologia **50**, 3156–3168 (2012)
23. Croxson, P.L., Browning, P.G., Gaffan, D., Baxter, M.G.: Acetylcholine facilitates recovery of episodic memory after brain damage. J. Neurosci. **32**, 13787–13795 (2012)
24. Kesner, R.P.: A process analysis of the CA3 subregion of the hippocampus. Front Cell **409** (2015)
25. Burkitt, A.N.: A review of the integrate-and-fire neuron model: I. Homogeneous synaptic input. Biol. Cybern. **95**, 1–19 (2006)
26. Fernandez, F.R., Engbers, J.D., Turner, R.W.: Firing dynamics of cerebellar purkinje cells. J. Neurophysiol. **98**, 278–294 (2007)
27. Kuznetsov, Y.A.: Saddle-node bifurcation. Scholarpedia **1**, 1859 (2006)
28. Tomkins, A., Vasilaki, E., Beste, C., Gurney, K., Humphries, M.D.: Transient and steady-state selection in the striatal microcircuit. In: Basal Ganglia: Physiological, Behavioral, and Computational Studies (2015)
29. Andersen, P.: The Hippocampus Book. Oxford University Press, Oxford (2007)
30. Wilson, H.R., Cowan, J.D.: Excitatory and inhibitory interactions in localized populations of model neurons. Biophys. J. **12**, 1 (1972)

Sparse-Network Based Framework for Detecting the Overlapping Community Structure of Brain Functional Network

Xuan Li[1], Zilan Hu[2], and Haixian Wang[1(✉)]

[1] Key Lab of Child Development and Learning Science of Ministry of Education, Research Center for Learning Science, Southeast University, Nanjing 210096, Jiangsu, People's Republic of China
{xuanli,hxwang}@seu.edu.cn
[2] School of Mathematics and Physics, Anhui University of Technology, Maanshan 243002, Anhui, People's Republic of China

Abstract. Community structure is one of the important features of complex brain network. Recently, major efforts have been made to investigate the non-overlapping community structure of brain network. However, an important fact is often ignored that the community structures of most real networks are overlapping. In this paper, we propose a novel method called sparse symmetric non-negative matrix factorization (ssNMF) to detect the overlapping community structure of the brain functional network, by adding a sparse constraint on the standard symmetric NMF (symNMF). Besides, we apply a sparse-network based framework by using non-negative adaptive sparse representation (NASR) to construct a sparse brain network. Simulated fMRI experimental results show that NMF-based methods achieve higher accuracy than methods of modularity optimization, normalized cuts and affinity propagation. Results of real fMRI experiments also lead to meaningful findings, which can help to promote the understanding of brain functional systems.

Keywords: Overlapping community · Non-negative matrix factorization (NMF) · Sparse-network · Brain functional network · fMRI

1 Introduction

Recently, it has been widely appreciated that the brain's functional and structural systems can be seen as complex networks [1]. Many efforts have been made to promote the comprehensive understanding of brain network structure. One important feature of the brain network is the community structure. Nodes are highly interconnected within each community while different communities are relatively sparsely connected. Popular algorithms as spectral clustering-based methods are able to detect the non-overlapping community structure [2,3]. However, they ignore an important factor that most real complex networks have

© Springer International Publishing AG 2016
C.-L. Liu et al. (Eds.): BICS 2016, LNAI 10023, pp. 355–365, 2016.
DOI: 10.1007/978-3-319-49685-6_32

overlapping community structure. Recently, we have applied the symmetric non-negative matrix factorization (symNMF) [4] to identify the overlapping community structure of brain functional network [5], which can be regarded as a soft clustering method. Moreover, symNMF is a part-based representation method due to its non-negativity. It only allows for additive combination of different parts and naturally group coherent parts together. For continuous NMF-based methods, an appropriate threshold is needed to decide the final network structure. However, symNMF is sensitive to the selection of thresholds.

Accumulating evidence has indicated that interaction of parsimonious functional representations can accomplish diverse neural functions. Many researches have taken sparsity into account when developing models [6,7]. Besides, sparsity can make it easier to interpret the physiological meaning of the results. Thus, in this paper, we develop a sparse network-based framework to identify the overlapping community structure of brain functional network. Specifically, we first apply the non-negative adaptive sparse representation (NASR) [5] to construct the brain functional network, instead of the traditional pairwise Pearson correlation method. More importantly, we propose a sparse symmetric non-negative matrix factorization (ssNMF) method based on symNMF by enforcing the sparsity of the learned parts, thus reducing its sensitivity to threshold settings.

In short, the contribution of this paper is two-fold. Firstly, we propose ssNMF by incorporating the sparsity into the symNMF while retaining the favourable property of part-based learning. Secondly, we develop a sparse-network based framework to discover the overlapping community structure of brain functional network.

2   Methods and Material

2.1   Sparse Network Construction with NASR

The brain functional network can be represented as an association matrix, which is generally computed by the pairwise Pearson correlation. However, it only considers the association between a pair of nodes and results in a densely connected association matrix with some negative values. Here, we adopt the NASR to construct the association matrix. It can calculate the association between one node and all other nodes simultaneously and lead to a sparse and non-negative symmetric association matrix which are easier to interpret.

Given a sample $y \in \mathbb{R}^d$ and a dictionary matrix $X \in \mathbb{R}^{d \times n}$, NASR aims to obtain a non-negative sparse solution $w \in \mathbb{R}^n$ such that it represents y with Xw. That means only a few samples in the dictionary matrix X that contributes positively are selected for the representation of y. Furthermore, the trace LASSO norm $\|X\mathrm{Diag}(w)\|_*$ [8] is used as the regularizer in optimization of NASR, where $\mathrm{Diag}(w)$ means a diagonal matrix with w as its diagonal elements, and the trace norm $\|X\mathrm{Diag}(w)\|_*$ computes the sum of all singular values of $X\mathrm{Diag}(w)$. The trace LASSO adaptively mediates between the great sparsity of ℓ_1-norm and the grouping effect of ℓ_2-norm [9]:

$$\|w\|_2 \leq \|X\mathrm{Diag}(w)\|_* \leq \|w\|_1. \tag{1}$$

The ℓ_1-norm and the ℓ_2-norm are two extreme cases when all samples in X are orthogonal or identical respectively. This optimization problem is formulated as

$$\min_{w} \|\text{XDiag}(w)\|_*, \ s.t. \ \|y - Xw\|_2 \leq \varepsilon, w \geq 0, \tag{2}$$

where ε denotes a given tolerance. It can then be reformulated as

$$\min_{w \geq 0} \frac{1}{2}\|y - Xw\|_2^2 + \lambda\|\text{XDiag}(w)\|_*, \tag{3}$$

where $\lambda > 0$ is a regularization parameter. A globally optimal solution of Eq. (3) can be achieved by alternating direction method (ADM), the same method as used in [5,9,10].

In the context of network construction using fMRI data, let the normalized fMRI data matrix be $X = (x_1, \ldots, x_n) \in \mathbb{R}^{d \times n}$ with d time points and n nodes and the sample x_i be the time series of the ith node. Then for x_i, its corresponding dictionary is the remaining part of X excluding x_i itself, i.e., $X_i = (x_1, \ldots, x_{i-1}, x_{i+1}, \ldots, x_n) \in \mathbb{R}^{d \times (n-1)}$ and its resulting solution $w_i \in \mathbb{R}^{n-1}$ characterizes the weights of the samples that positively contributes in the representation of x_i. The vector w_i is then padded with a zero in its i th position, denoted as $\tilde{w}_i \in \mathbb{R}^n$, indicating that the association between x_i and itself is set to zero. All $\tilde{w}_i$ $(i = 1, \ldots, n)$ are stacked as columns of a matrix $\tilde{W} \in \mathbb{R}^{n \times n}$. Then the sparse association matrix G is constructed by $G = (\tilde{W} + \tilde{W}^T)/2$.

2.2 Community Detection with ssNMF

The symmetric non-negative association matrix G obtained by NASR, representing the brain functional network, can be viewed as an undirected graph $\mathcal{G}$. Suppose an undirected graph $\mathcal{G}$ of n nodes consists of K communities. According to [4], symNMF can be applied to detect the community structure of $\mathcal{G}$ by solving the following problem:

$$\min_{H \geq 0} \|G - HH^T\|_F^2, \tag{4}$$

where $H = (h_1, \ldots, h_K) \in \mathbb{R}^{n \times K}$ and each column h_i indicates the extent to which all nodes belong to the ith community. Here, we propose ssNMF by adding a sparse constraint with the form of ℓ_1 norm as used in [11] on symNMF. Then the ssNMF problem can be casted as

$$\min_{H \geq 0} \|G - HH^T\|_F^2 + \beta \sum_{ik} H_{ik}, \tag{5}$$

where the parameter $\beta > 0$ controls the sparsity of H. In fact, the symNMF can be seen as a special case of the ssNMF problem when $\beta = 0$, which means symNMF enforces no extra sparse constraint on H. According to the algorithm of symNMF in [4], we can obtain the simple multiplicative update rules for the ssNMF problem:

$$H_{ik} \leftarrow H_{ik}\left(\frac{1}{2} + \frac{(GH)_{ik}}{2(HH^TH)_{ik} + \beta}\right). \tag{6}$$

The convergence of this algorithm is ensured based on the proof in [12]. We then normalized each row vector of the obtained solution H. The resulting H_{ik} can be considered as a posterior probability of belonging to the kth community for the ith node. At last H is converted into a binary membership matrix by applying a threshold on these probabilities. This allows ssNMF to assign one node to more than one community. In this way we can identify the overlapping community structure of brain functional network.

2.3   Data Preparation

In order to comprehensively assess the performance of ssNMF, we carry out the experiments on both simulated and real resting-state fMRI data sets.

The simulated fMRI data sets consist of a data set with overlapping community structure and one with non-overlapping structure ($S1$ and $S2$ respectively). Both data sets have a network size of 50 nodes and are available from [6] and [13] respectively. $S1$ consists of 40 subjects and 9 overlapping communities in the underlying network structure of different sizes. Each subject only include several communities (the number varying from 6 to 9). Note that the ground truth is slightly adjusted according to [5]. While, $S2$ of 50 subjects has 10 non-overlapping communities of the same size.

The real resting-state fMRI data set, Beijing_Zang, of 20 subjects used here can be downloaded from the 1000 Functional Connectomes Project online database [14]. The preprocessing procedures follows the steps in [10]. Here, we use 90 regions of interest (ROIs) in the widely used AAL template to define nodes of the network. Finally time series of 90 nodes are extracted for further computation.

2.4   Experiment

In the step of constructing the association matrix of brain functional network, the parameter λ in NASR is empirically set to 0.1 for all three data sets. In the following step of identifying the community structure, the proposed ssNMF is compared with symNMF and the other three popular clustering algorithms, i.e., modularity optimization [3], normalized cut (N-cut) [15] and affinity propagation (AP) [16]. The ssNMF is tested across a range of values of β from 0.01 to 0.2 with the stepsize of 0.01. The parameter k indicating the number of communities in ssNMF, symNMF, N-cut and AP is selected individually for each subject according to the ground truth in simulated data sets. For the real fMRI data, we set k to 8 according to the results in [17] that a number of studies have discovered around 8 functional resting-state networks (RSNs). Due to the randomness in the procedure of the initialization of NMF-based methods, ssNMF

and symNMF run 10 times in each computation. The best run with the minimum value of the objective function will be selected to participate in subsequent
analysis. Furthermore, the availability of the ground truth in simulated data
makes it possible for us to evaluate and compare the performance of different
algorithms quantitatively. Here, we use three metrics to compare the correspon-
dence between the identified communities and the ground truth, specifically,
the averaged F1-score [18], normalized mutual information (NMI) designed for
overlapping communities [19], and Omega index [20].

3   Results and Discussion

3.1   Simulated Data

For two simulated data sets, we identify both the individual community structure and the overall structure underlying all subjects by the group level analysis respectively. The group level analysis is conducted on the mean association
matrix averaged over all subjects within each data set. Figure 1 shows the clustering results of two randomly selected subjects and the group level results obtained
by all algorithms as well as the ground truth in $S1$. As can be seen, varying probability ensures the NMF-based methods to assign one node into more than one
communities. The non-negativity enforces them to naturally learns a part-based

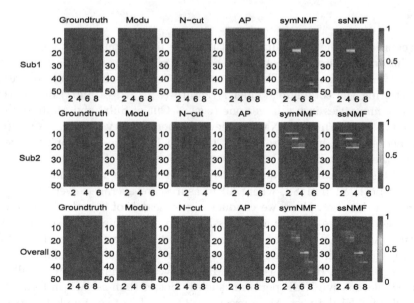

Fig. 1. Examples of identified community structure on the overlapping simulated data
set ($S1$). It shows the results from two randomly selected subjects (*on the first two
rows*). The group results computed on the mean association matrix averaged overall
subjects are shown *on the last row*. The x- and y-axis denotes the community index
and node index respectively.

Table 1. Individual level: measures of average F1-score, NMI, and Omega averaged over all subjects on the two simulated data sets.

	S1 (Overlapping)			S2 (Non-overlapping)		
	F1-score	NMI	Omega	F1-score	NMI	Omega
Modu	0.932*	0.844*	0.884*	0.817*	0.654*	0.659*
NC	0.900*	0.758*	0.824*	0.597*	0.353*	0.362*
AP	0.928*	0.823*	0.852*	0.651*	0.364*	0.333*
symNMF	0.945*	0.867	0.896	0.915*	0.819*	0.817*
ssNMF	0.948	0.859	0.897	0.932	0.850	0.845

Table 2. Group level: measures of average F1-score, NMI, and Omega on the mean association matrix of the two simulated data sets.

	S1 (Overlapping)			S2 (Non-overlapping)		
	F1-score	NMI	Omega	F1-score	NMI	Omega
Modu	0.928	0.782	0.859	1	1	1
NC	0.928	0.827	0.863	0.904	0.851	0.845
AP	0.928	0.827	0.863	0.788	0.627	0.553
symNMF	0.965	0.922	0.955	1	1	1
ssNMF	0.978	0.936	0.931	1	1	1

representation of the brain functional network by grouping the most coherent nodes into one cluster. By contrast, the other clustering methods fail to identify the overlapping nodes. This property may lead to some unpleasant results like scattering the community inner structure (e.g., AP of Sub2) or absorbing smaller communities into a larger one (e.g., N-Cut of Sub2 and Modu of Overall results). Furthermore, ssNMF achieves higher sparsity than symNMF (e.g., Sub1) and assign a higher probability (close to 1) to non-overlapping nodes to decrease the uncertainty (Sub1 and Overall results).

Table 1 summarizes the quantitative analysis of the individual and group results of both $S1$ and $S2$, where all measures are averaged over all subjects within each data set. Here, we conduct a grid search of β and τ according to the average F1-score individually for ssNMF to determine the best community structure. And symNMF can be seen as a special case when β is fixed to 0. Consequently, the obtained community structure can be used to calculate the NMI and Omega indices. It shows that ssNMF achieves the highest scores in all measures except that symNMF performs slightly better than ssNMF in term of the NMI index for $S1$ data set. More precisely, 22 out of 24 two-sample t-tests comparing ssNMF with the other four methods indicate that ssNMF performs significantly better than others ($p < .05$ marked with $*$) in detecting the overlapping and non-overlapping community structure. Table 2 shows the group clustering results with $\beta = 0.03$ for ssNMF. It can be seen that all methods have improved

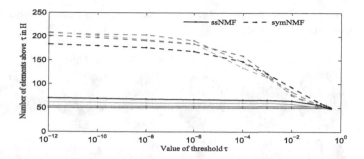

Fig. 2. The number of non-zero elements identified by ssNMF and symNMF on $S1$ varying with the threshold τ. Three randomly selected subjects (*in red, green and blue*) and the mean results over all subjects (*in black*) are shown here. Results of ssNMF and symNMF are drawn *in solid lines* and *dash lines* respectively. β of ssNMF is set to 0.1 for illustration. (Color figure online)

their performance in detecting the common underlying community structure of all subjects compared to the individual results, except the modularity method on $S1$. Especially the NMF-based methods achieve above 0.92 in all measures of both data sets and ssNMF achieves higher scores in terms of the average f1 score and NMI index than symNMF on $S1$.

We then analyze the sensitivity of ssNMF and symNMF to the threshold setting on the simulated data. Figure 2 shows the number of non-zero elements in the normalized matrix H under different thresholds (varying from 10^{-12} to 0.4). It shows that ssNMF is less sensitive to the selection of the threshold τ than symNMF. Specifically, the structure identified by ssNMF is stable across a wide range of τ while the number of nodes identified by symNMF decreases dramatically as τ increases. It indicates that without applying the threshold, ssNMF can extract the most coherent nodes and exclude the others naturally due to its sparsity constraint.

3.2   Real Resting-State fMRI Data

On the real resting state fMRI data, firstly eight communities are discovered for each individual. Then the group community structure is identified based on the mean association matrix averaged over all subjects. In the previous work [5], NMF-based methods show superiority compared to other methods. Here, we focus on the results of the ssNMF method. Figure 3 shows results of three different subjects and the group results, where β and τ are set to 0.1 and 0.3 respectively for illustration. As can be seen, the community structure of different subjects show high resemblance. In general, the 8 identified communities include the bilateral fronto-parietal, sensory-motor, default mode networks (DMN), anterior cingulate cortex (ACC), orbito-fronto-temporal, limbic, basal ganglia and visual networks. These functional modules are consistent with the results of [17] and literatures therein. Group analysis shows similar results in most communities

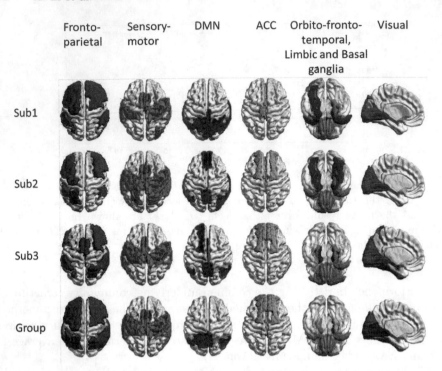

Fig. 3. Examples of eight identified communities obtained by ssNMF on real resting state fMRI data. Individual results of three different subjects are shown *in the first three rows*. The group results computed based on the mean association matrix averaged over all subjects are shown *in the last row*. Each color represent one community. The first four columns, the fifth column and the last column are viewed in ROIs from the dorsal axial, ventral axial and left sagittal views respectively. For illustration, β and τ are selected as 0.1 and 0.3 respectively for all the above results.

and reveals two main differences in some communities. Firstly, the orbito-fronto-temporal and limbic networks are combined together, which are thought to be extensively connected [21]. Another one is that it separates the visual networks into primary visual and extra-striate visual networks, as reported in [15].

Results of simulated data sets have shown that the group analysis of NMF-based methods on mean association matrix can achieve high accuracy on detecting the overall network structure of all subjects. Here, we further investigate the overlapping community structure on the group level by identifying the overlapping nodes. To eliminate the influence of the selection of β, for each condition of β the top 10 overlapping nodes with the largest probabilities of belonging to more than one communities are selected. β varies from 0 to 0.1 with a stepsize of 0.01. Then a majority vote procedure is adopted on all the top 10 overlapping nodes under all conditions of β. Only nodes reported by more than half the conditions are selected. Eventually, 9 overlapping nodes are identified and listed in Table 3. In general, frontal and parietal lobes have the most overlapping nodes, which

Table 3. Overlapping nodes occurring in both the individual and group-averaged community structures on the real fMRI data set.

Lobe	Central	Frontal			Parietal				Limbic
Region	PreCG.L	SFGdor.R	ORBsup.L	ORBsup.R	SMG.L	SMG.R	ANG.L	ANG.R	TPOsup.L

participate in multiple cognitive functions [22, 23]. These overlapping nodes play multiple roles in different networks. For example, the orbitofrontal cortex of the fronto-parietal network is also thought to serve for emotion process [24]. Besides, as parts of the DMN, the bilateral angular gyrus also takes part in fronto-parietal network, which is related to multimodal thoughts [25].

4 Conclusion

In this paper, we propose a ssNMF method and apply a sparse network framework to detect the overlapping community structure of brain functional network. We use NASR to construct a sparse graph and ssNMF to identify the community structure. Results of simulated data sets on both individual and group level indicate that NMF-based methods achieve higher accuracy compared with modularity optimization, N-cut and AP. On the real resting-state fMRI data set, the communities and overlapping nodes discovered by ssNMF are physiologically meaningful and easy to interpret. In sum, this framework can shed lights on the study of overlapping community structure detection of the brain functional network.

Acknowledgements. This work was supported in part by the National Basic Research Program of China under Grant 2015CB351704, the National Natural Science Foundation of China under Grant 61375118, and the Research Foundation for Young Teachers in Anhui University of Technology under Grant QZ201516.

References

1. Bullmore, E., Sporns, O.: Complex brain networks: graph theoretical analysis of structural and functional systems. Nat. Rev. Neurosci. **10**(3), 186–198 (2009)
2. Chen, Z.J., He, Y., Rosa-Neto, P., Germann, J., Evans, A.C.: Revealing modular architecture of human brain structural networks by using cortical thickness from MRI. Cereb. Cortex **18**(10), 2374–2381 (2008)
3. Newman, M.E.: Modularity and community structure in networks. Proc. Natl. Acad. Sci. **103**(23), 8577–8582 (2006)
4. Wang, F., Li, T., Wang, X., Zhu, S., Ding, C.: Community discovery using non-negative matrix factorization. Data Min. Knowl. Discov. **22**(3), 493–521 (2011)
5. Li, X., Hu, Z., Wang, H.: Overlapping community structure detection of brain functional network using non-negative matrix factorization. In: Hirose, A., Ozawa, S., Doya, K., Ikeda, K., Lee, M., Liu, D. (eds.) ICONIP 2016. LNCS, vol. 9949, pp. 140–147. Springer, Heidelberg (2016). doi:10.1007/978-3-319-46675-0_16

6. Eavani, H., Satterthwaite, T.D., Filipovych, R., Gur, R.E., Gur, R.C., Davatzikos, C.: Identifying sparse connectivity patterns in the brain using resting-state fMRI. Neuroimage **105**, 286–299 (2015)

7. Rosa, M.J., Portugal, L., Hahn, T., Fallgatter, A.J., Garrido, M.I., Shawe-Taylor, J., Mourao-Miranda, J.: Sparse network-based models for patient classification using fMRI. Neuroimage **105**, 493–506 (2015)

8. Grave, E., Obozinski, G.R., Bach, F.R.: Trace Lasso: a trace norm regularization for correlated designs. In: Advances in Neural Information Processing Systems, pp. 2187–2195 (2011)

9. Lu, C., Feng, J., Lin, Z., Yan, S.: Correlation adaptive subspace segmentation by trace Lasso. In: 2013 IEEE International Conference on Computer Vision, pp. 1345–1352 (2013)

10. Li, X., Wang, H.: Identification of functional networks in resting state fMRI data using adaptive sparse representation and affinity propagation clustering. Front. Neurosci. **9**, 383 (2015)

11. Hoyer, P.O.: Non-negative sparse coding. In: Proceedings of the 2002 12th IEEE Workshop on Neural Networks for Signal Processing (2002)

12. Wang, D., Li, T., Zhu, S., Ding, C.: Multi-document summarization via sentence-level semantic analysis and symmetric matrix factorization. In: Proceedings of the 31st Annual International ACM SIGIR Conference on Research and Development in Information Retrieval, pp. 307–314 (2008)

13. Smith, S.M., Miller, K.L., Salimi-Khorshidi, G., Webster, M., Beckmann, C.F., Nichols, T.E., Ramsey, J.D., Woolrich, M.W.: Network modelling methods for fMRI. Neuroimage **54**(2), 875–891 (2011)

14. Biswal, B.B., Mennes, M., Zuo, X.N., et al.: Toward discovery science of human brain function. Proc. Natl. Acad. Sci. **107**, 4734–4739 (2010)

15. Van Den Heuvel, M., Mandl, R., Pol, H.H.: Normalized cut group clustering of resting-state fMRI data. PloS one **3**(4), e2001 (2008)

16. Frey, B.J., Dueck, D.: Clustering by passing messages between data points. Science **315**, 972–976 (2007)

17. Van den Heuvel, M.P., Pol, H.E.H.: Exploring the brain network: a review on resting-state fMRI functional connectivity. Eur. Neuropsychopharmacol. **20**, 519–534 (2010)

18. Yang, J., Leskovec, J.: Overlapping community detection at scale: a nonnegative matrix factorization approach. In: Proceedings of the 6th ACM International Conference on Web Search and Data Mining, pp. 587–596. ACM (2013)

19. McDaid, A.F., Greene, D., Hurley, N.: Normalized mutual information to evaluate overlapping community finding algorithms (2011)

20. Gregory, S.: Fuzzy overlapping communities in networks. J. Stat. Mech. Theory Exper. **2**, P02017 (2011)

21. Price, J.L.: Definition of the orbital cortex in relation to specific connections with limbic and visceral structures and other cortical regions. Ann. NY Acad. Sci. **1121**(1), 54–71 (2007)

22. Fuster, J.M.: Prefrontal cortex. In: Comparative Neuroscience and Neurobiology, pp. 107–109. Birkhäuser, Boston (1988)

23. Culham, J.C., Kanwisher, N.G.: Neuroimaging of cognitive functions in human parietal cortex. Curr. Opin. Neurobiol. **11**(2), 157–163 (2001)

24. Beer, J.S., John, O.P., Scabini, D., Knight, R.T.: Orbitofrontal cortex and social behavior: integrating self-monitoring and emotion-cognition interactions. J. Cogn. Neurosci. **18**(6), 871–879 (2006)
25. Mazoyer, B., Zago, L., Mellet, E., Bricogne, S., Etard, O., Houde, O., Crivello, F., Joliot, M., Petit, L., Tzourio-Mazoyer, N.: Cortical networks for working memory and executive functions sustain the conscious resting state in man. Brain Res. Bull. **54**(3), 287–298 (2001)

Author Index

Printed in the United States
By Bookmasters